MANAGING
BUSINESS
IN HUNGARY

An International Perspective

Transition, Competitiveness and Economic Growth

1

PUBLISHED
IN ASSOCIATION WITH BUDAPEST UNIVERSITY
OF ECONOMIC SCIENCES,
INTERNATIONAL STUDIES CENTER

Series Editor:

JÓZSEF BERÁCS

In preparation:

Vol. 2

TEMESI, J. and ZALAI, E.(eds)

TOWARDS A MARKET ECONOMY

HUNGARY IN THE 1990s

MANAGING BUSINESS IN HUNGARY

An International Perspective

Edited by

JÓZSEF BERÁCS *and* ATTILA CHIKÁN

Budapest University of Economic Sciences

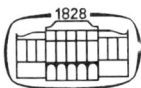

AKADÉMIAI KIADÓ, BUDAPEST

ISBN 963 05 7598 1
HU ISSN 1419-3159

© Akadémiai Kiadó, 1999

Published by Akadémiai Kiadó
H-1519 Budapest, P.O. Box 245

Printed in Hungary

CONTRIBUTORS

BUDAPEST UNIVERSITY OF ECONOMIC SCIENCES
(BEFORE 1990 KARL MARX UNIVERSITY OF ECONOMICS)
H-1093 BUDAPEST, FŐVÁM TÉR 8.

ATTILA ÁGH	Faculty of Social Sciences, Politology
RUDOLF ANDORKA	Faculty of Social Sciences, Sociology
ZOLTÁN ANTAL-MOKOS	Faculty of Business Administration, Management and Organization
GYULA BAKACSI	Faculty of Business Administration, Management and Organization
JÓZSEF BERÁCS	Faculty of Business Administration, Marketing
IMRE BRANYICZKI	Faculty of Business Administration, Management and Organization
ATTILA CHIKÁN	Faculty of Business Administration, Business Economics
ERZSÉBET CZAKÓ	Faculty of Business Administration, Business Economics
CSABA CSÁKI	Faculty of Business Administration, Agricultural Economics
KRISZTINA DEMETER	Faculty of Business Administration, Business Economics
MIKLÓS DOBÁK	Faculty of Business Administration, Management and Organization

MIHÁLY GÁLIK	Faculty of Business Administration, Business Economics
PÁL PÉTER GÁSPÁR	Institute for Continuing Education
PÉTER GEDEON	Faculty of Economics, Comparative Economics
HEDVIG HUSZÁR	Central Library
SÁNDOR KEREKES	Faculty of Business Administration, Environmental Economics
KRISZTINA KOLOS	Faculty of Business Administration, Marketing
ISTVÁN MAGYARI-BECK	Faculty of Social Sciences, Pedagogy
TAMÁS MÉSZÁROS	Faculty of Business Administration, Applied Economics
ZSUZSANNA NAGY	Central Library
ERNŐ TARI	Faculty of Business Administration, Management and Organization
LÁSZLÓ ZSOLNAI	Faculty of Business Administration, Business Economics

FOREIGN CONTRIBUTORS

INGWER BORG	Justus Liebig University, Giessen, Germany
AVISHAY BRAVERMAN	Ben Gurion University of the Negev, Beersheva, Israel
KAREN BROOKS	World Bank, Washington, U.S.A.
DOV ELIZUR	Bar Ila University, Ramat-Gan, Israel
ANDREW GROSS	College of Business Administration, Cleveland State University, Cleveland, U.S.A.
J. LUIS GUASCH	University of California, San Diego, U.S.A.
ROBERT HARTLEY	College of Business Administration, Cleveland State University, Cleveland, U.S.A.

LOUISE A. HESLOP	Carleton University, Canada
GRAHAM J. HOOLEY	Aston Business School, Birmingham, U.K.
RAYMOND HUNT	State University of New York, Buffalo, U.S.A.
NICOLAS PAPADOPOULOS	Carleton University, Canada
JONE L. PEARCE	Graduate School of Management, University of California, Irvine, U.S.A.
DENNIS A. RONDINELLI	University of North Carolina, Chapel Hill, U.S.A.
GYULA VASTAG	Univesity of North Carolina, Chapel Hill, U.S.A.
RICHARD WELFORD	University of Bradford, Management Centre, Bradford, U.K.

JÓZSEF BERÁCS

Having a Master's degree (1974) and a Ph.D. (1976) in economics from the Karl Marx University of Economic Sciences he is attached to the Department of Marketing at the Budapest University of Economic Sciences, where he has chaired the Department since 1992.

Professor BERÁCS has extensive international activities. As a visiting professor he has spent shorter or longer periods at many universities, e.g. Carleton University (Canada) 1984, the University of Texas 1988, London Business School 1995, etc. He is a member of the Executive Board of the European Marketing Academy and has various positions in other international and national organizations. He is the chairman of the Marketing-Theory Subcommittee of the Hungarian Academy of Sciences.

Professor BERÁCS has authored and co-authored more than 100 publications, issued in several languages. He is the co-author of the most extensively used marketing textbook in Hungary. Since 1990 he has been the founder-director of the International Studies Center of the Budapest University of Economic Sciences.

ATTILA CHIKÁN

Graduating in 1967 and earning a Ph.D. (1969) in economics from the Karl Marx University of Economic Sciences, he studied for one year (1971–1972) in the ICAME programme of the Graduate School of Business, Stanford University. Serving the Budapest University of Economic Sciences in different positions he was the chairman of Department of Business Economics between 1990 and 1998. Since the summer of 1998 he has been the Minister for Economic Affairs.

Professor CHIKÁN is a well-known personality in international academic and management life. Among many other positions he is a member of the Editorial Board of the International Journal of Production Economics and the International Journal of Quantitative and Operations Management, Senior Vice-President of the International Federation of Purchasing and Materials Management and First Vice-President and Secretary General of the International Society for Inventory Research since 1983.

Professor CHIKÁN has produced more than 200 publications; he is author and co-author of eight books, and editor of a series of Conference Proceedings at the Elsevier Science Publishing Co. He is the Director of the LÁSZLÓ RAJK College for Advanced Studies and a member of several Standing Committees, Editorial Boards, Advisory Boards and Boards of Trustees.

CONTENTS

FOR THE LAUNCH OF THE SERIES

The historically most marked change of the last decade of the 20th century seems to have been the political and economic transformation of the states of Central and Eastern Europe. Innumerable specialist articles, books and monographs have been written on this subject and innumerable Western and Eastern researchers (to use the old definition) have been engaged in the various aspects of the political and economic transformation. In spite of the dominance of a descriptive, positivist approach on the part of scholars, the pressures on decision-makers keep on producing new normative assertions. Economic policy-makers, politicians and businessmen are interested in highly practical problems. These problems include the correlation between inflation and the standard of living; the functioning of free elections and the democratic legal system; the effect of the market economy, ownership patterns and foreign capital investment, etc. Widely varying opinions are reflected in the answers to these and other questions, which can mostly be traced back to different judgments of the concept of "transition" by the different authors. There are domains where changes can be measured in months, while in others years or even decades are needed. The real problem is to find a basis for reference, a standard against which the situation of a society can be assessed. This line of thinking can be most tangibly represented by the terms "normal state" or, broadly interpreted, "state of equilibrium", widely used in economics, as well as by the trend labeled with the term "benchmarking" in the business world.

The new series to be published by Akadémiai Kiadó builds upon the philosophy that in Hungary the real transition occurred in the 90s. It did not affect all the spheres of society equally but the intensity of change cannot be expected to be the same in every field since there are national and regional peculiarities, cultural differences and divergences in consumption structure, history and so on. It is the task of scientific research to confirm or refuse the effect of all these. The new series is intended to give an insight into the process of competitiveness and economic growth for the wider professional community, relying upon the intellectual resources of the Budapest University of Economic Sciences, the most prestigious university of economics, business and social studies in Hungary. This process – particularly in the past – has been interwoven with the characteristic features of the transition. However, in view of the fact that the political and economic transformation has run its course in all fields, it seems important to give an account of the present situation. The first three volumes of this series are designed to render this account as a "chronicler" of the 90s, with a thematic selection from publications already issued.

The first volume emphasises business, the microeconomic sphere. Although we cannot render an account of its social impact, nevertheless it was here that the systemic change proceeded most rapidly.

The second volume focuses on macroeconomic systems and attempts to map the situation of the 90s by contrasting various economic theories.

The third volume will investigate from the political science, sociological and international aspects what has actually taken place in the past decade.

The further volumes will deal with the subject areas which directly or indirectly contribute to the economic growth and competitiveness of Hungary and which lend themselves to research by scientific methods. After the year 2000 practical work on joining the European Union will accelerate, though, innumerable theoretical issues have still to be settled, which the series aims to demonstrate using an interdisciplinary approach and presenting new ideas.

JÓZSEF BERÁCS
Series Editor

PREFACE

The history of Central Europe in the 20th century abounds in epoch-making events. At the beginning of the century its features were determined by the power of a great empire, the Austro–Hungarian monarchy, to organize society and the economy; at the end of the century, imminent accession to the European Union is opening up new prospects for the nations of the region, including the Hungarians. Because of the decisive role of economics and business the themes covered by the articles collected together in this volume of studies will be of interest to the wider professional community.

The occasion of this publication is the celebration in 1998 of the 50th anniversary of the establishment of the Budapest University of Economic Sciences as an independent specialized university. The staff of Hungary's number one economics university, which also plays a leading role on the international level, is very active in academic life. This prompted the idea of compiling a volume of articles published in English in the past decade by the University's teaching staff. Directly or indirectly, these articles relate to the management of business life. The varied nature of their themes reflects true interdisciplinarity. It expresses the intricate and complex situation in which, in a transition economy, an executive has to work.

These studies are characterized by a wealth of different academic approaches. Alongside conceptional – speculative and empirical – descriptive-type studies, others can be found that reveal historical interdependencies. Cooperation on the part of foreign researchers working in various parts of the world and the participation of Hungarian researchers in international programs ensure that the questions raised are not characterized by any sort of provincialism. Readers living in different countries will find themes discussed that belong to the mainstream of theoretical research. Therefore we are confident that the articles published at the beginning and at the end of the 90s will be greeted with an equal degree of interest, and we believe that experts, researchers and students working in these various fields will find their horizons expanded by this collection of articles imbued with the intellectuality of Central Europe and openness to the opinions of others.

October 1998   JÓZSEF BERÁCS–ATTILA CHIKÁN

HUNGARY ON THE THRESHOLD
OF A PROMISING DECADE

By

JÓZSEF BERÁCS, ATTILA CHIKÁN

"Future historians will record that the twenty-first
century belonged to the House of Europe."

LESTER THUROW, Head to Head 1992, p. 258

In business life, in the purchases of ultimate consumers and in consumption structures immense changes have taken place in the 80s and 90s. It will be the task of future historians to define which of these changes were crucial in the determination of the character and nature of this turn-around. Today we still consider that it was mostly the political transformation in 1989 in the Central European region which, due to its unexpectedness, shook the world and set these countries on a new path. The revolutionary changes can only be comprehended by understanding another concept, transition (MASON 1996). If we dig deeper into particular areas, we can see that certain revolutionary processes have undergone an evolution for several decades. One cannot understand the political situation in Hungary without the concepts of the Revolution of 1956 or of the reforming ideas implicit in the "New Economic Mechanism" of 1968.

1. THE TURBULENT LAST DECADE

Turning to the world of market products, it can be seen that a reversal took place in the proportion between physical sectors and the service sectors over the period 1980-1995 in Hungary. As far as the contribution to the Hungarian Gross National Product is concerned, in 1980 the share of the physical sector was 65% and in 1995 the share of services grew from its former 35% to 65%. For the first decade of the 15 years in question, the so-called socialist planned economy persisted whereas for the last 5 years a declared capitalist economy was functioning. The question can be raised whether these dramatic changes and the structural shift in the world of products by themselves stimulated the political changes. The abundance of information, the nature of products and the expansion of education probably also encouraged the changes that took place determining the environment in which companies and those active in business life have to operate.

The purpose of this book is to present the operations and environment of companies functioning in Hungary. The title "Managing the business world" refers not to the approach used by practical professionals, but to the traits specific to the operations of companies and the ways to describe them. In the case of a small country with open foreign trade (39% of GDP was exported in 1997) it is extremely important to know how its companies operate as compared to international standards, and to what extent they are able to integrate into the "European house" to which, as Lester Thurow said, the next century will belong.

If we cast a brief look back at the past decade, we can list beneficial and detrimental changes in the case of Hungary, too. The establishment of the fact that political and economic transformation did occur is positive. The most striking sign of this is that Hungary is already a member of the OECD, is expected to become a member of NATO in 1999 and as an associated country, began negotiations in the autumn of 1998 about joining the European Union. The legal and institutional system of a capitalist or free market economy has been formed. With the transformation of the legal system – when 100–150 new legal regulations annually (which had never existed before in any form) had to be approved by the Parliament – harmonization, adaptation to the legal formulas of the European Union played the key strategic part. Thus, for instance, the second competition act approved in 1996 is better adapted to the expectations of the Union than that of some countries within the Union. However, this is also true of several other Central European countries (SÁRAI 1998).

2. IMPROVING MACROECONOMIC CHARACTERISTICS

It was from the citizens that the political and economic transformation demanded the greatest sacrifice. Owing to the stagnation of economic activities, significant social strata (20 to 30% according to some estimations) hit the poverty line. Consumption in many product categories (e.g. milk, beer) declined by 30% over the past 8 years. GDP diminished significantly as compared to the 1989 level and in spite of a resumption of growth, it cannot be expected until 1999 to exceed the level of 10 years before. The benefits of the 10 years of transformation can already be seen in spite of or owing to the financial restrictions, including the high rate (over 10%) of unemployment, the fall in the number of those employed and the list of harmful processes could be continued. The macroeconomic indexes are beginning to improve. GDP of USD 4415 per capita in 1997 is estimated to grow by 5% in 1998. The new government ruled by the young democrats is determined to achieve GDP growth of 7% annually, unless the looming crisis in the world economy prevents it.

Economists and politicians do not agree on the recommended rate of economic growth or on the extent to which this can be achieved at the expense of stability.

We believe that JÁNOS KORNAI, Hungary's internationally most renowned economist is right in maintaining that stability and growth should be handled in parallel. In 1994 when the previous socialist government took power, KORNAI (1994) put forward in his message to economic policy-makers that continuous growth must be the government's highest priority. The 1995 analysis of Hungary by the World Bank also emphasised that structural reforms were needed for sustainable growth (Hungary, 1995). And slow economic growth did indeed begin. GDP growth in the years 1994 to 1997 was 2.9, 1.5, 1.3 and 4.4% respectively. As a matter of fact, these numbers are not very impressive, though other positive signs reinforce their impact. We should like to highlight two of them.

Perhaps the most important one is related to foreign capital investment. Numerous economic analysts expect the inflow of operating capital to encourage the transformation of the emerging markets. According to the EBRD (1998) report, among the transition economies Hungary leads in terms both of per capita and of cumulative FDI inflow *(Table 1)*. As a consequence of direct capital investments amounting to over USD 15 billion, twice the amount going into the Czech Republic, some industries, such as brewering and, car assembly, are entirely owned by foreigners. From banking to telecommunications, from the steel industry to public energy supply, every sector of the economy is permeated by foreign involvement.

The privatisation campaign came to an end in 1998. If we consider the distribution of GDP by ownership subsectors, we find that the public sector repesented only 30% in 1996. Alongside 54.4% domestic private sector ownership, the proportion of foreign ownership amounted to 15.6%. If we

Table 1. Foreign direct investments in transition economies

Country	Cumulative FDI-inflows 1989-1997	Cumulative FDI-inflows 1989-1997 per capita	FDI-inflows per capita in 1997	FDI-inflows as a % of GDP in 1997
	(in millions of US dollars)	(in US dollars)		(%)
Bulgaria	1 000	121	69	5.6
Croatia	1 276	267	105	2.7
Czech Republic	7 473	726	124	2.4
Estonia	809	557	90	2.8
Hungary	15 403	1519	207	4.7
Poland	8 442	218	79	2.3
Romania	2 389	106	44	2.9
Slovak Republic	912	169	28	0.8
Slovenia	1 074	538	161	1.8

Source: Transition Report Update, 1998, p. 12.

look only at the processing sector, the contribution of foreign-owned firms to GDP exceeds 25%. The large multinationals such as IBM, GM, GE, Philips, Audi, etc., beside conquering the domestic market, strive to export to other countries products manufactured in Hungary with less expensive Hungarian labour. It may be owing to this fact that about 70% of Hungarian exports are accounted for by firms with foreign owners. The volume is growing from year to year, though in 1996 export of USD 1541 per capita was only about one-fifth of that of Austria or one-sixth of per capita Danish exports, which amounted to USD 9273. Foreign capital investment also largely contributed to improving the employment effectiveness of Hungarian labour. The improvement in productivity in the processing sector since 1992 has outstripped the changes in this direction in other countries in the region. As *Fig. 1* shows, the highest growth was achieved in Hungary with 55% labour productivity, followed by Poland with 40%, while in the Czech Republic it actually stagnated.

The countries of Central and Eastern Europe are quite often compared, from the point of view of maturity for joining the European Union, as to how far they have gone in terms of catching-up. These comparisons are mostly made on the basis of macroeconomic figures and they underlie statements that Hungary, Poland or the Czech Republic is the leader in the favoured indices including foreign indebtedness, trade deficit, inflation, unemployment, etc.

(Index: 1989–100)

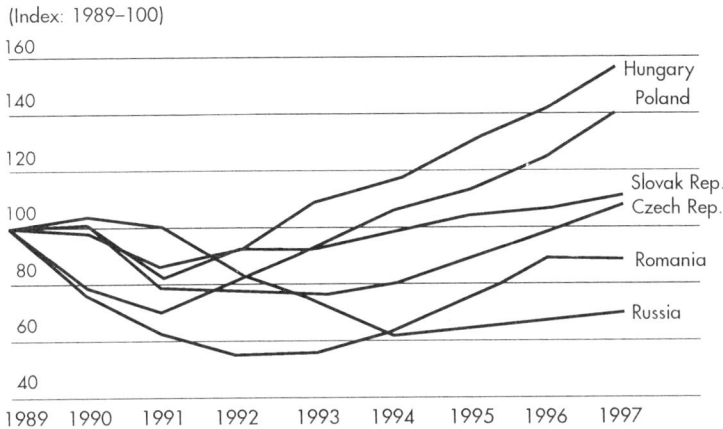

Figure 1. Labor productivity in manufacturing

(*Source:* Transition report update, 1998, p. 9)

We too recognise the significance of these parameters, as well as the economic and political changes underlying them. We are well aware that politics and the economy are interwoven in a multitude of ways. The overwhelming politicization of the former socialist economies has loosened considerably, though political and sociological analysis of the transition must be a starting point for any intended acitivty on the part of entrepreneurs. *Part One* of this book, providing a description of the socio-economic environment embedded in historic perspectives, is devoted to precisely this purpose. It also aims to convince the reader that the 40 years of the socialist régime did not identically "infect" the various areas of life and that the capitalist arrangements of the 90s do not automatically alter fossilized reflexes and attitudes.

3. A MICROECONOMIC APPROACH
TO BUSINESS PROCESSES

The articles contained *in the further three parts* of the book, on the other hand, suggest that one can understand the real functioning of the economy by analysing the microsphere, which comprises millions of business transactions. To comprehend this is to realise that the changes which have come about in the microsphere are now self-determining. It depends on the companies competing in a given market rather than on the will of economic policy-makers whether there will be growth in the sales of a particular product line or growth in efficiency. It may therefore be important to differentiate between the privatisation practices in each country. Macroeconomic analysts are inclined to regard growth in the role of private ownership as an advantage – ignoring other aspects. Thus, for instance, if they see that 70% of GDP is supplied by the private sector in Hungary compared with 75% in the Czech Republic, then this fact is indicated as a positive characteristic in favour of the Czechs. They do not consider that voucher privatisation creates lower motivation for change as against the natural person as the real owner. A foreign owner, in contrast to a domestic one, is able to introduce market economy know-how that spreads over to other firms, thanks to competition. URBÁN (1998) points out on the basis of the diverging characteristics of the Hungarian and Czech transformation that there is a trade-off between the macro-performance and the microstructure of the transitional economies. While in the former area the Czech economy has shown a better picture, in the latter field the Hungarian economy seems to lead the way.

In our opinion, the problem can only really be decided in the long run and in retrospect, or when we analyse the operation of companies in a comparative way. Michael Porter wrote a new Introduction to the 1998 edition of his work "Competitive Advantage of Nations" (1990). He emphasised that "Wealth is governed by productivity, or the value created per day of work". He explains why he used the concept of competitive edge rather than the comparative advantage common in economics. "Comparative advantage, as it had come to be understood, rests on endowments of inputs such as labor, natural resources, and financial capital. I argue that factor inputs themselves have become less and less valuable in an increasingly global economy." (PORTER 1998, p. XXI.) National competitive advantage, however, is determined not only by factor conditions but also by related and supporting industries, corporate strategy, structure and rivalry, "the role of chance" and the "role of government". In particular we highlight among the above factors strategy, which is subjected to more detailed investigation in the book in various functional areas such as production or marketing as well as management.

In the selection of specialty articles we have considered various points of view. We should like to call attention to four of these.

(1) A significant proportion of the articles rely on company surveys where the Hungarian sample constitutes usually just a section of a survey encompassing several countries, conducted by an international research group. This implies on the one hand that the study rests on a methodologically solid basis and, secondly, possibilities exist for international comparison including benchmarking.

(2) For some empirical surveys, longitudinal analysis has become possible as well on the basis of new data that has become available. It has to be stated that in international practice there are rather few repeated surveys relying on a representative sample and using consistent methodology. Nevertheless these are essential for drawing scientifically valid conclusions.

(3) The development of science is greatly assisted by intuition and speculation as well as theoretical argumentation. However, one can arrive at findings of general validity only if a real system underlies them which is not individual, but has dominant traits that can be found elsewhere. And this is now true of the Hungarian economy.

(4) The selected articles have been published in the last 8 years and thus they also reflect the changes which have taken place in this period. They show indirectly how far we have got and from where.

4. AFTER THE TRANSFORMATION
OF THE ECONOMIC SYSTEM

On the basis of the articles on the subject published in the second half of the 90s, we can draw the conclusion that the political and economic transformation was accomplished in the business sector of the Hungarian economy. Transition as a concept has lost its topicality in the business sphere. At least in the sense in which it was used in the special literature in relation to the Central and East European countries. It is, however, still needed in the way it is used for example by ESPING-ANDERSEN (1996) in relation to the Latin-American countries or the Scandinavian welfare states. Nevertheless, as far as the business world is concerned, it is more appropriate to speak about change management. This is, indeed, an evergreen subject of discussion among managers owing to the rise and fall of industries.

This statement was confirmed by the large academic research program conducted from 1995 to 1997 on the international competitiveness of Hungarian companies under the guidance of the Budapest University of Economic Sciences Department of Business Management. The concluding paper of the research program draws up 7 summarizing theses (CHIKÁN 1997) which at the same time mark the tasks to be accomplished as well as closing some debated issues. The seven theses are as follows:

(1) Transition has come to an end in the business sphere.
(2) The performance of the business sphere has greatly improved.
(3) Social acceptance of the market economy is low.
(4) Performance improvement can be attributed to the organising power of market mechanisms. The general impact of economic policy is negative.
(5) Critical direct obstacles to competitiveness are to be found in the fields of innovation and education.
(6) Sectoral structure does not impede competitiveness.
(7) Companies and company executives are strongly differentiated from the point of view of business management skills.

Finally, we ask the reader to approach the articles with an open mind. Those who wish to devote themselves entirely to a specific area such as production management or environmental protection can do so only to a limited extent. An interdisciplinary approach, on the other hand, provides an excellent opportunity for a better understanding of the background to phenomena. For example, managers' ethical attitude to environment protection reveals a lot about management's philosophy, too. This collection of articles, which appears eclectic on the surface, may become very logical in the hands who is able to think in terms of systems and to connect lines of argument built upon divergent schools of thought. To this end, we wish all our readers persistence and motivation.

Budapest, October 1998

REFERENCES

CHIKÁN, A.: Jelentés a magyar vállalati szféra nemzetközi versenyképességéről. (Report on the international competitiveness of Hungarian companies). "Versenyben a világgal" kutatási program, Budapest University of Economic Sciences, Dept. of Business Economics, p. 36, October (1997).

ESPING-ANDERSEN, G.: Welfare States in Transition, National Adaptations in Global Economies. SAGE Publications, London, p. 276 (1996).

Hungary: Structural Reforms for Sustainable Growth. A World Bank Country Study. Washington, p. 179 (1995).

KORNAI, J.: Lasting Growth as the Top Priority: Macroeconomic Tensions and Government Economic Policy in Hungary. EBRD, Working Paper No. 15, p. 42, December (1994).

MASON, D. S.: Revolution and Transition in East-Central Europe, Dilemmas in World Politics. Westview Press (2nd ed.), p. 242 (1996).

PORTER, M. E.: The Competitive Advantage of Nations, with a new introduction by the author. Macmillan Business, p. 855 (1990, 1998).

SÁRAI, J.: Versenypolitika, versenyjog EU-csatlakozásunk előzményeinek és környezetének tükrében. (Competition Policy – Calculating the Advantages and Disadvantages of Accession to the European Community.) Európai Tükör, Műhelytanulmányok 42., Integrációs Stratégiai Munkacsoport, Budapest, p. 146 (1998).

THUROW, L.: Head to Head, The Coming Economic Battle Among Japan, Europe and America. William Morrow and Company, Inc. New York, p. 336 (1992).

TRANSITION REPORT UPDATE. European Bank for Reconstruction and Development, London, p. 73, April (1998).

URBÁN, L.: Trade-offs between Macro-Performance and Micro-Restructuring in Transition Economies: Contrasting the Czech and the Hungarian Experience. CASE-CEU (Center for Social and Economic Research – Central European University) Working Papers Series, Warsaw, No. 5, p. 35, June (1998).

I

ECONOMIC
AND SOCIAL
ENVIRONMENT

INTRODUCTION TO PART ONE

Almost without exception, the specialized books on business activities attempt to show the investigated phenomena embedded in a wider economic, technological and cultural environment. If this is true in general, it ought to be even more true in a country like Hungary which has undergone a change of régime. This change in the system has profoundly altered the political, sociological and human circumstances in which company managers have to operate.

The first part contains articles that shed light on the process that has run its course during the 90s. At the same time setting it in a historical perspective, they show the conceptual framework that even before the change in the régime characterized professional Hungarian opinion. From this point of view the articles can be divided into three groups.

The first two articles were prepared before the change in the political system. Their tone, however, is no different from that of the ones that followed later. The key phrase is economic decentralization, which determined the scientific approach of the reformist thinkers. The article by MÉSZÁROS describes the tasks arising from the dismantling of the centrally-planned system, and the results already achieved. He points out that company operation must be given a central place. Briefly summing up Hungary's economic reforms, he provides an international survey showing that the East Central European states have not attained the same level with regard to what in some cases is their declared aim of developing mixed, planned-market economies.

It is the task of the professional academic community to dispel the national stereotypes that are interwoven into our lives at various levels. The first article stems from marketing, for it seeks an answer to the question how far the image of products and countries assists or impedes the sale of products on foreign markets, and domestic consumption. The PAPADOPOULOS–HESLOP–BERÁCS article is based on a population survey extending to 8 countries. Among its conclusions it is worth mentioning that a precondition for successful company product policy is the improvement of Hungary's image, to which the topics dealt with in the book's further chapters could significantly contribute.

The three articles forming the second block (Chapters 3, 4 and 5) were written at the beginning of the 90s. All three focus their examination on the problem of transition and seek handholds with the help of which society can achieve a permanent, stable condition. The BROOKS–GUASCH–BRA-

VERNAN–CSÁKI article analyzes the transition from the aspect of trends in the demand for and supply of agricultural and food industry products, which affect us all. It outlines the process that with the changes in ownership led to decollectivitization in the East Central European region. Emphasis is laid on the need for assistance from the international community in the form of technology and capital.

ANDORKA examines the economic, sociological and demographic changes in a historical perspective, from the viewpoint of the Hungarian intelligentsia. Touching on the institutional and legal system of higher education and academic research, he argues against oversimplifying assertions that describe as good everything that came into being after the change in the system, and condemn as bad all that existed before it. One indisputable good result, however, was the freeing of academic research.

In 1989 in many countries a peaceful revolution took place in the political system, but the story did not end there. The article by ÁGH vividly shows that in contrast to West-European democracy, an authority-based democracy sprung from historical traditions is evolving in the region. He presents a number of paradoxes of the transition period to prove that the game is not over yet. At least as far as the year 1994 and certain countries are concerned. ATTILA ÁGH's latest book (*The Politics of Central Europe.* Sage Publications, 1998) provides a many-sided illustration of how the characteristics of Central-Europeanness (and within this, the path of Hungarian development) have stabilized.

The third section of Part I consists of two articles (Chapters 6 and 7) written in the second half of the 90s. Both are characterized by a sort of pragmatic professionalism. The ANTAL-MOKOS article shows an episode in the virtually completed privatization process through the example of a Hungarian company. The story, which spans a period of one year, highlights the importance, in the privatization process, of politicization both inside and outwith the company structure. An interesting additional ingredient is provided by the "struggling through" scenario, in contrast to the "muddling through" type familiar in management literature.

The title of GEDEON's article is based on a play on words. With the economics of transition as his starting point, he raises the question what kind of transformation Comparative Economics as an academic discipline has undergone. He sums up his views in six theses and emphasizes the importance of interdisciplinary research, through which it may be possible to break down the rigid dividing walls between the various social sciences.

1

NATIONAL STEREOTYPES
AND PRODUCT EVALUATIONS
IN A SOCIALIST COUNTRY*

By

NICOLAS PAPADOPOULOS, LOUISE A. HESLOP, JÓZSEF BERÁCS

For Western businesses faced with saturated or stagnant markets at home and in traditional foreign markets, Eastern socialist countries represent a potentially lucrative new opportunity area. As early as 1973, MILOSH pointed out that these markets represent "...a vast industrial market of over 300 million people". Interest in these countries is likely to grow as a result of recent favourable developments in East-West relations.

East-West political and ideological differences have had a significant effect on the nature of research concerning socialist markets. Past studies have focused largely on such topics as descriptive surveys of Eastern marketing systems or macro-economic and trade issues (e.g. GOLDMAN 1961; BORNSTEIN and FUSFELD 1970; BARKSDALE and KELLY 1978). Most managerially oriented research was conducted from an external vantage point and was based on surveys of Western business (e.g. HISRICH and PETERS 1983).

More recently, there has been a noticeable increase in research that is more attuned to the needs of managers (e.g. ARTISIEN and BUCKLEY 1985; PAPADOPOULOS and BERÁCS 1985). Still, with only a handful of exceptions (e.g. BERÁCS 1984; NAOR 1986), most of the research to date has studied Eastern markets from without, rather than from within, and published empirical studies are virtually non-existent. This leaves a large gap in our knowledge and many questions about socialist markets. What are the crit-

* In *International Marketing Review,* 1990, Vol. 7, No. 1, pp. 32–47.

Acknowledgement: The authors wish to thank Canada's Department of Regional Industrial Expansion, the Marketing Science Institute and their respective universities, for helping to fund this study, and *IMR* reviewers for their helpful and insightful comments on earlier drafts of this article.

ical aspects of consumer behaviour? What factors influence purchase choices? Which marketing mix elements are important? A myriad questions remain to be answered if we are to understand socialist countries and their continued move towards decentralisation.

This article is among the first to report findings from empirical consumer research in Eastern Europe. Specifically, it reports on the views of Hungarian consumers about foreign products of Western origin, compares them to views about domestic products, and offers some comparisons between the attitudes of Hungarian consumers and those of buyers in seven other countries. The subject is important because it sheds light on an aspect of consumer behaviour in a socialist market based on empirical data, and also because it contributes to our knowledge about the potential influence of country images on product evaluations.

Over 20 years ago, DICHTER (1962, p. 116) commented that "the little phrase 'made in...' can have a tremendous influence on the acceptance and success of products". Since that time, over 100 articles have reported on country-of-origin studies. While many of these studies suffer from a variety of methodological problems (e.g. weak conceptualisation, extensive use of convenience samples, lack of a comparative perspective), the literature leads to the generalised conclusion that people do hold stereotyped images about various countries and that these images affect the way in which the countries' products are evaluated.

In this context, research into the views of consumers in an Eastern country is particularly important. Consumers in Western markets have an abundance of information about, easy access to, and considerable experience with, a large variety of products from virtually every corner of the world. Because of this, the potential country-of-origin effects on buyer behaviour are complex and difficult to discern. On the other hand, given the generally low level of penetration of Western products into socialist markets, it may be expected that Eastern consumers' attitudes regarding countries and their products are based less on experience and more on their perceived stereotyped images.

Questions that arise, then, include: What are the underlying dimensions along which domestic and foreign products are evaluated, especially in the light of relatively little consumer experience with foreign goods? What images do Eastern consumers hold about Western products, in terms of the evaluative criteria that are considered important? How similar or different are the images of products from various Western countries? How do consumer attitudes towards Western products compare with their attitudes towards domestic products? What opportunities or barriers to entry do these images, and their underlying dimensions, represent for Western businesses from various origins? These questions are dealt with in the present study.

BACKGROUND AND LITERATURE REVIEW

Past research in made-in images has been reviewed in detail in earlier studies (e.g. BILKEY and NES 1982; PAPADOPOULOS et al. 1987). Of interest here are three points:

(1) There is evidence that the importance of country images to consumers, marketers, and public policy makers has been increasing (e.g. JOHANSSON 1985). This may be attributed to the growing use of "made in" cues, (a) by consumers trying to simplify information processing, especially in light of the often-confusing array of products in today's markets; (b) by companies trying to define unique product positions in highly competitive markets; and (c) by governments aiming to protect domestic producers ("buy domestic" campaigns) or to promote their countries' products abroad.

(2) Consumers in some countries seem to prefer domestic over foreign products, while consumers in other countries generally do not. For example, Finnish consumers rated domestic products significantly higher than foreign good from major trading nations which hold dominant positions in world markets (DARLING and KRAFT 1977). The authors suggest that this is due to "...the intense national loyalty and pride of the Finnish people" (p. 529). It would seem reasonable to assume that such feelings are also held by other people. However, SEATON and VOGEL (1981) found that with other elements such as price being held constant, when a German car (such as the VW Rabbit) is manufactured in the US as opposed to Germany its "overall 'preference utility'" from the standpoint of American consumers declines significantly (also see JOHANSSON and NEBENZAHL 1986). Concerns about the quality of domestic goods in general have been reported in several other studies (e.g. ASQC 1980; WALL and HESLOP 1986; NAGASHIMA 1970).

(3) Consumers report foreign brand names as more recognisable than those that are expressed in their own language (e.g. NAGASHIMA 1970, 1977). NIFFENEGGER et al. (1982) suggest that this may be because for-

eign-language brand names "stand out" more than domestic ones (p. 286). This "memorability" factor underscores the importance of country-of-origin cues in international marketing.

METHODOLOGY

The study was a large scale cross-national consumer survey carried out in the capital and another major city in the US, Canada, Great Britain, the Netherlands, France, West Germany, Greece and Hungary. The overall purpose of the study was to investigate the country-of-origin effect in depth and from a transnational perspective. Hungary was included in order to examine the attitudes of consumers in an Eastern socialist market and to enable comparisons between consumers in Eastern and Western markets. The design of the larger study has been discussed in detail by PAPADOPOULOS (1986).

This article is based on a quota sample of 300 consumers from the Budapest area. National sampling frames, both in Hungary and in the other countries surveyed, were not selected since urban consumers were believed to be more knowledgeable about foreign products and also believed to influence their adoption within a country. The drop-off/pick-up technique was used to administer the survey instrument, resulting in a response rate of 94% (versus an average of 75% in the other seven countries that were sampled). Respondents in the Hungarian sample were somewhat upscale and generally fit the characteristics of opinion leaders (somewhat younger, better educated and with more prestigious occupations than the norm). Since opinion leaders influence the future views of all consumers, the sample's profile can, in fact, be seen as a positive element of the study.

The survey used a structured, self-administered questionnaire, which was identical in all eight countries and was translated and back-translated to ensure accuracy. The present article focuses on responses to two sections of the questionnaire, namely, those that asked respondents to evaluate countries and their products. Past research has been limited to examining attitudes towards *products* from various countries. The inclusion of evaluation scales for the origin *countries* themselves was an improvement initiated in the present study. Respondents were presented with one page containing 21 seven-point (1 = negative, 7 = positive) semantic differential (SD) items to evaluate products, and one page with 11 SD items to evaluate the respective countries, for each of five origins: Canada, the US, Japan, Sweden and their own (in this case, Hungary). The selection of these origins was dictated by the purpose of the larger study. The product evaluation scales were drawn from an initial list of over 100 items, derived from earlier studies (e.g. NAGASHIMA 1970; DARLING and KRAFT 1977). The country evaluation scales were drawn mainly from relevant research in the international behaviour literature (e.g. KELMAN 1965).

To prevent potential sequences bias and response routinisation, three ordering and scale rotations were undertaken; (1) the SD anchor points were randomly assigned to the left and right side of the scales; (2) the ordering of the SD items was different from one origin country to the other; and (3) the questionnaires were divided into five subgroups, each with a different pagination so that each of five respondent subgroups was exposed to different country sequences.

Mean scores for each of the SD items were computed and then summed to enable rating and ranking of the five origins for each variable and in total. Using the home country as a benchmark, *t*-test paired comparisons of the means were carried out to examine whether significant differences exist between domestic and foreign product evaluations. In addition, principal components factor analysis (VARIMAX rotation) was used to reduce that data and to identify underlying dimensions.

MAIN FINDINGS AND DISCUSSION

GENERAL OVERVIEW

To place the findings from the Hungarian sample in the context of the larger study, *Table 1* provides a summary of the attitudes of Hungarian respondents and compares them to those from the seven other countries that were sampled. Three significant observations can be made from this table:

(1) Japanese products were given the highest mean score by six of the eight samples (including the "tie" with the Netherlands). Hungary was among those giving Japanese goods top rank. The remaining two countries gave Japanese products the second highest rating. In five countries (Hungary, Canada, US, Great Britain and Greece) domestic products received a statistically significant lower rating than Japanese ones (at $\alpha = 0.001$ or higher) based on the paired-comparison *t*-tests.

Table 1. Summated means and ranks:
all origins, 21 variables

Evaluations	N	Own country	Canada	US	Japan	Sweden	Great Britain
			(a) Origin means				
Canada	272	4.7	–	4.7	*5.0*[d]	4.1[d]	4.2[d]
US	265	4.9	4.0[d]	–	*5.2*[d]	4.1[d]	3.8[d]
Great Briatin	243	4.6	3.9[d]	4.4[c]	*4.9*[c]	4.1[d]	–
France	287	*5.0*	3.7[d]	4.6[d]	4.9[a]	4.1[d]	–
West Germany	308	*5.2*	3.8[d]	4.4[d]	5.0[a]	4.3[d]	–
The Netherlands	245	4.9	3.9[d]	4.4[d]	4.9	*4.5*[d]	–
Greece	300	4.3	4.3	4.8[d]	*4.9*[d]	4.2	–
Hungary	300	3.8	4.2[d]	4.5[d]	*5.1*[d]	4.4[d]	–
			(b) Origin ranks				
Canada		2.5	–	2.5	1	5	4
US		2	4	–	1	3	5
Great Britain		2	5	3	1	4	–
France		1	5	3	2	4	–
West Germany		1	5	3	2	4	–
The Netherlands		1.5	5	4	1.5	3	–
Greece		4	4	2	1	4	–
Hungary		5	4	2	1	3	–

Means: The origin with the highest mean score is in italics. Statistical significance from the *t*-test paired comparisons between "own country" and the other four origins, is shown as: a = 0.05; b = 0.01; c = 0.001; d = 0.0001.

Ranks: Decimals indicate a tied score.

Note: Because the US and Canada were both origin and sample countries, Great Briatin was added to the questionnaires in these two countries as the fifth origin.

(2) With the exception of Hungary and Greece, domestic products were rated quite highly overall but only three of the eight respondent groups (French, German and Dutch) ranked them first. Examination of the mean of the individual SD items showed that higher ratings for domestic products were given mostly on such scales as "I know a lot about products from X" and "I buy a lot of products from X". It is reasonable to expect that buyers in any country buy more and know more about their own than foreign products. On the other hand, respondents expressed doubt about domestic products in certain key dimensions. For example, respondents in all countries except France rated

Japanese and/or Swedish products as better than their own on product performance aspects (e.g. workmanship, innovativeness, quality). Also, domestic goods received the lowest or second-lowest rank by all respondents except in France in price- and value-related considerations (e.g. "unreasonably/reasonably priced"). Such perceptions have also been reported in other studies (e.g. WALL and HESLOP 1986) and may be attributed to country-specific factors, such as perceptions of low productivity and cost inefficiencies in manufacturing.

(3) Concerning Hungary specifically, examination of the mean ratings of the individual SD items shows that, while giving generally higher ratings to foreign products, respondents do not consider domestic products to be poor as such (the means across the 21 seven-point items ranged from 2.8 to 4.9). Considering that Hungary is at an intermediate stage of development and that domestic products were being evaluated against those from some of the world's most advanced nations, attitudes towards domestic goods seem to be reasonably positive. This explanation is supported by the findings from Greece, which also is at an intermediate level of development and whose respondents also rated domestic goods lower than products from the four advanced foreign nations in the study.

UNDERLYING DIMENSIONS
(PRINCIPAL COMPONENTS ANALYSIS)

Although several variations exist, results of the factor analyses show a remarkable consistency in the underlying dimensions that Hungarian respondents used in evaluating foreign products. Based on the scree plot analysis and an eigenvalue criterion of greater than one, five interpretable factors emerged from the principal components analysis (VARIMAX rotation) of the *product* evaluation scales. The total amount of variance explained by these factors was fairly similar for all origins, ranging from 47.6% (Hungary) to 55.1% (US). The number of interpretable *country* factors was three for the US, Canada and Hungary, four for Japan and two for Sweden. The percentage of variance explained by the country factors ranged from 47.6% (Sweden) to 59.6% (Japan). *Table 2* shows the product factors and the variables with factor loadings greater than 0.4. *Table 3* gives a summary of the assigned product factor labels. *Table 4* and *5* show the same information for the country evaluation scales.

Table 2. Product evaluation factors

Variable	US I	US II	US III	US IV	US V	Japan I	Japan II	Japan III	Japan IV	Japan V	Canada I	Canada II	Canada III	Canada IV	Canada V	Sweden I	Sweden II	Sweden III	Sweden IV	Sweden V	Hungary I	Hungary II	Hungary III	Hungary IV	Hungary V
Poor/good workmanship	0.70					0.81					0.73					0.63					0.64				
Poor/good quality	0.67					0.68					0.62					0.72					0.54		0.51		
Technically not-/advanced	0.65					0.89					0.62	-0.44				0.78					0.73				
Unrecognisable/recognisable brands	0.54					0.41									0.57				0.69		0.75				
Initiative/innovative	0.68					0.51	0.43				0.64					0.69							0.72		
Not-/honest promotion	0.42						0.49				0.56					0.51							0.54		
Poor/good service	0.48		0.49		0.60		0.69				0.46					0.47							0.40		
Unreliable/reliable	0.69						0.51				0.64					0.58									0.52
Not proud/proud to own	0.66						0.63				0.66			0.40				0.43						0.76	
Overall not-/satisfied	0.76						0.58				0.61					0.51			0.52				0.40		
Know little/a lot about		0.81							0.65			0.82					0.82								-0.64
Difficult/easy to find		0.61							0.56			0.65					0.62						0.52		
Buy few/a lot of		0.79							0.69			0.84					0.73							0.63	
Appearance/performance					0.62								0.43							-0.67					
More for older/younger people					0.57					0.40			0.66					0.45		0.48		-0.68			
More for lower/upper class	-0.53		-0.53					-0.72					0.47							0.61		-0.71			
Expensive/inexpensive			0.46					0.77					-0.56			-0.42		-0.60				0.74			
Unreasonably/reasonably priced		0.66						0.67						0.73				0.53							
Necessity/luxury items		-0.72					-0.49				0.48			-0.58					0.43		0.45	0.53			
Narrow/wide choice				0.81						0.56			-0.50					0.66					-0.42		
Little/much advertising				0.82						0.80					0.83			0.68							0.66
Percentage of variance	22.7	12.1	7.9	7.2	5.2	19.7	12.0	7.6	6.3	5.6	24.6	10.7	7.8	5.7	5.1	23.0	10.9	7.5	5.7	5.5	19.0	9.6	7.2	6.5	5.3
Total percentage of variance	55.1					51.2					53.9					52.6					47.6				

Table 3. Summary – Product evaluation factors

Factor	Country				
	US	Japan	Canada	Sweden	Hungary
I	Product/market integrity	Product integrity	Product/market integrity	Product/market integrity	Product integrity
II	Experience	Market integrity	Experience	Experience	Status/value
III	Status/value	Status/value	Status	Market presence	Market integrity
IV	Market presence	Experience	Value	Market position	Domestic preference
V	Market orientation	Market presence	Market visibility	Status	Experience/ market presence

FOREIGN PRODUCTS

Views of products from the US, Canada and Sweden have one similar factor which explains between 22.7% and 24.6% of the variance. The scales which loaded on this factor were very consistent and include workmanship, overall quality, reliability, innovativeness and technical advancement. Pride in ownership (except for Sweden), and overall satisfaction also load here, suggesting that the technical aspects of product performance govern overall cognitive and affective responses to products from these countries. The fact that the variables "service" and "honest promotion" also tend to load in this dimension, albeit somewhat less strongly than the other scales, suggests that good products are seen to be well supported before and after the sale. As a result, this factor has been labelled "product and market integrity". For Japanese products these scales load on two distinct dimensions, "product integrity" and "market integrity", which together account for 31.7% of total variance. This proportion is substantially higher for Japan than in the corresponding single dimension of the other origins, suggesting that these constructs are perceived as more significant characteristics when evaluating Japanese products.

The four foreign origins also share an "experience" factor which is consistently represented by three variables ("know little/a lot about products from X", "products from X are difficult/easy to find", and "buy few/a lot of products from X"). This factor appears as the second dimension for American, Canadian and Swedish products and as the fourth dimension for Japanese products.

The survey instrument included four scales which deal directly or indirectly with the economic value and/or status of goods (expensive/inex-

Table 4. Country evaluation factors

Variable	US			Japan				Canada			Sweden		Hungary		
Factor:	I	II	III	I	II	III	IV	I	II	III	I	II	I	II	III
Admirable role in word politics	0.70					0.71		0.51	0.47		0.68		0.47		
Refined taste	0.51					0.66			0.59		0.55			0.71	
Likeable	0.75				0.41	0.49	0.46		0.75			0.66		0.81	
Trustworthy	0.70			0.67		0.43		0.57	0.44		0.70		0.73		
Industrious	0.59	0.40		0.77				0.63			0.66		0.71		
Managing economy well		0.72		0.61	0.49			0.71			0.61	-0.51	0.75		
Technically advanced		0.78		0.50	0.53			0.57			0.55	-0.52	0.60		
Agriculture/manufacturing		0.64		0.50				-0.43	0.45		NA				0.72
Industrial/consumer products			0.73				0.91			0.85		0.66			-0.67
Want more investment	0.45	0.46	0.56		0.77			0.70			0.52		NA		
Want closer ties		0.48	0.48		0.74			0.74			0.71		NA		
Percentage of variance	33.2	10.9	10.1	27.7	12.4	10.2	9.3	33.2	10.9	10.1	33.5	14.1	26.4	13.7	12.5
Total percentage of variance			54.2				59.6			54.2		47.6			52.6

pensive, unreasonably/reasonably priced, necessity/luxury and for the lower/upper class). Two or more of these variables load together in factor III for the US, Japan and Canada, accounting for slightly under 8% of the total variance. Hungarians view all products as rather expensive. The mean scores for one of the key variables loading in this dimension, "expensive/inexpensive", were very low ranging from 2.3 (US) to 3.1 (Canada) on the 1–7 scale. This finding seems reasonable especially in light of inflation (about 15%) and other economic problems that have affected negatively the Hungarian consumers' standard of living.

It should be noted that in separate factor analyses (not reported here) of the findings from the other seven countries that were sampled as part of the larger study, the price/value/status dimension usually appears as the second most important factor. The fact that for Hungarians the experience factor is more important in structuring their views probably reflects the low penetration level of Western products in socialist markets, which results in low levels of familiarity among consumers. It is also worth noting that, in the Hungarian sample, the price-value dimension did appear ahead of the experience dimension for Japanese products. This underscores the respondents' positive attitudes towards these products which, while being perceived as expensive as those from elsewhere, received the highest mean rating among all five origins on the scales "unreasonably/reasonably priced" (4.4) and "for the lower/upper class" (5.3).

Two other scales, dealing with product choice and amount of advertising, suggest a "market presence" dimension and appear in the assessments of American, Japanese and Swedish goods accounting for 5.6–7.5% of the variance. Some scales (recognisability of brands, appearance/performance orientation and for older/younger people) do not load consistently on the same or similar factors across the various origins. "Recognisability of brands" loads together with "much advertising" in the case of Canadian products in factor V which is clearly a "market visibility" dimension. "Appearance/performance" and "for older/younger people" load with "for the lower/upper class" in the fifth factor for Swedish products, which is similar to Canada's factor III and can be labelled "status".

In summary, the overall similarity in the percentage of variance explained by each of the product factors across the four foreign origins, and in the type and number of variables that load on each factor (i.e. the "richness" of the factors), suggests that Hungarian respondents used generally similar underlying constructs in evaluating foreign products. The four main dimensions are product and/or market integrity, value and/or status, and market presence or visibility.

DOMESTIC PRODUCTS

The dimensions used by respondents to evaluate domestic products are somewhat different from those used to assess foreign goods. The first factor represents a "product integrity" dimension. While being similar to the corresponding dimension for foreign products, it contains only four variables – workmanship, innovativeness, technical advancement and overall quality. Pride in ownership loads on factor IV with purchase level ("but a lot"), suggesting a nationalist preference for domestic goods. The "overall satisfaction" scale does not sit comfortably with any of the product assessment scales. It loads weakly with factor III, which also includes the variables of quality, recognisable brands, service, promotion, and difficult/easy to find. While being generally similar to the "market integrity" dimension of Japanese products, this factor appears third and explains only 7.2% of the variance. This suggests that satisfaction is derived from non-product performance factors, such as market availability and accessibility of service facilities.

A comparatively stronger status/value dimension emerges when evaluating domestic products. For Hungarian goods, three of the variables that reflect status and/or economic value appear together with the scale "for older/younger people" in factor II which accounts for almost 10% of the variance. It is possible that the price dimension is more important for Hungarians when they assess their domestic products, which are perceived to be almost as expensive as most foreign ones (a mean rating of 2.6 in the expensive/inexpensive scale, compared to a range of 2.3–3.1 for imports) and unreasonably priced (a mean rating of 3.0 on the unreasonably/reasonably priced scale, versus 3.8 or higher for the four foreign origins).

The three scales which emerged together as a distinct "experience" factor for foreign products are spread across three separate dimensions in the case of domestic products. One of these scales, "know a little/a lot about products from X" , loaded in factor V together with product choice and reliability, suggesting a different perspective on the respondents' experience with, or the market presence of, Hungarian goods.

THE ORIGIN COUNTRIES AND THEIR PEOPLE

As with the product evaluation dimensions, there is some similarity among the country evaluation factors. The first similar dimension is labelled as "affect" for the US (factor I), Japan (III) and Canada (II). The

Table 5. Summary – Country evaluation factors

Factor	Country				
	US	Japan	Canada	Sweden	Hungary
I	Affect	Industrial development	Industrial development	Industrial development and effect	Industrial development
II	Industrial development	Closer ties	Affect	Industrial orientation	Affect
III	Closer ties	Affect	Industrial orientation	–	Industrial orientation
IV	–	Industrial orientation	–	–	–

scales loading on this factor were very consistent and include the countries' perceived role in world politics and the trustworthiness, likeability and refined taste of their people *(Table 5)*.

The survey instrument included four scales intended to ascertain, directly or indirectly, perceptions about the origin countries' industrial development. These referred to the successful management of the country's economy, its technical advancement, its strength in manufacturing as opposed to agriculture, and the industriousness of its people. These four scales loaded together for the US (factor II), Japan, Canada, and Sweden (factor I). However, in the case of Canada and Sweden, this factor also contains several of the other country evaluation scales. One possible explanation for this is the relative lack of information in the Hungarian media about these two countries, resulting in less clear perceptions and providing evidence of uni-dimensional, stereotyped views about them among respondents.

The percentage of variance explained by the "affect" and "industrial development" factors varies considerably between the US and Japan. Development is clearly a more important consideration when evaluating Japan, accounting for a significantly higher proportion of the variance (27.7%) than in the case of the US (10.9%). Conversely, "affect" accounts for 33.2% of the variance in the case of the US, compared with only 10.2% for Japan. Examination of the mean scores of the variables shows that the US received the lowest rating among all five origins on the scales that comprise the affect factor. The range of means for trustworthiness, taste, likeability, and role in world politics was 3.1–4.3 for the US compared to 4.2–5.9 for the other four origins. This suggests that the consumers' affective responses can have a significant negative impact on the ability of US producers to enter the Hungarian market.

The behavioural dimension of attitude was examined by including, for the foreign origins only, the following two scales in the questionnaire: "I would not/would welcome more investment here from X" and "We should not/should have closer ties with X". These variables tended to load with the "industrial development" dimension for the US (factor II), Canada and Sweden (factor I). In the case of Japan, they are contained in factor II together with technical advancement, strength in manufacturing and likeability of the people, perhaps reflecting Japan's attractiveness to the Hungarians as a potential trade partner in light of its orientation towards producing high value-added, technically advanced products.

A scale anchored by the terms "heavy, industrial goods/light, consumer products" was included in the survey instrument. It was expected to load together with the scale "agricultural/manufactured products" and to provide an indication of the respondents' perceptions of the origin countries' industrial orientation. With the exception of Hungary, however, where the two scales loaded together on factor III, these variables did not load consistently on any one factor and they do not seem to make any contribution to our understanding of how Hungarians view foreign countries.

The Hungarians' views of themselves are generally similar to their views of other countries, although some differences do exist. The first factor concerning Hungary itself is the "industrial development" dimension. It contains the same four variables as the foreign origins and also Hungary's role in world politics. The second factor is an "affect" dimension which, however, contains only two of the four affect variables (trustworthiness and likeability). As mentioned above, the third dimension reflects Hungary's orientation towards agricultural and industrial goods (as opposed to manufactured consumer products).

IMPLICATIONS AND CONCLUSION

THE IMAGE OF WESTERN PRODUCTS

Prevailing public perceptions in Western countries, formed in large part by mass media reports, suggest that Western products epitomise much that is desired by consumers in Eastern socialist markets. In this context, and especially in view of the Hungarian consumers' relative lack of experience with products from Western developed nations, one might have hypothesised that all such products would be held in equally high regard.

An alternative hypothesis might have been that, due to the important international role of the US and the high visibility of American products, the latter would be seen more favourably than products from other Western origins. Significantly, among the four Western origins studied, the US is the most important exporter to Hungary, being its 10th largest supplier overall and accounting for 2.5% of its imports. By contrast, Japan and Sweden are, respectively, Hungary's 19th and 20th largest suppliers accounting for only 1.1 and 1.0% of its imports, and Canada represents less than 0.5% of Hungarian imports (*Statistical Pocketbook of Hungary*, 1986).

However, the findings from this study do not support either of these two hypotheses. Hungarian consumers' views about Western products and their origins are not uniform, neither do they coincide with the comparative importance of these origins as suppliers of the Hungarian market. Japan is seen most favourably by the respondents as a product source, a view that is shared by consumers in the seven other Western countries where this study was conducted (see *Table 1*). Japan's products were rated highest of all origins in 14 of the 21 SD product items, and second-best in five of the remaining items, by the Hungarian sample. Likewise, Japan received the highest rating in 10 of the 11 SD items in the country evaluation scales. An obvious conclusion from these findings is that Japanese products have succeeded in creating a universally positive image for their products and themselves among not only Western, but also Eastern consumers. This image can be seen as representing a significant amount of goodwill towards Japanese products, which must be taken into account by producers who find themselves in competition against manufacturers from Japan.

Base on the paired comparison *t*-tests (at α = 0.05), American products were rated as second overall (see *Table 1*) and were seen as superior to Swedish goods, which ranked third overall, in eight of the 21 SD product variables (technical advancement, innovativeness, product choice, "know a lot", more for younger people, recognisable brands, advertised a lot, and "buy a lot"). On the other hand, Swedish goods were rated significantly higher on seven variables (reasonably priced, honest promotion, service, workmanship, appearance/performance, necessity/luxury, and inexpensive). Swedish and US products received identical ratings on the remaining six variables.

The image of Swedish goods seems to be almost as strong as that for American products, in spite of the comparatively low-key presence of Swedish products in Hungary. One possible explanation for this finding may be that Hungarians transpose their favourable image of Sweden and its people to their views of Swedish products. Sweden was rated significantly higher than the US (at $\alpha = 0.05$) in seven of the 11 country evaluation scales, including the affect variables as well as the scales, "We should not/should have closer ties with X" and "I would not/would welcome more investment here from X".

Canadian goods received the lowest rating among the four Western origins in the study, sharing fourth or fifth place with Hungarian goods on most of the variables. Although Canada was rated relatively high on the variables comprising the "affect" factor in the country evaluations, its perceived agricultural orientation and comparatively low level of technical advancement appear to influence negatively respondents' perceptions about Canadian products.

DOMESTIC VERSUS FOREIGN PRODUCTS

As discussed earlier, the factors and variable loadings for Hungarian products differed in several respects from the criteria used to evaluate foreign products. Given that pride in ownership loads together with purchase level, it is possible that for some Hungarian consumers national pride plays a significant role in terms of their attitudes towards domestic products. Clearly, however, the dimensionality of responses that Hungarians hold towards domestic goods is complex and differs from how they view foreign products.

Domestic products were rated as "best" by only three of the eight respondent groups in the larger study (see *Table 1*). Much like respondents in Greece, which is at a similar stage of development with Hungary, Hungarian consumers rated domestic products significantly lower than products from foreign origins. Surprisingly, however, respondents also rated Hungary and its people lower than Japan on all but one of the country evaluation scales (the exception was on "role in world politics", where Hungary received the highest score while Japan was ranked fourth). Considering the cultural and geographic distance between the two countries, it is difficult to explain why Hungarians would rate Japan higher even on such variables as likeability, trustworthiness and taste. One plausible hypothesis is that unlike Sweden, where the country's image seems to be transposed to its products, for Japan Hungarians transpose their positive attitudes towards Japanese products to the country itself and its people.

IMPLICATIONS FOR INTERNATIONAL MARKETING

This study provides a number of significant insights into the nature of the country-of-origin effect as well as on Hungary as a potential market for various Western producers. One significant conclusion must be that consumers do hold strong and distinct images about foreign (Western) products, notwithstanding the relative lack of information about and experience with them. These images are generally in line with those held by consumers in the seven other (Western) countries that were part of the cross-national study. The low penetration of Western goods in Hungary, coupled with the presence of distinct images about them, strengthens the theoretical suggestion concerning the presence of a "country-of-origin effect".

The findings for Sweden and Japan suggest that this effect may well be bidirectional. That is, it is possible that attitudes towards a country and its people may affect attitudes towards the country's products, as in the case of Sweden; however, the reverse may also be true – a country and its people may come to be appreciated as a result of positive views towards the products they produce. This would suggest that causal relationships, which in earlier made-in studies have been assumed to be unidirectional (image of country leads to image of products), may be considerably more complex than previously thought.

Concerning international marketing strategy, prevailing perceptions in Western countries are that the willingness of consumers in Eastern socialist countries to buy Western products is constrained largely by income considerations and lack of availability. However, the findings suggest that not all Western producers will find ready markets in socialist as East-West trade grows. Assuming an increasing ability on the part of consumers to access Western products (because of greater availability due to market liberalisation), existing lukewarm or even negative perceptions about an origin country's level of technical advancement, or about the quality and performance of its products, are likely to constitute perceptual barriers to entry in Eastern markets as much as they do in Western ones.

Therefore, export activity towards Hungary (and probably other Eastern European markets) needs to be planned as carefully as any such activity addressed to Western markets. Careful consideration of consumers' attitudes also seems to be necessary concerning investments. In stating their views about countries with which they would like to have closer links, Hungarian respondents expressed positive attitudes for all four foreign origins but also indicated a clear preference for certain origins. The mean scores for these two seven-point scales were 6.5 and 6.1 for Japan, 5.9 and 5.6 for Sweden, 5.4 and 5.2 for Canada, and 5.2 and 5.2 for the US. These two SD items loaded strongly with variables related to industrial development (e.g. manufacturing orientation, technical advancement) in the factor analysis for the foreign origins, suggesting that an ability to produce high value-added products is an important consideration governing the respondents' attitudes.

SUMMARY AND CONCLUSION

Similar to their Western counterparts, Hungarian consumers hold strongly positive attitudes about Japan and its products. The factor analyses suggest a certain degree of consistency in the underlying dimensions used by consumers to assess products and their origins. A significant product and/or market integrity dimension is followed by an experience and/or status/value factor. In assessing countries and their people, two key factors emerged – affect and industrial development. Contrary to what might have been expected, the views of respondents were found to be neither the same for various Western-origin products nor universally positive.

This study contributes to our understanding of the underlying dimensions along which products are evaluated. By including distinct country evaluation items for the first time in this field of research, the study also provides some tentative evidence that product images may influence, and/or be influenced by, country images. The findings suggest that the direction of causality between these two constructs is less clear then previously thought.

It goes without saying that the present research has only scratched the surface in terms of insights into behavioural aspects of consumers in socialist markets. Questions that may be asked, in addition to those that have been raised so far in this article, include the relative importance of made-in images in making purchase decisions, the potential use of these images in market segmentation decisions, and a better understanding of the correlations between respondents' views about country versus product images. Insights into these types of questions will enable managers to identify strengths and weaknesses of their particular products, and to make more informed decisions regarding the development of "global" marketing and communication strategies.

REFERENCES

ARTISIEN, P. F. R., BUCKLEY, P. J.: "Joint Ventures in Yugoslavia: Opportunities and Constraints", *Journal of International Business Studies*, Spring, pp. 111–135 (1985).

(ASQC) American Society for Quality Control: *Consumer Attitudes on Quality in the US*, ASQC, Milwaukee, Wisconsin (1980).

BARKSDALE, H. C., KELLY, W. J.: "The Marketing Concept in the US and the USSR: An Historical Analysis", *Journal of the Academy of Marketing Science*, Vol. 6, No. 4, Fall, pp. 258–277 (1978).

BERÁCS, J.: "Marketing Activities of Hungarian Industrial Companies", *Working Paper Series*, School of Business, Carleton University, December (1984).

BILKEY, W. J., NES, E.: "Country-of-origin Effects on Product Evaluations", *Journal of International Business Studies*, Spring-Summer, pp. 89–99 (1982).

BORNSTEIN, M., FUSFELD, D. R. (eds): *The Soviet Economy*, Irwin, Homewood, Illinois (1970).

DARLING, J. R., KRAFT, F. B.: "A Competitive Profile of Products and Associated Marketing Practices of Selected European and Non-European Countries", *European Journal of Marketing*, Vol. 11, No. 7, pp. 519–531 (1977).

DICHTER, E.: "The World Customer", *Harvard Business Review*, Vol. 40, No. 4, July–August, pp. 113–122 (1962).

GOLDMAN, M. I.: "The Marketing Structure in the Soviet Union", *Journal of Marketing*, July, pp. 7–14 (1961).

HISRICH, R. D., PETERS, M. P.: "East-West Trade: An Assessment by US Manufacturers", *Columbia Journal of World Business*, Winter (1983).

JOHANSSON, J. K.: Presentation at the 1985 Conference of the *Academy of International Business*, October, New York (1985).

JOHANSSON, J. K., NEBENZAHL, I. D.: "Multinational Production: Effect on Brand Value", *Journal of International Business Studies*, Fall, pp. 101–126 (1986).

KELMAN, H. C. (ed.): *Internartional Behaviour: A Social-Psychological Analysis*, Holt, Rinehart & Winston, New York (1965).

MILOSH, E. J.: "Imaginative Marketing in Eastern Europe", *Columbia Journal of World Business*, Winter, pp. 69–72 (1973).

NAGASHIMA, A.: "A Comparison of Japanese and US Attitudes Toward Foreign Products", *Journal of Marketing*, January, pp. 260–266 (1970).

NAGASHIMA, A.: "A Comparative 'Made-in' Product Image Survey Among Japanese Businessmen", *Journal of Marketing*, July, pp. 95–100 (1977).

NAOR, J.: "Towards a Socialist Marketing Concept – The Case of Romania", *Journal of Marketing*, January, pp. 28–39 (1986).

NIFFENEGGER, P., WHITE, J., MARMET, G.: "How European Retailers View American Imported Products: Results of a Product Image Survey", *Journal of the Academy of Marketing Science*, Vol. 10, Summer, pp. 281–291 (1982).

PAPADOPOULOS, N.: "Development and Organisation of a Cross-national Study: The Country-of-origin Effect", in BRADLEY, M. F. and PAPADOPOULOS, N. (eds): *Proceedings, Workshop on International Marketing Strategy*, European Institute for Advanced Studies in Management, Brussels, pp. 42–56 (1986).

PAPADOPOULOS, N., BERÁCS, J.: "Expanding the Geographic Scope of Research to Eastern European Shortage Economies", *Broadening the Uses of Research,* 38th Congress, European Society for Opinion and Marketing Research, Wiesbaden, September, pp. 1–21 (1985).

PAPADOPOULOS, N., HESLOP, L. A., GRABY, F., AVLONITIS, G.: "Does 'Country-of-origin' Matter? Some Findings from a Cross-cultural Study of Consumer Views About Foreign Products", *Working Paper Series,* No. 87–104, Marketing Science Institute, Cambridge, Massachusetts (1987).

SEATON, B., VOGEL, R. H.: "International Dimensions and Price as Factors in Consumer Perceptions of Autos", paper presented at the 1981 Annual Conference of the Academy of International Business, Montreal, October (1981).

Statistical Pocketbook of Hungary: Central Hungarian Statistical Bureau (annual) (1986).

WALL, M., HESLOP, L. A.: "Consumer Attitudes toward Canadian-made versus Imported Products", *Journal of the Academy of Marketing Science,* Vol. 14, No. 2, Summer, pp. 27–36 (1986).

2

CHANGES IN ECONOMIC MANAGEMENT SYSTEMS IN HUNGARY AND OTHER EAST EUROPEAN COUNTRIES*

By

TAMÁS MÉSZÁROS

Taking Hungary as an example, this article examines changes taking place in economic management systems in Eastern Europe. Developments in the political, institutional and economic sectors of Hungarian society are analyzed, and current trends and problems are presented. Countries of Eastern Europe are classified into three categories in order to show how a need for change emerges under different constraints.

The last few years, and particularly the last few months, have been a period of relatively rapid change in Hungary. There have been contrasting views in Hungary and elsewhere about the speed of the changes, but there is no doubt about the rapidity with which new developments are occurring.

The declared goal of the different developments is not only to halt the decline of the Hungarian economy, but also to find the best ways of improving economic performance. The decisions of the last few months were designed to lead the country out of its crisis. Although Hungary's policies are extraordinary and important it is not alone in facing serious economic problems and in looking for ways to resolve them. Most East European countries have decided to implement – to various degrees – economic management reforms during the past decade.

If we thoroughly examine the measures implemented and results achieved by the various countries, we find substantial differences. Naturally there are some common aspirations, first of all in recognizing the need for change and in increasing the role of market forces. However, with regard to directions, solutions, methods and even results, the differ-

* In *Futures* Dec. 1989, pp. 632–639.

ences tend to be major. The main reasons for these differences can be found in political and historical backgrounds, traditions, different levels of technical development, behaviour of leadership, relationships with Western countries (in the case of East Germany for example), participation in the CMEA, and so on.

In this short article I cannot analyze the situation in depth; instead I try to show through the example of Hungary how the East European nations are moving from centralized planning to a market-oriented economy. I go on to describe briefly the attempts, plans, recent results and problems of some of these countries.

In trying to do so, an important question must be answered: how can we characterize an economic management system and how can we describe its development process? I have selected a few key economic management factors which were generally used in Hungary. In addition I will discuss some other features to show the impact of the system on enterprises.

The economic management factors I have chosen are as follows:

- *The national planning system,* which defines the general role of the national plan and its specific impact on enterprise management.
- *The regulatory system,* which concerns taxation and the regulation of capital investment and wages.
- *The institutional and organizational system,* which is the structure and authority of different organizations at both central and enterprise (including banks) levels. An important issue in this system is enterprise autonomy.
- *The main enterprise goals,* which refer to how enterprise performance is evaluated and how the various interests in an enterprise are coordinated.
- *The price and exchange rate system,* which refers to the types of consumer prices, the relationship between the world market and domestic prices and exchange rates.
- *The nature of competition,* which refers to competition in the different markets (domestic, rouble and dollar areas) and also to competition between domestic enterprises.

To provide an overview of the various developments in Hungary, I shall discuss events in three different time periods: before 1968, after 1968, and the 1980s. The period before 1968 can be characterized as the period of centrally planned instructions. These instructions were based upon the principle that all important decisions involving economic activity must be made by central institutions such as the National Planning Office. During the period after 1968 the so-called new economic mechanism was introduced in Hungary. The measures of 1968 were the first major steps towards a market-oriented economic management system. The most recent period (the 1980s) is still taking shape. I therefore describe the most recent measures and currently planned changes in the economic management system.

CHARACTERISTICS OF THE ECONOMY DURING THREE MAIN PERIODS

BEFORE 1968

The national planning system was the basic instrument for managing the economy, with the enterprise plan an integral part of the national plan. All important decisions involving economic activities were made in central institutions (i.e. the National Planning Office). Detailed instructions about production, investment, and so on , were transmitted through the different levels of the hierarchy to the enterprises. The key element was control through the central plan.

The regulatory system was used by the state to withdraw and redistribute all income from the enterprises. Decisions about investments and wages were centralized.

The institutional and organizations system was characterized by centralization and monopolization. State-owned enterprises were dominant; enterprises had little autonomy and their establishment or elimination was a prerogative of the state; enterprises were excessively large and concentrated; foreign trade and banks were monopolized by the state; cooperatives existed primarily in the agricultural sector; the role of the private sector was slight; there was a large number of ministries and other central organizations.

The main goal of the enterprises was the quantitative fulfillment of the plan, which was determined by the higher administrative levels.

The Price and exchange policy was centralized. There was no relationship between prices (i.e. all consumer prices) and the domestic market, let alone the world market. All prices were fixed. The situation was the same for exchange rates. There was a complete lack of competition.

AFTER 1968

The national planning system formed plans at two separate levels: national and enterprise. Their relationship was to be indirect. Mid-year and annual plans were required of the enterprises. In practice, the role of the national plan was dominant. Many bureaucratic elements of the system remained. Consequently, the basic instruments for managing the economy were the national plan and regulation of the enterprise. The enterprise plans were formal and uninformed. Still, some attempts at strategic planning appeared.

There were many changes in the regulatory system. A complicated and frequently changing tax system was instituted and the regulation of wages varied greatly. Provision and withdrawal of resource support for enterprises was confusing, which caused great difficulties in evaluating enterprises. The government determined about half of all investments. Possibilities for mobilizing capital were very limited.

In the system of institution and organization there were only a few fundamental changes. Some enterprises were able to be directly involved in foreign trade, although the state monopoly remained in control of hard currency. The private sector increased, especially in the retail area. The number of ministries was reduced. A process of excessive concentration was continuing in industry and even in agriculture. Enterprise autonomy was increasing but dependence on ministries and other central organizations remained high (ministries appointed enterprises' top management). Most members of agricultural cooperatives had household plots, and their collective and private production worked well together.

In theory, the main goal of enterprises was increased profit. In practice this was not the case because of price distinctions an subsidies.

The central regulation of the price system was maintained because market conditions were backward and imperfect and because of social conditions and the living standard policy. There were three forms of consumer prices: fixed prices, which were defined by the authorities; ceiling prices; and free prices. The proportion of free prices grew, although some obstacles were applied (eg. requirements for reporting price rises and consulting with the Central Price Office about the level of price rises). There were strong connection between prices and supply and demand within the country but tenuous relations with world market prices. Different price systems were implemented in three different markets: domestic, rouble, and non-rouble. An inflationary tendency became evident at the end of this period.

In its exchange rate policy, Hungary made a gradual adaptation to hard currencies. There were no changes within the CMEA. There was only limited competition.

RECENT PLANS AND TRENDS

There is debate about the role of the national plan. Some specialists recommend a significant reduction on its future role with a focus on only some of the economy's monetary processes. Others agree with the need for change but are unsure about restricting it to a solely monetary role. Enterprise plans are formed independently, including decisions about the type of plan, time frame, and so on. Ideas about enterprise planning are changing and strategic management is improving. The basic instrument for managing the economy is the regulatory system.

The regulatory system sow focuses on monetary instruments. New taxes – a value added tax (VAT) and a personal income tax (PIT) – became effective on 1 January, 1988. The government initiated a new entrepreneur profit tax in 1989. Though decisions about investments are generally to be determined by enterprises, at present this is greatly limited because of the fiscal deficits. Possibilities for capital mobilization, both domestic and foreign, are increasing significantly. The government is planning a complete reform of the wage system, so that in future wages will depend on agreements between employers and trade unions.

In the last eight years there have been a number of serious changes in the institutional and organizational system. Three separate ministries were fused into the Ministry of Industry in 1980; some large industries and trusts have been decentralized (up to 1985, 10 trusts and 47 big companies were modified); a number of new small private enterprises, novel cooperatives, and corporations have been established. New forms of enterprise management have been introduced (enterprise council, assembly of delegates). This generally means complete independence from the ministries, except for certain important enterprises and crucial sectors of the economy. The top management of most enterprises are elected by the enterprise council or the assembly of delegates. A two-level banking system and commercial banking hours have been established, thereby changing the bank monopoly. In October 1988, the Hungarian parliament passed a corporation law, which makes it possible to establish different forms of companies: private enterprises (the maximum permitted number of employees has been raised from 30 to 500 if the owner is Hungarian, and the ceiling has been removed altogether for foreign owners); joint stock companies; limited liability companies; and joint ventures with foreign firms (of which there are at present 111, the most in Eastern Europe).

The main goal of enterprises is economic growth and increased assets.

Table 1. National income[1] according to different forms of property[2]

Type of property	1970 %	1980 %	1986 %
Socialist sector (total)	97.4	96.5	93.0
of which:			
state owned	70.7	69.8	63.4
cooperative	23.6	23.0	23.0
employees' complementary economy	3.1	3.7	6.6
Private sector (total)	2.6	3.5	7.0

Notes

[1] National income or net national product (NNP).
[2] *Hungarian Statistical Almanac, 1987.*

As far as the price policy is concerned no fundamental changes have occurred although much research is being done. The main goals are to approach world market prices and to eliminate the so-called "three markets equals three prices" construction. However, there are some results, such as the increasing approximation of world market prices in the area of raw materials, and the growing proportion of free prices. In 1988 double-digit inflation reached 17%, which necessitates a change in the exchange rate policy. The government expected double-digit inflation for 1989 as well.

The possibility of competition is growing, mainly in the domestic market. However, many obstacles remain; there is no competition within the CMEA, and competing in Western markets is difficult for Hungarian firms, because of the relatively low level of technology of their products.

PRESENT ECONOMIC ISSUES

One of the key current issues is the question of property rights. This issue is not simply economic, but also political and ideological. It is being raised not only in Hungary but even in the USSR, Poland and other socialist countries. Current approaches to this issue represent significant changes, and today in Hungary a new corporation law allows the establishment of private enterprises. Crucial barriers to private enterprises are being eased or removed, such as the increased limit on number of employees, as mentioned above. According to the new corporation law companies may sell

Table 2. Index of Hungary's gross domestic product, 1981–1988

Year	GDP	Domestic use
	(Index: 1980 = 100)	
1981	102.9	101.4
1982	105.8	101.3
1983	106.5	99.6
1984	109.4	99.9
1985	109.1	100.3
1986	110.7	104.2
1987	115.2	107.5
1988 (projected)	115.3	104.5

Source: Hungarian Statistical Almanac, 1987.

Table 3. Index of Hungary's national income, 1960–1988

Year	National income (actual prices)	Domestic outlays	Material consumption	Net investment
	(Index: 1950 = 100)			
1960	177	183	168	251
1970	300	316	273	522
1980	467	450	39	66
1988 (projected)	521	442	435	373

Source: Hungarian Statistical Almanac, 1987.

Table 4. Living standard indicators, 1970–1988

Year	Real income (per capita)	Real wages (per capita)
	(Index: 1960 = 100)	
1970	159.4	129.3
1980	217.2	157.8
1988	240.2	146.3

Source: Hungarian Statistical Almanac, 1987.

Table 5. Retail price indices, 1985–1988

1987	1985	1986	1987	1988 (projected)
(1980 = 100)	(Annual index: previous year = 100)			
159.1	107.0	105.3	108.6	116.5

Source: Plan Econ Report, 9 September, 1988.

shares, and the legal framework for a fully fledged stock exchange has been established. It is now possible to transform state enterprises into joint stock companies, and this is already happening. The new corporation law and the accompanying measures will probably cause significant changes in the structure of ownership in Hungary. *Table 1* illustrates the current trends.

The development of the so-called "socialist market economy" is an urgent task for the Hungarian leadership. Despite the good annual results achieved at the beginning of the 1970s, such as the rise in living standard, the increased assortment of consumer goods, the relative independence of enterprises, and the generally continuing improvements during the last decade, Hungary today confronts a stagnant and even declining economy.

There are several aspects to this development. There are problems with economic growth (illustrated in *Tables 2* and *3*). The standard of living is declining (see *Table 4*), and there is an upward inflationary trend (see *Table 5*). Hungary has a relatively high external debt, namely, US$17739 million in 1987 [1]. Unemployment has become a problem: there were 11500 registered unemployed at the end of the second quarter of 1988 [2]. The basic structure of the economy in particular is ineffective as it is changing too slowly. There is a growing income differentiation, resulting in more poor people.

The recognition of these problems has led to the following expectations of the rapid changes in Hungary's economic management system:

- to mobilize dormant capital, create a favourable investment climate and lure Western investors with money and know-how;
- to increase economic growth and the living standard; and
- to develop a social support system for poor people.

Having spelt out the expectation, I should add that there are no illusions about how fast all of this can take place. There is general agreement in Hungary that it is impossible to reform the economy without political reforms. This means that in the process of implementing economic reform we have to expert resistance, because the new measures will lead to an additional decline in the standard of living during the early years. The ways, the possibilities, and even the consequences of the reform are not yet completely understood.

There are many risks, contradictions and hardships in the process of implementation. Social problems, new competitive pressures, and the continual increase of external debt through imports are just a few illustrations of this. The conditions needed for real competition are generally limited, for various reasons. There is no competition within the CMEA, and the conditions for competition (i.e. a real convertible currency to replace bilateral trade) are missing. Most Hungarian products cannot compete in Western markets because of their poor technical quality, and the relatively small domestic market.

These are facts, but, of course, they do not mean that Hungary cannot change the situation and take advantage of the opportunities. This view is held in other East European countries as well, and this is a crucial factor.

SITUATION IN OTHER EAST EUROPEAN COUNTRIES

When we discuss the changes in economic management system in Eastern Europe, we have firstly to distinguish between declarations and facts. Undoubtedly, there are very different pressures for change in these countries as well. On the basis of what is actually happening, one can group these countries into three different categories, described below.

COUNTRIES REJECTING DEVELOPMENT OF NEW ECONOMIC MANAGEMENT SYSTEM

These include the German Democratic Republic (GDR) and Romania. These countries do not admit their economic problems in public, and so they see their current political-economic direction as a proper one. To deal with problems and tensions they tend to strengthen centralization.

The system of the GDR has two basic elements. One is a strict requirement for the quantitative fulfillment of plans and balancing the books, and the other is the high degree of operational independence of the so-called middle management organizations (for example combines). This system, in spite of its overregulation, is flexible because of certain informal solutions.

In Romania, the leadership wants to solve its crisis in the Stalinist manner. The basic elements of the management system are the "natural economy" and major central decisions. In recent years Romania has significantly reduced its foreign debt, but the problems of the domestic market are increasing and the living standard is continuously declining. Various authorities (including the IMF), however, believe that the country could archive important and fast results through the elimination of current practices.

COUNTRIES WHERE CONTINUITY IS PREDOMINANT

We can define this group as nations which profess to be making reforms, but where, in reality, the changes undertaken are not fundamental. Czechoslovakia and Bulgaria belong to this group, despite significant differences.

In the 1970s Bulgaria could be characterized as a highly centralized economy. In the last decade the leadership has declared spectacular changes as part of its "new economic approach" (involving changes in the price system, and self control of enterprises). The new measures are frequently withdrawn because of their unexpected consequences. Direct state interference with management decisions is viewed as undesirable, but the state maintains control over the direct allocation of materials, trade balances, and other central decisions, including large investments.

The Czechoslovakian leadership plans some major changes in 1991. Recent measures show that it intends to create an indirect type of economic management system, rather than a market-oriented one. There is no intention, for example, to make changes in the system of national planning. In Czechoslovakia there is no urgent need for reform because of the relative equilibrium of the economy. However, signs of economic problems are beginning to appear. Economic growth is slowing (in 1986 annual growth was 2.6%; in 1987 it was 2.2%; and in the first half of 1988 it was about 2.0%, instead of the average 3.5% achieved in recent five year plans).

COUNTRIES DEVELOPING A MARKET ECONOMY

This group of countries is trying to create a market-oriented economy, but the manner in which they have worked towards this objective during the last decade is full of contradictions. Poland and Hungary represent this group. The other common characteristic of their approach is that so far they have not developed a successful model of a socialist market economy. Both countries have relatively high foreign debts. This results in the postponement of important decisions which limits technical development. The general opinion at present is that their performance does not support the attempts at change promoted by the USSR. Naturally, there are significant differences between these two countries.

A headline in *The New York Times* of 10 October 1988 read: "Hungary sets the pace for East bloc change". Hopefully, the analysis presented in this article can serve as a basis for a precise evaluation of future trends in the new socialist world.

REFERENCES

[1] *Plan Econ Report,* 9 September 1988.
[2] Figyelő, Economic and Political Weekly, 16 September 1988.

3

AGRICULTURE AND THE TRANSITION
TO THE MARKET*

By

KAREN BROOKS, J. LUIS GUASCH,
AVISHAY BRAVERMAN, CSABA CSÁKI

Agricultural sectors in Eastern and Central Europe are large, and a substantial number of people are directly affected by changes in producer prices, farm employment, and land ownership. Retail food markets are among the most distorted in the pre-transition economies, and the needed adjustment are correspondingly large. The decollectivization of agriculture and return of land to former owners are among the most dramatic and emotive elements of the economic transition.

Food, moreover, is highly politicized. Citizens of Eastern Europe and the USSR were for decades offered stable, subsidized food prices and a steadily improving diet as an indicator of the superiority of socialism over capitalism, and compensation for deficiencies in other aspects of material life. It is paradoxical that food assumed this political importance, since the economic organization of agriculture in socialist economies was particularly ill-suited for production of cheap food.

The agricultural transition requires substantial adjustments on the demand and on the supply sides of the food economy. Institutional and technological change on the supply side must bring down traditionally high costs of production and increase efficiency and quality. Price liberalization confronts consumers with the real costs of food, and these costs are for some commodities two and three times the former subsidized prices. Domestic demand is reduced by the removal of food subsidies, and producers lose the protection that insulated them from competitors on world markets. Such price liberalization is well under way in Poland,

* In *Journal of Economic Perspectives*, Fall 1991, Vol. 5, No. 4, pp. 149–161.

Czechoslovakia, Hungary, Romania, and Bulgaria.[1] The demand side adjustment, although still incomplete, has been swift and less painful for consumers than many people had feared. The supply adjustment is slower, and complicated by depressed demand on both domestic and foreign markets.

Decollectivization and distribution of property rights in land is an important component of the supply adjustment, and merits careful attention. The essence of the agricultural transition, however, is the withdrawal of the state from its traditional role as residual claimant of (positive and negative) rents to the use of agricultural resources. That role will pass in stages to owners of land, where it ordinarily resides in a market economy. A discussion of the new land laws and distribution of land would be incomprehensible without attention to conditions that shape the value of land, the income that owners can earn from it, and the decisions that private owners make regarding land management.

The macroeconomic stabilization, associated liberalization of prices and interest rates, and depressed demand on domestic and foreign markets creates an atmosphere of acute economic uncertainty and declining farm incomes that forms the context for the distribution of agricultural land. Romania leads with swift implementation of a land law passed in February 1991. Many owners expect to take possession of their land after the harvest in fall of 1991, although few report plans to remove their lands from collective production next season. The Bulgarian land law was also passed in February 1991, but implementation has been delayed and the approach taken implies a more lengthy process. Land laws in Hungary and Czechoslovakia were passed in April and May of 1991, respectively. In this paper we place the agricultural transition in its larger context, and treat the distribution of land more briefly.

A FRAMEWORK FOR THE AGRICULTURAL TRANSITION

CONDITIONS AT THE OUTSET OF THE TRANSITION

The countries of Eastern and Central Europe comprise a large and diverse agricultural region. In the northern tier – in Poland, the Czech and Slovak Federal Republic, and the former GDR – grains (except for maize), roots,

---

[1] Yugoslav food prices were less controlled even prior to the current period than was the case in other Eastern and Central European countries.

and specialty crops dominate the field crops, and imports augment domestic production of feed to sustain a large livestock industry. In Hungary, Romania, and northern Yugoslavia, moisture and warmth are adequate for maize and oilseeds, and mixed grain/livestock farming predominates. Farther south in Yugoslavia and Bulgaria irrigation becomes more important, as do viticulture, orchards, and tobacco production. If the Soviet Union is included, the agroclimatic range of Eastern and Central Europe is replicated, and augmented by the largest area of irrigated agriculture in the world, in Soviet Central Asia.

To draw lessons that transcend the particularities of the individual countries, we create a stylized country with the general features of each, but the particular uniqueness of none. We take this country through an agricultural transition, indicating how various initial conditions affect the path of transition.

Agricultural production in the stylized country was collectivized. Approximately one-third of farms were state farms, and two-thirds were collective farms (cooperatives), but there was in practice little difference between the two. Many members of collective farms in theory retained title to collectively managed land, but ownership rights in the past were so attenuated as to be meaningless. (The exception to this pattern is the USSR, where all land was nationalized.) On both state and collective farms, workers had a high degree of job and wage security, little responsibility for the financial performance of the farm, and little incentive to improve productivity. Both types of farms were protected from bankruptcy by a soft budget constraint.

Farm employees managed a household plot of about one-half hectare in addition to their work on the large farm. The structure of production was thus dual, with very large units of 2,000 and 3,000 hectares plus many mini-farms. The private and socialist sectors were intimately linked in one agricultural system, and each would have faced significantly higher costs of production if forced to function independently of the other. For example, the socialized sector contracted out labor-intensive tasks to the private households, and they, in turn, relied on the larger farms for provision of many inputs for which markets did not exist.

This dual structure and the constraints on private landholding that produced it had the greatest impact on the livestock sector. The highest value that many households could extract from their tiny plots was in livestock products, but they could not grow feed on a half hectare. The large farms rarely had the flexibility or incentive to make high quality pasture available for private use, and the livestock sector, both collective and private, became dependent on concentrate feed. The livestock sector faces the most extreme adjustment on both the demand and the supply sides.

Agriculture employed 25% of the work force, and produced 20% of GNP in this country. In developed market economies, agriculture is capital intensive and the share of agriculture in the labor force is smaller than its contribution to GNP. In our stylized country, capital investment in agricultural production has also been substantial. Investment was in part necessitated by the political decision to replace small-scale private agriculture by large-scale collective agriculture, with the resulting need for land reclamation, large buildings, and large machines. Although the investment increased output and domestic self-sufficiency in food, only rarely was it guided by a calculus of economic returns. The capital/labor ratio in socialist agriculture is lower than in developed market economies, but this reflects inefficiency of investment, rather than its lack.

Poor incentives and relatively low capital stock per worker in the stylized economy reduced labor productivity. Severe price distortions make it difficult to measure agricultural labor productivity and the contribution of agriculture to GNP, but it is likely that labor productivity was lower than in industry. Agricultural wages were in rough parity with those of other sectors. When earning from private plots were taken into account, agricultural incomes exceeded those of other workers on average. High wages were sustained by regular increases in controlled prices paid to farms for agricultural products, plus recurrent loans and grants.

Yields of grains and field crops per hectare were not as high as in western Europe, where farmers receive the support of the Common Agricultural Policy, but they equaled yields of major commercial exporters in other parts of the world (see *Table 1*). Fertilizer use per hectare was lower than in western Europe, but higher than in North America. Use of other agricultural chemicals was quite low, but poor storage and management practices resulted in environmental damage and health problems even at low levels of application. Technical productivity in the livestock sector was lower than in crops. Lags in breeding and protein-deficient feed rations reduced productivity. Milk yields per cow lagged those of western Europe by about one-third.

Table 1. 1985–1988 Average yields
(in metric tons per cow or metric tons per hectare)

Country	Milk	Rye	Sugar Beet	Wheat
Bulgaria	3.385	1.718	17.636	3.638
Czechoslovakia	3.843	3.556	35.854	4.936
GDR	4.312	3.398	31.196	5.282
Hungary	4.803	2.116	37.435	4.765
Poland	3.098	2.492	33.632	3.584
Soviet Union	2.395	1.773	25.029	1.747
Yugoslavia	1.750	1.771	38.813	3.726
Austria	3.804	3.728	54.471	4.780
Canada	5.444	1.539	39.027	1.782
France	3.603	3.345	61.123	5.790
Greece	1.890	2.085	61.320	2.387
USA	6.159	1.749	46.539	2.415

Source:
FAO Production Yearbook, 1989. Romania is not included because revised Romanian data for 1985-1988 are not yet available.

Use of labor, fertilizer, and feed grain was high per unit output, reducing efficiency and raising costs of production. With the drastic realignment of exchange rates at the outset of the transition, costs of production and prices received by farms no longer look high in comparison with world trading prices. With the increased ability to compare domestic prices to world trading prices that a reasonable exchange rate brings, it appears that agricultural producers are substantially discriminated against, since semi-controlled producer prices lag world prices. For example, most Romanian wheat will be purchased this season at $35 per ton at the market and interbank exchange rate of 200 lei to the dollar. (The official exchange rate is still 60 lei to the dollar.)

These costs and prices, however, still embody distortions in input prices, since fertilizer, energy, and machinery are not yet priced at world trading prices. Part of the distress of the early transition is caused by the more rapid approach of input prices to world levels and slower adjustment of producer prices. As the economies make their ways in fits and starts to a price structure more consistent with world trading prices, it appears that agricultural incomes will increase less than the general price level. This is not necessarily a manifestation of a textbook type of urban bias, although some of the instruments for restraining agricultural earnings, such as Bulgaria's ban on the export of some food products, are standard tools for the transfer of income from rural to urban people (BRAVERMAN and GUASCH 1990). Falling farm incomes now are a symptom of partial liberalization, but they also signal the needed longer-term adjustment; more efficient production of products for which domestic and foreign demand exists under the new price structure.

Agroindustry in our stylized country was highly concentrated, and food processing, distribution, and input supply were managed by several large state monopolies. With pervasive excess demand for food, processors paid little regard to product definition and quality.

The stylized country was a middle income country, with per capita GNP of about $6,000 using the purchasing power parity methodology, and $2,500 using the exchange rate methodology. In recent years, the country sustained aggregate consumption despite declining aggregate growth by borrowing heavily abroad. Agriculture's contribution to the growth in net foreign indebtedness derived from increased demand for imported feed grains, and diversion of food from export markets to (subsidized) domestic consumption.

Per capita consumption of food was comparable to countries with income levels considerably higher (see *Table 2*). Caloric consumption was the same as that in market economies with higher levels of income, and consumption of meat exceeded that in many more prosperous market economies. This consumption pattern was a result of food subsidies, particularly for livestock products. Retail food prices changed little in nominal terms for several decades, despite growth in nominal incomes. Real food prices (at official prices) thus declined. Since markets did not clear at these official prices, the actual prices that people paid were higher than official prices. Consumers' expectations about what they should be able to purchase, however, were formed on the basis of official prices.

The most highly subsidized food items were meat and dairy products, and official prices for these products were approximately half the cost of delivery. Subsidization of items with low income elasticities is often considered to benefit poorer people, but the most highly subsidized items in the stylized economy were those with high income elasticities. The food price subsidy delivered more benefits to the wealthier groups who consumed more of the most highly subsidized products, and fewer benefits to poorer people.

Each country camouflaged the growing gap between costs of consumption and production by passing the costs to the state through subsidies, and increasing imports or reducing exports of food. The increase in

Table 2. Per capita average food consumption, 1985
(kilograms annually)

Country	1984–1986 Calorie Per Day	1984–1986 Protein Gram/Day	Meat	Milk[a]	Sugar[b]	Grain and Bread
OECD						
USA	3642	106.5	118	129	30	65
Japan	2858	88.0	38	36	21	108
Austria	3416	96.6	90	142	37	68
Finland	3080	95.6	68	182	37	73
France	3273	111.3	106	84	34	80
FR Germany	3476	101.0	100	112	37	74
Spain	3365	96.5	75	102	33	77
United Kingdom	3218	88.0	74	141	37	83
CMEA						
Bulgaria	3634	106.3	77	250	35	144
Czechoslovakia	3473	103.3	86	239	35	111
GDR	3800	112.7	96	–	40	99
Hungary	3541	101.7	77	175	35	110
Poland	3298	101.8	67	403	41	118
Romania	3358	104.3	60	–	26	143
Yugoslavia	3542	101.5	55	–	35	175
USSR	3394	105.6	62	295	42	133

Source:

FAO *Production 1987*, pp. 291, 293. Food and Agriculture Organization of the United Nations, 1988. *Food Consumption Statistics 1976–1985,* OECD, Paris, 1988. *COMECON Data 1988.* Wiener Institute für Internationale Wirschaftsvergleiche, 1989, pp. 157–163.
[a] For OECD countries, excludes processed dairy products. For CMEA countries, includes milk equivalent of all dairy products.
[b] Excludes other sweeteners, and syrups.

consumption of food and other goods that came with the post-Stalin thaw was one that the underlying productive economies could not deliver on a sustained basis. The degree of subsidization varied by country and its impact on the macroeconomy also varied, but in each case the burden of food subsidies was very high. Subsidized sausage for the relatively wealthy cut into budgetary funds available for investment in education, health care, physical infrastructure, and environmental protection.

THE TRANSITION

Thus, the agricultural sector on the eve of the transition was characterized by:

(a) large inefficient farms with high costs of production (primarily fertilizer, labor, and feed);
(b) high levels of food consumption relative to market economies of comparable prosperity;
(c) subsidized food prices;
(d) excess demand for food at those prices;
(e) macroeconomic imbalance, including budge deficit and foreign debt;
(f) pervasive monopoly in food processing and distribution.

The macroeconomic imbalance in the stylized country was substantial, and the transition is initiated by a program of stabilization. Fiscal outlays are reduced, the money supply tightened, and the overvalued currency devalued. (For an exposition of the programs of stabilization and reform more generally, see BLANCHARD et al. 1990.)

The macroeconomic stabilization affects the agricultural sector in several ways. (For parallels in other adjustment processes, see COMMANDER 1989.) The food subsidy, at approximately 5% of GNP, is a visible target for significant fiscal savings. Although governments throughout the region approached removal of food subsidies with great trepidation, all (except for the USSR) have by now eliminated direct consumer food subsidies. Partial direct income compensation accompanied the removal of subsidies. Without the subsidy, meat prices approximately double, and food prices rise on average by 50%. Demand for food declines due to the partial compensation, and consumers purchase less and different food at the higher relative prices. The price increase does not reduce caloric intake on average, but does induce shifts away from more expensive foods, particularly meat and cheese.

The price liberalization frees processors with market power to act like monopolists, and many respond by raising prices to consumers and pressuring producer prices. The price increase that accompanies liberalization is thus in part due to removal of subsidies, and in part due to the exercise of market power.

The price liberalization does not raise prices that producers receive. In an open market economy, devaluation will raise agricultural producers' prices, since most food and fiber is tradeable. However, this economy is not fully open yet, and transmission of changes in world prices and exchange rates is weak. Moreover, producer prices in the past exceeded retail prices by the amount of the subsidy. The increase in retail prices removes the wedge that formerly divided them from producer prices without appreciably affecting farm level prices. In fact, the formal freeing of retail food prices is sometimes accompanied by retention of controls at the wholesale level, as governments try to insure themselves against too rapid a rise in food prices. Processors' market power allows them to pass controls back to producers. Partial decontrol is reported in Romania and Bulgaria, although statistical monitoring of price movements is weak now.

Producers are unable to push the former volume of production through markets at lower prices, since for products requiring processing, they cannot bypass the processing monopolies. Producers are thus hostage to the pace of change in the processing, marketing, and distribution of food and fiber. The hope of a quick improvement in agriculture that will facilitate change in other sectors is illusory unless a concerted effort to increase competition and the technological performance of food processing and marketing brings early results.

Excess supply appears at the farm level. Some of this can be exported, and it is more competitive than in the past, due to the devaluation. Institutional linkage between producers and international markets, however, is weak, and product definitions and quality are not conducive to quick switching between domestic and export markets. Producers face higher costs for fertilizer and imported animal feed, and the combination of higher costs and reduced demand puts pressure on farm income.

The crucial variables in determining the impact of macroeconomic stabilization on the agricultural sector are the relative magnitude of the food subsidy; the amount of excess demand for food before liberalization; the degree of concentration in processing; and the openness of international markets to products redirected from domestic markets. If the food subsidy is small, if its removal approximately absorbs excess demand, and if processors have limited market power, the adjustment process will be less disruptive for producers. However, if the shock to the demand side is large and the economy shifts abruptly from excess demand to excess supply, producers will face a substantial adjustment. The adjustment will be particularly difficult if exports cannot be readily expanded. Agriculture, like other sectors, has been hard hit by the disruption of trade with the USSR and the Middle East.

Problems in food processing are apparent even prior to the transition, and many participants in the food economy have argued for increased investment to modernize food processing. The investment is sought both from domestic and external sources, and the goal of the investment is usually construction of new plants and/or purchase of more modern equipment. A visitor assessing the "needs" of food processors of Eastern and Central Europe can amass requests amounting to several billion dollars in a few weeks in the field.

Few of these, when viewed as commercial investments rather than "basic needs", pass careful scrutiny. Unless price liberalization is well under way and changes in food demand are better understood, new investment in food processing is likely to respond to the wrong signals. It will be devoted to the wrong commodities, placed in the wrong locations, and purchase technology inappropriate for the post-transition factor costs.

Some kinds of food processing stand out as particularly poor targets for investment in the early period. Plants that operate wholly or in part with imported raw materials but sell their products on the domestic market, such as oilseed crushers, will be particularly hard hit as foreign exchange risk is passed to them but domestic prices lag world prices. Meat processors and dairy plants in areas dependent on subsidized imported feed are poor targets. Investment in simple packaging technology and materials for products with export markets can be relatively safe and productive. The focus of change in food processing in the early period of the transition should be to augment competition through dismantling monopolistic processing trusts and expanding small-scale private transport. New investment should promote competition rather than simply expand or modernize processing capacity. After the price liberalization has settled down, alternative investments in food processing will be easier to assess.

If producers have poor access to markets because reorganization of processing and distribution is stalled, they will demand direct government subsidies to forestall declines in farm income. Governments will be pressured to embark upon programs of price support that they can ill afford. Tariffs are costless to the budget, but have obvious implications for inflation. Moreover, if producers' difficulties stem in part from lack of domestic competition in processing and marketing, tariffs will not address the basic problem, and may worsen it. Poland, which has led in many aspects of the economic transition, issued agricultural tariffs in

May 1991, designed to protect the troubled dairy industry. (For an exposition of the Polish experience in the early transition, see World Bank, 1990.)

Given the inherited concentration in food processing, a concerted demand for tariff protection against imported food is a predictable feature of the political economy of agriculture during the transition. Producers may well be drawn into alliance with processors when their longer term interests are not well served by protection of processors' monopolies.

DISTRIBUTION OF AGRICULTURAL LAND

In Czechoslovakia, Hungary, Romania, and Bulgaria, recognition of rights of landowners prior to collectivization has been universal.[2] Debate on the legal foundation for reaffirming property rights in land proceeded throughout the region in 1990, and until late in the process it was not obvious that restitution would be the outcome. Parliaments passed land laws in Romania and Bulgaria in February 1991, in April in Hungary, and in May in Czechoslovakia. Each of these laws recognizes the rights of landowners just prior to collectivization, and sets up a procedure for reinstating the property right.

Since most agricultural land is being returned to people perceived to be rightful owners, recipients do not pay, and the land distribution has little impact on macroeconomic balances. In the parts of the Soviet Union in which land was nationalized in 1917 and collectivized between 1929 and 1933, it is difficult to imagine how rights of former landowners could be reinstated. The course of decollectivization is thus likely to be quite different in much of the USSR.

The Romanian land program embodies the judgment that costs of delay are greater than those of moving ahead before all complications are foreseen and forestalled. Local land commissions in each district were established quickly after passage of the law, and began receiving claims. Households can claim a maximum of ten hectares, and can submit a variety of evidence to support their claims. The period for submission and

---

[2] This section is based on field interviews during May 1991. The interviews were part of an ongoing study organized by the World Bank and partners in member countries. The study analyzes changes in land tenure and use in Romania, Hungary, Bulgaria, and Poland.

judgment of claims ended on May 20, 1991. When possible, claimants will be given the land actually owned prior to collectivization. When this is not feasible, a piece of equivalent size and quality will be returned. When the original land was broken into parcels, the parcelization is deliberately duplicated in the returned land; many households in the Danubian plain will receive four or five hectares divided into several parcels. Holdings in the hill areas will be larger, and broken into more parcels.

Romanians who receive land through restitution of their rights can sell it immediately if they so choose, or buy more up to a maximum holding of 100 hectares per household. Family members and neighbors have rights of first refusal on farm land for sale, a restriction on free sale that is intended to address the fragmentation problem. Since in the densely settled areas of intense agriculture almost all land will be distributed through restitution, an active land market could develop rather quickly.

There appears to be little intent in the law or its implementation to create farms of an optimal size, or to look forward to how farming will take place after the land is distributed. This at first appears economically myopic, but may in fact show a more profound sophistication. The Romanian approach to the land distribution is more like a voucher scheme than a land reform, since it widely disperses claims to the land, but carries little expectation that people will work the land in the units they receive. A small number of people receiving large holdings (for example, eight to ten hectares) plan to manage them as households. Most people plan to keep the land in collective management this season and next. The distribution thus opens a trading period during which households can buy and sell their land, consolidate holdings, and prepare to leave the collective when the infrastructure for individual management is more developed and the economic outlook for the sector has improved. In the meantime, the collective will continue to work the land, and landowners will receive a share of returns to land proportionate to their share of the farm's total area.

The land law in Bulgaria was also passed in February 1991, but political stalemate and administrative inertia delayed its implementation. The National Land Commission, the main administrative organ of implementation, was not appointed until May 31, 1991, and appointment of local land commissions was attendant upon the formation of the national commission. As a consequence, people who wanted to claim land in the first half of 1991 had nowhere to take their claims. Many of the records showing who brought land into the collectives are held by the farms, and even managers who wanted to speed the restitution of land rights could not submit them to nonexistent local commissions.

Administrative delay has hindered the implementation of the Bulgarian law. The philosophy of land distribution embodied in the law and the implementing regulations is slow by nature. Rather than relying on market trades to improve a quick and imperfect distribution of rights, the Bulgarian approach attempts construction of appropriate holdings through administrative assignment. Local and commissions accept and adjudicate claims, and when a substantial number of claims have been verified, turn them over to a team of specialists who draw up a local map of the allocated holdings.

The Bulgarian law prohibits purchase and sale of land by private individuals for three years, thus precluding market-based solutions to the land fragmentation problem.[3] In many places the amount of land that can be restored is only a proportion of that claimed, since development has changed the contours and use of land, and agricultural area has declined. In these areas all claims will be prorated by proportionate adjustment. The effort to achieve justice and economic efficiency through administrative meticulousness can be contrasted with the Romanian priority on speed. The costs and benefits of each approach are not yet clear. The slower distribution of land in Bulgaria and the severity of the agricultural contraction suggest that in Bulgaria, as in Romania, management of the land will remain largely collective in the coming seasons despite the change in property rights.

In Hungary, the initial attempt to return agricultural land to prior owners in 1990 was struck down by the Constitutional Court, with the ruling that restitution of ownership of agricultural land must be considered along with that of other assets. In April 1991, landowners, along with dispossessed owners of other property, were granted vouchers redeemable for agricultural land or other assets. Landowners who continued to hold title to lands managed by the cooperative are granted the return of their managerial rights unconditionally. In Hungary, thus, the restitution for those who relinquished title is essentially monetary, and the impact on demand for land depends on economic agents' assessment of the value of land compared to other assets.

---

[3] The economic implications of this restriction have received attention, and amendment of the provision is under debate. As this is written in July 1991, the restriction remains.

In Czechoslovakia, the law mandating return of agricultural land to prior owners who will cultivate it passed only in late May 1991, and at the time of passage, little interest in claiming land was reported. In Czechoslovakia the agricultural sector is a relatively small part of the national economy, due largely to the industrial development of the Czech republic and its dominance in the aggregate measures. Agriculture is more important in Slovakia. Food markets approximately cleared even prior to the price liberalization, and few citizens of the country perceive that they have had or now have a "food problem". Thus recognition of the need to change the inherited structure of agricultural production has been late in coming, although a fully open trade regime would demonstrate its high cost relative to world levels.

The agricultural contraction is just beginning in Czechoslovakia, and difficulties in marketing meat and milk are pulling farm incomes down. Pressure for change is increasing, but it is early yet to predict whether the form of change will be protection of the old structure, or the start of decollectivization. Since the agricultural sector is a smaller share of the Czechoslovak economy, and given the complications of federal politics, pressures for protection and subsidy will be great.

In Poland, the state sector owns only about 20% of agricultural land, since the remainder of land was never collectivized, and remains in fragmented private ownership. Although the proportion of marketed output that originated in the state sector was greater than its share of land ownership, the excess supply of food occasioned by the Polish big bang diminished the perceived urgency to reorganize state farms. Those most agitated about the fate of state farms were their employees. The disposition of land in state farms throughout the East and Central European region has lagged and followed a different course than that of land held by collective farms.

In summary, the land distribution programs in practice are quite diverse, and are not what most people outside the region expected. In surveying the economic options, few outside economists would have chosen physical restitution of rights to prior owners as the preferred solution. The economic difficulties are evident. The restitution approach does have some redeeming features to complement its apparent political appeal, and counter some of the economic problems it raises. Had land been distributed without payment to the agricultural work force with no higher principle than "land to the tiller", it would have been easy to exclude rural people from further distribution of state-owned assets. Since landowners have instead received back property judged to have been rightly theirs all along, there can be little justification for excluding rural people from a fair share of assets accumulated by the state. Thus, when privatization swings into full force through vouchers or distributed shares, rural people will be integrated into the new capital markets. (For discussion of privatization more generally, see VICKERS and YARROW 1991.)

CONCLUSION

The agricultural transition is an essential part of stabilization and adjustment in Eastern and Central Europe because agricultural sectors are large and food is important. Decollectivization is a highly visible component of the agricultural transition, yet the course of decollectivization is strongly influenced by the economic environment in which it proceeds. The economic environment is at present dominated by depressed demand, economic uncertainty, and interest rates higher than agricultural producers in the region have ever seen. The emerging private sector is particularly vulnerable; it is poorly endowed with inherited capital and still has poor access to markets for inputs and outputs. Many producers are therefore choosing to delay their emergence into fully private individual production, and are instead staying with cooperatives until the economic force of the agricultural contraction weakens.

Despite the very clear difficulties, significant progress in the agricultural transition is evident. Liberalization of food prices is not yet everywhere complete, but has proceeded with surprising speed and social acceptance. Redefinition of property rights in land, the first step in decollectivization, is under way. Progress already achieved in Eastern and Central Europe provides instructive lessons and cautious optimism for the USSR. The international community has shown its readiness to support the agricultural transition with capital and technical assistance. The effectiveness of each would be enhanced if the generosity extended to market access.

REFERENCES

BLANCHARD, O., DORNBUSCH, R., KRUGMAN, P., LAYARD, R., SUMMERS, L.: "Reform in Eastern Europe." Report of the WIDER World Economy Group (1990).

BRAVERMAN, A., GUASCH, J. L.: "Agricultural Reform in Developing Countries: Reflections for Eastern Europe." *American Journal of Agricultural Economics,* December, pp. 1243–1251 (1990).

COMMANDER, S. (ed.): *Structural Adjustment and Agriculture.* London: Overseas Development Institute (1989).

VICKERS, J., YARROW, G.: "Economic Perspectives on Privatization." *Journal of Economic Perspectives,* Spring, pp. 111–132 (1991).

The World Bank: *An Agricultural Strategy for Poland.* Report of the Polish-European Community, World Bank Task Force, Washington, December (1990).

4

INSTITUTIONAL CHANGES AND INTELLECTUAL TRENDS IN SOME HUNGARIAN SOCIAL SCIENCES*

By

RUDOLF ANDORKA

This paper is focused on developments and problems in three social sciences in which the author has some experience, namely sociology, economics, and demography. These sciences are practiced in universities and in research institutes, among which are the institutes of the Hungarian Academy of Sciences. To understand developments in these fields, it is necessary to study the characteristics of the stratum of professionals or, as they are sometimes called in Eastern Europe, intellectuals, and to understand this stratum a brief look at general political, economic, social, and cultural developments in Hungary is needed, all in historical perspective.

POLITICAL, ECONOMIC, SOCIAL, AND CULTURAL DEVELOPMENTS AND CHANGES IN HUNGARY

Since 1919 the political system of Hungary has fluctuated between extreme totalitarianism and various forms of authoritarianism. The brief totalitarian Communist regime in 1919 was followed by a similarily oppressive counterrevolutionary regime, which soon evolved into an authoritarian system that maintained such attributes of democracy as a multi-party parliament. With the occupation of Hungary by the German army in 1944 an extremely oppressive totalitarian regime was established, which ended with the defeat of Germany the next year.

For about two years after the war the hope remained that Hungary would become a democratic society, even though the Communist party

* In *East European Politics and Societies*, 1993, Vol. 7, No. 1, pp. 74–108.

had managed to occupy the most important positions of power as early as 1945. The first arrests of opposition leaders happened in 1945 and the first fake political process took place in the spring of 1947. For the next six years until June 1953 a savagely totalitarian system was imposed. The Communists not only suppressed every sign of political opposition, but also attempted to regulate the everyday of Hungarians and to control their private opinions. About a million persons were arrested, criminally prosecuted, and imprisoned or deported, affecting about one-third of all Hungarian families directly. A series of fake political trials, ending with a great number of executions, occurred where defendants were accused of acts that they obviously did not, even could not, commit. Confessions were usually extracted from the defendants through torture, which resulted in death in some cases.

The Communist regime inherited a very backward economy in which more than half of the population earned its living from agriculture, and the leadership attempted to follow the example of the Soviet Union and implement a program of forced and very rapid industrialization. This was a sound goal and had been accepted as such by most political groups in the interwar period. The Communist industrialization, however, was strongly concentrated on heavy industry and was burdened by the inefficiencies of the centrally planned economy based on state ownership of productive assets.

The social structure reflected the characteristics of a backward society: in 1949 only 1.3% of the population had education beyond secondary school and thus the intellectual base of science was very narrow. In addition, the Communist party implemented strong policies that were anti-professional in intent, because most professionals would not support the oppressive regime. Many were imprisoned and many others, including outstanding university professors, lost jobs and had to get employment as manual workers. Many emigrated.

All intellectual influence coming from outside of the "socialist camp", conservative or moderate or liberal, was declared to be hostile to the state and highly dangerous. All members of society were isolated from any Western influence, with the exception of news on Western radio stations, often jammed.

Only dogmatic Marxist scientific publications were permitted and even GYÖRGY LUKÁCS was criticized for not being a "true" Marxist. Only "socialist realist" literature, art work, and music was published or presented to the public.

Immediately after the death of Stalin in 1953 the first rifts appeared in the totalitarian system as the new minister-president, IMRE NAGY, installed by order of the Soviet leadership, attempted to alleviate the worst aspects of the system. This development toward a milder authoritarian system was stopped by the Stalinist first secretary of the Party in Hungary, MÁTYÁS RÁKOSI, and resulted in the exclusion of IMRE NAGY from the Party. RÁKOSI and his new minister-president, ANDRÁS HEGEDŰS, were not able to reestablish the totalitarian system completely, however, mainly because of the resistance of the "revisionists" (today we would call them the "reformists") in the Party and in the population. The revolution in October 1956 broke out in a typically "Tocquevillean" situation: the oppression had begun to be softened, but not as rapidly as society hoped and there was widespread fear that the political elite intended to reintroduce severe oppression. The revolution, during which NAGY again became minister-president with a multiparty coalition government, was crushed after twelve glorious days by the Soviet army. Severe repression followed during which 350–400 persons were executed, about 22,000 persons were convicted by criminal courts, and 13,000 persons were interned without sentence by any court [1]. In spite of the cruelty of vengeance after this brief revolution, in terms of the number of executions and arrests the oppression was less severe than in the Stalinist period of 1947–1953, the accusations were usually based on facts, and torture was not used systematically to obtain confessions. Between 100,000 and 200,000 persons emigrated, professionals and children of professionals overrepresented among them.

Although the revolution was defeated, all of the developments in the next decades, which were in many respects different from the developments in the other Eastern and Central European socialist countries, can be understood only against the background of this revolution.

The Soviet leadership insisted upon changes in the power structure in Hungary. The new leader of the Party, JÁNOS KÁDÁR, who belonged to the "home" wing of the Party (that is, spent the years before 1945 in Hungary, not in Moscow) and who was himself imprisoned in the Stalinist years, seems to have recognized that a return to the severe totalitarian system of those Stalinist years would result in a new revolution, which, even if crushed again, would sweep him out from the political leadership, similarly to RÁKOSI who went to live a simple pensioner's life in the Soviet Union after his removal in 1956.

Thus, after the first period of severe repression, KÁDÁR attempted to implement a tacit compromise with the Hungarian masses. Some economic bonuses were offered, mainly through the decrease of the rate of state investment, and the standard of living began to increase moderately. The turning point toward a less repressive regime was in 1962–1963, when a political amnesty was given to the majority of political prisoners, and KÁDÁR, at a Party conference, paraphrasing Christ, expressed the new approach; "those who are not against us, are with us". These were the workers and peasants, who tried to attain a higher level of living by engaging in income-supplementing activities in the second economy, and, above all, the professionals.

In order to understand the politics of this power elite, it ought to be remembered that KÁDÁR was always distrustful of the Soviet leadership, most of all of BREZNEV. His attitude can be guessed from the short remark quoted in the book of ZDENEK MLYNAŘ [2]. Talking with ALEXANDER DUBČEK during the Prague spring, on the reforms in Czechoslovakia and on the hopes expressed by DUBČEK concerning the benevolence of the Soviet leadership, KÁDÁR asked DUBČEK, "Do you really not know with whom you are dealing?". As KÁDÁR was not daring nor willing to rely on the Soviet Union, he had to seek some support from Hungarian society, or at least the tolerance of his leadership by the Hungarians, based on their belief that any other Communist leader would be worse than KÁDÁR. In addition, KÁDÁR did not have a unified Party behind him. Because he was not willing or was not able to achieve the unity of the Party by coercion (through the political police), since 1956 three groups or "fractions" became more and more visible in the Party:

(1) the "hardliners", who preferred a return to a totalitarian or at least strongly authoritarian system;
(2) the "center" around KÁDÁR; and
(3) the remnants of the revisionists around NAGY, who wished for a less oppressive system, and who were gradually reinforced by the younger generations entering the Party in the 1960s and 1970s.

These "reformists" were themselves not united, for at least three groupings can be distinguished:

(1) the economic reformists around REZSŐ NYERS, a former Social Democrat;
(2) the agricultural pressure group, around LAJOS FEHÉR; and

(3) the intellectuals around GYÖRGY ACZÉL, who was, in fact (although not always formally), the head of culture, education, and science in the Party leadership and who formulated the "intelligentsia policy" of the Party. Although these reformist groups suffered a setback in 1972–1974, in the 1980s they were able to regain their influence on political developments.

The old "hardliners" simply died out or were pushed back by KÁDÁR, while almost all of the new younger members of the power elite supported the reformists. The reformist camp again became differentiated into three groups:

(1) the economic reformists or technocrats, headed, in addition to the earlier leader NYERS, by MIKLÓS NÉMETH, the last socialist minister-president;
(2) the intellectuals who remained around ACZÉL; and
(3) the intellectuals around IMRE POZSGAY, who was the first Party leader who stated, and forced the Party to accept, that 1956 was not a right-wing "counterrevolution", but a popular uprising, based on justified complaints.

The dividing line between these last two groups of intellectuals was really very vague; their opinions on the main political issues were similar, but based essentially on personal relations, sympathies, and antipathies, going back to the interwar period, when the progressive (anti-Nazi and reform-minded) intelligentsia of Hungary was divided into a more urban-based and a more rural-based pairing. This division remained important also after the change of regime, as in the 1980s, when the oppositional movements were cautiously appearing in Hungary. These were themselves divided into two groups:

(1) the urban group that had personal contacts with the ACZÉL group in the party;
(2) the rural group that had personal contacts with the POZSGAY group. The first became the Free Democrats and the second became the Hungarian Democrats.

Parallel with these political developments toward a less authoritarian one-party system, the economic system developed toward a market oriented system. When economic growth slowed down in the mid-1960s, NYERS was able to convince KÁDÁR and the Party leadership that a "socialist market system" would produce better economic achievements. In the "new economic mechanism" proposed by the economic reformers the state-owned enterprises would have operated on a more or less free market similar to the privately owned enterprises on the capitalist markets [3].

The new economic mechanism might be evaluated both as a failure and as a success. It was obviously a failure in that it proved to be an illusion that state-owned enterprises in a socialist system will operate like private enterprises, for the basic characteristic of the socialist economic system, the weak budget constraint, was not eliminated, and, at best, diminished somewhat by the new economic mechanism [4]. In the 1980s the reform economists began to recognize that in the absence of privatization of most of the state-owned sector the Hungarian economy will not operate like a capitalist market economy. This recognition was followed by another, namely that the privatization of the productive assets cannot be achieved in the existing one-party political system, therefore political democratization is a prerequisite of economic efficiency.

On the other hand, the economic reform was a success in the sense that – as an unintended but tolerated side-effect – the second economy began to expand and to prosper in Hungary. Second economy is defined here as those welfare-producing and not-illegal (at least semi-legal, that is, tolerated) activities performed outside of the socialist sector, mostly as a "second job" or moonlighting after the regular working hours in the "first" socialist economy. The second economy began to develop in the 1960s, first in agriculture, but slowly expanded to other sectors and began to be encouraged by the government in the 1980s in order to avoid a serious decline of the level of living, when the real wage level began to decline after 1978. In 1988 81% of the adult males and 70% of the adult females stated that they were participating in some area of the second economy. About 33% of the total input of working time was in the second economy and at least 20% of the personal income of the households came from activities in the second economy in 1987 [5]. The second economy not only helped the Hungarian society to avoid a deep decline of the standard of living, but in addition provided the opportunity to learn the behavior of a private market and slowly to develop the basis of a "civil society", as those, who earned part of their income in this semi-private second economy, became less dependent on the state. SZELÉNYI hypothesized that the development of the second economy represents the continuation of the embourgeoisement process that began in the interwar period and was interrupted by the Communist period, among other ways, by the collectivization of agriculture [6].

We arrive at the crucial question: How did the Hungarian society develop in these years of fluctuation between a harder and a softer authoritarianism and of a messy half-market–half-centrally-planned economy? In other words: Did the bases of a democratic society emerge, and the characteristics of a civil society develop?

One of the relevant questions in this respect was raised by KONRÁD and SZELÉNYI: Were the intellectuals really on the road to class power in Hungary in the 1970s? [7]. In a certain sense the answer is clearly yes. The "Kádárist compromise" with Hungarian society implied a special compromise with the professionals or intellectuals (the social stratum whose members have a tertiary diploma and a job that accords with that education). All negative discriminatory measures against professionals were gradually abolished. Persons having a tertiary diploma were assured of an appropriate job and relatively high salaries. Their per capita income was the highest among the social strata, except the high bureaucrats and managers [8]. In terms of inter- and intragenerational mobility chances they were clearly privileged as compared to the other strata, similarly as in Western societies [9]. They were gradually permitted to travel – partly on official trips, partly as tourists – to Western countries. They were not commanded to write strictly Marxist scientific works and to produce "Socialist realist" novels, art, and music. The slogan of the "three Ts" of ACZÉL illustrates well the policy toward intellectual creation: Marxist and socialist works were supported (támogatott), openly anti-Marxist and antisocialist works were prohibited (tiltott), other works were tolerated (tűrt). This third "tolerated" category permitted the birth of many outstanding scientific and artistic works. In an interview given to an American newspaper ALEXANDER SZALAI stated (somewhat over-optimistically) around 1980 that there are only three "taboos" for Hungarian social scientists: It is not permitted

(1) to say that Marxism is false;
(2) to question the Socialist character of the Hungarian system;
(3) to criticize the Soviet Union.

On the other hand, the Party and state bureaucrats were a clearly distinct class from the powerless professionals. In a later auto-critical article SZELÉNYI himself recognized that the East European New Class Project had failed: the professional class was not able to push the bureaucrats out from power [10].

It ought to be mentioned, nevertheless, that the bureaucratic power elite became more and more professionalized in Hungary (probably much more than in the other Eastern European socialist countries), as its new young members were increasingly recruited from professionals having tertiary education. In consequence the professionals became less and less antagonistic toward the bureaucrats, while the bureaucrats behaved increasingly as professional experts. Their self-definition also approached that of the experts, and in consequence they were probably clinging less to their bureaucratic power positions and willing to abandon them in favor of real expert positions. NÉMETH, the last socialist minister-president, might be considered as an ideal type of these new Party and state bureaucrats: he had a diploma in economics and studied some time at Harvard; upon becoming minister-president he cleverly built up the image of the president of an expert government, and soon after the election in 1990 changed his position of minister-president for the position of deputy director of the European Bank in London.

Parallel to these developments at the top of the social hierarchy deep changes occurred slowly in the whole social structure. The society became more and more independent of the hierarchy of the authoritarian state. In terms of the theory of SZELÉNYI a "dual structure" developed, the structure of state redistribution and the second structure of the market, an important part of the society being involved in both structures [11]. In terms of the theory proposed by KOLOSI the Hungarian society was structured in two dimensions:

(1) in the dimension of state redistribution and
(2) in the dimension of the market. According to both theories the importance of the market structure or dimension was slowly growing [12].

Using (and somewhat transforming) the concepts of PIERRE BOURDIEU, SZELÉNYI interpreted this change in the following way: in the Stalinist period the "political capital" was the predominant factor of social position, in the "KÁDÁR" period the importance of "cultural capital" was increasing, and in the 1980s "economic capital" began to gain importance [13].

These social developments had a great influence on the culture of Hungarian society. Culture on all levels again became completely Western-oriented. The best Western novels were translated into Hungarian and were widely read by the Hungarian public (for example, HEINRICH BÖLL, MARGUERITE DURAS, E. L. DOCTOROW), arts and classical music followed the new styles of the West, classical and new works in social sciences were translated (for example, the series of Nobel Prize winning economists), psychoanalysis had a renaissance, phenomenology gained adherents in philosophy, popular youth music imitated the Western styles, even fashions followed the Western models, hippies appeared in Hungary similarly as some years later yuppies did. There is usually a lag of about ten years between the West and Hungary.

In consequence of all these slow changes the basis of a civil society was created.

ECONOMICS, SOCIOLOGY, AND DEMOGRAPHY IN THE POSTWAR DECADES

The history of the three social sciences treated in this paper was deeply influenced by developments of political, economic, social, and cultural history. All three were reduced to the state of apparent death in the totalitarian period and all of them went through a renaissance in the softer authoritarian period, although always struggling for the opportunity to do serious research.

Economics has a long and productive history in Hungary, although most of the best Hungarian economic scientists achieved their successes in foreign countries (BALOGH, KÁLDOR, SCITOVSKY, KATONA, BALASSA, HARSÁNYI, QUANDT). After the Communist take-over the Institute of Economic Research directed by ISTVÁN VARGA, a "bourgeois" economist, was dissolved. The Faculty of Economics of the Technical University of Budapest was separated from the Technical University and made an independent University of Economic Sciences, strictly dominated by orthodox Marxism–Leninism. Its first rector was the philosopher LÁSZLÓ RUDAS, who both in the 1930s in the Soviet Union and in 1948 in Hungary led the attack against LUKÁCS, declaring him to be revisionist. Nevertheless, the right to existence of economics as a science (although in the form of Marxist political economy) was never denied, and institutions of scientific research in economics existed, like the Research Institute of Economic Sciences of the Hungarian Academy of Sciences.

Thus serious economics was reborn rather soon. The book of JÁNOS KORNAI, written in 1956 and first published in 1957, on the overconcentration of economic management is a visible indicator of the reappearance of economic science [14]. This book and the works of many other economic researchers arose from the realization that the economic policy and the centralized planning system of the Stalinist years had resulted in serious economic troubles. KORNAI was severely criticized and, for some time, lost his job in the academic research institute.

As KORNAI stated in the introduction to the second edition written in 1989, in this book he neglected the treatment of questions of property, political power, and socialist ideology. The avoidance of the treatment of basic theoretical questions and the concentration instead on the analysis of the reality in Hungary remained characteristic of economic research in the following decades.

Outstanding works were published on economic cycles in socialist Hungary, on the level of economic development in Hungary since 1937, and on the history of the Hungarian economy in the postwar period [15].

Mathematical economics and econometrics were the other fields where the achievements of Hungarian economists were approaching the world level [16]. Modern Western economic ideas entered the Hungarian economic sciences through these channels, as mathematical equations, coefficients, and optimalization techniques could be attacked on the basis of Marxism more difficultly than verbal theoretical works. In addition, mathematical economists and econometricians could always claim that their models will contribute in future to the improvement of national economic planning, and thus neoclassical economics slowly became dominant in economic thinking.

The great theoretical questions of economic sciences were tackled only by the later works of KORNAI on anti-equilibrium and on chronic shortage in the socialist economies [17]. It should be noted though that KORNAI, at the time of writing his great theoretical works, spent about half of his time in Western countries, as visiting professor at several fine universities. Nevertheless, his theories were very influential in Hungary, most of all among young researchers and students of the University of Economic Sciences.

Some of the Hungarian economic researchers played important roles advising the government and writing proposals for the reform of the Hungarian economic system, partly invited by the governments, partly independent of any official call. The content of their reform proposals was sometimes rather vague and changed rapidly from year to year [18]. Recently KORNAI himself, who usually kept his distance from politics, published an important reform program [19]. Only some of these reform proposals were accepted and implemented, but they had the important additional function of helping to convince the political elite and the general public that thoroughgoing reforms were needed.

Demography was a well-developed scientific discipline in Hungary since the end of the nineteenth century, mostly based on the high-quality census and vital statistics of the Central Statistical Office. In the Stalinist period, when almost no statistical data were published and the work of the Central Statistical Office was concentrated on the monitoring of the fulfillment of the economic plans, no demographic research was performed. Beginning in 1958 a quarterly demographic journal of high-quality, *Demográfia*, was published and after 1960 a Demographic Research Institute was established in the Central Statistical Office. Being located in the statistical service entailed that the science of demography was concentrated on the analysis of statistical data (among others, numerous surveys of fertility and family planning) and in later years on advising the government.

Two remarkable tendencies presented themselves for scientific research to the Hungarian demographers:

(1) the early decline of fertility (declining in 1958 below the replacement level) and

(2) the deterioration of adult mortality, beginning in the mid-1960s.

The facts of these tendencies were very well documented [20]. The explanation of their causes was much less successful because the basic characteristics of the socialist system might have been pinpointed among those possible causes, and because theoretical work was a weak point of Hungarian demography. (It might be added that demographic theories are much less developed in international scholarship than the economic and sociological theories.) Nevertheless the advice given to the government (and not always followed by the government) in the field of fertility was sound: no limitation of the freedom of abortion, increasing the access to contraceptives, and important monetary benefits, including family allowances and the like, for the families having children [21].

Sociology in Hungary has a much less fortunate history than that of the economic sciences and of demography, both of which were cultivated almost continuously during the twentieth century. No such continuity existed in Hungarian sociology; each time sociology returned it had to start from scratch. The sociological school thriving before the First World War essentially disappeared during the postwar Communist revolution and the counterrevolution. Some of its members became world-famous scientists in other countries (KARL MANNHEIM, KARL POLÁNYI, OSZKÁR JÁSZI), but had no followers in Hungary. The "discovery of Hungary" movement of the 1930s was disrupted by the Second World War and discontinued after 1945.

A chair of sociology was established at the Eötvös University of Budapest; the professor of sociology, ALEXANDER SZALAI, who had been a prisoner in the ill-famed concentration camp of Bor in Serbia during the war, was arrested in 1949 and sentenced to death, although (or because) he was a left-wing Social Democrat. Fortunately he was not executed, and came out of prison in 1956 and then could play an important part in Hungarian and international sociology in the 1960s and 1970s. After his arrest, however, the institutional basis of sociology was abolished and sociology was declared to be a hostile bourgeois science, not needed in socialist Hungary, because the discipline of "scientific socialism" can explain all the social phenomena in Hungary.

After 1960, however, it seems to have been slowly recognized, at least by the more enlightened groups in the political elite, that a science describing and analyzing social reality would be useful, among other reasons, to draw the attention of the leadership to potential sources of social discontent and other trouble. With the establishment of the Sociological Research Institute of the Hungarian Academy of Sciences in 1963 (the year of the great political amnesty) sociology was officially reborn. The first director of the Institute was HEGEDŰS, the former minister-president of 1955–1956 under the fist secretaryship of RÁKOSI, who was therefore expected to be a bulwark against any revisionist deviations. Nevertheless he soon began to criticize the existing system from a Marxist standpoint.

It was clear from the beginning, however, that no theoretical heresy would be permitted, neither of the revisionist Marxist type, nor – and much less – from the point of view of other sociological theories. When the first reader from the work of MAX WEBER was published in 1967, the book itself, and even more the positive evaluation of WEBER in the preface written BY ISTVÁN KEMÉNY, provoked violent criticism from the side of the representatives of "historical materialism" and "scientific socialism".

The taboo of challenging Marxism and criticizing the whole Hungarian system led the majority of Hungarian sociologists to concentrate on empirical research. An important part of the empirical research, for example, the great surveys of income distribution, social mobility, and time budget, were performed by sociologists in the Central Statistical Office (ZSUZSANNA FERGE, LÁSZLÓ CSEH-SZOMBATHY, RUDOLF ANDORKA). The conditions of the Central Statistical Office were especially immune to ideological demands but did not encourage theoretical works in any way.

Very slowly courses of sociology were introduced into the teaching program of the Eötvös University of Budapest and the University of Economic Sciences. Other research institutes were founded, which did chiefly empirical research, like the mass communication research center of the radio and television and – surprisingly – the Research Institute for Social Sciences of the Party, which did the bulk of stratification research using multivariate methods in the 1970s and 1980s.

In consequence, the greatest achievements of Hungarian sociology were in the field of empirical research of Hungarian society. Among others, the following facts, debunking the claims of official ideology were demonstrated:

(1) poverty exists in Hungary [22];
(2) the income distribution is far from equal [23];
(3) inequalities in the field of housing are especially great [24];
(4) the openness of the society of social mobility opportunities is similar (not greater) to Western capitalist societies [25];
(5) the educational system and the health care system work in very dysfunctional ways [26];
(6) the daily use of time of the Hungarians is characterized by very long working hours, caused by participation in the second economy and long household chores [27];
(7) certain types of deviant behaviour, all belonging to the retreatism category of Merton (like suicide, alcoholism, and mental disorders) continuously increased from the first half of the 1950s and attained very high levels in the mid-1980s [28];
(8) serious problems developed in the field of the quality of life, more especially in human relations and in the dimension of anomie and/or alienation [29].

Two main theoretical orientations can be discerned in the background of Hungarian sociology in these decades. On the one hand, the "Budapest school", that is, the students of LUKÁCS and the students of his students ("the grandchildren of LUKÁCS"), some of whom worked in sociological institutions (ÁGNES HELLER, MÁRIA MÁRKUS), declared themselves to be Marxists in the 1960s. Their Marxism was, however, often in conflict with the official Marxist ideology. After the death of LUKÁCS in 1971 the school began to disintegrate and distance itself from Marxism, adopting phenomenological and liberal standpoints. Some members of the school emigrated. With them the influence of Marxism on Hungarian sociology began vanishing.

The classical sociologist having the greatest – not open, but tacit – influence in Hungary was MAX WEBER. His ideas were very attractive for the Hungarian sociologists for several reasons:

(1) his anti-dogmatism: WEBER's works are all full of new ideas, often contradicting each other and therefore offering themselves for further development;
(2) his emphasis on power as an important dimension of social hierarchy;
(3) his theory of bureaucracy, which seemed to be applicable to the Hungarian society;
(4) the role of non-material factors, like religion, in his theories, which seemed to be a healthy counterbalance to the "basis and superstructure" dogma of Marxism.

No theoretical synthesis of the empirical findings of Hungarian sociology could be published in Hungary. When KONRÁD and SZELÉNYI finished their manuscript, which was intended to be a synthesis, with theoretical ambitions, on Hungarian society, they were arrested and detained for some days by the political police and it was suggested to them that they ought to apply for permission to emigrate. SZELÉNYI emigrated and KONRÁD lived for some time in foreign countries; the manuscript was first published in English and much later in Hungary [30].

Some sociologists were engaged in advising the government through a comprehensive research program on social policy [31]. The proposal was, however, not implemented. Sociologists in general participated much less in direct advisement of the government than economists and demographers.

Thus in the 1970s and 1980s economics, demography, and sociology had developed a rather important institutional basis for doing empirical research. They were relatively well endowed with financial resources, partly through the Hungarian Academy of Sciences, partly through other institutions like the Central Statistical Office, and partly through government research contracts. The financial resources and research possibilities of the universities were much more limited. The separation of research (in the research institutes) and of teaching (in the universities) was due to the Soviet model, which recognized that some open, innovative, and free research is needed, but it ought to be isolated from the students, so that students should not be "infected" by new and potentially non-Marxist–Leninist ideas and critical research results.

In contrast to the relatively good possibilities to do empirical research, theoretical work was hindered by the taboos of openly criticizing Marxism–Leninism and openly criticizing the socialist system.

The relation of social scientists to politics was ambivalent. Most social scientists defined themselves as members of the opposition or at least reformists, but were willing to give advice to the power elite. The politicians, most of all the reformist groups in the party, were willing to ask for advice from the social sciences, but often did not follow the advice obtained, and indeed were willing to sacrifice social scientists, who became too critical of the system, in order to appease through this sacrifice the "hardliners".

THE REGIME TRANSITION IN 1990,
AND THE TWO POST-TRANSITION YEARS

The regime transition, which occurred very rapidly and completely peacefully in Hungary in 1988–1990, was not foreseen and predicted by anybody. In retrospect it is, however, quite understandable.

On the one hand, deep dissatisfaction was widespread in society. According to a sociological survey in 1988, only 2% of the interviewed adults considered that economic reforms were not necessary and 7% considered that the political system must *not* be changed, while 76% considered the changes of the economic system and 40% the changes of the political system highly necessary and desirable. When it became clear that GORBACHEV would tolerate thoroughgoing reforms of the system and certainly would not interfere by arms in the process of change in Hungary, the last remaining element of the legitimation of the KÁDÁR system disappeared. KÁDÁR was persuaded to abdicate from his position as the first secretary of the Party and went into retirement. In the following months the political elite first permitted the reburial of NAGY and the four other persons executed at the time. The great mass attending the reburial ceremony convinced the political elite to accept the idea of round-table talks in which the conditions of the transition to a multiparty democracy were discussed and finally agreed upon. These talks led to the parliamentary election of spring 1990, which resulted in the following distribution of seats in the parliament: Hungarian Democrats, 43%; Free Democrats, 24%; Smallholders, 11%; Socialists, 9%; Young Democrats, 5%; Christian Democrats, 5%; independents, 3%. The government was formed by the Hungarian Democrats, the Smallholders, and the Christian Democrats.

Thus the government coalition had a stable, but not too-large majority. Minor shifts of party affiliation have occurred since the election, but the government seems to be stable and will probably be able to remain in power till the next election in 1994. It is possible that the parties at present in opposition will win at the next election the majority of the seats in the parliament. Thus the basic precondition of democracy, the possibility of the peaceful change of government, is attained.

The economy, after stagnating in the pre-1990 years, went into a recession after the regime transition; the GDP declined by about 5% in 1990 and by somewhat more in 1991. The decline seems to continue in 1992, but is expected to be stopped around the end of the year. The recession was caused by several factors:

(1) the need to abolish state subventions of the deficit-ridden state-owned enterprises;
(2) the breakdown of the export market of the former COMECON countries;
(3) the world-wide slowing of economic growth.

The average per capita personal income of the population declined somewhat less than the GDP. Income inequalities, however, increased. All those who relied mostly on fixed salaries and pensions from the state sector suffered a loss of real income, while those who became private entrepreneurs changed over from the state sector to the private sector or simply were able to extend their activities in the second economy and in the private economy in the form of part-time work and were able to increase their real income.

The results of a survey in 1991, in which adults interviewed in 1989 were reinterviewed about their income, give an idea of the income changes [32]:

From April 1989 to April 1991	%
The nominal income declined	7
The real income declined	42
The real income remained unchanged	13
The real income increased slightly	18
The real income increased strongly	15
The real income more than doubled	5
Total	100

These data explain both the widespread complaints about income decline and pauperization and the visible signs of affluence of part of the population: the increase of the number of Western personal cars, the construction of rather luxurious private houses, and the volume of expensive luxury goods sold.

The transition to a market economy based on the private ownership of most productive assets demands the privatization of the state-owned enterprises and a reduction of the state budget as compared to the GDP. This necessitates the limitation of the expenditures of the state, including its expenditures on education and science. This simple fact demands deep-going changes not only in the financing of, but also the organization of, education and science.

What kind of changes of the social structure and what kind of social mobility processes result from these political and economic changes? Are new social strata replacing the former power elite at the top of the social hierarchy? Is the elite exchanged as a result of the regime transition? While on the basis of the rapidity of the transition and the radical structural changes the process might be called a revolution, it was indeed a peaceful revolution, and it might be asked whether a peaceful revolution produces a similarly radical exchange of the elite of the society, as bloody revolutions used to do?

The social structure is rapidly transformed. In terms of the theories of SZELÉNYI and KOLOSI the dual structure continues to exist, but the second structure or dimension of the market is rapidly growing and the first one of state redistribution is rapidly declining. At the medium and lower levels of the society the number of small private entrepreneurs, of the petty bourgeoisie, is increasing. At the top the government bureaucrats and managers of state-owned enterprises are joined, to a certain extent replaced, by great private entrepreneurs and by the managers of private (mostly foreign) enterprises. Earning in private business are at present much higher than earnings in the government bureaucracy. Universities and research institutes are on a level similar to the bureaucracy.

Only a few data are available on social mobility after the regime transition. (The next national mobility survey will be performed in Autumn 1992.) On the basis of the survey reinterviewing in 1991 those persons interviewed in 1989, RÓNA-TAS and KOLOSI found that the members of the power elite under the socialist system are able to obtain advantageous positions either as private entrepreneurs or as managers in private and foreign enterprises or as professionals [33]. The regime transition resulted in the almost complete removal of the top political elite affecting from a hundred to three hundred persons, while at lower levels the change in personnel is proceeding very slowly. The reason for the relative success of the former elite in maintaining its privileged position is that it has the expertise, the tertiary education, and the practical knowledge to manage a business enterprise and to run a government office, for example, a ministry department. Also an important part of the former elite actively promoted the regime change or at least did not oppose it, and this applies even more to the scientists and university teachers. Thus I would guess that not much more change will happen at the top levels of the social hierarchy than is usual in advanced societies in consolidated non-revolutionary periods.

In terms of the concept of three types of capital, the importance of economic capital greatly increased while the importance of political capital declined and the importance of cultural capital as a background-determining factor remained unchanged. During the socialist period the party and state bureaucrats were increasingly recruited from the professional stratum; now the new private entrepreneurs and managers of private enterprises come overwhelmingly from that professional stratum, and the new political elite consists mostly of former scientists and other professionals.

Culturally Hungary is now completely open toward the West but Western influence is much more visible in mass culture influenced by the mass media and much less visible in high culture and in the sciences. The publishing of scientific books and journals declined for financial reasons, as state subventions were largely abolished. In addition the hectic economic and political changes do not seem to promote the careful study and evaluation of serious scientific works. Therefore I would think that the Hungarian intellectual and scientific scene lags behind the leading world science by about ten years. Hungarian social scientists often discover scientific works written ten or fifteen years ago in the West and consider them to be the most up-to-date achievements of science, although in the West they are often considered outdated.

In society an even deeper problem is that a market economy needs the widespread acceptance of some basic norms of business behavior, and political democracy needs the general acceptance of the rules of the democratic game. Rather unexpectedly – but really not surprisingly – a widespread lack of the values of honest business is evident, and the virtues needed in a democracy, like tolerance, honesty in public debates and a certain consistency of political principles, seem to be widely absent in the political forums, the press, the television, even in the day-to-day life of the workplaces. Thus the development of a democratic civil culture seems to be very much needed.

Summarizing the experience of the first two post-transition years, one might agree with DAHRENDORF that

(1) the formal process of constitutional reform, that is the political regime change, can be achieved in six months;
(2) a general sense that things are moving up as a result of economic reform is unlikely before six years have passed; but
(3) sixty years will be barely enough to lay the social foundations of a democratic system [34].

This not very pleasant conclusion, however, ought to increase the feeling of responsibility of social scientists, as it would be to an important degree their function and duty to help to lay these foundations.

INSTITUTIONAL CHANGES AND PROBLEMS IN SCIENCE AND HIGHER EDUCATION SINCE THE TRANSITION

The social sciences have to face these increased responsibilities in a period when their institutions have to undergo absolutely necessary changes that are sometimes rather troublesome. The three types of main institutional actors are:

(1) the Hungarian Academy of Sciences and its research institutes;
(2) the universities and other higher educational institutions;
(3) the newly created Hungarian Research Fund.

The Hungarian Academy of Sciences is in the middle of a reform process. As the 1992 report of a group of OECD experts suggested in Western countries, an academy of sciences usually exerts only one or two of the following functions; it is either:

(a) a learned society, consulted as a group of highly qualified experts, to advise the government on important science policy issues;
(b) a scientific association regrouping the scientific community and defending its interests;
(c) an organism of accreditation of doctorate diplomas;

(d) an agency providing money for basic research on a contract basis; or
(e) a research organization running its own laboratories.

The concentration of several of these different functions in a single organism is not safe.

The Hungarian Academy of Sciences, created in the first half of the nineteenth century, was originally an association of the best scientists and literary authors and its activity consisted of organizing scientific meetings and providing some guidance and advice on scientific questions. The post-1945 reorganization gave it a great number of scientific institutes, the right to give the scientific degrees (including the "kandidátus" degree which was intended to be equivalent to the Ph.D.). It played the role of a ministry of science, giving money to research projects selected by the academy and performed mostly in the institutes of the academy. Researchers in the academic institutes were among the most privileged in terms of income, research resources, possibilities of travel abroad and regular contact with scientists of other countries. The whole range of activity of the academy was dominated by the Party and the state bureaucracy; the newly proposed members of the academy had to have the approval of the highest Party organizations before being elected, the nomination to higher positions in the research institutes all depended on the approval of the Party. The power elite, however, considered it more and more desirable that the academy and its institutes present the image of serious scientific bodies, so that at least some of the new academicians and some of the researchers were outstanding scientists.

The draft of the new law on the Hungarian Academy of Sciences, not yet accepted by the parliament, makes it clear that:

(1) The academy maintains its research institutes (function e) although cooperation with the universities will be strengthened and some of the institutes abolished.
(2) The academy will continue to fulfill its original function of a learned society (function a).
(3) Several trade unions of scientific researchers and university teachers at the academy are competing to fulfill the function of defending their interests (function b).
(4) The question of giving doctorate diplomas, that is, scientific degrees, is not yet fully decided on. The organization of Ph.D. training programs and the giving of Ph.D. degrees will be left to the universities for now, but the academy will maintain the right to give a higher-level scientif-

ic degree of "doctor of sciences" while the universities will have the right to implement "habilitation" or "tenure" type procedures for the selection of university professors (function c).

(5) Although part of the responsibility to provide money for basic research was given to the Hungarian Research Fund, the academy has some possibility to finance the researches performed in its institutes (function d).

This reorganization obviously would cause serious problems in the Hungarian Academy of Sciences. If research institutes were to be abolished, it is hard to decide which institutes should not operate within the academy. The research institutes in the social sciences are obvious candidates for being abolished or given to the universities. As the number of researchers in the academy will probably diminish and certainly not increase, the possibility to recruit new young researchers becomes very restricted. The renewal of the personnel encounters great obstacles also at the academy, which has 200 members below the age of seventy. Members aged 70 and over maintain their rights and privileges but are not calculated into this total of two hundred. Because new members can be elected only when academicians attain the age of seventy or die, it will be a long time before new members dominate in the voting at the academy.

The necessity to change over to a grant application system for research resources, instead of having an assured budget for research from the academy, involves a change in attitude in the planning of research in competition with other researchers, including those in the universities, on equal terms.

Higher educational institutions in Hungary are of two types, after the German model:

(1) the university with a teaching program of four to six years and
(2) the college or *főiskola* similar to the German *Fachhochschule*.

They are fragmented into relatively small units (for example, several universities of medical sciences, a separate university of economics sciences), that is, no universities in the sense of containing faculties for all sciences. The reason for this fragmentation implemented after 1945 was probably that the political elite could more easily control these fragmented units. University teachers had very little chance to engage in research and students did not participate in research because there were no postgraduate studies at the universities. Political considerations played an important role in the selection of the teaching staff, for the political police had a veto over the employment of each new university teacher. Nevertheless, due to the "soft authoritarianism" of the Hungarian system, more and more able scientists were teaching at the universities and some universities and faculties played the role of "think tanks" in the process of transition.

After an initial period of expansion the growth of the number of students slowed down and virtually stopped at the end of the 1970s. In consequence the enrolment ratios in higher education are among the lowest in the advanced societies (about 10% of the appropriate age groups being enrolled in day-time courses). The explicit argument for keeping the enrolment ratios down was the need for manpower planning: it was assumed that Hungary would not need more professionals in the next few decades. The implicit reason, however, was probably the fear of unemployment of university graduates, who might become dangerously critical of the socialist system.

The universities and other higher education institutions are undergoing at present a turbulent period characterized by the sometimes violent antagonism between demands for rapid changes and the forces of resistance and immobility.

It is obvious that the curricula and the content of the courses have to be changed according to the new conditions created by the market economy and democratic politics. As the autonomy of the higher educational institutions is now much greater than some years ago, the fight on the curricula and content is decided within each educational institution separately, and progress in the renewal of curricula and content varies greatly.

Changes of curricula and of teaching programs often necessitates changes in the teaching staff. The Hungarian universities and other institutions of higher education do not seem to favor an evaluation and radical purge of part of the teaching staff with one blow, as carried out in Eastern Germany. A more gradual approach through pensioning off and the natural turnover of the staff seems to be followed. Not only the dismissal of teachers who are not able to comply with the demands of the new conditions, but also the recruitment of new teachers cause serious problems, as the salaries of university teachers are very low. Most of all the younger teachers are disadvantaged, as they are usually less able to supplement their income by second jobs, research contracts and so on. On the other hand, the demand in business for young and well-educated professionals is very high, and some of the best young university teachers are seduced by the much higher (sometimes four times higher) salaries in business.

It is usually stated that student-teacher ratios at the Hungarian institutions of higher education are quite low [35]. That might be a further argument in favor of the dismissal of part of the teaching staff. At the same time, however, a growing demand is expressed both by the ministry of education and by society to increase the number of students, so that the enrolment ratios in higher education should attain the lower level of the range of this ratio in the advanced Western societies (that is, at least 20 or 25%). This would improve at once the student-teacher ratios and therefore brush aside the need for the massive dismissal of the staff.

The problem of the number of students is made more acute by the fact that from 1993 to 1997 cohorts of 20–30% greater numbers of the population are entering the age group of nineteen, that is, the age of entering higher education institutions. Therefore the maintenance of the present 10% enrolment ratios in the ordinary day-courses would require an important increase in the number of students. The greatest obstacle of the increase is the shortage of buildings and other infrastructure and immediate investments in university buildings and infrastructure would be needed.

It is planned that the number of ordinary day-course students will be increased from 77,000 in 1990 to 133,000 by the year 2000. (The number of all students, including evening and correspondence students, will increase from 102,000 to 180,000.) The rate of increase will be somewhat higher in the universities than in the colleges, and will be differentiated by universities and faculties, economists and lawyers increasing at a higher than average rate. That would produce in 2000 an enrolment figure of 16% in day-courses for the birth cohorts 1976–1980 and of 21% in all courses (assuming that the evening and correspondence students are all aged 20–24, which is obviously not the reality). As the subsequent birth cohorts are smaller, the maintenance of these student numbers after 2000 would result in an enrolment of about 21–22% in day-courses of the population aged 20–24. This development plan of higher education is obviously very ambitious and necessitated important investments in infrastructure and budget expenditure for current expenses. Yet it is far from overambitious as compared to student ratios in other advanced societies [36].

This raises the question of financing tertiary education. At present the institutions of higher education receive the overwhelming part of their financial resources from the ministry of education. This financial support follows the "basis principle": many years ago a certain allotment to each institutions of higher education was decided and this "basis" sum was increased from year to year by a certain percentage. Recently the ministry would give some additional sums, if the university were willing to increase the number of students. Obviously it would be desirable to go over to normative financing, that is, to a system in which each higher education institutions would obtain financial resources according to the number of students (the per student financial support would obviously be differentiated by types of institutions, for example, medical universities need a higher sum per student).

Universities and other higher education institutions ought to cover a larger part of their expenditures from other sources. One obvious potential source is tuition. Similar to other advanced societies, the children of well-to-do parents are overrepresented among the students of the Hungarian higher institutions. There is, indeed, "no real justification for using tax revenues collected from working people to provide a free education for the children of well-to-do parents" [37]. On the other hand there is a strong resistance among students in Hungary against any tuition. Stipends and loans given to students might help to mollify the resistance of the students.

The financing by the state budget and the introduction of tuition are related to the question of private universities. There are some initiatives partly by private groups and partly by the Roman Catholic Church to establish private universities. Two important problems are mentioned in the discussions about these projects:

(1) how should the supervision and accreditation of these universities be performed and
(2) how much, if any, support from the state budget should be given to the private universities?

In addition to these acute questions of higher education, there are some deeper problems, which have to be handled by the universities and other higher education institutions as well as by the government and the parliament. Most of these problems were treated by the experts of the Citizens Democracy Corps, which visited Hungary in October 1991 [38]. Some of these problems might be solved by the Law on Higher Education, the draft of which is still hotly debated.

(1) Universities and other higher education institutions at present are completely autonomous. The rectors of the universities and the directors of the colleges are nominated by the president of the Republic and by the minister-president on the basis of the election at the university or college, usually by the council of the educational institutions, and the

agreement of the minister of education. Election results are very rarely overruled and only on the basis of lack of scientific achievements (appropriate degree and so on). Professors are nominated on the basis of the vote of the university council and college council by the president of the Republic and the minister-president, who examine only the scientific achievements necessary for the nominations. Docents (associate professors) are nominated by the rectors and directors on the basis of the programs and on the content of the courses are made by the university and college councils. Students are represented at the councils and have maximum of 30% of the vote. The present practice, however, ought to be confirmed by a law, so that it cannot be changed in future.

(2) The present fragmentation of higher education is clearly inefficient from the point of view of administrative costs and disadvantageous from the point of view of interdisciplinary cooperation and exchange of ideas. The process of forming university federations has already begun, but goes on very slowly, because each university and college jealously defends its autonomy and interests.

(3) Some universities adopted the "American" system of undergraduate studies (usually three years) ending with a bachelor of arts or sciences diploma, and graduate studies (usually 2 years) would end with a master of arts or sciences diploma. It is not clear at present how this 3+2 system would fit with the colleges having usually a four-year undergraduate program.

(4) Postgraduate studies, including Ph.D studies, have to be introduced and expanded urgently in the universities. In the Ph.D. programs the institutes of the Hungarian Academy of Sciences are organized to participate together with the universities, but the degree will be given by the universities. In order to elevate the Ph.D. training to the Western level, it would be desirable to cooperate with Western universities, perhaps by sending the Ph.D. students for one two semesters of study at Western universities.

(5) The whole higher education system of Hungary has to catch up with higher education in Western Europe and other advanced societies of the world. Curricula and content of courses ought to be compatible, degrees ought to be equivalent. Exchange of students is an important way to promote this catching up, as it necessarily stimulates the Hungarian universities. From this viewpoint the introduction and expansion of teaching courses in foreign languages in Hungarian universities, in which foreign students can participate, is of very high importance.

In the socialist period the financing of research went either through the Hungarian Academy of Sciences toward its research institutes, or through the government and the Party, which made five-year plans of scientific research in the social sciences and selected the research topics and the scientists responsible for leading research in the topic.

For example, in the five-year period from 1986 to 1990 the following four topics were selected in the fields of sociology and demography within the framework of these government-financed programs:

(1) social structure and social policy;
(2) social values;
(3) population policy;
(4) deviance.

The party financed research in the field of the conditions of the working class and the conditions of youth and young adults.

Thus no grant application system and no competition for research funds evaluated by peer review existed. In 1984 the government and the academy introduced a system of grant applications for the financing of basic research. The allocation of the grants was decided by the committees of the academy.

In 1991 a Hungarian Research Fund independent of the Hungarian Academy of Sciences was created [39]. Following the advice given by an expert group of the World Bank, which contributed the resources of the research fund through a "human resources project" provided to Hungary, the Hungarian Research Fund is an autonomous body, independent of the government, the academy, and the universities [40]. Its president is nominated for a five-year period by the government. All the members of the scientific committees and juries deciding about the research grant applications are nominated by the president on the basis of opinions expressed by the scientific community and partly on the basis of opinion polls. All researchers have the right to present research grant applications for a period of one to four years. The applications are evaluated by peer review with the juries and scientific committees deciding on the basis of clear criteria.

Four types of grant applications exist at present in the framework of the Research Fund:

(1) so-called thematic research applications, that is, resources for the investigation of well-defined research topics;

(2) applications for instrumental infrastructure;
(3) applications for informational infrastructure;
(4) special support for young researchers below the age of thirty-five.

In 1991 the Research Fund obtained 1.8 billion forints from the state budget. 1.2 billion forints was distributed for thematic grant applications, 18.7% to the social and cultural sciences, 36.5% to the life sciences, and 44.8% to the natural sciences. 40% of the 1.2 billion forints was given to institutes of the Academy, 60% to universities and other research units. The remaining 600 million forints was used to finance applications for instruments and informational infrastructure, as well as the grant applications of young scientists. The World Bank contributed about 18 million US dollars in a three-year period to the financing of applications for instruments, informational infrastructure, and young researchers.

In 1992 the Research Fund obtained 2 billion forints from the state budget, that is, in real terms (taking into consideration the inflation rate of about 36% in 1991) less than in 1991. For comparison it might be mentioned that the allotment of the Hungarian Academy of Sciences from the state budget was nearly 4.5 billion forints and the allotment of the research institutes of the ministries (for example, health, agriculture) was 1.2 billion forints.

It ought to be added that the financial resources of the social sciences coming from the government-financed projects were extended by the government to 1991, but not continued in 1992, so that great problems emerged in the financing of research. New projects, but with much smaller research funds, were decided by the government in 1992.

The greatest problem of the Hungarian Research Fund is at present the shortage of research funds. If the allotment from the state budget will not increase at least parallel with the rate of inflation, almost no new grant applications can be accepted in 1993 and even the financing of the earlier-accepted grant applications extending until 1994 will be in danger. The shortage of research funds makes the competition more fierce, good applications must be rejected or much smaller amounts of funds can be alloted to the individual applications than they originally applied for. This clearly contributes to the deterioration of the general atmosphere in the scientific communities.

Peer review and decisions by the juries and the committees are made difficult by the smallness of the country and of the scientific community. Applicants for research funds and the reviewers and member of juries and committees know each other and are sometimes dependent on one another. Thus impartiality might be in danger. An obvious solution to this problem would be to involve experts from other countries in the process of reviewing. For that purpose applications ought to be written in Hungarian and English.

The committees of the Hungarian Research Fund are at present not in a position to decide major research priorities, that is, which fields of research ought to be especially supported in Hungary and which of the scientific disciplines in Hungary are at the top world level and promise important new research results. An overall review of Hungarian science would be highly desirable, but in view of the interests of the different science lobbies this review also seems impossible without the involvement of foreign scientists. In addition to the very great input of work demanded of the foreign reviewers the question of language and translation again appears.

In addition to special problems faced by the Hungarian Academy of Sciences, the higher education institutions, and the Hungarian Research Fund, there are some general, but very concrete, difficulties that all social scientists have to face:

(1) The financial support of the state for research in the social sciences diminished and became much less secure because of the introduction of the system of competition for research funds. This endangers the existence of some research institutions, but at the same time helped the emergence of new and innovative research collectives.
(2) The diminution of state subsidies for the publication of scientific books and journals resulted in a sharp decline in their publication. The Hungarian public is not accustomed to the much higher prices of scientific books and journals, necessitated by the decline of state subventions. The support by private foundations and business enterprises will need a longer time to develop, although the first hopeful signs are already visible. Publishing in major languages would be highly desirable.
(3) A great part of the new top political elite came from the scientific elite. Many social scientists became politicians: ministers, high-level bureaucrats, parliamentarians, and leaders of parties. A great number of social scientists are regularly writing articles for daily and weekly newspapers. All these researchers are, at least temporarily, lost for the social sciences.

(4) Formerly most social scientists had a feeling of "togetherness", as if they were in a besieged fortress attacked by the power elite and the dogmatic ideologues and felt that they had to defend each other in case of an outside attack, which might have resulted in a loss of their scholarly position. This feeling disappeared after the regime transition, nay, fierce, fights between the social scientists joining different parties appeared, which are highly disadvantageous for objective scientific discourse. The deeper cause of this infighting in science might be conceptualized as a general confusion of the role of the politician and of the role of the social scientists, a problem MAX WEBER had already tried to clarify.

(5) The general lack of democratic civic culture also affects the community of social scientists. It ought to be accepted by scientists that in science the main value and goal is scientific truth and not power, and that the political or scientific opponent is not an enemy who ought to be eliminated by all available means. It has to be understood that these antidemocratic thought and behavioral patterns were obviously inherited from the previous totalitarian and authoritarian period and the innate absorption of the democratic civic culture is obviously a long process, yet the heritage of patterns learned in the totalitarian and authoritarian period hinder painfully and daily the progress toward a democratic scientific climate.

PRESENT INTELLECTUAL TRENDS AND PROBLEMS IN THE HUNGARIAN SOCIAL SCIENCES

The complete intellectual freedom brought about by the change in regime provides new possibilities but also causes problems for economics, sociology, and demography. Some of the new tasks and problems are:

(1) The taboo of criticism of Marxism in the socialist period resulted in the avoidance of theoretical equations in the social sciences and in the avoidance of a serious analysis of classical Marxist and modern Western Marxist ideas. The only serious Marxists in Hungary were the members of the "LUKÁCS school". In the totalitarian and authoritarian period it was perhaps a healthy self-defence strategy to avoid the theoretical questions and, most of all, the Marxist theories, but now a profound critical evaluation of classical and modern Marxism is needed

because these are, in spite of all their failures, serious and influential theoretical schools, perhaps more in sociology and less in economic sciences and in demography. I do not think that it is a scientifically sound attitude to declare that MARX and all of the Marxists are to be simply "non-persons". It is characteristic that only VAJDA, a member of the LUKÁCS school, attempted to face his Marxist past and describe his intellectual distancing from Marxism, and that among sociologists SZELÉNYI, who teaches at the University of California at Los Angeles, refers most frequently to MARX and used to say that the utility of some Marxist concepts ought to be at least reconsidered [41].

(2) Liberalism is today the dominant intellectual tendency in Hungary. This is completely understandable, for the negative experiences of totalitarian and authoritarian regimes obviously convinced the great majority of Hungarian society and, most of all, the social scientists that the values of liberalism (freedom, tolerance, and dignity of the individual, non-interference of the state into the personal matters of individuals and families) are superior to the values of either nationalism or socialism. Two remarks seem to be appropriate, however:

(a) There are many variants of liberalism around the world: in politics from the American liberal democrats through the English social liberals to the Italian rather right-of-center liberals and in the social sciences from HAYEK and FRIEDMAN to POPPER, RAWLS, and DAHRENDORF. With the important exception of a short book by KÖRÖSSÉNYI I do not know of any work that presents to the Hungarian public these variants of liberalism, and those who define themselves as liberals (and usually their opponents as nonliberals, although these opponents often emphasize their own liberal values) usually forget to specify the variant of liberalism to which they wish to belong [42]. A scientific discussion about the different meanings of liberalism and their implications for the social sciences would be a very important need.

(b) It would be somewhat ridiculous, but somewhat sad, if liberalism would replace Marxism as an index to point to the "good guys", as opposed to non-liberal "bad guys", and if citations from HAYEK and FRIEDMAN would be used to decide scientific debates in a way similar to the way earlier citations from MARX were used. Thus it would not be desirable if some dogmatic variant of liberalism would replace dogmatic Marxism in the Hungarian sciences.

(3) In the economic sciences the neoclassical synthesis seems to play the dominant role right now. This is again understandable, if the pure logical structure of neoclassical economics, based on some assumptions like the homo oeconomicus, were to become a very healthy remedy against the obfuscations of twentieth-century Soviet Marxism. On the basis of neoclassical economics, based on mathematical models, it was easy to demonstrate the impossibilities of the economic policies proposed by the dogmatic Marxists. It would be dangerous now, though, to believe that the real market economies operate exactly according to the models of neoclassical economics, and to neglect the new insights of such recent schools of economic sciences as new institutional economics, the theory of public choice, the concepts of public good and of externalities, the theories of satisfying behavior of the firms, disequilibrium theories, and the like. Recent works of KORNAI might serve as a means to mediate these new approaches of the economic sciences.

(4) No similar theoretical orientation seems to dominate in sociology. Weberian and Neo-Weberian theories, which were the "secret" theories of most sociologists, seem to have lost some of their influence among younger sociologists, maybe because of their relative similarity to the Marxist approaches. Also the example of American positivist sociology seems to have lost its attraction. New structural-functional theories (LUHMANN), theories of rational choice (COLEMAN), phenomenological and interpretative approaches and the theories of BOURDIEU are known and enthusiastically accepted by some younger sociologists, but the critical comparative evaluation of all these theories is lacking.

(5) Although the critical evaluation of these new theories would be highly desirable in the Hungarian social sciences, I would warn against an overemphasis on theoretical work as a reaction to the empiricism of the previous period. Theories without facts would lead the Hungarian social sciences into very dangerous directions, and the temptation is great because the new intellectual freedom abolished all obstacles to theoretical investigation and because the shortage of research funds hinders empirical investigations.

(6) A new attitude is needed toward giving political advice to the government, to parties including the opposition parties, trade unions, and so on. In the soft authoritarian system most sociologists defined themselves as belonging to the opposition, but were willing to give advice to the government. The simple criterion of "good" advice was that it proposed a greater role of the market and more democracy in politics

and in society. The problem is much more complicated since the regime transition. Should a social scientist give advice to the government if he favors one of the parties in opposition? Is it permitted to give advice to other parties than the one which you belong? What should be your opinion of your colleague who gives advice to the party you do not like? Does a social scientist have to go completely into politics and be an activist of one of the parties or should he maintain his independence from political parties? Or should he choose some middle-ground between complete involvement and complete distance from politics? Can the role of political activist and the role of social scientist be reconciled? What kind of institutions could facilitate the discourse between social scientists and politicians, so that the knowledge produced by social sciences could somehow enter the political decision-making processes, without endangering the independence of the sciences and the scientists?

(7) Ultimately the self-definition of social sciences is to be formulated in new terms. In the authoritarian period economists, demographers, and primarily sociologists defined their scientific discipline as a critical science, the main function of which is the critique of existing economic, demographic, and social conditions. The highlighting of positive developments during the authoritarian period brought always the suspicion that one was an apologist. The question became much more complicated in the post-transition period. The neglect of the positive developments since the regime transition and the overemphasizing of the undeniable social and economic problems like pauperization, the decline of the financial resources of the health care system and of education and science and so on might easily result in the semblance that the pre-transition system was indeed better. It is not easy to find such a balanced evaluation of recent changes as the concept of "creative destruction", borrowed from SCHUMPETER and proposed by KORNAI recently to characterize the present situation [43].

CONCLUDING REMARKS

The transition of the social sciences in Hungary parallel with the regime transition is a much more complicated process than an outsider might believe. There are relatively few perfect "good guys" and perfect "bad guys", there are no good and democratic institutions and bad and authoritarian institutions, the former socialist regime was not completely "black" and the conditions after the transition are not completely "white". This results from the peaceful and gradual character of the Hungarian transition. Without this "messiness" of the Hungarian system the transition could not have happened without strong outside influence. Therefore the "messiness" has to be accepted also now. In consequence there are no clear-cut recommendations and no simple solutions – neither in politics, the economy and the society, not in the scientific field.

The second possible conclusion to be drawn might be that the difficulties that the Hungarian social sciences have to face are so enormous that the development toward the scientific conditions of advanced democratic societies is almost hopeless. I would not agree with this conclusion, although my emphasis on the difficulties might contribute to it. My emphasizing the difficulties is, however, the result of the disenchantment coming after the euphorie of 1990, when I and other social scientists had to tackle the difficult everyday problems of the transition in the sciences and in the universities. Therefore I would like to add a rather personal and subjective note. In spite of all the difficulties described above, the regime transition and the two years that have passed since the political moment are wonderful experiences for me, and probably most Hungarian social scientists, for two reasons:

(1) Complete freedom of scientific research was achieved, which was never before dreamed of.
(2) We are witnesses of extremely interesting economic, social, and political changes; it might be said that we live in a laboratory of social sciences. By studying the causes of the collapse of the authoritarian system and the interrelations of market-oriented economic changes, the development of political democracy, and the development of civil society, Hungarian social scientists could really contribute to worldwide knowledge of economic, social, and political changes and developments.

REFERENCES

[1] GYÖRGY LITVÁN: *Az 1956-os forradalom* (Budapest 1991).
[2] ZDENEK MLYNAŘ: *A prágai tavasz... és ősz* (Budapest 1989).
[3] REZSŐ NYERS: *Útkeresés – reformok* (Budapest 1988); FERENC BÖRÖCZFY (ed.): *Vélemények, viták. A magyar gazdaságirányításról*, Vols 1 and 2 (Budapest 1983).
[4] JÁNOS KORNAI: *A hiány* (Budapest 1980).

[5] RUDOLF ANDORKA: "The Importance and the Role of the Second Economy for the Hungarian Economy and Society", *Aula Society and Economy* 12: 2, pp. 95–113 (1990).

[6] IVÁN SZELÉNYI: *Socialist Entrepreneurs: Embourgeoisement in Rural Hungary* (Madison 1988).

[7] GYÖRGY KONRÁD, IVÁN SZELÉNYI: *The Intellectuals on the Road to Class Power* (New York 1979).

[8] RUDOLF ANDORKA: "Die Nutzbarkeit des Schichtkonzepts für die Untersuchung der heutigen ungarischen Gesellschaft" in PETER A. BERGER and STEFAN HRADIL (eds): *Lebenslagen, Lebensläufe, Lebensstile*, pp. 271–294 (Göttingen 1990).

[9] RUDOLF ANDORKA: "Changes in Social Mobility in Hungary, 1930–1983", in MAX HALLER (ed.): *Class Structure in Europe* (Armonk, N. Y. 1990), pp. 198–232; ROBERT ERIKSON and JOHN H. GOLDTHORPE: *The Constant Flux* (Oxford 1992).

[10] IVÁN SZELÉNYI: "The Prospects and Limits of the East European New Class Project – An Autocritical Reflection to The Intellectuals on the Road to Class Power", *Politics and Society* 15, pp. 103–144 (1986–1987).

[11] IVÁN SZELÉNYI: *Új osztály, állam, politika* (Budapest 1990).

[12] TAMÁS KOLOSI: *Tagolt társadalom* (Budapest 1987).

[13] IVÁN SZELÉNYI: "Merre tartunk a posztkommunizmusból?", *Magyar Hírlap*, november 17 (1990).

[14] JÁNOS KORNAI: *A gazdasági vezetés túlzott központosítása*, 2. edition (Budapest 1990).

[15] TAMÁS BAUER: *Tervgazdaság, beruházás, ciklusok* (Budapest 1981); KÁROLY ATTILA SOÓS: *Terv, kampány, pénz* (Budapest 1986); ÉVA EHRLICH: *Országok versenye, 1937–1986* (Budapest 1991); IVÁN PETŐ and SÁNDOR SZAKÁCS: *A hazai gazdaság négy évtizedének története 1945–1985, I. Az újjáépítés és a tervutasításos irányítás időszaka* (Budapest 1985).

[16] JÁNOS KORNAI: *A gazdasági szerkezet matematikai tervezése* (Budapest 1965); ANDRÁS BRÓDY: *Érték és újratermelés* (Budapest 1969).

[17] JÁNOS KORNAI: *Anti-equilibrium* (Budapest 1971); KORNAI: *A hiány.*

[18] TIBOR LISKA: *Ökonosztát* (Budapest 1988); LÁSZLÓ LENGYEL: *Végkifejlet* (Budapest 1989).

[19] JÁNOS KORNAI: *Indulatos röpirat a gazdasági átmenet ügyében* (Budapest 1989).

[20] ANDRÁS KLINGER: "The Impact of Policy Measures, Other Than Family Planning Programmes, on Fertility", *Research Reports of the Demographic Research Institute*, No. 18 (1984); PÉTER JÓZAN: *A halálozási viszonyok alakulása Magyarországon 1945–1985* (Budapest 1988).

[21] RUDOLF ANDORKA: "Politiques démographiques natalistes et leur impact en Hongrie", *Politiques de population*, 4: 3, pp. 87–125 (1991).

[22] "A többszörösen hátrányos helyzetű rétegek vizsgálata. A Magyar Szociológiai Társaság tudományos ülésszaka, 1981. április 23–24." *Szociológia*, 10, pp. 279–332 (1981); ÁGNES BOKOR: *Depriváció és szegénység* (Budapest 1985).

[23] ZSUZSANNA FERGE: *Társadalmunk rétegződése* (Budapest 1969); TAMÁS KOLOSI: *Státus és réteg* (Budapest 1984).

[24] GYÖRGY KONRÁD, IVÁN SZELÉNYI: "A lakáselosztás szociológiai kérdései", *Valóság* 12: 8, pp. 28–39 (1969).

[25] RUDOLF ANDORKA: *A társadalmi mobilitás változásai Magyarországon* (Budapest 1982).

[26] ÁGNES LOSONCZI: *A kiszolgáltatottság anatómiája az egészségügyben* (Budapest 1986).

[27] RUDOLF ANDORKA, BÉLA FALUSSY: "The Way of Life of the Hungarian Society on the Basis of the Time Budget Survey of 1976–1977." *Social Indicators Research*, 11, pp. 31–74 (1982).

[28] *Társadalmi beilleszkedési zavarok Magyarországon* (Budapest 1986).

[29] RUDOLF ANDORKA: "Causes of the Collapse of the Communist System, Present Situation and Future Prospects in Hungary" (Paper presented at the Conference on the Legacies of the Collapse of Marxism, Washington, D.C.) (1992).

[30] KONRÁD and SZELÉNYI: *Intllectuals*.

[31] ZSUZSANNA FERGE: *Társadalompolitikai tanulmányok* (Budapest 1980).

[32] TAMÁS KOLOSI, PÉTER RÓBERT: "A rendszerváltás társadalmi hatásai", *TÁRKI Gyors-jelentések*, 5 (1991).

[33] ÁKOS RÓNA-TAS, TAMÁS KOLOSI: "The First Shall Be Last? The Social Consequences of the Transition from Socialism" (unpublished manuscript) (1992).

[34] RALF DAHRENDORF: *Reflections of Revolution in Europe* (London 1990).

[35] World Bank, *Hungary: The Transition to Market Economy: Critical Human Resources Issues* (Washington 1990).

[36] *A magyar felsőoktatás fejlesztése 2000-ig* (Budapest 1992).

[37] DEREK BOK: *Universities in transition: observations and recommendations for Hungary and Czechoslovakia* (Citizens Democracy Corps Report, p. 7, 1992).

[38] BOK: *Universities*.

[39] RUDOLF ANDORKA, ISTVÁN LÁNG: "Hungarian Research Fund: Experiences and Perspectives" (Paper presented at the United States–Hungarian Science Policy Workshop, Washington 1991); RUDOLF ANDORKA, ZSUZSANNA GILYÉN: "The first 18 months of the autonomous Hungarian Research Fund (OTKA)" (Paper presented at the German–Hungarian workshop on science policy, Berlin 1992).

[40] World Bank, *Hungary*.

[41] MIHÁLY VAJDA: *Orosz szocializmus Közép-Európában* (Budapest 1989); MIHÁLY VAJDA: *Marx után szabadon, avagy miért nem vagyok már marxista?* (Budapest 1990).

[42] ANDRÁS KÖRÖSSÉNYI: *Liberális vagy konzervatív korszakváltás?* (Budapest 1989).

[43] RUDOLF ANDORKA: "Hungarian Sociology in the Face of the Political, Economic and Social Transition." *International Sociology*, 6, pp. 465–469 (1991).

5

THE PARADOXES OF TRANSITION: THE EXTERNAL AND INTERNAL OVERLOAD OF THE TRANSITION PROCESS*

By

ATTILA ÁGH

The countries of former communist East-Central Europe are experiencing an imposed set of over-generalized and over-simplified institutional and value systems, whose relevance is not self-evident to the populations concerned, and whose successful implementation cannot be assumed. A range of possibilities exist, from formalist, elitist and "partyist" democracy, or to tyrannical majoritarianism, authoritarianism or west European-style democracy. In the current world-wide wave of authoritarian renewal, overcoming the authoritarian history of the region is an added dimension of the struggle for democracy.

FORCED DEMOCRACIES IN EAST-CENTRAL EUROPE

The revolutions of 1989 in the countries of East-Central Europe were events of global importance. In the first place these countries (Poland, the Czech lands, Slovakia, Hungary and, possibly, Slovenia and Croatia) made great efforts to liberate themselves from the captivity of the Soviet empire, and their resistance weakened the whole empire fatally. The events of 1989 and the collapse of the Soviet empire have made all the contradictions of old world order outdated and have created a great number of new domestic and international contradictions. Yet basically these relatively small countries were, and still are, over-dependent on external factors; they have remained captives of the international system and over-sensitive to all external changes. Thus, despite all of their efforts and contributions, their democratic transition was a direct result not of their own action but of the disintegration of the bipolar world system. Parado-

* In *The Journal of Communist Studies and Transition Politics*, September 1994, Vol. 10, No. 3, pp. 15–34.

xically, although countries such as Poland and Hungary mostly "liberated" themselves, their liberation from the Soviet empire was, at the same time, a "defeat" for them. Because of their structural and conjunctural weakness, they have had to accept the model of Western democracy that has been the fundamental precondition for their acceptance in the international system. We can therefore consider these emerging new democracies as "forced" or "imposed" ones. They were, in fact, "forced to be free".

Of course, forced democratization is not a new situation in political history. The same happened to some countries (Germany, Italy and Japan) in the early post-war period when this term was used first for the model of "democratization through defeat" [1]. Samuel Huntington has identified three European waves of global democratization in all. After the first wave of the Anglo-Saxon countries and the second, post-war wave of democratizations (Germany, Italy and Japan), the recent ones in Southern Europe, Latin America and the eastern half of Europe have been classified as "The Third Wave" (as the title of Huntington's book suggests). Between these waves of democratization there were two "reverse periods" and Huntington also sees the possibility of "The Third Reverse" (perhaps the title of his next book, five years hence). There is no doubt for him that the waves of democratization have been functions of the world system as such and not only the result of internal developments. This is why and how the countries of the second and third waves have been forced to be free. In this context, inside the third wave, the East-Central European democratizations represent the third generation after the South European and Latin American ones. The East European case is completely different, however, in that it may be either the fourth generation or the next reverse wave [2].

The forced democratizations in the early post-war period took place in the emerging bipolar world system, in the old world order. The United States then had a very strong vested interest in supporting the new democracies through the Marshall Plan for a simultaneous transformation of economy and polity, or in other words for the creation of both a market economy and democracy. The 1989 revolutions, in turn, meant not only the collapse of the external Soviet empire but of the whole bipolar world and the emergence of the new world order. However, the forced democratization of the East-Central European countries has been more paradoxical. The first paradox is that, although the Western powers were very much interested in the defeat of state socialism, because they did not have an enemy image of the East-Central European countries, they have not shown any particular engagement in supporting their new democracies.

To begin with, these countries tried to be free on their own, then they were forced to be free, and now they have been abandoned. This leads us to the second paradox: the East-Central European countries have been forced to play a role expected from outside which has not been the optimal way of democratization from the inside.

The paradoxes of democratic transition had already appeared in the second wave but they were solved in the circumstances of the cold war confrontations by massive US political and economic assistance. Claus Offe clearly formulates this paradox as the principle of the necessity of simultaneous transition in politics and the economy:

> The only circumstance under which the market economy and democracy can be simultaneously implanted and prosper is that one in which both are forced upon a society from outside and guaranteed by international relations of dependency and supervision for a long period of time. This, at least, is arguably the lesson offered by the war ruined post-war democracies of Japan, and, with qualification, of the Federal Republic of Germany.

Therefore Offe is very pessimistic about the fate of the East-Central European developments, since "there is no obvious 'patron power' that would be a natural candidate for the task of supervising and enforcing the peaceful nature of the transition process" [3].

In my opinion, however, the failure of the East-Central European democratizations has not been predetermined at all, although the paradoxical nature of transition appears in a much more marked way. This forced democratization has been negative for the East-Central European developments in many respects, by imposing alien standards upon them which are based on the over-generalizations and over-simplifications of international organizations. At the same time it has been positive in creating a "forced-course development" for democratization which has provided protection against anti-democratic forces and influences coming from inside. This positive aspect of forced democratization has been dominating so far, but with so many disturbing "side effects" that it remains an open question whether the East-Central European countries will follow the success story of the South European forced democratizations or whether they have to face a period of reversal, that is, the breakdown of democracy, after this current short period of re-democratization.

History shows that the process is not predetermined either way. Even the United States failed in the post-war period in most cases of forced democratization throughout the world, and in Europe above all in Greece and Turkey. The special compromise, *the façade or formal democracy,* which developed there has a relevance also for the recent developments in the eastern half of Europe. Where the internal political and economic circumstances for substantial democratization were not present, the forced democratizations were detailed and produced a minimum democracy consisting of the constitutional formalities as a façade for what was actually an authoritarian regime. This was clearly the Greek case in its "ally phase" when the United States accepted Greece as an ally in the bipolar European security order and did not impose democracy as a model upon it.

The turning-point for Greek democratization came in the mid-1970s. The "transition trigger" resulted from the combined effect of external and internal linkages, including both the global and the domestic economic crisis. In this respect the Greek transformation is the closest to the East-Central European developments, except for the main thing: the engagement of the EC countries in the democratization process, which was extremely strong in Greece and surprisingly weak in East-Central Europe. In the mid-1970s the Greek political elite suffered defeat from outside (the Cyprus conflict) as well as from inside (the crisis of the colonels' regime), and it was simply forced to change its political system dramatically by a radical adjustment to West European standards. In other words, it had to give up the formal or façade democracy and change it into one of substance. The forced or imposed character of systemic change was not new at all in Greek political history and the crisis was solved by a shift from US dependency ("ally") status to the EC "model" of substantial democracy. The forced democratization in Greece was the first EC "promotion of democracy" in the third wave, followed by Spain and Portugal, but it has remained the most difficult one. Greece was a very special case of "democratization through defeat". This time, however, the EC forced its Greek partner to be democratic not mainly by military but by economic means. The "capitulation" of Greece to forced democratization by the European Community was mostly based on the Greeks perception of, and accommodation with, their own "penetrated society" and external dependence:

> The Greeks themselves, however, take for granted an explicit connection between the political regime and its external links... it often seems as if a considerable proportion of the populations views the polity as an only partially autonomous sub-unit of its broader inter-

national environment. Long before political scientists recognized the importance of linkages between national and international systems, the Greeks believed that the nature of their regime was largely determined by the "foreign factor" [4].

The experiences and perceptions of the East-Central European populations have been historically very similar, yet the present situation is fundamentally different. Many alien and artificial elements were imposed upon the countries that underwent forced democratization, but after some time these "inorganic" elements became mostly "organic" and they produced or triggered a real democratization effect. However, the forced democratization by the EC in East-Central Europe at present lacks both the means and the resources to trigger a successful democratization. Thus the East-Central European countries are left in the middle of nowhere, and the East European countries, in turn, have only a façade of democratization.

This contrast of high expectations and lack of support gives rise to an external overload for the East-Central European democratizations, while the crisis of the East European "façade" democracies means a special burden for them, in addition to this external overload. Forced democratization can be successful only if either the external pressure (as in Japan) or the internal social potential (as in Germany) is great enough to trigger a positive spiral of simultaneous changes, so that the changes in the political and economic systems are able to reinforce each other in democratization and marketization. In the East-Central European region both have been missing so far, and if both factors are insufficient in the long run, then the slide back to a façade democracy would seem to be unavoidable. As we know from post-war history, façade democracies can result either from the failures of forced democracies or from situation where the external patron, or "victor", accepts a pseudo- or superficial democratization with an external façade which looks "democratic" from outside. This is the case with East European countries today and this situation is a great danger for the East-Central European semi-democracies.

It is very important to emphasize the fundamental differences between forced and façade democracies, but at the same time also those between façade democracies and authoritarian regimes, because even limited and formalistic human rights matter a lot compared to conditions under authoritarian regimes. Still, our main concern here is to point out that façade democracies represent a blind alley in the democratization process.

Therefore the divergence between the forced but substantial democratization (Italy) and superficial façade democratization (Greece before the mid-1970s) is absolutely vital for our argument. The later type of "promotion of democracy" meant its "third-worldization" by the United States, and this is what we are witnessing today in the East European countries.

The Western powers have offered an easy compromise for the East European region. If they build up a thin democratic façade and provide some domestic political stability, then they are considered democratic countries and eligible for Western assistance. In this case the crucial issue is whether these façade democracies can be consolidated in their deep economic crisis and with minimal Western assistance, or whether the breakdown of democracy is unavoidable, as it has been so in many countries of the same kind in the post-war period. The international organizations treat the East European countries in the way they usually treat underdeveloped countries, but this treatment may not be sufficient for their stabilization. Actually these countries now embody the biggest danger both for the new European order and for their neighbours, the whole East-Central European region. Yugoslavia and Russia alike represent the failure of the EC crisis management, although in different ways, and Yugoslavia may indicate the future of the former Soviet Union, since the Serbian and the Russian empires had a lot in common [5].

The East European countries, in deep crisis even now, can explode at any time and disturb the build-up of the new European "post-war order", unless they are more effectively "forced" at leat to take formal democratization seriously. Obviously some East European countries, such as Serbia, Romania and Russia, have not been able to build a credible façade of democracy. They are not stable domestically at all, they are politically delegitimized, and their political elites seek a solution in aggressive and militant emotional nationalism in order to create some legitimacy for themselves. In this drive for stability by aggressive nationalism they need external enemies in the neigbourhood as well as at home, and also a myth of global conspiracy against their countries.

The unstable East European façade democracies have been the worst possible environment for the democratic transition of the East-Central European countries. Yet, in the Central European region the democratization process in some fundamental features has become irreversible. The real question here is whether this process can be accomplished or must remain a half-democratization. In the East European region, however, this point of no return has not been reached yet, and the former state socialist regimes have only been transformed to a new kind of "national communism" with the old paternalistic étatism. The East European region, of course, is not homogeneous. Yugoslavia (or Serbia) may represent the worst, Bulgaria the best case, but the whole East European region is still in the period of the "original crisis" and has not yet begun the real democratic transition.

If we change the comparative focus, the difference between Southern Europe and East-Central Europe is as great as that between East-Central Europe and Eastern Europe. It is not so much the internal points of departure but rather, above all, the external conditions that are different between South-East and East-Central Europe. As discussed above, in the South European case the EC adopted a "model" approach (the mandatory acceptance of the EC model of democracy and market economy) but this is more doubtful in the Central European case. More importantly, however, the South European democratic transition took place in a stable region and in the balanced international system of the old world order while the Central European transition is attempting to stabilize itself in the troubled waters of the not yet emerging new world order [6].

The external conditions in the neighbouring regions are even more detrimental. Altogether, from a narrow economic point of view, the following difficulties stand in the way of the East-Central European democratic transition:

(1) the inertia of the former system with its tremendous debt burden, dead industries and passive economic mentality;
(2) the price of opening up the closed economy which has devalued its products and production units on the world market;
(3) the transition costs of economic system change, the destruction of the old and construction of the new economic structure and employment;
(4) the collapse of the international trade and monetary network, and the trade diversion towards new markets and partners; and
(5) the economic loss produced from the series of international crises globally (the Gulf crisis with high oil prices and the collapse of Soviet market with a debt never really repaid) and regionally (the Yugoslav war with its disastrous effects on trade, travel and transport).

Paradoxically enough, although for the most part unwittingly, the EC produces also much trouble for the East-Central European countries. On the one hand there is an expectation on the part of the EC that the East-Central European countries will overcome the economic crisis, provide regular debt servicing and expand exports, but on the other hand the EC is sophisticated enough to discover non-tariff measures to protect its markets from successful East-Central European export industries such as meat or steel. The EC has not been too eager to include the East-Central European countries in its East European assistance programmes, it has not created an East-Central European regional clearing system for solving the currency issues, and, in general, it has been too preoccupied with its own birth-pangs in the post-Maastricht Europe. While the new vision of East-Central European integration has not yet emerged, small-mindedness and "short-termism" still prevail. In 1992 total East-Central European exports made up only 1.6% of EC imports, while Austrian exports alone made up 1.9%. Indeed, the economic recovery of the East-Central European countries would not threaten the EC markets because of the relatively small size of their economies. The whole question of East-Central European integration into the EC still awaits a political decision [7].

I see four possible scenarios for East-Central European development:

(1) *Germanization* as the partial integration of East-Central European into the EC through a semi-formalized German sphere of influence. This partial integration can be established as part of an intensive economic relationship of currency, trade and investment issues, bordering on dependency. The EC passivity towards the East-Central European countries invigorates their efforts to join the dynamic German economy, and Germany may take this opportunity to seriously extend its activity to this region after having fully absorbed its eastern provinces. This back-door entrance to the EC economic system, however, also has some negative consequences in terms of relationships with other EC countries, and, as a unilateral economic connection, it leaves open the questions of the political and military integration of this turbulent region into the EC. However, this scenario can be helpful to economic stabilization and could lead to a genuine democratic transition in the event of a more marked German effort in favour of East-Central European forced democratization.

(2) *Turkization* means just the opposite option: the formal integration into Western military organizations (NATO, WEU or both) which can provide military security for the EC against the permanent East European crisis zone on its borders, but all the other issues of integration would remain unresolved. The Turkish case shows, in fact, that some countries can be kept in this half-way situation for decades and they are not

eligible for the other aspects of integration, although they may even have an association treaty with the EC. The East-Central European countries are in many ways different from Turkey, most evidently in their geographical proximity to the EC, but this could be a major reason to turn them into a fortress, a buffer zone between the island of calmness and the sea of turbulence. This scenario in the long run would reduce the East-Central European democracies to the East European type of façade democracies with some formal rules of democratic behaviour such as "electoralism".

(3) *Yugoslavization* is obviously the worst-case scenario for the East-Central European region. It is very unlikely but it cannot be excluded. This low-probability scenario presupposes the complete abandonment of the East-Central European region by the EC and the intensification of low-intensity conflicts by Serbia into high-intensity ones within the whole region. This escalation of regional conflict threatens everywhere in the Western part of the former Soviet Union from Moldova to the Baltic States, and above all, in Russia itself where fragmentation as "bantustanization" can turn into a desperate effort of re-centralization by which Russia may attempt to reconquer its previous sphere of influence. In the rimlands of the East-Central European region there have been so many unpredictable events that this "absurd" scenario cannot be excluded, and the EC has not fared at all well in its role of crisis management in the East European region. This collapse would also mean the breakdown of democracy in the East-Central European countries with little hope that in the next re-democratization wave the EC would have better prepared neighbourhood policies.

(4) *Europeanization* is the optimal scenario for the East-Central European region, in which all the aspects of European integration would be treated in a coherent way. This would presuppose a strategic vision or "grand design" on the EC side and a concentrated effort of the East-Central European countries to overcome the "post-communist" crisis. The victory over short-termism and narrow-mindedness on both sides could lead to the full accomplishment of the forced democratization in the coming ten to fifteen years. This is a medium-probability scenario because the Europeanization process has already begun in many fields, but very controversially on both sides and with many setbacks [8].

There are two major requirements for this positive turn in the East-Central European region: first, the elaboration of the "grand design" of the East-Central European integration by the EC and, second, the emergence in the East-Central European countries of a new professional political elite with a firm commitment to Europeanization. After having discussed the external overload, we have to turn now to the internal overload of the democratic transition.

THE INTERNAL PARADOXES OF DEMOCRATIC TRANSITION

The East-Central European countries have also created some obstacles to democratic transition for themselves. Even the word "transition" has become doubtful since it seems to imply a prediction of progress to full democratization. Today, with the crisis of "transitology", most analysts use the terms of the transformation and change interchangeably with transition, or they abandon the word "transition" completely. In my view, it is too early to adopt that pessimistic conclusion about the future developments of East-Central Europe. The positive outcome – the consolidation of the young democracies – is still very likely, but we now see the whole democratization process with more scepticism and sophistication than some years ago. From the very beginning, however, there have been some conceptual uncertainties and observers have used competing notions to discuss the East-Central European developments, for example in terms of revolution, transition, transformation and restoration. These new doubts on "transition" have emerged before the conceptual framework of system change could be "consolidated" [9].

I suggest that this intellectual tradition could and should be retained for East-Central Europe, although the questioning of the term "transition" does reflect a new crisis. This new crisis is not a prolongation of the previous one; it is not the deepening and widening of that crisis which led to the collapse of the state socialist systems, but it is absolutely new as a *crisis of crisis management*, a failure in the reaction to the former crisis. I would call this "post-communist" crisis the "crisis of neo-traditionalism", of the re-awakened past, a late nineteenth-century response to the late twentieth-century challenge. In some ways the new paternalistic étatism is not new but represents very strong continuity with state socialism. Since the mid-nineteenth century all the political courses or regimes in East-Central Europe have represented a changing mixture of half-democratic and half-authoritarian systems in which the democratic features have been reduced to constitutional formalities. At most they have existed only for the elites, but the "overweight" role of state has remained intact.

On the question of the recent "post-communist" authoritarian renewal, Adam Michnik argues that "our fight against the totalitarian communism has ended. But our fight for freedom has just begun" [10]. We realize more and more that after the collapse of state socialism only a formalist, elite democracy has emerged, in which the democratic features have been overshadowed by our authoritarian heritage. The authoritarian renewal has threatened the democratization process by offering a blind alley of neo-traditionalism and anti-European provincialism. Therefore the real fight for democracy has only now begun, but this time against the newly emerging neo-traditionalist regimes. The traditional "political class" with its anti-democratic political culture has returned to power in East-Central Europe. It makes a claim to have a monopoly of power and to have a historical vision and a mission to rule. The authoritarian character of politics is presented as the most valuable part of the national tradition. This traditionalist elite has returned to power with all the paraphernalia of symbols, slogans, mental and ideological simplicities, claiming that it can save the nation in the present "moral" crisis.

The paradoxes of transition in the East-Central European countries have appeared in the following major ways and forms:

(1) The inside of the political system as a contradiction between the democratic form and anti-democratic content, between the elite democracy and the alienation of people from politics, between the democratization of macro-political institutions and clientelism as an anti-democratic fusion of economics and politics.

(2) The structural contradiction between westernized macro-politics and the weak dependent economy with a sluggish privatization and re-invigorated state sector, re-nationalized by the new political elite in order to extend its political power.

(3) The increasing battle between politics and society, the growing gap again between "us" and "them", state and nation, macro-politics and other spheres of socio-political life, between the demobilizing efforts of the new ruling elite and civil remobilization against the new regimes [11].

Obviously, there is no coordination between the three major aspects of systemic change – the economic, political and social dimensions. Instead, politics has been running amok, and as a result it has produced a new crisis, in which:

(i)   the priorities of the new ruling elite have been fundamentally different from those of society, therefore economic crisis management as a priority has been mostly abandoned;

(ii) the new elite has not been ready to accept society and its representatives as partners, so all-round social warfare has broken out between state and society;

(iii) finally, the political system has underperformed; it has worked with very low efficiency, and the effectiveness of political system change has been tragically defective and faulty.

Political culture as the "software" has actually played a more important role in the East-Central European transformations than have the legal institutions as the "hardware". The subjective factor can change the institutions very quickly, but itself changes very slowly. This is why it is so difficult to cope with the authoritarian heritage. But democrats are the results and not the preconditions of the democratic transition. The mass emergence of democrats can be observed only after a long process of democratization when the democratic culture permeates all walks of life. This is the fundamental turning-point in the establishment of the self-sustaining democracy – what has been called in Spain "the invention of democratic tradition". The dynamic model of democratization attributes a great role to the subjective factor in both elite and mass transformations: first "there must be a conscious adaptation of democratic rules" and then "both politicians and electorate must be habituated to these rules". Consequently, as Dankwart Rustow argues, "Circumstances may force, trick, lure or cajole non-democrats into democratic behavior" [12].

No doubt the Latin American and Southern European political elites had the same authoritarian heritage to overcome for democratization to occur, but they also had more possibilities to manoeuvre during the democratic transition than did the East-Central European elites in the conditions of benign neglect. After the capitulation of state socialist regimes it was "pre-determined" that the new political system had to be acceptable to the Western governments, and compatible with their own patterns of elite behaviour. Also, since the populations of the East-Central European countries were attracted by the demonstration effect of Western democracies, they set up expectations to which the new political elite had to conform. In this situation a double paradox has emerged with positive and negative effects: on one side the new elites could not avoid some kind of westernization, but this has remained on the surface, since they neither know western political culture properly, nor accept it completely. On the other side the West has also imposed upon them certain rules that have been alien and detrimental to their national development.

As a result, the new elites have become double-faced, and all the contradictions and limitations of the democratic transition have been concentrated in their actions and patterns of behaviour. Of course, the new elites have been very fragmented in many ways, but they have acted towards the masses in their elite roles as almost one unitary actor. They have underperformed in their modernizing and democratizing roles, since they have been unable to produce a programme of modernization and they have not been ready to mobilize the masses for democratization. Nancy Bermeo may in general be correct when she argues that "democracy is always the fruit of popular struggle, and this must be never forgotten, but the *design* of formal democratic *institutions* is, of necessity, the work of a political elite". However, the East-Central European new elites, in particular, have not yet prepared either the design of the new democracy or the mobilization plan to accomplish it [13].

The new elites so far have been hostages to the old political system, the state socialism in their mentality and their drive for full power. As such, they have become the major obstacle to the further progress of the democratic transition. This is the reason why in the East-Central European countries a new tension has emerged between the elite and the masses, rather similar to that in the former system. If we overcome the simplistic view of elite–mass linkages, according to which the East-Central European transformations as negotiated transitions have only been elite games without mass movements, then we cannot fail to notice that a turning-point occurred after the change-over of elites or power transfer: there were very active mass movements everywhere in East-Central European countries before the collapse of state socialism, and they pushed forward the elite negotiations and legitimized them in advance, but the new elites coming to power then tried to stop and demobilize them. Unlike in the South European countries, the East-Central European elites have not yet concluded social pacts because they have refused to accept other social actors as partners representing the interests of the articulated and organized civil society in the democratization process [14].

In the first phase of democratic transition, inside the fragmented political elite, the group that has dominated so far has been the one representing authoritarian renewal as the intellectual and political heritage of the traditional political class. Their intellectual–moralist opposition, with its historical roots in the former hard opposition to the state socialism, has been unable until now to elaborate a viable and widely supported political alternative to this traditional conservatism and paternalist étatism. Their weak abstract–doctrinaire presentation of the ideas of westernization and Europeanization has been pushed into the background by the neo-traditionalist new rulers who are believers in the strong state and tough power politics. This "new-old" political class has no real idea about late twentieth century Europe, which is, at the same time, alien to their "archaic" mentality. They would like to return to a "Christian Europe" of the kind the West no longer knows, and to a Golden Age of the National History that Never Was [15].

The danger of this detour from real democratization has been present since the end of the pre-transition crisis, but we have not noticed it properly until now. This means that while the left–right political spectrum is still valid in East-Central Europe, for a full analysis it has to be complemented by a spectrum ranging from Europeanization to traditionalization. The major political actors, above all the political parties, can be characterized by using only these two axes, which result in four types of parties: Traditionalist Right, Traditionalist Left, European Right and European Left – a typology which has been quite common in Poland with its "multi-party system". The dominant political forces belong to the neo-traditionalist Right while the centre-right Europeanizing parties are still too weak to govern and to formulate the grand design for democratization. Thus, in contrast to the common wisdom, it is the Right which has been in deeper crisis, since it has not been able to produce a real and strong European type of centre-right party. The Left has also been similarly split between the traditionalists and modernists (if the Stalinist conservatives can be called Left at all). Therefore the political fight has been going on not only between Left and Right, but also between Traditionalizers and Europeanizers, although the first cleavage still dominates over the second. In the East European region the leftist and rightist traditionalist conservatives, the friends of paternalistic étatism, have already found their common denominator in national communism. This danger of an unholy alliance between different forces of the authoritarian renewal is present also in the East-Central European countries, but the modernizing political parties are not yet ready on both the left and right sides of the political spectrum to form an alliance with each other in order to defeat the authoritarians and to clear the ground for normal competition within a modern political system of the European type.

Summing up, there are four types of degeneration or distortion of democracy which threaten the democratic transition in the countries of East-Central Europe as semi- or pseudo-democracies:

(1) *Formalist* democracy in which there is no actual counter-elite as an organized and institutionalized opposition which could offer a radically different political alternative. Therefore the electorate "freely" re-elects the same political class – organized in a hegemonic party system in Sartori's terms – with a rather large degree of popular participation (for example, Mexico).

(2) *Elitist* democracy in which there are some competitive elites – organized in a party system, with many competitive parties, but where one of them is predominant – sharing the whole political scenery among themselves and excluding any meaningful popular participation from policy-making in general (the early British polity or the recent Indian system).

(3) *Partyist* democracy (*partitocrazia* in Italian) in which there are real competitive parties but they are the only political actors and they try to exclude all the other social and political actors – above all, organized interests – from the decision-making process, so that politics becomes a "chamber drama" of the party oligarchies, interwoven with their "clienturas" in the economy (Italy, Japan).

(4) *Tyrannical majorities* which are the distortions of majoritarian democracies, excluding all consensual measures for political, ethnic and cultural minorities – found in young democracies where the first random majorities make an effort to monopolize all powers and, as new governments, refuse all compromises with the new oppositions.

In East-Central European we have a tradition of formalist democracies with a hegemonic party system in which the political class almost completely merges with the public administration, and in the new wave of democratization we have experienced all four types of distortions listed above. The "old-new" political classes have tried to build up a formalist democracy with a very active tyrannical majority, above all in Hungary, but, so far, "checks and balances" have constrained these tendencies to some extent. In order to overcome the present deadlock in democratization, we need a social pact to open up politics for meaningful popular participation and the co-option of social and political actors.

In this situation our four scenarios for the East-Central European reappear from inside as two modernization–Europeanization and two retraditionalization–"provincialization" scenarios with markedly different elite–mass linkages:

(1) "Germanization" as a semi-modernization scenario, in which the economic mobilization of the large parts of the population can go ahead but under the leadership of the "comprador" bourgeoisie emerging from joint ventures and foreign enterprises, and also organizing a political pressure group. The national bourgeoisie remains weak, the middle classes develop in a controversial way, but still relatively large masses are involved in the modernization process. Some national independence parties would emerge as a political opposition to balance the unilateral dependence on the German giant. In would be necessary to look for more coherent and wider integration strategies to keep open the option of real Europeanization.

(2) The "Turkization" scenario would mean a political takeover by a narrow modernizing elite ("reform–dictatorship") in the spirit of a strong state, as the best agent of modernization, to suppress popular discontent with the tacit approval of the Western powers. This modernizing elite has been present in its technocratic forms but it has not yet received political support. The economists demanding shock therapy have not yet found their counterparts in uniforms, although in the "creative chaos" of the democratic transition some intellectuals and entrepreneurs have already called for a strong man. This scenario of "first market, then democracy" seems feasible if the economic crisis continues to deepen drastically and populism from below as a form of popular pressure threatens law and order. This scenario is, in my understanding, an anti-modernization scenario, because it would lead not only to the breakdown of democracy but also to the breakdown of a genuine developed market economy. In the European environment an oppressed population cannot develop a full-scale market economy either [16].

(3) The "Yugoslavization" scenario can enter into force if the confrontation with the neigbouring East European countries turns from low- to high-intensity conflicts. It can also be the result of domestic develop-

ments if the extreme Right, in the form of "populism from above", takes over and creates a regime similar to national communism. If we visualize the political spectrum as a horseshoe model, the extreme Right and the extreme Left are not so far apart and not so different from each other. The extreme nationalist–populist part of the present East-Central European political elites has produced similar declarations to those in power in the East European countries and they need each other as enemies for their own domestic support. This clearly anti-modernization scenario is very unlikely: although the extreme nationalist–populist Right has been present in the East-Central European political life, it is very weak compared to the aggressive and powerful East European nationalist elites, and it has not received any international support either.

(4) The "Europeanization" scenario is, at the same time, the real democratization scenario, entailing an emerging professional political elite and an articulated civil society organized into legitimate social organizations and actors. A coherent European integration process would produce rather broad middle classes, a broader modernizing elite and a balanced political system with dominating centre-left and centre-right parties. This full modernization scenario can be accomplished, of course, only in the long run and not necessarily in its ideal form, but the crucial issue is whether, in the second phase of democratic transition, the present neo-traditionalism can be overcome by an unambiguous Europeanizing orientation.

So far, the different East-Central European countries have had different combinations of the above scenarios. Further differences can easily be predicted but it is also clear that the whole region has to engage in a more or less common action in favour of Europeanization in the form of some kind of regional integration. Again, for the diversity of the East-Central European democratic transition, experience has shown so far that the different types of transition lead to markedly different kinds of democracy. The emerging young democracies may be more "corporatist", "populist", "consociational" or "electoralist", but in order to be sustainable or consolidated they have to be based on a broad social transformation and political participation [17].

We can characterize the particular Hungarian developments in the framework of the general East-Central European framework through a series of paradoxes.

(1) Hungary was the first among the East-Central European countries to embark upon socioeconomic reforms and significant results were achieved even before 1989 in economic legislation for marketization and privatization. Yet it was the first freely elected Hungarian government that then most neglected economic crisis-management and ignored the fundamental necessities of the economic and social system change as opposed to the political transformation. In other words, it was a situation of "politics running amok".

(2) Hungary had an early multiparty system, emerging already in 1988–1989, and has had the least fragmented party system so far in the East-Central European region. Nevertheless it has witnessed the most sustained attempt to have a new ruling party – a state-party with a party-state – through the Hungarian Democratic Forum as an umbrella organization. Although this ruling party fell apart, the danger of the rise of a new conservative "successor" party still exists. This can be described as the "state-party syndrome".

(3) In the 1980s a new, non-ideological technocratic elite came on to the scene and a large intelligentsia was born in Hungary. Nevertheless, the comeback of the traditional political class was the most marked phenomenon here, with its late nineteenth-century ideas on conservative "national liberalism" and "Christian Europe". At the same time, as a contrast to the "Return to the Past" syndrome in the East-Central Europe, we can see here the strongest modernizer-Europeanizer liberal parties (the Alliance of Free Democrats as a social-liberal party and the Alliance of Young Democrats as a self-proclaimed conservative liberal party) and the earliest radically reformed "successor" party (the Hungarian Socialist Party) with a clear social democratic profile. This can be described as an "ideologically polarized multiparty system".

(4) The national-ethnic minority issues are most relevant for Hungary in the East-Central European region because of the three to four million Hungarians living in the neigbouring countries, with their minority rights largely unsettled in the countries concerned. These circumstances gave rise to the strongest form of extreme right-wing nationalist populism which remained inside the governing coalition for three years. But the marginalization of this political force has also occurred first and foremost in Hungary. There has been no real danger that it could become a significant political factor in that country, where most people are immune to militant nationalism.

(5) The conflict of values between Europeanizers and traditionalizers broke out first in Hungary, has been the most vehemently there, and has also been first solved there, in the basic terms of a "Europeanization *cum* democratization". In a drive to acquire full powers on behalf of the "national interest", the first ruling coalition accepted the principles, but refused the practice, of separation of powers and the inclusion of organized interests into the policy-making process. Still, the first Spanish-type social pacts have been concluded here, transforming the multiparty system into a "multi-actor" system step by step. That is, following the establishment of a political dialogue, the social dialogue has now become one of the fundamental processes of Europeanization. In other words, there has been a new opening from macro-politics to meso-politics.

There is today a new international wave of authoritarian renewal, first of all in Latin America and perhaps in Eastern Europe as well [18]. The real fight for democracy has just begun, not only in Hungary, but also in the other East-Central European countries. The major task is not simply to defeat the first neo-traditionalist regimes, but to overcome the whole "history" of our own region with its deeply embedded authoritarian traditions. At the same time, it is necessary to reinvigorate the existing democratic heritage in order to be able to invent a new democratic tradition of the East-Central European civil societies. The idea and the normative features of "transition" can be and should be kept, since the new crisis, in the form of the emergence of neo-traditionalism, is only a temporary phenomenon, although the struggle against its aftermath may last for many years to come.

NOTES

[1] I have dealt with the problems of the post-war forced democratization in much more detail in my paper "The New World Order and the Young East European Democracies", *Budapest Papers on Democratic Transition*, No. 48 (1993). I should indicate here that it is not about the "dependency" of small states in the world system in general, but about a development model in particular which can be discussed, in terms of J. Rosenau, as "linkage politics" and "penetrated societies".

[2] SAMUEL P. HUNTINGTON, *The Third Wave: Democratization in the Late Twentieth Century* (Norman, OK, and London: University of Oklahoma Press, 1991). HUNTINGTON has been the best-known representative of the theory of forced democratization, using the very term "forced to be free".

[3] CLAUS OFFE, "Capitalism by Democratic Design? Democratic Theory Facing the Triple Transition in East Central Europe", *Social Research*, Vol. 58, No. 4 (1991), pp. 874, 889.

[4] SUSANNAH VERNEY, "To be or not to be within the European Community", in GEOFFREY PRIDHAM (ed.), *Securing Democracy: Political Parties and Consolidation in Southern Europe* (London: Routledge, 1990), p. 205. See also SUSANNAH VERNEY and THEODORE COULOUMBIS, "State-International Systems Interaction and the Greek Transition to Democracy in the mid-1970s", in GEOFFREY PRIDHAM (ed.), *Encouraging Democracy: The International Context of Regime Transition in Southern Europe* (London: Leicester University Press, 1991).

[5] See BOGDAN SZAJKOWSKI, "Will Russia Disintegrate into Bantustans?", *The World Today*, Vol. 49, Nos 8–9 (Aug.–Sept. 1993).

[6] I have tried to make a point about the similar starting conditions between South-East and East-Central Europe in my paper, "The 'Comparative Revolution' and the Transition in Central and Southern Europe", *Journal of Theoretical Politics*, Vol. 5, No. 2 (April 1993). I have discussed the problems of East-Central Europe's attempt at European integration in my chapter, "Difficulties and Obstacles for the Construction of Europe: Observations from the Central European Countries", in MARIO TELO (ed.), *Towards a New Europe?* (Brussels: Editions de l'Université de Bruxelles, 1992).

[7] The EC has always reacted to the East-Central European problems very slowly, with a long delay and lack of empathy. In spring 1990 there were some efforts to create a strategy for the whole eastern part of Europe (Dublin summit, 28 April 1990), but they returned to this issue seriously only three years later (Copenhagen summit), and the real results of any new decisions cannot yet be seen.

[8] For a Hungarian contribution to mutual understanding, see FERENC GAZDAG, "Does the West Understand Central and Eastern Europe?", *NATO Review*, Dec. 1992. The major problems of the East European crisis zone are summarized in KONRAD J. HUBER's paper, "The CSCE and Ethnic Conflict in the East", *RFE/RL Research Report*, Vol. 2, No. 31 (30 July 1993).

[9] The framework was first suggested by Dankwart Rustow as the three stages of initial crisis, democratic transition and consolidation. This was further elaborated by the authors of *Transitions from Authoritarian Rule* (1986) and completed by the analysts of the East-Central European countries. ANDRZEJ TYMOVSKI, in his paper, "The Unwanted Social Revolution: Poland in 1989", *East European Politics and Societies*, Vol. 7, No. 2 (1993), has summarized this conceptual controversy.

[10] ADAM MICHNIK, "Zwei Visionen eines posttotalitaeren Europas", in R. DEPPE et al. (eds), *Demokratischer Umbruch in Osteuropa* (Frankfurt am Main: Edition Surkamp, 1991), p. 350. See also JADWIGA STANISZKIS, "Dilemmata der Demokratie in Osteuropa", in the same volume. It is not by chance that the Poles discovered the new crisis first, because they have been the frontrunners of the political transformation in East-Central Europe.

[11] I have described these three contradictions of the new political system and the new ruling elite in my papers, "The Premature Senility of the Young Democracies: The Central European Experience", and "From Nomenclatura to Clientura: The Emer-

gence of New Political Elites in East-Central Europe", *Budapest Papers on Democratic Transition*, Nos 68 and 69 (1993).

[12] D. RUSTOW, "Transition to Democracy", *Comparative Politics* (April 1970), pp. 344–345 and 361. See also my paper, "The Invention of Democratic Tradition in Hungary", *Budapest Papers on Democratic Transition*, No. 65 (1993).

[13] NANCY BERMEO, "Democracy and Lessons of Dictatorship", *Comparative Politics* (April 1992), p. 276. See also TIMUR KURAN, "Now out of Never: The Element of Surprise in the East European Revolution of 1989", in NANCY BERMEO (ed.), *Liberalization and Democratization* (Baltimore, MD, and London: Johns Hopkins University Press, 1992). Kuran emphasizes with justification that these new elites were taken by surprise and were not prepared for the takeover. The major worry is, however, that they are not prepared after four years, either.

[14] TYMOWSKI, op. cit., pp. 184–198, describes this sharp turn to demobilization in Poland very well, including the moment when economic changes were forced upon the society against the former programme of Solidarity and following the dictates of Western powers. MARCIN KRÓL in his paper, "Marginalisierung der Politik", *Neue Gesellschaft-Frankfurter Hefte* (March 1992), gives a similar analysis of the post-Solidarity crisis. See also GERT WEISSKIRCHEN, "Paradoxien in Transit", *Neue Gesellschaft-Frankfurter Hefte* (May 1992).

[15] For example, J. ANTALL, prime minister of Hungary (1990–1993), declared in a speech on the national holiday (20 August, Saint Stephen's Day) that there has been a very strong historical continuity between the ancient Hungarian kingdom and the present parliamentary republic, since the former was not a tyrannical power, but a constitutional, democratic state in terms of its particular historical period: see *Népszabadság*, 21 Aug. 1993.

[16] In the last year there have been widespread debates on whether the East-Central European countries would follow the Latin American path of the breakdown of democracy: see, for example, "Is Latin America the future of Eastern Europe? A Symposium", *Problems of Communism*, May–June 1992; DIRK MESSNER and JÖRG MEYER-STAMER, "Lateinamerikanische Schwellenlaender: Vorbild für Osteurpa?", *Vierteljahres Berichte*, Friedrich Ebert Stiftung, Sept. 1992.

[17] PHILIPPE C. SCHMITTER and TERRY KARL, "The Types of Democracy Emerging in Southern and Eastern Europe and South and Central America", in PETER VOLTEN (ed.), *Bound to Change: Consolidating Democracy in East-Central Europe* (New York and Prague: Institute for East-West Studies, Westview Press, 1992).

[18] There is also a "new wave" of international conferences on the authoritarian renewal: see, for example, the paper by STEVE C. ROPP (University of Wyoming), "New Authoritarian Tendencies in Latin America: Their Dynamics and Implications" (presented to the 34th Annual Convention of the International Studies Association, Acapulco, Mexico, 23–27 March 1993).

6

POLITICKING AND PRIVATISATION*

By

ZOLTÁN ANTAL-MOKOS

This article charts the privatisation process in a Hungarian firm. It was a long, compli-cated and high profile journey, typifying what the author calls a "struggling through" scenario, as distinct from "going through" and "muddling through". The case under-lines the fact that privatisation in Central and Eastern Europe (and elsewhere) needs to be considered in the context of a political view of organisations, as a complement to the dominant economic model based on agency theory.

In the context of Central and Eastern Europe, a basic assumption of policy and academic work is that privatisation brings about stronger incentives, and hence improves management and performance: that this is both the purpose and the effect of privatisation. One would expect that a priva-tised enterprise could no longer be effective without being efficient. But comparing the distinct states of "before" and "after" privatisation ignores the path "in between". This may be an appropriate way of looking at mass-privatisation in the long-run, but is misleading for short-term issues at the level of the firm. Central European transformation is not happening overnight. It is important to chart the changes in the behaviour of firms which privatisation encourages *during* this systemic transformation – which has been taking place in an institutional context in a state of flux, in a politically overheated environment, and which exceeds any previous experience in size, scope and speed (ESTRIN 1994).

This article presents a case history of privatisation in Hungary. It is one of a series of in-depth longitudinal case studies designed to explore the relationship between privatisation and the behaviour of the firm in the

* In *Business Strategy Review*, Spring 1997, Vol. 8, No. 1, pp. 23–30.

context of national (social, political, economic) transformation. The case illustrates two properties of politics during the process of privatisation: *politicisation* of the environment in which privatisation is taking place, and *politicking* within organisations.

INTRODUCING FIRM AND INDUSTRY

"Pluto" (pseudonym after the planet) operated in an industry with a handful of major suppliers, all having licence agreements with Western firms. For Pluto, brands licensed from its Western "Licenser" accounted for more than a third of sales and profits. Prices were fully liberalised in 1989. Demand rose until 1991, but declined sharply later. Four of its competitors had already been privatised by 1991, with foreign companies holding majority stakes in each.

When the process of Pluto's privatisation began, it was the third largest supplier of its products in Hungary; it was also an important local employer and a significant taxpayer. Since 1985, Pluto had operated as a self-governed enterprise under the general management of an Enterprise Council (the main governing body of a firm, authorised by law to make strategic decisions including hiring and firing the general director; consisting of the general director, representatives of the management, and elected representatives of the employees; often acting as a rubber-stamp to the management's decisions; see KORNAI 1992, Ch. 20).

Pluto's journey down the path of privatisation dragged out for several years. It was a "struggling through" process rather than a consciously planned and implemented, straightforward business transaction. It cannot be said to typify "the" Hungarian privatisation, but it illustrates some general features. To one degree or another all – or almost all – cases of privatisation in Hungary (as well as in the rest of Central and Eastern Europe) have been subject to forces similar to those which the case of Pluto illustrates to the extreme: forces which all too often are not explicitly considered by either academics or managers. Those who have been involved in the privatisation process in Britain and elsewhere will also recognise features of this case.

We pick up the story or Pluto in March 1989.

THE "SPONTANEOUS" START-UP

This was the era of the so-called "spontaneous" privatisation. In March 1989 the Enterprise Council authorised Pluto's General Director to explore the possibilities of establishing a joint venture with the Licenser. By November 1989, negotiations had led to an offer. In order to inject finance, the Licenser would acquire a 35% equity stake; benefits were promised for managers and employees. The necessary legislation was already in place, and interest was exhibited by both parties. So Pluto's privatisation could have been concluded relatively quickly and smoothly.

As it turned out, the journey had only begun. After preliminary talks with government officials, an Expatriate Investor (Hungarian by birth, representing a firm with headquarters in a remote tax haven) also submitted a formal offer. He met the General Director to present two alternatives: he would either purchase 100% of Pluto's assets, or acquire 50% of the equity by putting in finance to an amount equal to Pluto's asset value. Promises were made to modernise equipment, to keep the incumbent top management and to increase wages.

In effect, the meeting of the Enterprise Council in early December 1989 settled the future for Pluto. It was presided over by the Enterprise Council Chairman, himself a top manager, a locksmith by profession with no higher degree, who was understood to be an associate of Pluto's General Director. Six issues had been discussed before the General Director reported on the talks he had had with possible investors. In his comments he favoured the Expatriate Investor's offer. He appealed for the members' "good decision", adding that "I can state in my full responsibility that this management is not committed to anyone, only to the Enterprise Council, and to all the employees of the firm". The Licenser's offer was rejected with the result that the choice was reduced to one of the Expatriate Investor's alternatives. The Enterprise Council voted for the second one.

The Expatriate Investor was pleased to learn about the Enterprise Council's decision, but only 36 hours later he asked that the first alternative be accepted instead. He reasoned that "it seems much simpler [and] the final outcome is the same" since he, eventually, wanted to own 100% in any case. Another Enterprise Council meeting was called at unlawfully short notice. This modified the previous resolution. One of the interviewees for this case history believed the Enterprise Council members "could not differentiate between the alternatives".

High level government officials also committed themselves to the Expatriate Investor's offer. One official assured the Expatriate Investor that he would "intercede with the responsible ministers in order that the necessary permissions be issued out of turn". As the "quickest and least difficult" way of getting the transaction done, an assistant minister proposed that Pluto be drawn under ministerial control, turned into a limited liability company with the state as the sole owner, and sold to the Expatriate Investor. This procedure, he argued, would give the foreigner assurance, and at the same time would be public and would provide protection against an accusation of "squandering" (viz "selling the family silver for nuts"). Another proposal argued that only privatisation in this way could ensure Pluto's development. At this time the Expatriate Investor sought an option for six months, pointing out that he could not responsibly mobilise finances until his position as a purchaser was secured.

YOUNG TURKS' GAME

What happened next was a variant of the young Turks' game. This is depicted in academic research on organisational power as a zero-sum game fought for all or nothing, ranging deeply into the organisation. It is usually initiated by a small but critical group from within the organisation which needs to seek influential external supporters (MINTZBERG 1983). In Pluto's case, the coup was initiated by a few middle managers and eventually resulted in the blocking of this "ethically challenged" (MAHONEY 1994, p. 13) acquisition attempt. "It was a period of big fights, internal strife, ... external supports [lobbying]", remembered the Leader of the soon-to-be-established Independent Union, a middle manager himself. "The management did not give much attention to the firm, because everybody was engaged in these internal problems. This was a very baleful, stormy period."

The General Director stated that "my personality is the guarantee that I have always represented and will represent the interest of Pluto's working collective". Not everyone was impressed by this assurance. A small group of "rebels" protested against the planned deal, challenging the legitimacy of the incumbent top management. Their seemingly quixotic fight subsequently developed into a microlevel movement of social resistance. They argued in a letter to a Member of Parliament (MP) that assets had been undervalued, the Expatriate Investor's financial background was questionable, the sale would solve the problem of "some missing stock", etc. The "young Turks" started a fight against what they saw as fraud and dark prospects for Pluto. They believed that a fulfillment of all the promises made by the prospective acquirer, coupled with his need to tap Pluto's cash flow in order to repay debts, would suck out resources and lead to an eventual collapse.

They were accumulating support from within and below, and from "outside influencers". Tactics used to enlist external support included further letters that were sent to another MP, to the county chief police commissioner, the county public prosecutor, the Ministry, the State Audit Office and, when established, the State Property Agency (SPA, created in March 1990 to oversee privatisation and represent the state as owner, replacing the ministries in this role). Five members of the Enterprise Council entered an action in court, requesting that the Enterprise Council's resolution be judged null and void since "management deliberately misled the Council". A press campaign began. One day the General Director called the commencing resistance a "manifestation of resentment, increasing desire for power, weakness of mind and character"; on the next day a heated public demonstration was held. The young Turks were out and vocal.

But to no avail. The firm was drawn under ministerial control, losing its self-governing status. The authorities' earlier commitment was cemented in a letter from the Ministry, promising that a closed call for bids would be announced, and the Expatriate Investor would be granted a right of first refusal. He was also assured that the SPA, once it came into operation, would regard the outcome of the negotiations with the Ministry as binding.

These developments might have daunted Pluto's rebels. On the contrary. They redirected their efforts towards the newly formed SPA. However, the SPA first had to establish its own authority against other state agents. The Ministry argued that the Expatriate Investor's offer was the best possible, and favoured a closed (invitational) tender. The SPA suggested an open call for bids, "according to the rules, contrary to prior government-level (or seemingly government-level) commitments", and stated: "It is the SPA's right to make a decision", while itself seeking support from an MP.

Only a couple of weeks before the 1990 general election, an open call for bids was advertised, albeit in a somewhat low-key brief announcement, letting it be known that "purchase of the firm in 100% will be favoured". The deadline for submitting offers was in two weeks.

Only two bids were submitted: the Licenser and the Expatriate Investor confirmed their earlier offers. The Ministry proposed that the Expatriate Investor be given an option, strongly arguing in favour of the Expatriate Investor's offer and referring to earlier commitments. The price difference between the two offers, as presented by the Ministry official, reflected a direct comparison of differently structured deals. In fact, in relative terms the Licenser's offer valued Pluto significantly higher than that of the Expatriate Investor, and the Licenser was prepared to pay a better relative price even for a minority stake. Yet, the presentation of the offers as set out in the Ministry official's argument suggested quite the opposite. In other words a case for the Licenser's offer could have been made just as strongly if the Ministry had so wished. In any case, an official was soon able to inform the Expatriate Investor in a hand-written letter that he "managed to contact [highest government level] and I assure you your option is firm and will be honoured".

The Expatriate Investor was given an option for six months. He promptly became involved in decision-making at Pluto. For example, he mediated a purchase of imported used equipment. This deal was presented to the SPA by the General Director as exceptionally favourable. Middle managers later attacked the purchase as a waste of money on junk. At about this time the county police terminated an investigation into allegations of missing stock. To keep the story simple, we pass over the investigations by police and tax authorities (there were a couple of these during the year, without any "serious" outcome).

The young Turks, growing in number and fortified by increasing employee support, kept pressing. In a letter to an MP they attacked the General Director, the Expatriate Investor and, now that the option had been given, the SPA as well. They claimed that the Expatriate Investor conducted "most of his negotiations in week-ends, or after working hours, at the General Director's apartment or his [wine] cellar". Critics pointed out the remarkable speed with which state bureaucracy had made commitments in late December and early January 1989–1990: "it seems the point in all this was only that the transaction could be managed still by the old Government".

Although some letters presented him as having ample resources, the Expatriate Investor was in fact engaged in a vain search for money and bank guarantees. It was at this point that the Independent Union was founded by 85 members, although only some 40 turned up to the founding meeting. "Forty-five did not dare to come", said its Leader. "On the next day we were up to 200"; membership kept increasing and was soon to exceed that of the old union which appeared to support the General Director. Following the election, new leaders were appointed at the Ministry and the SPA. Triggered by objections raised by representatives of the largest party in the new Hungarian coalition who had been contacted by middle managers, Ministry officials became concerned about the deal. In concert with the SPA, however, they decided to wait since "it would not be advisable, in the interest of good foreign reflection of the Hungarian economic conduct", to withdraw the Expatriate Investor's option.

As a preparation for the sale, Pluto was transformed into a limited liability company with the SPA as its sole owner. Timing was of essence here. Pluto's operating profits were at a peak when the transformation (corporatisation) occurred. Pluto had to pay tax on its peak-level profits as of the day of transformation. Later it turned out that the outstanding results of the period were considerably lower when properly offset by tax arrears and irrecoverable debts.

One of the core young Turks was appointed to the Supervisory Board on the proposal of the General Director himself. This move was later described by the person concerned as an attempt to satisfy the quarrelsome, which itself was to be only part of an "if you cannot beat them, try to enlist them" tactic. This proved to be a mistake in the game, since it meant that the challenged was himself responsible for allowing the challengers to get close to information: they got the data to make a reasoned case. Other efforts by the General Director to placate the opposition, again mistaken, included "incentive trips" and promises of promotion. Some of the General Director's close associates became uncertain whether it was worth remaining loyal; after all, it was their positions that the General Director was promising to his opponents.

As the option period was about to expire, the Expatriate Investor and the SPA signed a sale contract on option-terms. Payment was due in 25 days, and the deadline was extended twice. But the Expatriate Investor failed to come up with the funds. This provided the young Turks with ammunition for a final attack. They pointed out that what they had said was now proved true: the emperor had no clothes. They had also by now enlisted to their side the vice-mayor of the town where Pluto was located and one of the General Director's deputies. The time had come to increase pressure on the SPA. "The control over [this] privatisation has fallen out of your hands", wrote the Independent Union Leader, threatening to call a strike. Some parts of this letter became public knowledge via the press, an additional pressure on the SPA.

The SPA abandoned the sale contract because the Expatriate Investor missed the very last deadline. He continued to ask for more time in a personal letter to a high level state bureaucrat, expressing his appreciation of "your abilities and the grasp you have of complicated situations and the high standard at which you operate to protect the interests you represent". Similarly, he hoped that "you have a reasonable estimation of my standards and what I have to offer". But by this stage all this elicited was an even firmer rejection.

For the young Turks, the problem was no longer the Expatriate Investor but the General Director. The Leader of the Independent Union demanded his replacement in a letter carrying signatures of hundreds who were prepared to strike. Pluto's contract with a business partner was said to serve the self-interest of the General Director, who sat on the partner's board.

The General Director set about defending himself. But his eroded legitimacy meant he had no chance to mobilise backers as influential as those of the young Turks. Instead, he orchestrated an inflow of supportive letters from customers, and attempted to cover an unfavourable purchase of used equipment with an expert's technical report. It was all too late. The SPA suspended him from his position. Allegedly, he was then moving documents in cardboard boxes out of the firm. Middle managers described him in a report to the SPA as "old fashioned, building on his network, keeping everybody around him in a state of being intimated, following only his self-interest". As even the traditional union's leader acknowledged, "The trust in the General Director has crumbled". The General Director went on sick leave and after his recovery was allowed to take early retirement.

Having won a job tender against an outsider, the leader of the young Turks was soon appointed Managing Director. In a restructuring programme, management ranks were completely reorganised within a few weeks. A new position of General Deputy was created for the closest associate of the new Managing Director.

Meanwhile the Expatriate Investor was fighting an endgame, claiming that the SPA was acting under pressure from Pluto's "troublemakers". He sought justice for himself from both domestic and foreign high-level politicians – which triggered some correspondence between ministries and embassies. Referring to "a most reliable source" in an appealing letter, he accused middle managers of colluding with the Licenser to block the deal with him, and claimed that they had intervened at the Hungarian bank involved to try to stop it from providing a guarantee. Articles in a press campaign took up positions on both sides. Some pictured a palace revolution led by "ambitious self-appointed executive-candidates". The Expatriate Investor was portrayed as a victim who was "cornered with impossible deadlines" and had to "fully drink the poison cup which had been mixed for him by 'bartenders' heated by adverse political and personal ambitions". Others presented the opposite story: "the General Director used every opportunity to make Mr. Expatriate Investor popular for the employees. It is said that the [Enterprise Council's] members had been worked on well in advance". The Expatriate Investor also published his version in a paid full-page advertisement. At this time he was described as "a swindler with a gift of the gab but with no money" in a letter which prompted inter-office correspondence within government but whose sender and his address turned out to be non-existent.

These actions had no effect on what was to come. The SPA Board of Directors reviewed the case once more and kept up its rejection. The firm had already gone a long way down the privatisation path. But it was still only half the journey.

TIME IS PASSING

After all the scandals came slow progress and meticulous adherence to rules. In April 1991 the SPA selected an advisor and a valuation report was ready by September. The advisor's Sales Recommendations were prepared and approved by the SPA in late November. The condition that "special attention must be paid that the Licenser-relationship does not have a negative influence on sales opportunities" was presciently included in the privatisation strategy for Pluto.

A dozen major firms were interested in the acquisition, including foreign owners of other Hungarian firms directly competing with Pluto. The firm's bitter experience was that the owner of one of its competitors used due diligence, granted for all who bought the information memorandum from the SPA, only to get confidential business information without ever wanting to submit an acquisition offer.

The year 1991 ended with Pluto's transformation into a joint stock company limited by shares – an attempt to ease the sale procedure. We now enter the fourth year of Pluto's privatisation process.

PLUTO SLOWLY GOES PRIVATE

Of the 17 companies invited only one submitted a bid – so much for the competitive bidding that the SPA was hoping for. This was a Consortium led by the Licenser. The SPA rejected it because it offered insufficient cash proceeds and because the Consortium demanded cancellation of debt and tax arrears. Nevertheless, talks began. The SPA emphasised Pluto's strategic prospects; the Consortium pointed at its current financial and market difficulties.

Pluto's management and employees (M&E) themselves put in a bid. The buy-out vehicle was structured so that Pluto's directors and board members controlled an interest of about 30%, the rest being widely spread. Around this time attitudes on privatisation shifted in the direction of Hungarian and employee ownership, which may have signalled to management how to present their bid. The M&E buy-out proposal emphasised the importance of "the emergence of a group of Hungarian owners [which] could also be welcomed politically". The idea of a pure management buy-out without employee participation had been dropped: "The press would have jumped on us immediately, saying that the previous managers wanted to squander [the company], and now the new ones want to steal it for themselves".

The SPA and the Bank were supportive to the M&E buy-out idea. The Bank's help was essential since M&E could line up only limited funds. The proposal included a statement of intent to draw in external capital after the privatisation which the management was confident they could do better than the SPA. According to the SPA's advisor, the Licenser was playing for a liquidation sale while deterring other potential bidders. The Consortium's revised offer was still conditional – on a debt-equity swap – which the Bank was reluctant to accept. The tender was announced unsuccessful, and the parties entered into negotiations freed from binding tender rules.

Although the SPA advisor proposed a different financial structure for the deal and favoured equity raising to be managed by the SPA instead of being attempted by M&E after privatisation, the SPA decided to sell 80% of the shares to M&E. Payment was made mostly from a loan from the Bank. It was only a formality to sell the remaining shares for so-called compensation notes a few months later. M&E assumed all debts of Pluto and there were no conditions, making the deal look better than a sale to the Consortium. However, the form in which the privatisation was structured brought no new resources but created the need of M&E to tap Pluto's sources so as to repay its debts to the Bank, and secured none of the tax concessions available to firms with at least 30% foreign ownership (like all but one of Pluto's competitors).

Pluto was at last 100% privately owned. The privatisation process might at this stage have been considered complete. However, the new story which begins here about a private firm's efforts to solve the problems of a critical financial situation, and still to retain majority ownership by M&E, was largely dependent on the nature of the privatisation process which had gone before.

THE SEARCH FOR AN INVESTOR

Optimism was prevalent in interviews conducted at about this time. This proved to be a false dawn. Pluto's management was seeking investors but opportunities were missed or, rather, mismanaged. A promising offer was obtained from a major foreign company. Partly because management attempted to avoid becoming subordinated to that company's other Hungarian acquisition, and partly because they have been going for the big win, another offer was also obtained. It was hoped that the two potential investors would engage in competitive bidding.

Market demand continued declining in 1993; competitors backed by foreign investors made the market a tough place to live in. Commercial depots that had been separated as independent limited liability companies were abusing Pluto's resources. There was tension in management ranks between those in top positions who were in charge of negotiations with potential investors, and those who remained middle managers and represented some several hundred employees as co-owners. As Pluto's financial and market position worsened further, one of the potential investors lowered its offer and raised conditions to the point that management terminated negotiations. Meanwhile, the Licenser took away its brand from Pluto and switched to one of Pluto's competitors while denying that it did so because of Pluto's talks with investors. The other potential investor soon announced that it had lost interest in the acquisition, denying that it did so because Pluto had lost the licence. Acquiring Pluto in Hungary was only a minor scuffle in the backyard of the battle that foreign companies were fighting against each other.

For a while, management dropped the whole idea of getting a foreign investor on board. They hoped that later they might be in a better position to negotiate, or even have an opportunity to not merely "stay upright" but to "stand on our own feet". They succeeded in finding a replacement for the Licenser, but on worse terms. The Bank was getting impatient and started tightening control over the firm. The Managing Director was reported to be "not worried". Yet, news about possible layoffs leaked out as the Bank demanded that the management take "every necessary step without delay and with appropriate firmness", pointing to the example of some competitors. Privatisation of the last two firms still in state owner-ship was also to be completed soon. Both were sold to foreign investors, and thus obtained funds to repay debts, qualified for tax benefits and immediately started restructuring. All of Pluto's competitors were able to take advantage not only of additional resources but also of owners com-ing from outside the firm's dominant coalition and having the power to break any existing coalition if necessary in order to improve efficiency. But how could Pluto's management impose redundancy on a couple of hundred people, proud owners themselves, when they had reached the top with the support of the very same people? Decisions made on the basis of mutual favours and interpersonal commitments do not necessari-ly reflect economic rationality.

FORCED SELL-OUT

The Bank submitted an ultimatum to management: unless certain targets (increased sales volume, and successful capital raising) were achieved, it would take over the shares at an "acceptable price". It became more and more urgent to attract foreign capital into the firm so that it would be enti-tled to tax concessions. There was no investor in sight. Instead, manage-ment was taught a lesson by a potential acquirer who, having conducted due diligence examinations of the target, elaborated on managerial mis-takes and inadequacies in a long letter which ended with its withdrawal from any possible acquisition.

Management intended to use Pluto's resources to repay the M&E's debt due to the Bank. The Bank would not tolerate further delay in stem-ming the losses and objected to the tapping of Pluto's resources. So Pluto was taken over by a domestic investment group, brought in by the Bank. If the takeover had been rejected, the Bank would have simply discontin-ued loans to Pluto. At a speed which suggests thorough preparations beforehand, the new owners sold slightly more than 30% of the shares to an offshore company in only two weeks, thus qualifying the company for tax benefits.

Management knew they had no choice. Some argument within their ranks arose: the top management was accused of mismanaging the search for investors, and neglecting the business itself. As a member of the young Turks (still a middle manager) commented: "We made a big fuss three years ago but the team has entirely fallen apart by now. There should have been teamwork in the running of Pluto, but unfortunately there was no sign of it."

RESTRUCTURED, THEN SOLD AGAIN

In the first half of 1994 the new owners drastically restructured Pluto. The former top management was retained in second-level positions; some others were fired. They introduced tight financial control, sold some of the assets, completely renewed the managerial information system, and re-established Pluto's control over distribution. The Bank converted some debt to equity and extended the deadline for debt repayments. The owners, enjoying substantial support from the Bank, managed to re-negotiate arrears with the Tax Authority. By May 1994 an Information Memorandum for investors had been prepared, and in the summer Pluto was once again sold. The buyer was a large foreign firm that had already made a large acquisition in Hungary but never formally bid for Pluto. Its two Hungarian acquisitions combined to create the largest player in the industry. A major capital expenditure programme was launched, while the workforce was substantially reduced.

CONCLUSION

Throughout the privatisation process politicking was rife. The *tactics of organisational politicking* and some of the variants that appear to have been used by players are summarised below:

- *Building a coalition.*
- *Manipulating information:* withholding, concealing, and excluding others from access to information, and providing false information, setting the agenda, swaying opinion, hinting.

- *Manipulating time:* delaying a process, or pushing through an issue towards a favoured outcome; cementing biases by putting the unfolding events on a path that seriously limits the range of subsequent choices; setting deadlines with a hidden agenda.
- *Going public:* press campaigns, public demonstrations, court litigation, protesting letters.

The research programme of which the case of Pluto forms a part has led to the formulation of three generalised privatisation scenarios: the less extreme *"going through"* and *"muddling through"* scenarios, and the *"struggling through"* scenario of which Pluto is an example (ANTAL-MOKOS 1997, forthcoming).

In the "struggling through" scenario, firms have to survive several years of interregnum. They are in a constant state of flux emanating from long-drawn-out strife between clashing interests that remain undisciplined in the absence of effective corporate governance, self-control and forbearance. The bargaining power of the contenders may be raised by taking advantage of the high politicisation of the privatisation process. Politicking drag on and on. Efforts are diverted from managing the business and consumed in the political arena, leaving performance to be determined by the momentum of habitual routines. Strategy making is vague, producing strategy of a drifting kind. The firms gets entangled in a downward spiral where unrestrained power contests and lack of resources exacerbate drifting. This leads to further deterioration in the firm's position; which may intensify the strife over the slices of the shrinking cake.

Helpful comments from Saul Estrin, David Chambers and Jonathan Levie on an earlier draft of this paper, as well as financial support from the World Bank Graduate Scholarship Program and the Know-How Fund are gratefully acknowledged. This work could not have been completed without support from many people at various business organisations and institutions that need to remain anonymous. Their invaluable co-operation in highly appreciated. The usual disclaimers apply.

REFERENCES

ANTAL-MOKOS, Z.: *Privatisation, Politics and Economic Performance*, Cambridge University Press; based on *Privatisation and Firm Behaviour in National Transformation: the Case of Hungary,* unpublished PhD thesis, London Business School, October 1995 (1997, forthcoming).

ESTRIN, S. (ed.): *Privatization in Central and Eastern Europe*, London and New York: Longman (1994).

KORNAI, J.: *The Socialist System: The Political Economy of Communism*, Oxford: Clarendon Press (1992).

MAHONEY, J.: What Makes a Business Company Ethical? *Business Strategy Review*, Vol. 5, No. 4, pp. 1–15 (1984).

MINTZBERG, H.: *Power in and around Organizations*, Englewood Cliffs, NJ: Prentice-Hall (1983).

7

THE ECONOMICS OF TRANSITION AND THE TRANSITION OF ECONOMICS*

By

PÉTER GEDEON

1. Comparative economic systems (CES) was a discipline that focused on the economic structure of the socialist economies within a comparative framework. Socialist economies were contrasted to, and measured on, the variations of Western market economies. Due to the nature of its subject this approach was sensitive to the importance of institutions, to the qualitative aspects of economic analysis. However, the institutional approach developed by CES, just because it was more enforced on the discipline by its subject than deduced from its theoretical premises, represented a different version of institutionalism in respect to new institutional economics. The institutional approach in CES was less analytic and more descriptive, less deductive and more inductive, processing empirical data and describing historical events in an empirical narrative.

The socialist system could not be and was not a source for categories neither of neoclassical economics, nor of new institutionalism, since the socialist system was a structure that was not based on private property and market coordination. As a result it seemed to lie outside of the conceptual framework that was worked out by the other two economic sciences. CES was separated or isolated from the economic discourse carried on in analytic terms.

On the other hand CES remained distinct from political economy analyzing the interrelationship of economy and polity in modern economic systems in historical-institutional terms. The distance of CES from comparative political economy was partly due to the separation of subjects, partly due to differences in method of research. CES was not an analytic

* In *Economic Systems*, 1997, Vol. 21, No. 1, pp. 72–77.

version of economics, but it was interested in quantitative analysis and applied the concepts of neoclassical economics on the socialist economy when it was possible. All in all, CES could be seen as a mix of qualitative and historical description of the institutions and organizations and a quantitative analysis of micro- and macroeconomic phenomena in the economy, but mainly in the socialist economy. The family of sciences within which CES can be placed is shown in the *Table*.

The science group embedding CES

	Institutional	Non-institutional
Analytic-deductive Empirical-historical	New institutional economic Political economy+	Neoclassical economic Application of neoclassical theory on the socialist economy

+ The historical-institutional versions of political economy.

CES can be placed in between political economy and the direct application of neoclassical theory.

2. The collapse of the socialist system has eliminated the traditional subject of CES, and the postsocialist transformation has created a new one. However, the study of the new subject invites new and competing approaches. The process that may lead to the reintegration of the former socialist systems into the mainstream of Western capitalist development may be coupled with the parallel process of reintegration of CES into the mainstream of economic and social science. The transition from socialism to capitalism brings about a deep and radical institutional change both on macro and micro level. It has created a unique opportunity for neoclassical economics to apply its insights on market economy developed in the ivory tower of theory onto a real process of making markers, and for new institutionalism to develop and verify an *analytical* theory of contemporary *historical* change. In other words, there are competing theories and paradigms that look at the postsocialist transition as their legitimate subject. It is going to lead to the blurring of boundaries among the different subeconomics, and may generate new interactions among them. Interdisciplinarity in a narrower sense, within the family of economics, is in the air.

3. The postsocialist transition is about modernizing the socialist econo-mies, about a new effort to cope with economic and social backwardness of the former socialist countries. The erection of the institutions of private ownership and market coordination is understood as the main task of the transition. This situation creates incentives to nurture constructivist plans for the introduction of Western models in Eastern Europe. What is seen as a necessary institutional framework for successful modernization is exact-ly the institutional setting having been emerged in the historical process of the formation of modern capitalism. Postsocialist states should and do work on implementing these institutions. This transformational process generates a new series of research questions.

3.1. Although the end of the transition is historically open, it is theoret-ically closed. The end station of transition need not be constructed: the present of modern capitalist countries shows the future termination point of the transition. Constructivism only comes into play about the uncertain roads leading to at theoretically certain future. The task of importing Western institutions is coming out of the fact that these countries, due to historical circumstances, have deviated from the mainstream of Western development. As a result, the preconditions having led to the emergence of modern market economy in the West are missing or different in the East. This situation gives rise to constructivist techniques for building up new institutions in the postsocialist transition. The outcome of institution-al change should be the same, but the path leading to it must be different from that of Western development. Institutional change in general and constructivist experiments in particular put the problem of evolution on the agenda. Is institutional change a result of rational human action or an unintended outcome of the actions of more or less ignorant individuals? Can the new institutions be implemented as a result of a comprehensive social plan or will they emerge out of an evolutionary process? The study of postsocialist transition underlines the importance of a broadly con-ceived evolutionary approach. The interest in the evolutionary approach reinforces the interdisciplinarity of research on the postsocialist transition. This approach is able to rely on different sources and traditions of social sciences. Evolutionary theory is by now firmly rooted in institutional eco-nomics in conservative philosophy, in macrosociology, in organizational theory, etc. [1].

3.2. The theoretically closed end of the transition becomes open if in-stead of thinking about the postsocialist transition in general terms of private property and market coordination we ask the question: what type of capitalism, what type of property and market economy is going to emerge in this process? This question opens up research about the institutional diversity of the transition and sets the agenda for a comparative analysis. The integration of the research on the postsocialist transition into the research on modern capitalism is taking place parallel with the process of the integration of postsocialist countries into modern capitalism. As a consequence the former boundaries of CES are going to disappear. No specific discipline may declare the postsocialist transition as its exclusive domain of investigation. On the contrary, the study of this specific subject reinforces the blurring of boundaries between social sciences and gives place to partly competing, partly supplementary research projects of interdisciplinary nature.

This way the traditional economic approach is being challenged and broadened at the same time by other social sciences.

4. The postsocialist transition as an extrication from socialism [2] assigns a significant role to the state in this process. The understanding of the role of polity in the transition of economy is crucial for the analysis economic phenomena. The different branches of political economy formulate important questions and answers on this subject. There are at least three different political economies:

(1) the historical-institutional version of political economy coming out of political science;
(2) the historical-institutional version of political economy coming out of economics;
(3) the analytic-institutional version of political economy called public choice (it may also be classified as a branch of new institutional economics) [3].

4.1. The historical-institutional version of political economy distinguished among the market-led, state-led and negotiated subtypes of modern mixed economies after the Second World War. The different characteristics of these models were understood along the dimension of state versus civil society and were traced back (1) to the degree of centralization of the state and functional interest groups of business and labor; (2) to the existence or the absence of clear boundaries between state and society. The emergence of these models was explained by the historical conditions of industrialization (early versus late industrialization) and by the formation of different social coalitions [4]. The transformation of these models was shown as a result of the internationalization of the economy and the process of long-term technical change. The postsocialist transition can be evaluated from the perspective of the existing Western models of market economy [5]. Are the different postsocialist states heading toward any of the developed Western models or not? What are the social coalitions that may select the new institutions for the postsocialist economy? What is the role of interest groups in the transition? Are governments autonomous players in the economic game or are they captured by particular interest groups? How does the effect of simultaneity, the simultaneous necessity of forming and sustaining political democracy, market economy and a welfare state influence the transition [6]?

4.2. The political economy reemerging from economics can be exemplified by the works of KORNAI [7]. In the analysis of the socialist system KORNAI applied the categories of neoclassical economics, like that of budget constraint, to the socialist economy, in order to explain the phenomena of shortage that determined the economic logic of the socialist system. The concept of soft budget constraint was linked to economic and political institutions like bureaucratic coordination, state ownership, one-party system, etc. This way a broader institutional context could be introduced into the description of the socialist system: an originally non-institutional category of neoclassical economics was given institutional content. Analytical economic analysis became integrated into a historical institutional-theoretical framework explaining the interrelationship of polity and economy within the socialist system. This research strategy can also be fruitful for the research of postsocialist transition in showing the effects of politics on economic policy and reforms [8].

4.3. The third version of political economy, also called public choice, is coming out of new institutional economics relying on the rational choice approach. Public choice applies the tools of economics on the political sphere and follows an analytic-deductive research method based on methodological individualism. Public choice is not sensitive to the historically rooted qualitative differences across different cases, but may be powerful in analyzing the generic characteristics of the political system as opposed to the economic system, and can be applied for comparative exercise. The public choice literature analyzes among others how political parties and politicians try to maximize their votes, how bureaucrats within bureaucracies seek to maximize their utilities, how collective action emerges from the individual decisions of the members of interest groups, how institutions may come into existence as a result of constitutional decisions made behind the veil of uncertainty. This research perspective is able to generate a series of research questions for the study of postsocialist transition. Just to name a few: why do governments pursue radical or gradual reform strategies? What is the role of interest groups in setting up the institutions of market economy? How do party systems emerge and change in the postsocialist countries? Why are new social rules in some of the postsocialist countries enforced not by the state but by the mafia? How do governmental bureacracies try to maintain their decision making power [9]?

5. The different versions of political economy took seriously the dichotomy of state and society, state and market, polity and economy [10]. However, within sociology a new way of thinking has been spreading since the mid-eighties. Sociologists say that there is a third social form of coordination that is beyond the state versus market dichotomy. Economic activities are embedded in social networks of individuals. These networks enter and inform individual calculations and their economic outcomes [11]. Economic activities and economic institutions cannot be understood without taking into consideration their social aspect. These insights can be utilized in the analysis of postsocialist transition. Investigating the privatization process in Hungary, DAVID STARK has put forward the argument that privatization cannot understood in terms of the private versus public dichotomy. Privatization of state-owned assets neither leads to the elimination of state-ownership, nor to the creation of real or pure private ownership. What is coming out of the process is the recombinant property based on the network of private, semi-private and public cross-ownership of different organizations and individuals [12]. Recombinant property is based on the parallel existence of bureaucratic social form of coordination among the economic actors. STARK thinks that the existence of this mix is the specific feature of the postsocialist transformation. His argument links the emergence of recombinant property to the concept of path dependent institutional change, i.e. to the concept of social evolution. New structures cannot be introduced by constructivist reforms, they emerge as the recombination of the elements of existing structures. The collapse of the socialist system destroys the structures of the politicized economy and sets free its elements for recombination. Recombination does take place, because the

destruction of the former coordination mechanism does not create a new market coordination. The analysis of the postsocialist transition seems to prove for the sociologist the importance of social forms of coordination beside other forms.

6. This list of research questions, interdisciplinary effects and links incited by the postsocialist transition is far from being exhaustive. The study of the collapse of the socialist system and the consequent economic and political transformation reinforces the insights and confirms the importance of the evolutionary approach within economics in particular and social sciences in general. It gives new incentives for interdisciplinary research blurring the boundaries among the different social sciences. In the process of studying the postsocialist transition social sciences learn a great deal not only about their subject, but about themselves, too.

NOTES

[1] See for instance HANNAN and FREEMAN (1986), HAYEK (1948), Luhmann (1992), MURELL (1992), NELSON and WINTER (1982), OAKESHOTT (1962), and PARSONS (1967).
[2] See STARK (1992).
[3] For the distinction between (1) and (3) see PONTUSSON (1995).
[4] See for instance KATZENSTEIN (1985), ZYSMAN (1983), and SCHMITTER and LEHMBRUCH (1979). The results of this research were reflected in Hungary by BRUSZT (1987) and GEDEON (1992).
[5] An early attempt toward this direction can be found in COMISSO (1991).
[6] This problem was analyzed by OFFE (1991).
[7] See first of all KORNAI (1992).
[8] See KORNAI (1995) who provides a political economy explanation for "gradualism" in Hungary.
[9] Some of these question are addressed by MUELLER (1991), MURRELL and OLSON (1991), PEJOVICH (1995b), and PRZEWORSKI (1991).
[10] Although there appeared also within political economy a new approach that focused instead of macro level analysis on the meso and micro level. See for instance KITSCHELT (1991), SCHMITTER and STREECK (1985).
[11] See first of all GRANOVETTER (1985).
[12] See STARK (1996).

II

BUSINESS PROCESSES AND FUNCTIONS: PRODUCTION, LOGISTIC, MARKETING

INTRODUCTION TO PART TWO

In this part, among the business functions production and marketing are subjected to deeper analysis. Both are rather broad concepts, so that stockpiling can also be included alongside them, and logistics ties in with the communications market on the one hand, and the business information market on the other. The shared feature of the articles dealing with the different areas is that they are based on empirical surveys. On the basis of the opinions reflected in the questionnaire surveys, it is possible to formulate the strategic courses followed by companies in the fields of production or marketing. Analysis of Hungarian data is supplemented by international comparisons, so that developments in Hungary can be judged in a wider context.

Although this period of the past is not very long, there is still a need for longitudinal analyses, which enable changes in company behaviour to be traced. The selected articles give the reader an opportunity directly or indirectly to compare changes through time.

Not one of these articles was written before the change in the régime. In Chapter 8 CHIKÁN examines the production and stock management systems in the Hungarian processing industry. Companies carried out their planning in a manner determined by the operating characteristics of the socialist or "shortage" economy (KORNAI J.: *The Economics of Shortage.* North-Holland, Amsterdam, 1980). Signs of adaptation to the market were nevertheless discernible even then, since late delivery (caused by production or planning problems) to the developed market countries was less typical than to the COMECON countries.

In Chapter 9 CHIKÁN and DEMETER provide a longitudinal analysis, rare even in the international specialized literature, based on empirical data collected in 1986, 1990 and 1994. Examining the constituents of manufacturing strategy, they show that after the change in the system, improvement of the quality of products and of production came to occupy the top place in the list of strategic aims. Though much still remained to be done in the application of modern production methods (JIT, MRP), managers made considerable progress in recognizing what was needed.

Because of the growth of the service sector, it is particularly interesting to read about the survey described by CHIKÁN and DEMETER (Chapter 10), focussing on the so-called service factory. The problem is found to have its roots in marketing, because they investigate what kind of services production can offer to internal and external customers. The results are similar to those of the British survey, which concluded that the dispatcher-service activity of fulfilling orders is the most important.

The peculiarities of the operation of a market economy can best be observed through marketing activity practice. Satisfying the ultimate consumer is the paramount motivator in society. This must motivate companies as well, and determine the activity of the marketing function. Chapters 11 and 12 present the Hungarian data from an empirical survey of several East Central European countries carried out in 1992 and 1996. This uniquely extensive survey based on the example of representative national companies provided an opportunity to make a comprehensive evaluation of the marketing situation and to describe the marketing strategies employed. In 1992 HOOLEY–BERÁCS–KOLOS revealed five distinguishable types of marketing strategy. Two-thirds of companies followed a defensive-type strategy.

The influence of foreign capital investment and privatization is also reflected in the HOOLEY–BERÁCS article, in which on the basis of the 1996 survey the authors describe the marketing strategies of top-performing companies. Their main conclusion is that the strategies of leading companies are the same as those to be found in advanced market economies and expected in the 21st century.

The changes that have taken place in mass communication equipment have affected advertising costs, which represent the greatest proportion of marketing costs. It is no accident, therefore, that the big media empires have sought to establish suitable positions in the developing markets. On the basis of his analysis of both the electronic and the printed press up to 1996 (Broadcasting and Magazine Publishing), GÁLIK comes to the conclusion that the day of the ideal, democratic media has not yet arrived. He regards a continued inflow of foreign capital as desirable in the interest of breaking state monopolies.

The boom observable in the information market should be accompanied by an upswing in business. HUSZÁR and NAGY compare the results of a questionnaire survey carried out in 1992–1993 with the general information market situation up to 1995. Making a thorough analysis of the participants in the demand and supply markets, they call attention to a number of trends. One of these, for example, is that while on the demand side large-scale restructuring has taken place, on the supply side state-type institutions seem still to be dominant. Locally-developed databases have appeared on the market, but they need to be perfected. The infrastructure and professional expertise of libraries make them suitable to become suppliers of business information.

8

CHARACTERIZATION OF PRODUCTION-INVENTORY SYSTEMS IN THE HUNGARIAN INDUSTRY*

By

ATTILA CHIKÁN

The paper reports the main characteristics of the production-inventory systems of Hungarian industrial companies. After a brief discussion of the general economic background some results of a survey are provided. We used a questionnaire developed from an international project aimed to carry out cross-national comparison. The results discussed here will be part of this project.

The main conclusion is that the general character and relatively low level of development of the production-inventory systems in Hungary are direct consequences of the specific environmental challenges companies in our country must face. The level of production-inventory management can be – and should be – raised considerably but attempts aimed to improve the situation can be successful only if the environmental conditions are appropriately taken into consideration. More advanced systems with a chance of successful implementation must utilize many conceptual and methodological elements of the internationally known integrated systems efficiently operated in the Western world but efforts to simply copying them would definitely lead to failure.

1. INTRODUCTION

Attending conferences where production management problems are discussed one can see that the involvement of companies in implementing up-to-date concepts of integrated manufacturing is so wide-spread that one gets the impression: no companies can gain nowadays sustainable competitive advantage without applying some variances of JIT or MRP systems. This is obviously not true – however, it would be hard to deny that a well-operated integrated production-inventory system can be a decisive factor of success under a variety of conditions.

* In *Engineering Costs and Production Economics*, 1990, Vol. 18, pp. 285–292.

The Hungarian economy is not a particularly successful one, and among the major short-comings which are usually quoted as characteristic to our economy there are two which are in close connection with the application of integrated production-inventory systems:

- the general methodological level of management is considerably lower than that of the Western countries;
- inventory investments are high; but even the high inventories cannot defend companies from the effects of shortages of necessary inputs.

From these two facts one could conclude that a major task is to improve inventory management. This is of course true but for being able to suggest ways of improvement we had to learn more about the causes of the present situation. A project was started about a year ago, the final goal of which is to develop principles for production-inventory systems and methodology which can be efficiently used at Hungarian industrial companies.

First we made an overview of the general situation, partly on theoretical grounds and partly using the results of various previous surveys of different kinds. During this work we learned about the international project initiated by Professor CLAY WHYBARK of Indiana University. This project aims to explain cross-national differences in production-inventory control practice. We decided to take part in this project and used this survey as a means to get deeper knowledge of the reasons of our present situation. At this stage we can report on the main findings of the evaluation of the questionnaire in Hungary. We still do not have the results of other countries – the cross-national analysis will certainly enrich our understanding of the Hungarian situation as well.

2. GENERAL ECONOMIC SITUATION INFLUENCING PRODUCTION-INVENTORY MANAGEMENT

When starting the survey we already knew that the results would show a rather dark picture – not because we are too critical, but because we know both the actual operation of the average Hungarian company and the theoretical explanation of their behavior. There are several well established reasons why companies in a shortage economy do not – and reasonably cannot – go in trying to implement advanced management technologies, including such systems like MRP and JIT.

What are these reasons? Why can't the majority of our companies apply these successful ideas?

It is a fact discussed many times (mainly based on the theory of JÁNOS KORNAI [1]) that companies in shortage economies are in a special "paternalistic" relationship with the state (or better to say, with the organizations representing it). The main form of appearance of this paternalistic relationship is the redistribution of the companies' income: a very large proportion of this income is first centralized and than redistributed according to principles which cannot be derived from profitability requirements. The rules of this redistribution are to a great extent "tailor-made", i.e. the fate of a particular company depends on its general judgement by governmental institutions, based on a complex set of quantitative and qualitative, formally and informally used measures, which can just by chance coincide with profitability requirements.

The main reason behind low methodological level of management is therefore that managers are much more involved in external "political" activity (to ensure good judgement and in this way central preferences) than in internal development of company operations, which latter can produce results only at the margin, while good relations to central government can result in incomparably higher rewards.

The second track of thinking is about high inventories. A shortage economy is characterized by a seller's market, where easy to sell but hard to buy. It is again a fact discussed many times that such a market which is characterized by a general overdemand leads to relatively much higher inventory levels (in particular, much higher input inventories) than the buyer's market which is characterized by an oversupply [2]. It is quite obvious that changing this situation is beyond the control of any company – the real question is how can they accomodate themselves to this given environment.

Finishing this extremely short and necessarily superficial overview of the Hungarian situation, I just want to refer to the well-known thesis of organization theory, namely that open organizations (like companies) form their internal activity according to the requirements of their environment. From this it comes that even though we are not happy at all with the concepts and methods used in production-inventory systems in Hungary, it must be admitted that the present situation is adequate with the actual everyday interest of the majority of our companies. This fact must be taken into consideration if we want to effectively improve their operation.

3. THE SURVEY

A questionnaire consisting of 96 questions in the following structure was used in the survey:

   I. Company profile.
  II. Sales forecasting.
 III. Production planning and scheduling.
 IV. Shop floor control.
  V. Purchasing and materials management.
 VI. Inventory control.

The structure and the vast majority of the questions simply reflects the questionnaire used by CLAY WHYBARK and his colleagues in several other countries. We wanted to have a comparable questionnaire; but a few questions must have been changed because of the specific situation at the Hungarian companies. Also we have included some direct questions about inventory control, to fulfill the special interest of the author of this paper.

Seventy-eight companies have filled out the questionnaire. This is not a very high number but the structure of the sample reflects quite well the industrial structure in Hungary. The results were not sensitive neither on branches of industry nor on size of the companies.

It has to be added, that since we wanted to get a picture which reflects the situation of the average Hungarian companies, we have deliberately left out those outstanding companies, which for one reason or another enjoy a special situation and usually are more advanced in their general operation, including production-inventory management. This way we got a less favourable but more characteristic result.

4. RESULTS OF THE SURVEY

The results of the survey did not cause any surprise but contributed to deepening our knowledge about the details. An extended study is under preparation – here we report about some of the most characteristic results.

The results are presented in two parts: first, policy questions, and then methodological issues.

4.1 PRODUCTION-INVENTORY POLICY

Results of the survey show that production planning to a great extent depends on resource availability. Since companies mainly produce on order, sales forecast does not play a very important role. (As for the companies of our sample, production on order represents more than 80% of total production in case of 85.9% of the companies, so this policy can be considered as overwhelmingly dominant.) Sales forecasts are prepared usually for a one-year period and are updated quarterly. (Quarters play a very important role in production planning. Based on traditions, this can be considered as a time period of fundamental importance in company operations.) Forecasts are usually made on the basis of actual knowledge of sales orders or on their judgement based on long-term relations with consumers.

The evaluation of the question on the factors influencing production plans are presented in *Table 1*.

Table 1. Relative weight of factors influencing production plans

Factor	Weight/% of companies						Average weight
	0	1	2	3	4	5	
Actual orders/backlog	1.2	0.0	3.8	3.8	16.7	74.4	4.64
Production capacity	1.3	0.0	1.3	7.7	28.2	61.5	4.52
The forecast	3.8	1.3	9.0	24.4	41.0	20.5	3.73
Level of inventories	2.6	3.8	15.4	34.6	28.2	15.4	3.37
Costumers' plans	1.3	7.7	19.2	30.8	28.2	12.8	3.19
Previous sales	1.3	6.4	23.1	39.7	23.1	6.4	3.0
Other	93.6	0.0	0.0	0.0	2.6	2.6	4.5

Note:
Factors could have been weighted 1–5, 0 means no answer.

As a direct consequence of the fact that our companies operate in a shortage economy production in the vast majority of cases goes on to order and not to stock.

Companies' behavior is much different depending on which market they want to sell on. In case of domestic and COMECON market they usually promise long delivery time, while in case of selling to market economies these lead times are much shorter (see *Table 2*). This situation is of course not the consequence of something like a subjective preference of

Table 2. Delivery time promised in different
market orientations

Market	Delivery lead time in days		
	−60	60–180	180–
Internal	29.8	54.3	15.8
Market economies	40.8	44.9	14.3
COMECON countries	20.0	44.4	35.6

Table 3. Determinants of delivery lead times

Lead time is mainly determined mostly by	% of companies		
	Internal consumers	COMECON countries	Market economies
Consumer	37.2	41.0	73.1
The company	23.1	10.3	0.0
Negotiation	37.2	30.7	14.1
Other way/no answer	2.5	18.0	12.8
	100.0	100.0	100.0

Table 4. Priorities in production scheduling

Aspects	Percentage of companies indicating the various aspects as important
Consumer order due dates	91.0
Processing time required	35.9
Similarity of set-ups	3.8
Material availability	61.5
Marketing preferences	16.7
First-come first-served	9.0
Selling price of item	6.4
Management directive	17.9

the companies, but the different requirements of the markets. This is illustrated by *Table 3*, answering the question "How the delivery lead times are determined?".

Another result illustrating the importance of sales direction is the analysis of factors influencing priorities in production scheduling, which is shown in *Table 4*.

Combining the information provided by *Table 4* with that of *Table 2*, one can conclude that since priorities in production mainly depend on due dates and in the same time sales to market economies are subject to a much tighter schedule, these priorities have a very basic influence on the actual operation of the production system. This conclusion is in correspondence with our everyday experience.

Further consequences of the situation discussed above for the production system:

(i) companies offer long delivery times for consumers to have time to ensure the availability of resources;

(ii) since there is a great difference between the various market relations, those companies which sell for more than one type of markets (and this is the majority of the Hungarian companies) make themselves flexible by rescheduling their production when necessary to ensure the timeliness of delivery to the more important relation. As an illustration for this see the survey results regarding the timeliness of delivery (*Table 5*).

Table 5. Percentage of orders late

Market type	Percentage of orders late		
	−10	10−20	20−
Internal	30.8	39.7	29.4
Market economies	78.2	16.7	5.1
COMECON countries	62.8	23.1	14.1

However, this production scheduling policy leads to two major consequences, against an efficient operation:

(i) Since companies want to protect themselves against frequent rescheduling as much as possible they build up high input stocks. (Which on the other hand, prevents them from holding appropriate output stocks and so from short capital which can be invested in stocks is also limited.)

(ii) Since rescheduling depends mainly on material availability, which is a random factor, companies must have a rather flexible internal operation which can always adjust production to the resources. The answers to the questions which asked about priorities in production scheduling are shown in *Table 6*.

Table 6. Factors influencing delivery times
promised to consumers

Delivery time depends on	Market type		
	Market economies	COMECON countries	Internal
Product complexity	38.5	32.1	35.9
Production load	44.9	38.5	56.4
Importance of costumer	50.0	39.7	56.4
Material availability	56.4	50.0	66.7
Other	1.3	2.6	3.9

The general tendency is that the dominant factor is the availability of input materials – in case of the internal and COMECON oriented production on the second place one can find capacity availability, while in case of export production to Western countries the second place is for the importance of consumer so if companies have orders from this direction, they try to find the way of fulfilling it.

The flexibility of the above type supposes that companies react rather fast. For that there are two necessary conditions:

(i) availability of slacks of production resources;
(ii) organizational flexibility.

As for the question of slacks, attention has to be given to the fact that they are in close connection with shortages. Slacks of production resources on the one hand serve as buffers against shortages, to protect production against the disturbances, while on the other hand slacks can be consequences of shortages: the shortage in one kind of resource for example can cause unusability of another resource, this way causing non-intended slacks.

Theoretical studies as well as an other survey which was carried out a few years ago show that slacks play a very important role in the production system of Hungarian companies. ZELKO [3] in his often cited book even states that having appropriate slacks belongs to the four basic policy goals of Hungarian companies [besides (i) high level of wages of employees, (ii) growth and expansion, (iii) favourable image]. The high rate of investment in input inventories supports this statement.

As for the use of slacks, or the short-term adaptation to the situation our survey shows that it mainly goes on by using overtime: if short term shortages occur in input materials or parts, companies wait until the necessary input arrives and then they try to catch up by working overtime.

As for the required organizational flexibility, the above mentioned situation leads to two important consequences:

(i) the operation of an informal decision system, built organically into the system [4];
(ii) the integration of the sales – production-inventory – purchasing processes in the vast majority of cases goes on under the leadership of a production manager, who is usually at a high level in the hierarchy (in most cases at the position of a first deputy of the CEO).

The integration is actually dominated by the production, the interest of which is a smooth operation, which can be ensured by high input stocks. An interesting result of the survey shows that those companies which have a top-level manager in charge of all or most of the production and logistics operations tend to have considerably higher inventories than the group of companies which do not have such a leadership. The reason is, that the interest of smoothing production by stocks can be followed more efficiently when this interest is represented consequently by some top manager. Another interesting fact is, that inventory plans are better met at these companies, which result supports the existence of the above mentioned effect.

4.2 OPERATION-METHODOLOGY

The discussion of methodology is started with admitting that the generally known up-to-date concepts of operation of the production-inventory systems have not penetrated the Hungarian industry (see *Table 7*). Knowledge of some companies which more or less successfully apply forms of MRP was available, however, these companies have not been in the sample. We do not know about any company which would have tried JIT. General conditions presented in the introduction fully explain this situation.

Let's consider three aspects of the methodology according to which companies' operation of their production-inventory systems can be judged.

Table 7. Exposures of companies to up-to-date
production concepts

Exposures to MRP/JIT	MRP (%)	JIT (%)
Never heard of it	39.7	56.4
Using it and benefiting from it	10.3	0.0
Using it but not benefiting from it	2.6	19.2
Understanding it, but feeling no necessity of introducing it	20.5	0.0
Just starting to introduce it	2.6	1.3
Trying to introduce it, but having difficulty doing so	3.8	11.5
Considering its introduction	17.9	0.0
No answers	2.6	6.4

(i) Systematic character of operation

Under this heading the problem of how systematic is the control of operation (as opposed to an always changing, irregular, ad-hoc management) is dealt with.

For the time dimension of operation, companies' activity shows a rather regular annual, and within that quarterly cycle. Almost all activities are time-phased first on an annual basis and than figures or plans are broken down to the quarters of the year (59% of the companies in the sample make forecast and 66.7% plan production on that basis – and 47.4% do so both activities).

This uniform behavior has both advantages and disadvantages: it is simple and the processes can be coordinated well, while on the other hand it is not very adaptive. This can be illustrated by the fact, that companies adjust their forecast with a rather random character, and this is only partly connected to changes in the production plan.

Table 8 shows that a large proportion of the companies modifies the production plan independently of the sales forecast – which means that

Table 8. Frequency of changes in forecasts and plans

How often is modified (annually)	1	2	3	4	4–
Sales forecast	10.3	26.9	15.4	24.4	10.5
Production plan	3.8	9.0	16.7	47.4	12.8

they have some other reason for correction (this can be explained in connection with their preferences discussed in the previous chapter).

Purchasing is connected to the processes discussed through the ordering rule. Answers from the questionnaire indicate that this connection is very close: the vast majority of the companies (79.5%) says that their input material order is based on their production plan, 25.6% says that the basis for ordering is the sales forecast. (There is an overlap among the answers, so they do not sum up to 100%.) However, only a small proportion of the companies use formalized ordering mechanism: reorder time-order level (t, S) system is used at 16.6% of the companies, while reorder point-order quantity system (s, q) is introduced at 5.1%.

(ii) The use of computers

Computerization in Hungary is rather backward in comparison with the industrialized countries – there is a time-lag of a decade in hardware. Knowing that, the result was not surprising: only 23.1% of the companies in the sample uses computers in forecasting and only 10.3% of the companies say that they cannot carry out production planning without a computer because it is so strongly nested in their system. (Though it is remarkable that an additional 33.4% says that the computer plays a role: the system is operated partly on computer; by 69.2% it would lead to considerable results in their efficiency in production planning.)

A question which has been added to the original questionnaire is oriented to the general computerization of companies. Companies had to give a weight to the computerization of 13 activities: "1" means that computer is not used at all, "5" means that the activity is fully computerized. The following averages were obtained:

Inventory recording	3.1	Production planning	2.2
Material accounting	2.8	Capacity planning	2.0
Sales order recording	2.5	Purchase order recording	1.9
Wage recording	2.5	Quality control	1.6
Material usage planning	2.4	Production design	1.6
Job-shop order recording	2.3	Sales forecast	1.4
Production scheduling	2.2		

(iii) The application of "hard" methodology

The field we are examining is one of the favourite ones of the O.R. people; though, there are permanently complaints about the lack of practical implementation. We cannot tell any good news to researchers about the Hungarian situation.

In sales forecast the results obtained from the questionnaire are illustrated in *Table 9*. The result is quite acceptable (in comparison with the other areas) – the cause may be that appropriate models can be found in practically all computer software packages.

Table 9. Methods used for sales forecast

Method	% of companies
Simple time series	31.6
Causal models	9.0
Complex time series models	5.0
Other/no answer	54.4

Table 10. Methods used to determine inventory standards

Method	Type of inventory		
	Materials + purchased parts	WIP	Finished goods
Technical calculations	29.7	16.2	5.4
Subjective judgement	25.0	6.3	12.5
Statistical evaluation	29.0	3.2	3.2
Mathematical models	9.1	9.1	5.9

The results are much less favourable when we take a look on the techniques used to determine inventory standards *(Table 10)*. This shows that the majority of companies build up their inventories according to rules determined on a technical (engineering) and not an economic basis. This is in connection with the fact that the whole area is dominated by managers who consider technical relations much more happily willing to hold rather high inventories.

An interesting results has turned out when we carried out a series of cluster analyses (which at the time of writing this paper is still not fully evaluated yet). There is a rather strong correlation between the hierarchical level where decisions are made in the production-inventory – purchasing system and the methodology used in the decision process: the higher the level of the decision the less advanced methodology is used.

5. CONCLUSION

Results of the survey are not favourable neither if one thinks in terms of the theoretical possibilities nor if we consider the actual efficiency of the average Hungarian companies. However, the survey supports the concept outlined in the introduction: the behavior of companies reflect the conditions and requirements of the environment. Vast majority of the characteristics given above can be well explained with causes stemming from the situation of companies in the Hungarian economy described very briefly in the introduction.

A more complete evaluation can be given when the results of the survey carried out in other countries are available.

What to do next? The question comes absolutely naturally since the above described situation do not promise any good to the average Hungarian firms in their international competitiveness.

The first and far most important way of approvement is to change the environment. That is the question of economic and political reforms, which are on the agenda in Hungary – to discuss these goes far beyond the scope of this paper.

The second and more direct task is to construct such systems of operation which conform adequately with the very special Hungarian circumstances. It is impossible to simply adapt even the most efficient concepts and methods worked out under the different circumstances of the leading countries of the world though we can and have to take into consideration many elements of them. We have just started a project to promote the research on this field – the survey reported about above belonged to the first steps of this project.

REFERENCES

[1] KORNAI, J.: The Economics of Shortage. North-Holland, Amsterdam (1980).
[2] CHIKÁN, A.: Market disequilibrium and the volume of stocks. In: A. CHIKÁN (ed.): The Economics and Management of Inventories, Part A. Inventories in the national economy. Akadémiai Kiadó, Amsterdam/Budapest, pp. 73–85 (1981).

[3] ZELKÓ, L.: Vállalatelmélet és politikai gazdaságtan. The Theory of the Firm and the Political Economy (in Hungarian). Közgazdasági és Jogi Könyvkiadó, Budapest (1979).

[4] BARANCSI, É.: Formal and informal systems of inventory management in Hungary: A case study. In: A. CHIKÁN (ed.): Inventory in Theory and Practice. Elsevier/Akadémiai Kiadó, Amsterdam/Budapest, pp. 303–313 (1986).

9

MANUFACTURING STRATEGIES IN HUNGARIAN INDUSTRY:

THE EFFECTS OF TRANSITION FROM PLANNED TO MARKET ECONOMY*

By

ATTILA CHIKÁN, KRISZTINA DEMETER

INTRODUCTION

There have been fundamental economic and social changes in all Eastern and Central European countries in the last half decade. These changes have obviously had a great effect on manufacturing strategy. In this article we briefly summarize the essence of these changes and their consequences in the Hungarian manufacturing industry.

The article is organized as follows: first we describe those main features of the transition which affect manufacturing most; second, the framework of SKINNER [1] is used to assess the changes experienced in Hungary in the three main fields of manufacturing strategies. To illustrate the changes we shall use data from a recent survey conducted as part of a global research project. Finally, some conclusions will be drawn.

MAIN COMPONENTS OF ECONOMIC DEVELOPMENT IN HUNGARY

It is obviously not the task of this article to analyse the general process of economic transition – we concentrate on those issues which are most closely connected with manufacturing. For a recent analysis of the Hungarian transition see KORNAI [2] and for a more extended description of the economic tendencies discussed here see CHIKÁN [3].

* In *International Journal of Operations & Production Management*, 1995, Vol. 15, No. 11, pp. 5–19.

GENERAL ECONOMIC TENDENCIES

There are four main tendencies which should be mentioned here as most important factors influencing manufacturing strategies:

(1) *The general decline of production:* in all the transition economies the general level of economic activity has fallen sharply as a consequence of the elimination of non-economical activities; the collapse of the Council for Mutual Economic Assistance (COMECON), the economic integration of the "socialist" countries; the enduring world recession including the declining demand in the domestic markets.

(2) *Changing microstructure:* the structure of the microsphere of the economy is undergoing fundamental changes in three very important dimensions: by ownership: about half of the total state property has been privatized and many new private firms have been established; by size structure: large, monopolistic, state-owned companies have broken up or shut down several plants and a number of small enterprises were started; by sector: trade and service companies have increased their part in production of GDP, manufacturing has fallen behind and the proportions of its subsectors have changed.

(3) *Change of market relations:* in the traditional shortage economy there was a permanent overdemand, as a result of which sellers have been in a superior position to buyers. However, in consequence of increased supply (mainly because of liberalization of imports) and decreased demand (because of the fall of production and buying power of households) this relationship has changed – now we have a buyers' market.

(4) *Uncertain environment:* the above mentioned economic effects, the fundamental political changes and the changing relations with our neighbouring countries together created a rather uncertain environment for company management.

It is easy to see that these changes together created a completely different environment for manufacturing companies compared to the one to which they were accustomed.

MANUFACTURING IN DEVELOPED MARKET ECONOMIES
AND HUNGARY

In order to help the reader to understand the weight and importance of changes going on in Hungary let us give a brief summary of the differences between the structure and operation of the manufacturing industry in Hungary and in the developed market economies on the eve of the transition. These differences are exactly those which must be gradually decreased and finally eliminated during the transition. (It should be added that the other Central and Eastern European countries face basically similar tasks, though there are rather important differences also as far as the depth of the gap and the speed of building a bridge is concerned.)

Some of the differences are of structural character. In planned economies, "large is beautiful" was the accepted slogan, due to the logic of central planning, and even though Hungary had already departed from central planning about 30 years ago, its industrial structure still suffered at the end of the 1980s from oversized mammoths. The structure of the industry was like a reversed pyramid, so the number and role of the small and medium-sized companies had to be increased. This started to happen immediately at the turn of the 1990s.

Another structural difference was sectoral. The overweight of the sectors producing investment goods and industrial supplies as opposed to customer goods is also diminishing in the ongoing processes.

There were (and still are) a number of behavioural differences. Companies in the developed world had to face the need of permanent changes, while the long term COMECON contracts and the slowly changing internal demand made Hungarian firms too comfortable. There was certainly a need for adaptability – but this meant mainly adjusting to the scare resources (mainly material and labour shortages), so companies were more input than output oriented. Under these circumstances quantity was more important than quality and there was no pressing need for innovation. That was true not only for technology but also for management systems: MRP, JIT and other new approaches could hardly penetrate Hungarian industry.

Obviously, there were important differences among companies even within the Hungarian industry. It was especially important that – being part of an always very open economy – many Hungarian companies maintained close ties with Western partners. These ties helped a great deal in getting a quick start when circumstances made it possible.

Despite the early departure from the traditional planned economy and the aforementioned contacts with the developed world, the Hungarian manufacturing industry had and still has to meet great challenges in the transition process. Some of these challenges and the achievements up to now are summarized in the following sections.

COMPONENTS OF MANUFACTURING STRATEGY

In our analysis we shall use the framework provided by SKINNER [1]. According to that, we examine the following components of manufacturing strategies:

- *Selection of plant location and manufacturing hardware:* this element generally leads to an investment problem and thus it is very closely connected to financial strategy.
- *Determining critical focuses of managerial control (quantity, quality, cost, productivity, etc.):* this aspect is very important from the point of view of establishing the objectives which should be followed and the main measures of performance are also derived from here.
- *Selection of control systems and organization:* this determines the means by which management wants to achieve its goals, and also reflects the forecasted response of the organization.

In the following sections we shall analyse how manufacturing strategies, reflected in actual behaviour, have changed during the transition process in Hungary.

THE GLOBAL MANUFACTURING RESEARCH GROUP SURVEY AND THE STRUCTURE OF THE SAMPLE

To illustrate the changes in manufacturing strategy we use the results of a series of surveys conducted in the framework of a global research project. The project started in 1986 and since then basically the same survey has been conducted in over 20 countries (for details of the project and the analysis of the first results see WHYBARK-VASTAG [4]).

The survey was completed in Hungary three times: in 1986, 1991 and 1994. This was a very fortunate timing since we were and are able to monitor the effects of the transition, which has been continuous in Hungary. We used the same questionnaire in all three cases, with slight modifications (which did not prevent comparability of the results).

As for the sample, we had about the same number of companies each time (78, 77 and 75, respectively). We tried to maintain comparability also in respect of the structure of the sample but we have had serious difficulties. As a consequence of the changes mentioned before, in 1994 we simply did not find the companies we visited in 1986 and 1991 (the first two surveys included basically the same set of companies), so we can not draw any conclusions about the developments at the individual firms' level. However, since the sample itself reflected in all three cases the structure of the Hungarian manufacturing industry, valid conclusions can be drawn at the aggregate level. Let us now see the structure of the sample (*Table 1*).

Table 1. Characteristics of the sample

	1986	1990	1994
Number of companies	78	77	75
Average number of employees	2,712	1,732	640
Average annual sales			
(million HUF, current prices)	2,749	2,744	1,555
Percentage of exports	26.0	38.8	39.0
Value of purchased goods			
(million HUF, current prices)	NA	1,526	596
Percentage of imports	29.0	31.7	38.3

As shown in *Table 1*, the average size of companies in the sample became smaller progressively. The difference is even more dramatic if one considers that between 1990 and 1994 annual inflation was well over 20%. The other characteristic change in the sample is that companies became much more open: the proportion of both exports and imports have increased.

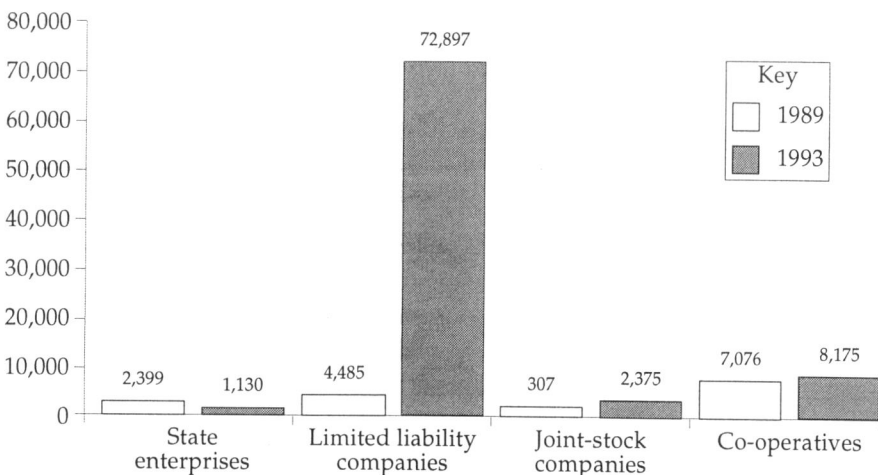

Figure 1. The number of economic organizations with legal entity

The change of size structure reflects the processes in the Hungarian economy: *Figure 1* shows the general structural changes.

As for the sectoral structure of the sample, it contains basically three groups, one third machine industry, one third textile industry and one third other industries. This sample is such because the first two groups are the focus of the Global Manufacturing Research Group project. However, all analyses (see [4]) show that in the vast majority of cases sectoral differences are much less important than many others – this experience is supported by our previous analyses.

CHANGES IN THE MANUFACTURING STRATEGY OF HUNGARIAN COMPANIES

First of all we have to emphasize that there appear to be many different company strategies in our economy. Several groupings of companies can be given based on various factors. We shall concentrate on those general features which can be attributed to the transition process, disregarding some further features which can be very important in other dimensions of analysis (like ownership, relation to the privatization process, main markets, management attitudes, etc.).

In this section we go through the three main areas of manufacturing strategy discussed previously. Let us note here that the following data were drawn, with only minor changes, from CHIKÁN [3]. This section does not contain any survey data, since plant location and manufacturing hardware issues were not part of the survey.

PLANT LOCATION AND MANUFACTURING HARDWARE

We shall first discuss issues related to the location of production, i.e. the plant structure of manufacturing, then turn to the questions of hardware.

Location and plant structure. One of the characteristic features of Hungarian companies before the transition was that many of them had a great number of plants, the actual operations of which were connected only very loosely. These companies were conglomerates of horizontal character, in which the main marketing and development decisions were made at a central location (which physically was usually on the site of the largest plant, in the vast majority of cases in Budapest, the country's capital), while operational decisions were more or less decentralized. This situation has caused attempts to separate the plants, which were very seldom successful before 1990. However, these attempts became not only more frequent but also more often successful in the transition process. Besides the general process of liberalization, there are two specific reasons for this development:

(1) Many or most Hungarian companies were simply too big to be privatized in one, therefore it was quite common for the original mother company to be transformed to a state owned holding plus a number of limited liability companies in which the holding had a majority ownership. This new organization was then privatized piece by piece.
(2) The extent of fall of demand for products of the various plants of the same company was in many cases rather different. This has changed the power structure within the company, making it possible for the more successful plants to survive as independent companies, while the original big company faces serious problems.

From the point of view of manufacturing strategy the above processes led to the following consequences:

• The profile of Hungarian companies is more homogeneous than before. This in most cases leads to a better position for introducing elements of "lean production", a very necessary process after many years of cost-insensitivity and volume-orientation (as opposed to quality-orientation).
• The pyramid of organizations became flatter and decision making became simpler – very positive developments, since the management of the previously existing large organizations was in many cases rather bureaucratic.
• The management of the new smaller companies had to face new challenges. This, on the one hand, was very inspiring, leading to extra efforts and to discovering new resources; on the other hand, however, it required skills which were not readily at hand for the management of the majority of companies.
• With the appearance of many players in the economy, companies had to face new partners at both the input and the output side of their production. These new partners were much smaller than before, more flexible in most cases, and also more demanding. This meant new requirements for most fields of company operations, with special emphasis on production.

- The change of characteristics of partners has led to important changes in the logistics processes. New transportation routes and new needs for materials handling have also had an important impact on the organization of manufacturing processes.

Issues of production hardware. The actual status of production hardware at the time of the start of transition is among the most important differentiating factors among the formerly fully state owned manufacturing companies. Since in recent years there were very few new investments in hardware at these companies, today's (and to a great extent the near future's) opportunities depend on past investments in fixed assets. There are at least three main dimensions of evaluating production hardware which are of basic importance in the strategic opportunities of companies:

(1) The first is modernity. Since investment in fixed assets under the conditions of the planned economy depended mostly on and was financed to a great extent by, state authorities, those companies which were lucky enough to have obtained support for such investments in the last few years of the old regime, now have an imminent advantage compared to those who did not get the necessary support. One further issue related to this is the form of financing for the above mentioned investments. The situation of some of the major manufacturing companies became extremely uncertain after the start of the transition, because they just could not pay their debt services during a recession – while others, whose financing portfolio was more favourable, easily paid their dues, taking advantage of the inflationary conditions. However, from the strategic point of view, the main thing is that some companies have up-to-date production hardware, while some others have not.

(2) The second hardware-related issue is convertibility. The transition requires an extremely large amount of flexibility and adaptability on the companies' side. The collapse of the COMECON market and the internal recession have changed the structure of markets of practically all companies. The more convertible the hardware the higher the chance of survival.

(3) The third issue is integration. Ironically, under the current circumstances integrated production capacities are not always an advantage. Since Hungarian manufacturing companies were usually oversized, as has already been mentioned, those companies had and still have better

chances of being privatized (and through that, obtaining the often badly needed fresh capital) where the various units of the companies were not so closely connected to each other that it would prevent their separation and privatization piece by piece.

FOCUSES OF MANAGERIAL CONTROL

Under the changing conditions described previously, only those companies which have been able to accommodate themselves to the new environmental challenges could survive. This, among other things, required refocusing priorities of managerial control. Under the conditions of the planned economy the main emphasis was on meeting the demand of consumers in terms of quantity, other characterizing factors of the delivery being mostly at the will of the supplier (including lead time and quantity). This behaviour cannot be continued now. Completely new delivery patterns and new production management practices are required.

Our analysis shows that the first steps have already been taken in the majority of companies *(Table 2).*

Table 2. Importance of various strategic goals

	Average weight
Product quality	4.41
Production quality	4.39
Reliable delivery	4.33
Low production cost	4.30
Fast delivery	4.27
Customer service	3.91
Adaptation to individual customer demand	3.88
Fast product innovation	3.84
Fast quantity adaptation	3.32
Wide product line	3.32

Table 2 shows how companies now consider quality issues of first priority and the reliability and speed of deliveries are also taken very seriously. (This question was only asked in 1994, so there is no possibility of comparison with previous periods.) *Table 3* and *Figs 2–3* show that the com-

panies we have interviewed in the two recent surveys not only say that consumer service is important, they actually behave much more effectively in this respect.

Table 3 shows that they promise much shorter delivery times. This table does not contain 1994 data, since in this case we put the question differently: what is the minimum, maximum and usual delivery time you offer to your customers? The average of the answers is 13.8, 28.9 and 63.2 respectively for the internal market and 22.2, 69.9 and 35.9 for export, which is an even better performance than the one reflected in *Table 3*.

Table 3. Usual delivery time promised in various markets
(in percentage of companies in the survey)

Market		Delivery time in days		
		<60	60–80	>80
Internal	1986	29.8	54.3	15.8
	1991	51.3	43.2	5.4
Market economies	1986	40.8	44.9	14.3
	1991	52.7	41.8	5.4
COMECON countries	1986	20.0	44.4	35.6
	1991	32.2	50.8	17.0

Besides the fact that they make a better offer, it is also important to notice that previously there was a large gap between the various markets, which has now been almost eliminated. It is easy to see that this is very healthy for manufacturing.

As can be seen in *Figs 2–3* companies not only promise shorter delivery times than the ones in the previous periods, but their actual performance is far better. (Again, note how the markets have been unified.)

As regards the causes of lateness, *Table 4* illustrates that those reasons which are connected with the shortage of production factors – capacity, production bottleneck, material and labour shortage – have lost a lot of their weight (answers were given on a 1–5 scale), while the only reason increasing in weight, even though slightly, is the due date changes, i.e. a factor originating from the market.

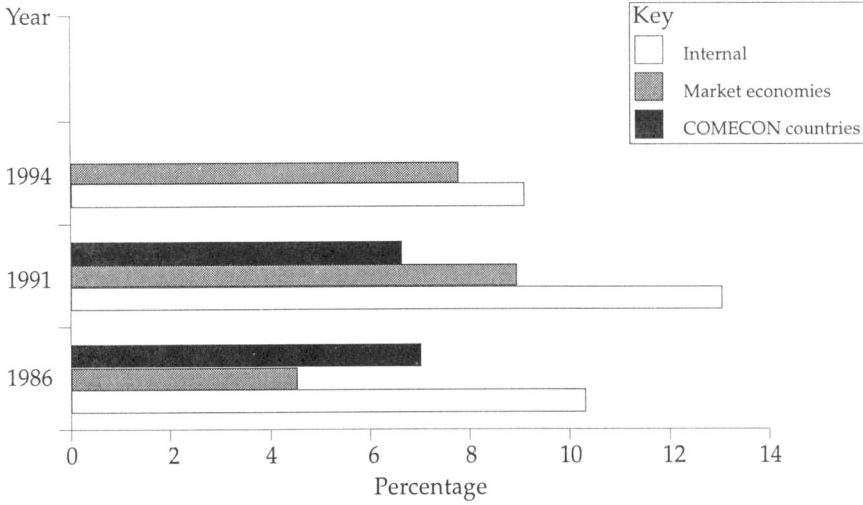

Figure 2. Late deliveries in proportion to total deliveries

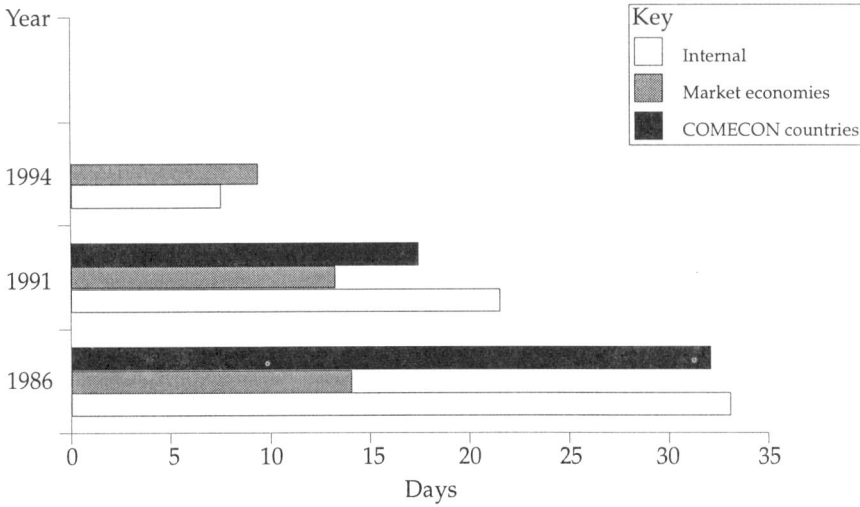

Figure 3. Average days late

Table 4. Causes of late delivery

	1986	1991	1994
Due data changes	2.30	1.97	1.89
Quality problems	2.96	2.36	1.97
Materials shortage	3.13	3.07	2.79
Production bottlenecks	4.37	3.92	3.03
Labour shortage	2.77	2.94	2.65
Insufficient overall capacity	2.51	2.76	2.78

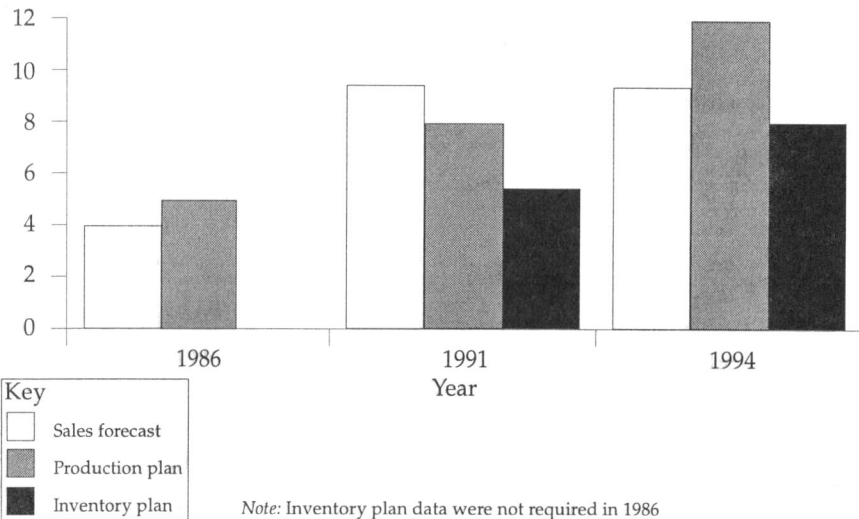

Figure 4. Average number of revisions per year

The better delivery performance is supported by a more flexible operation. This is shown by the data regarding the approach to sales forecasting, production and inventory plans *(Fig. 4)*. The average number of revisions has increased substantially, and this provides a much better basis for adjustment processes.

The survey shows that companies today are much better integrated in the market environment than before. Sub-contracting became a more widely applied policy (the proportion of fabricated parts purchased has increased from 42.8 to 61.8% between 1986 and 1994). Increased cost sensitivity, quality and delivery requirements all encourage companies to move in this direction *(Table 5)*.

Table 5. Reasons for sub-contracting

Reasons	Average weight (1–5)		
	1986	1991	1994
Production load	3.3	2.8	2.9
Production difficulty	3.2	3.1	3.3
Company policy	2.6	2.6	2.1
Lower costs	2.9	2.6	3.5
Higher quality	2.5	3.3	3.3
Faster production	2.5	2.9	3.2

Stronger market-orientation is also reflected in the management of internal processes. As an example, scheduling priorities in the past were determined mainly on the basis of resource availability, while today they are based on market processes *(Table 6)*.

Table 6. Causes of priority changes

Cause	Average weight (1–5)		
	1986	1991	1994
Pressure from marketing	3.4	3.9	3.9
Pressure from consumers	3.3	3.9	4.0
Orders from management	2.9	3.4	2.9
Changes in delivery dates	3.7	3.8	3.8
Sudden surges in demand	2.8	3.6	3.8
Manufacturing problems	3.5	3.5	3.1
Material shortages	4.3	3.8	3.6
Changes in sales plan	2.8	3.4	3.4
Engineering problems	2.7	2.9	2.9
Average	3.27	3.51	3.49

CONTROL SYSTEMS AND ORGANIZATION

Manufacturing management also uses new approaches and methods in execution corresponding to the new strategic goals. A good example of the changing attitude is given in *Table 7*, showing the new approach to the adaptation process. In the "old system" manpower resources were hardly used in this process, while these days they seem to be as important as any other option.

Table 7. Alternative ways to change capacity

	Average weight (1–5)		
	1986	1991	1994
Increases			
Hire additional workers	2.8	2.5	2.6
Use overtime	3.0	3.8	3.8
Subcontract production	2.9	3.0	2.6
Backorder the production	2.7	2.1	2.1
Lease temporary capacity	1.9	2.2	1.6
Decrease			
Lay off extra workers	1.7	2.2	2.3
Idle time	1.6	2.1	2.9
Reduce the work time	1.6	2.5	2.3
Build inventory	2.0	2.4	2.4
Lease capacity to others	2.0	2.5	2.4

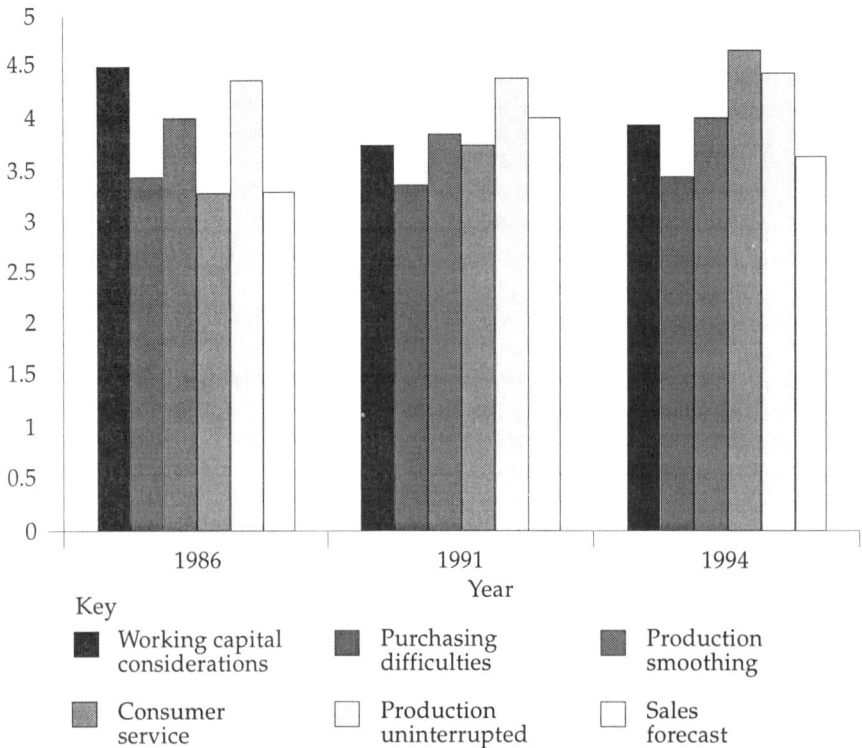

Figure 5. Factors of inventory planning

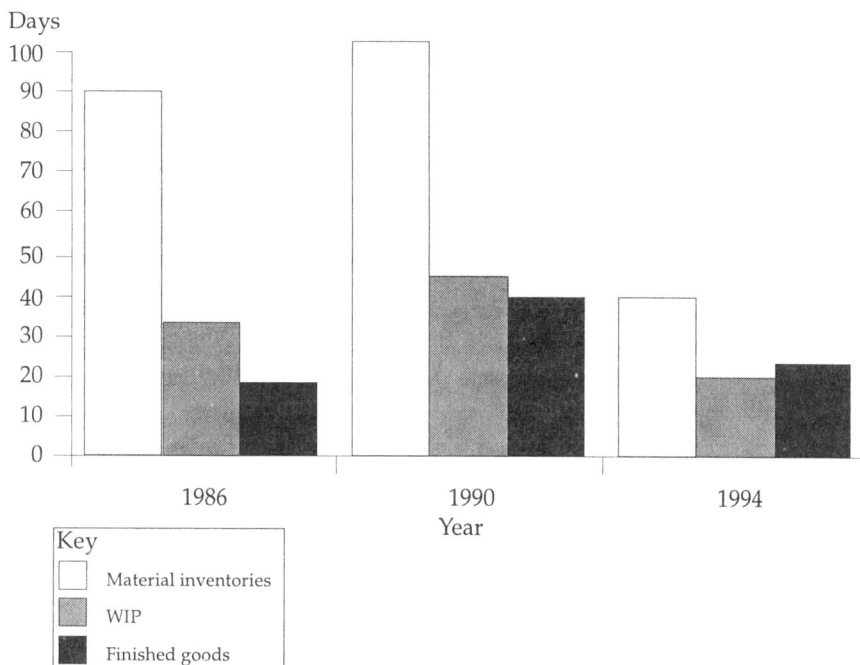

Figure 6. Inventory turnover

One can observe that the average weights given to the means of decreasing production have increased substantially. This shows the adjustment of companies to the fall in production.

The new approach is reflected also in *Fig. 5,* which shows the various factors involved in inventory planning: the importance of customer service is clearly reflected and for 1994 it has surpassed in importance the issue of smooth input supply. These new preferences are also demonstrated by the fundamental change of inventory structure. (See the increase of the proportion of finished goods in total inventories in *Fig. 6.*)

It should also be noted here how much inventory turnover rate has increased, which is certainly a sign of greater process efficiency. The latter is demonstrated also by the fact that the proportion of actual manufacturing time within the delivery lead time has increased form 52 to 61%.

The use of computers dramatically increased between 1986 and 1991, and remained at the same level in 1994. If one considers that the 1994 sample contains much smaller companies with fewer financial resources, this is a good result *(Table 8).*

Table 8. Degree of computerization

Activity	Average weight (1–5)		
	1986	1991	1994
Sales forecast	1.4	1.8	2.1
Production planning	2.2	3.0	2.8
Capacity planning	2.0	2.6	2.5
Material usage planning	2.4	3.1	3.0
Job shop order recording	2.3	2.4	[a]
Production scheduling	2.2	2.4	2.6
Quality control	1.6	1.6	2.4
Production design	1.6	2.1	2.4
Sales order recording	2.5	3.7	[a]
Purchase order recording	1.9	2.9	2.7
Inventory recording	3.1	3.5	3.4
Material accounting	2.8	3.1	[a]
Wage recording	2.5	4.3	[a]
Average	2.0	2.6	2.7

Note: [a] not questioned

Table 9. Exposure to MRP and JIT

Statement	MRP		JIT	
	1986	1991	1986	1991
Never heard of it	39.7	24.1	56.4	17.1
Using it and benefiting from it	10.3	6.3	0.0	5.2
Using it but not benefiting from it	2.6	2.5	0.0	1.3
Understanding it but feeling no necessity to introduce it	20.5	10.0	19.2	5.2
Just starting to introduce it	2.6	3.8	1.3	2.6
Trying to introduce it, but having difficulty doing so	3.8	4.9	0.0	3.9
Considering its introduction	17.9	15.2	0.0	19.7
It can not be introduced under present conditions in Hungary	[a]	26.6	[a]	43.4

Note: [a] not questioned

Table 10. Investments in progress in order
to improve efficiency

	Average weight
Productivity	3.81
Computer hardware and software	3.60
Customer relations	3.47
Cellular production	2.92
TQM	2.88
Recycling	2.85
Throughput time reduction	2.84
MRP	2.70
SPC	2.68
Workforce involvement	2.65
Set-up time reduction	2.65
Set-up time reduction	2.65
Shopfloor automation	2.45
JIT	2.41
Process analysis	2.31

However, systemic changes in methodology and organizations are still somewhat far from the thinking of managers. This is reflected in *Table 9*, which shows that the level of information about MRP and JIT has increased very substantially between 1986 and 1991 (this question has been left out of the 1994 survey), but their use did not spread at all. *Table 10* shows that they are rather low in the hierarchy for frequency of current development projects. This table also shows that ill-defined objectives like productivity and customer relations development lead together with computerization – these three are far ahead of those development areas which can be considered specific means to increase productivity and improve customer relations.

CONCLUSION

This article demonstrates that Hungarian companies have adjusted fairly rapidly to the new circumstances, as far as both the goals and the means are concerned. This rapid adjustment also demonstrates for us the importance of the existence of some "general rules" which guide the behaviour of players in the economy. The global research, some results of which have been used in this article, is to a great extent oriented to the discovery and explanation of these rules. It has to be added that despite the rapid changes, most Hungarian companies still have a long way to go before they reach the level of competitiveness required by the always increasingly demanding world market.

REFERENCES

[1] SKINNER, W.: "Manufacturing – missing link in corporate strategy", *Harvard Business Review,* May–June, pp. 136–145 (1969).

[2] KORNAI, J.: *Lasting Growth as the Top Priority: Macroeconomic Tensions and Government Economic Policy in Hungary,* European Bank for Reconstruction and Development, Working paper No. 15, December (1994).

[3] CHIKÁN, A.: "Consequences of economic transition on manufacturing strategies", *International Journal of Technology Management* (forthcoming).

[4] WHYBARK-VASTAG: *Global Manufacturing Practices,* Elsevier, Amsterdam (1993).

FURTHER READING

CHIKÁN, A., DEMETER, K.: "In the attraction of the market economy: manufacturing strategies in Hungary", in VOSS, C. A.: *Manufacturing Strategy,* CHAPMAN and HALL, London, pp. 211–219 (1992).

CHIKÁN, A., DEMETER, K.: "Manufacturing practices in a transition economy", in WHYBARK-VASTAG: *Global Manufacturing Practices,* Elsevier, Amsterdam, pp. 341–352 (1993).

10

SERVICES PROVIDED BY MANUFACTURING: THE HUNGARIAN CASE*

By

ATTILA CHIKÁN, KRISZTINA DEMETER

The paper is built on an empirical study of the service factory concept in Hungary. The importance of the possible service roles that manufacturing can play, and the general service features that a manufacturing company can posess are examined at Hungarian companies. The results show that service is still not the strongest competitive factor in Hungary, quality and costs get much more emphasis. Comparing the results with those of an English survey, the main tendencies are similar, except that the laboratory role seems to be more important in Hungary, possibly due to the relatively low capacity utilization.

1. INTRODUCTION

As service sector started to grow some decades ago, its specific problems attracted the attention of many researchers. The problems first were handled by classical operations and marketing management tools. Later on, however, specific characteristics of services were discovered and the special field of service management was developed [3, 4].

Nowadays an opposite direction can be found [5, 6, 10]. Operations managers, manufacturers of tangible products, have started to use the management tools of services. This phenomenon is the result of the increasing competition which forces companies to employ new and new competitive weapons. After price, delivery, flexibility, and time competition services represent the newest weapon.

In this paper we examine the level of services in some Hungarian factories. Before the survey our hypothesis was that the concept of the service factory, or even the weapon of service itself have not really affected

* In *International Journal of Production Economics*, 1996, Vols 46–47, pp. 489–496.

Hungarian manufacturing companies yet. In general, the decades of the "shortage economy" did not stimulate the intensive use of any weapons of competition.

The main question of our survey was: What kind of services does production give to its internal and external customers? The idea to look at this question came from [6], where the same problem was analyzed for English companies. (*Table 1* provides the scope meant by "services" in our case.) In this paper the method of the research (which followed that of Voss) will be described first. Then, the Hungarian results will be analyzed and compared to the English survey. Finally, we draw some conclusions.

Table 1. The questions of customer questionnaires
and the service roles of the company

Factory as a laboratory: *Manufacturing's ability to furnish critical data on processes and their costs, for example, through providing fast accurate process feedback to R&D and providing fast product-built feedback to marketing.*

    1. Testing new products.
    2. Debugging new processes.
    3. Making new products available faster.
    4. Customized adaptations of products.

Factory as a dispatcher: *The ability of manufacturing to support customer delivery needs, to support the distribution function, and to support other customer needs after the sale, such as status tracking and feedback and engineering-change order management.*

    5. Packaging minimizes handling difficulty and the likelihood of damage.
    6. Packaging minimizes potential for pilfering.
    7. Keeping to agreed delivery dates.
    8. Keeping to agreed quantities.
    9. Delivering punctually at the agreed delivery time.
    10. Notification of any actual or potential delivery problems.
    11. Changing order mix/volume/time-of-arrival at short notice.
    12. Clear labeling on packaging.

Factory as a consultant: *Manufacturing's ability to assist internal and external groups in problem solving in areas such as quality improvement, cost reduction, new uses for the firm's products.*

    13. Training of sales people.
    14. After sale's help with use (includes installation, maintenance, etc.).
    15. Accuracy of advice.
    16. Objective assessment of competitors' products.
    17. Speed of response with advice.
    18. Advice by telephone.

Table 1 (continued)

Factory as a showroom: *Manufacturing uses its facilities to support sales through showing off its products and processes, people, quality commitment.*

    19. Demonstrating how their operation works.

    20. Identifying who does what in the operation.

    21. Demonstrating all the features of the product.

    22. Promotional material (catalogues, videos, etc.).

    23. Technical detail of promotional material.

    24. Accuracy of promotional material.

    25. Clarity of promotional material.

Other service features *(overall company related):*

    26. Reputation of the company's products you buy.

    27. Image of the company's personnel project.

    28. Prompt telephone response at switchboard.

    29. Prompt telephone routing to appropriate person at the company.

    30. Competence of the company's employees.

    31. Trustworthiness of the company's employees.

    32. Courtesy of the company's employees.

    33. Friendliness of the company's employees.

    34. Availability of the company's employees.

    35. Someone at the company who understands how you use their product.

Source: Ref. [6] and the questionnaire.

2. SURVEY DESCRIPTION

Eight diverse companies were involved in the survey, from small to large size companies, from automated delivery systems producer to consumer goods producers.

The first step of the survey was to make semi-structured interviews. 30 altogether. The interviews were made with production managers (one for each company), and with managers of other functions (marketing, sales, finance, 10 altogether) in order to see the role of internal services, and with 12 customers. (Here we have to note that there were no significant differences in the answers of the managers of different functions.)

Beside the interviews customers also filled in questionnaires. These questionnaires examined the four service roles of manufacturing as defined in [5]. The essence of these service roles and the structure of the questionnaire can be see in *Table 1.* All the factors listed in the table had to be answered from three aspects:

(1) How important is it to the customer?

(2) What is the performance of the company comparing it to the expectations of the customer?

(3) What is the performance of the company comparing it to other suppliers?

Answers were measured on a five-point scale from low (1) to high (5) importance/performance.

After the interviews and the questionnaires a discussion workshop was organized just like in England, where those companies who took part in the survey were represented. The initial question of the workshop was: What kind of service do you expect as a user from your industrial supplier? Firstly, the participants collected and explained the various factors (more than 40 items) they expect as service from their suppliers. Then they had some additional tasks:

(1) to create 3–4 groups of the factors;

(2) to identify the 10 most important factors; and

(3) after counting which factors are the most important on a group level (after summarizing the individual factors 11 were selected) they were asked to rank these factors. Results are described below.

3. RESULTS FROM THE SURVEY

Before presenting the results obtained, we have to mention some general conclusions, which affect the evaluation of the results.

Companies did not really make a difference between services and the tangible characteristics of the product itself. That is, in most cases they used the term "service" in a broader sense. This is e.g. the explanation why they thought price and product quality as the most important features of their service.

Although all the participants interviewed were informed that the role of production is examined, they rarely considered the company and its production as separate entities. (It is especially true for small companies where the different functions are not really separated.) That is why it is very difficult, if possible at all, to draw conclusions on the services provided for internal customers; therefore, only external customers are considered in this analysis. It also means that the possible origins of services provided – the distribution chain, the after sales service operations and the services from factory (see VOSS) – are not really separated in the paper.

The performance of companies involved in the research was evaluated by their partners higher than average. The overall average of the comparison question (the third question) was 3.89, while the score of "3" had the meaning of the average supplier. In principle, this shows that the companies in the sample do not represent the Hungarian average.

Service literature says [3, 7] that satisfaction of customers comes when real service performance is equal or higher than expectations. Having a look at our answers, we can see that importance factors are in all but one case higher than performance. It supports both the everyday experience and our main hypothesis, namely that service is still not a fundamental weapon of competition. In order to show the most important discrepancies, we collected the factors where the difference is higher than half point in *Fig. 1*. The average of factor differences for the service roles are shown in *Fig. 2*.

It seems that neither the suppliers nor the customers do know exactly what they expected from the other. They have impressions and good or bad experiences. That is, when customers filled in the questionnaires they generally could not really make differences between the importance of various factors of services. What made the difference were the bad experiences. In these cases they gave high scores for importance to be able to give sign of their dissatisfaction in performance. This means that it was not the absolute level of importance or performance but the difference what they really mattered. (It also means that in case of factors left our from *Fig. 1* the difference between importance and performance values are minimal.) The difference has shown significance at a 5% level of statistical *t*-test in case of six factors (see the * in *Fig. 1*).

To support the importance of discrepancies, a good example is to focus on the consequences of the generally *poor infrastructure*, which is a well-known cause of dissatisfaction. There are three points in the questionnaire dealing with telephone: advice by telephone: prompt telephone response at switchboard: and prompt telephone routing to the appropriate person at the company. All of them had large difference between importance and performance. Hungary still needs some years until companies can base their connections and their work on telephone and forget the bad experiences.

Our results are very similar to those of the English survey in the aspect that the role of *dispatcher* is considered to play the most important role

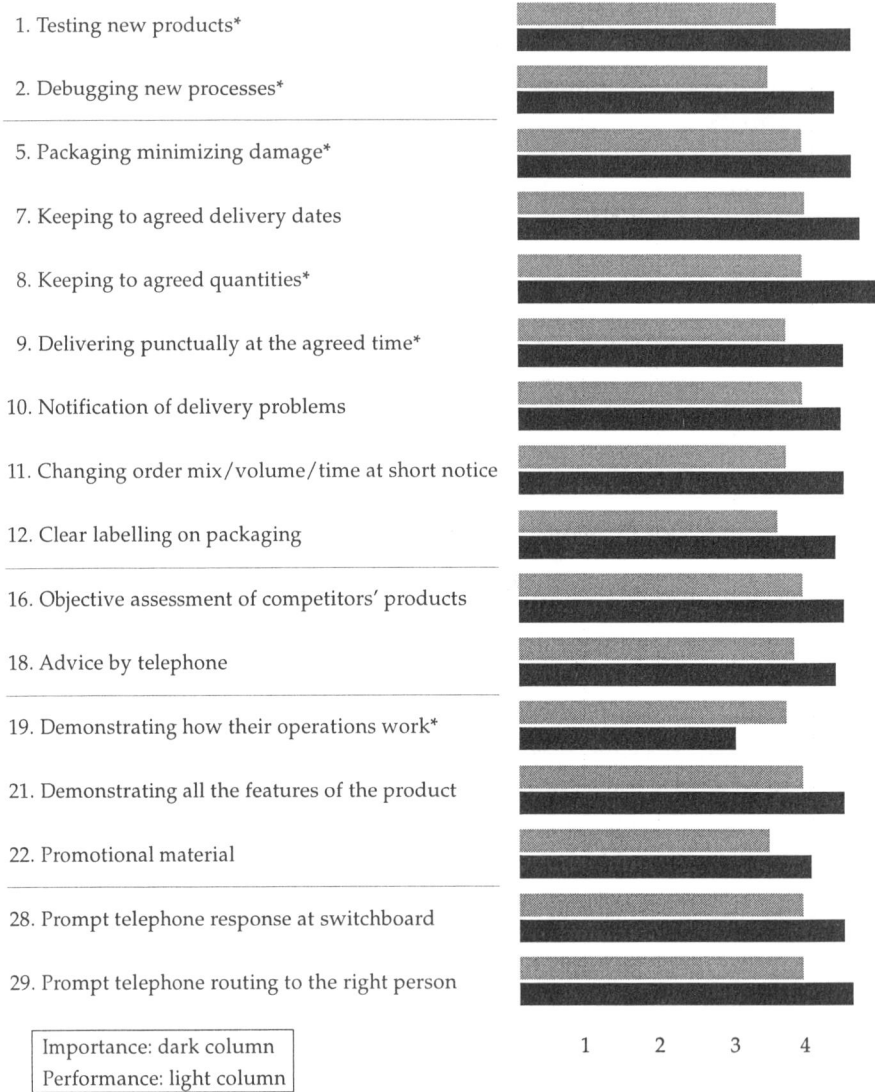

1. Testing new products*

2. Debugging new processes*

5. Packaging minimizing damage*

7. Keeping to agreed delivery dates

8. Keeping to agreed quantities*

9. Delivering punctually at the agreed time*

10. Notification of delivery problems

11. Changing order mix/volume/time at short notice

12. Clear labelling on packaging

16. Objective assessment of competitors' products

18. Advice by telephone

19. Demonstrating how their operations work*

21. Demonstrating all the features of the product

22. Promotional material

28. Prompt telephone response at switchboard

29. Prompt telephone routing to the right person

Importance: dark column
Performance: light column

1   2   3   4

* Significant at 5% level with *t*-test.

Figure 1. The largest discrepancies between importance and performance

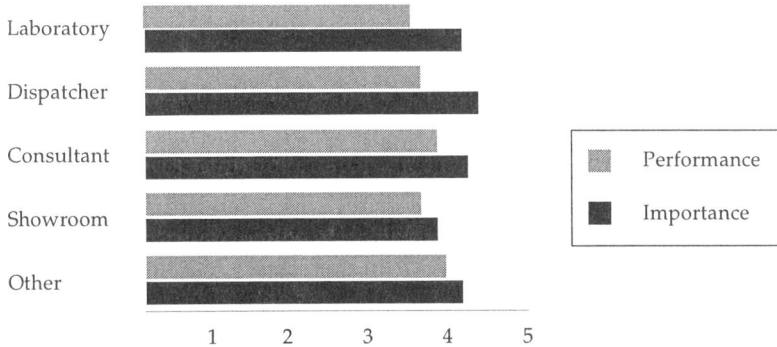

Figure 2. The summarized importance and performance results of service roles

and, in the meantime, it is the least satisfactory. Except pilferage preventive packaging all the factors are at least with half point higher in importance than in performance.

An interesting results is that the role of *laboratory* got a higher importance in our survey than in the English one. Although it is only an assumption, since English results are not shown numerically in the article of Voss, however, the low importance is mentioned there. This result can be the consequence of low capacity utilization in Hungary. In this situation companies try to fulfill every possible order to keep their factories busy. In this case the cooperation of R&D, engineering and production gets a higher emphasis.

In *Fig. 2* we can see that the role of *showroom* is the least expected and one of the best fulfilled. The factor of "demonstrating how their operations work", which is the lonely factor having positive difference, belongs into this group. Customers do not feel the need of this service and if they do they generally get it.

In case of the *consultant* role two things have to be mentioned:

(i) two very important factors belong to this group: training of sales employees and the speed of response with advice. The latter was also mentioned as very important during the workshop.

(ii) Large difference in importance and performance exists in the objective assessment of competitors' products. It can be explained with the rapid changes in competitive situation (which still did not leave enough time to organize this task within companies) and with the lack of well-established strategy at most Hungarian companies (see [8]).

Table 2. Factors with the highest scores

Importance	Performance against expectations	Performance against others
1. Keeping to agreed quantities	1. Trustworthiness of the company's employees	1. Customized adaptations of products
2. Prompt phone routing to the right person	2. Training of sales people	2. Trustworthiness of the company's employees
3. Keeping to agreed delivery dates	2. Availability of the company's employees	3. Someone who understands how you use their products
4. Packaging minimizing damage	4. Competence of the company's employees	4. Competence of the company's employees
5. Competence of the company's employees	5. Speed of response with advice	5. Courtesy of the company's employees
6. Someone who understands how you use their products	5. Clarity of promotional material	5. Friendliness of the company's employees
7. Testing new products	5. Courtesy of the company's employees	5. Availability of the company's employees
8. Delivering punctually at the agreed time	5. Friendliness of the company's employees	8. Reputation of the company's product to buy
8. Training of sales people	5. Someone who understands how you use their products	
8. Speed of response with advice	10. Reputation of the company's product to buy	
8. Demonstrating all the features of the product	11. Keeping to agreed delivery dates	

The group of *others* contains factors which characterize the whole company not only production. Some of these factors seem to be quite important and some of them seem to be quite well performed.

Ranking of the highest scored factors on the basis of their importance, companies performance against expectations and against other suppliers can be found in *Table 2*. The table illustrates that the companies examined outperform other suppliers mainly in the field of customer service (in the narrower sense). Only one factor, customization of products, takes place among the best from another role than the general service characters group.

If we compare the list of the most important factors with the performance against expectations, quite a lot of factors can be found in both of them: keeping agreed delivery date, competence of employees, existence of a person who understands customers' as users, training of sales people. However, the most important factors, like keeping to agreed quantities, prompt phone routing and packaging minimizing handling difficulty and damage do not appear in the list of performance. It can be an important source of dissatisfaction.

4. RESULTS FROM THE WORKSHOP

An important proposal made by companies was to make a difference between materials and equipment suppliers. Expectations towards these two groups of producers can be quite different. While the group of material producers should concentrate on issues like punctual deliveries (sometimes measured in hours), continuous and consistent product quality, etc. equipment producers should focus their efforts, for example, on after sale service, or accurate documentation. These characteristics shows the difficulties to make a uniform valuation of expectations.

We have to consider size differences as well. Small firms are expected to be very flexible in their information flows and products (technical flexibility), with fast deliveries and competitive prices. This expectation is very logical, thus it is not a coincidence that managers of these companies have to concentrate their efforts to manage time and costs. On the other hand, large companies, are expected to provide superior quality, and volume flexibility (both large and small batches). They have to concentrate their efforts to manage their internal information flow, and training of their sales personnel.

The workshop unambiguously showed that there is a rather large difference between the performance of foreign and domestic suppliers because of which those companies who have connections with both parties considered it very important to handle them separately. It can be interesting, how companies grouped the collected (approx. 40) service items, being an important aspect to decide where to put the emphasis of the strategy. (The following four groups were given by the participants.) The participants gave

(a) leadership aspects, technical aspects, customer–supplier relationship;
(b) economic aspects, quantity, quality, technical aspects, human, partnership aspects;
(c) information aspects, quality aspects, company's position, performance aspect;
(d) database aspect, supplied product certification, supplier analysis aspect.

All of these groups are different somewhat but they have some similarities. Information related aspects (the first in each row), product-specific aspects (the second), and human relations aspects (the third) always went together. That is, only the category titles are different, the meaning behind them is very similar (although not identical).

From a managerial point of view, this grouping can offer some help in finding the ways to improve of our services: we need good information management tools to collect and distribute all the necessary information within and outside the company (it is the core); we have to keep tight relationship with our current and potential customers: we have to know our product the need of our customers for these products (quality, quantity, technical, informational, customer service aspects are the most important).

At the end of the workshop, company representatives arrived to the following ranking of the most important factors:

1. Consistent and continuous quality.
2. Reliability of the partner.
3. Dependable delivery.
4. Favourable paving conditions.
5. Confidential relationship.
6. Fast response to seasonally changing requirements.
7. Fast response to changing requirements.
8. Keeping the requirements of the contract.
9. Flexibility of requirement handling.
10. Fast response to changing quality requirements.
11. Customer service.

The scoring which created this ranking inevitably shows the importance of the first three factors which are positioned significantly higher than the others. These are the most important factors, the weapons of competition, the factors to be analyzed and to monitor in every case, before or during contracts.

Another interesting result is that customer service (in the narrower sense) has the eleventh place only in the rank of 40 factors. The undervaluation of this aspect is further supported by the fact that warranty and after sales service were put on the list of expectations only at the very end of the discussion of the factors.

5. CONCLUSIONS

Hungarian companies still need some time to be competitive in the field of services. This statement is supported by the results of the workshop and also by the high discrepancies of importance and performance scores in the questionnaires.

Our results are similar to the English survey in the sense that the service role of dispatcher is the strongest. The laboratory role seems to be more important in Hungary than in England. We think this fact is due to the low-capacity utilization of companies caused by the current strong recession. Companies have to do extra tasks, to fulfill special orders in order to survive. It can also lead and already have led to improvement in the field of services.

At last, we have to emphasize that the small sample may deviate the results in any direction. However, we think, that they support everyday experience, so if any distortion exists it cannot be too large.

REFERENCES

[1] LEVITT, T.: Production-line approach to service. Har. Bus. Rev., pp. 41–52 (1972).

[2] LEVITT, T.: The industrialization of service. Har. Bus. Rev., pp. 63–74 (1976).

[3] LOVELOCK, C. H.: Managing Services, 2nd ed., Prentice-Hall, Englewood Clifts, NJ (1992).

[4] HESKETT, J. L., SASSER, W. E., HART, C. W. L.: Service Breakthroughs. The Free Press, New York (1990).

[5] CHASE, R. B., GARVIN, D. A.: The service factory. Har. Bus. Rev., pp. 61–69 (1989).

[6] VOSS, C.: Applying service concepts in manufacturing. Int. J. Oper. Prod. Mgmt., pp. 93–99 (1993).

[7] BITRAN, G. R., LOJO, M. P.: Framework for analyzing service operations, manuscript (1993).

[8] DEMETER, K.: Changes in Hungarian manufacturing strategies. In: D. C. WHYBARK, G. VASTAG (eds): Global Manufacturing Practices. Elsevier, Amsterdam (1993).

[9] CHASE, R. B., ERIKSON, W. J.: The service factory, Academy Mgmt. Executive 2, pp. 191–196 (1988).

[10] MATHE, H., SHAPIRO, R. D.: Integrating Service Strategy in the Manufacturing Company. Chapman & Hall, London (1993).

11

MARKETING STRATEGY TYPOLOGIES
IN HUNGARY*

By

GRAHAM J. HOOLEY, JÓZSEF BERÁCS, KRISZTINA KOLOS

The identification and evaluation of alternative business and marketing strategies has received increasing attention in the marketing and business strategy literature in recent years. Two main approaches have been adopted to identify strategic types. The first may be termed *a priori*, in that strategic types are created based on some theoretical, conceptual model and then, typically, tested using empirical data. The second approach is *post hoc*, in that types are sought through pattern searching within empirical data. Both are discussed briefly below.

Under the a priori approach theoretical models are developed of the different strategy types expected. There are two prime examples of this approach. The first, derived primarily from economic theory, was that proposed by PORTER [1] over a decade ago. He used case observations to suggest four main strategies based on market scope (across the entire industry or focused on specific market segments) and an emphasis on internal efficiency (cost leadership) or external customer attractiveness (differentiation). The combination of the two dimensions resulted in four main approaches which PORTER used to classify alternative strategies. The second example is that of MILES and SNOW [2] who again used case data to suggest four main strategies, based on strategic ambition in their approach to the market: defenders, prospectors, analysers, and reactors. The key dimension that distinguished these strategies was the degree of adaptive capability in product or market development.

More recently, WALKER and RUEKERT [3] have combined the PORTER typology with that of MILES and SNOW to create a "hybrid typology of

* In *European Journal of Marketing*, 1993, Vol. 27, Nos 11/12, pp. 80–101.

business unit strategy". Two dimensions were used for this hybrid: first, intensity of product market/development (high to low); second, the basis of competitive advantage (cost or differentiation). The resulting three strategic types were "prospectors", "low cost defenders" and "differentiated defenders".

The post hoc approach is more firmly embedded in more extensive empirical work to identify typologies which exist in particular industries (see, for example [4, 5] or across industries (for example [6, 7]). Each of these approaches first postulates the important dimensions of strategy to be considered in creating the typologies. In the case, for example, of the study by DOUGLAS and RHEE the focus was on competitive strategy variables such as degree of vertical integration, relative market scope or breadth of the product line. HOOLEY et al. focused on objectives, strategic focus, market targeting and positioning in creating their five "generic marketing strategies".

To date these studies of strategic types have been concentrated in Western markets where Western theories and marketing techniques prevail. There has been, to our knowledge, no attempt to examine strategic types in non-Western economies.

This study seeks to extend our understanding of strategic types by focusing on differences in approach and strategy by firms operating in the Hungarian market. Using the approach developed by HOOLEY et al. [7] in the UK, a typology of marketing strategies is sought and compared with that found by those authors in the UK.

ECONOMIC BACKGROUND

Before going further, however, it is important to set the economic context of the current study.

Democratic and subsequent economic reforms began in earnest in Hungary in 1986, but were spurred on in 1989 by the collapse of the Iron Curtain and the freeing of the economies of many countries in the region (e.g. Poland, Czechoslovakia) from control by the old Soviet Union. Indeed, it is true to say that Hungary has been reforming longer (but at a less rapid pace) than any other East European country (see [8]). Progress towards a Western-style free market economy has been sure but steady.

A major aspect of the move to free up the economy has been the privatization programme of the Hungarian Government. Though most companies remain state owned, the privatization programme has made substantial progress over the past few years. In 1980, 5–6% of GDP was accounted for by private enterprises. By 1990, that figure had risen to 25% and is expected to reach 50% by the middle of the decade. In 1989, there were 15,169 legally constituted commercial entities in Hungary. That figure doubled to 29,405 in 1990, almost doubled again to 52,694 in 1991 and was predicted to reach 70,000 by 1992.

Leading this process of privatization has been a substantial inflow of foreign investment in the form of joint ventures and wholly-owned subsidiaries. In the first quarter of 1993 alone, 1,069 joint ventures or wholly-owned foreign companies were set up. Of these, around 700 were joint ventures between Hungarian companies and foreign partners, which offered the opportunity both to implant Western management techniques and approaches and to infuse Western capital for investment purposes [9]. McDonald [10] has argued, on the basis of experience in Poland, that the single most successful way of transforming industry in Eastern Europe is through the introduction of Western shareholders with both financial resources and managerial know-how.

Despite these changes, however, the Hungarian economy remains in recession. While the Polish economy is predicted to grow at about 5% in 1993, predictions for Hungary are less optimistic. The first three months of 1993 saw Polish output 5.5% higher than the same period in 1992; Hungarian output fell by 3.5%. Particularly damaging to the Hungarian economy has been the recession in Germany, the market which has been seen as the natural successor to the collapsed Soviet market.

OBJECTIVES

The overall research project, funded by the European Commission under its Action for Co-operation in the Field of Economics (ACE), set out to examine the state of the art of marketing in Hungary. This article examines one aspect of that. The objectives of the article are to examine the different strategic approaches evident in the Hungarian market and, specifically, to create a typology of approaches to marketing.

CONCEPTUAL FRAMEWORK

Fundamental to the post hoc approach to identifying strategic types is the selection of the strategy variables on which to base the types. It is necessary to select a relevant set of variables, pertinent to the environment in which the firms operate. There are a number of characteristics that have been suggested in the marketing literature as fundamental aspects of marketing strategy choice. These are shown in *Fig. 1* and are discussed below.

The need to set clear marketing objectives as a fundamental to establishing strategy is well documented in the literature. Leading marketing textbooks (see, for example [11]) stress the need for objective setting as a starting point for strategy determination. In reality the range of objectives open to any company is limitless. For our purposes, however, three main alternatives were considered, following DOYLE et al. [12].

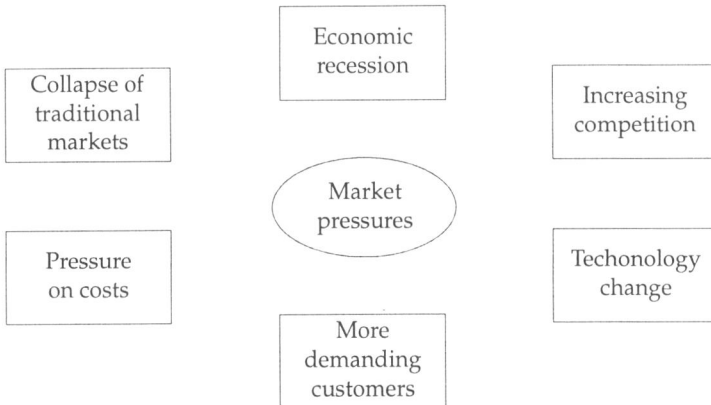

Figure 1. Marketing strategy variables

The first set of alternatives can be grouped as being predominantly defensive. These objectives include "hold position", "prevent decline", "defend against competition", "prevent decline". Both the MILES and SNOW, and WALKER and RUEKERT typologies explicitly recognized defensive objectives as setting strategic direction and both include "defend" as elements of the labels of their strategic groups. The depth interviews conducted in Hungary, reported below, revealed a high proportion of companies adopting essentially defensive objectives as a result of both the harsh economic climate and increasing levels of competition.

The observe of defensive objectives are expansion or growth objectives. These were separated into two types of growth objectives: steady growth;

and aggressive growth. The reason for the split was the significant difference found by DOYLE et al. in performance between companies adopting modest objectives and those adopting more aggressive, or market domination, objectives. Indeed, the recent literature on strategic intent (see, for example [13]) suggests that a critical factor differentiating high from low performers is the aggression with which they attack their markets (and competitors).

Having set objectives, be they defensive or expansionary, the focus for how they will be achieved needs to be decided. Logically, expansion can be achieved either through expanding the total market or through winning market share from competitors. From DOYLE'S [14] discussion of the product life cycle, a focus on market expansion might be expected more in growth markets, while a focus on winning market share might be more appropriate in mature or declining markets where gains will come, by definition, at the expense of competitors. The in-depth interviews conducted showed that defensive objectives were often pursued through an internal focus on cost reduction and/or productivity improvement. These approaches may be complemented by measures to fortify the position to be defended [15]. Defence may be pursued through proactive attempts to enter newly emerging market segments prior to competitors, or to replace lost business in other declining segments.

Related to strategic focus is the market targeting adopted. A firm's marketing may be aimed at the whole market, selected market segments or individual customers. Targeting policy is likely to be dependent on size of firm (the larger companies are more likely to target more widely across the market), market position (leaders being more likely to target more widely) and the nature of customer wants and needs. Where the latter are segmented, targeting becomes more critical. Where needs are highly fragmented (as in some industrial markets), individual targeting is more likely. The need to tailor the targeting to market conditions has been stressed by HOOLEY and SAUNDERS [16].

The final strategy variables considered were concerned with price quality positioning in the marketplace. While positioning is, in reality, determined by a number of factors in addition to price and intrinsic product quality, and the actual position achieved is best measured from a customer, rather than company perspective [17], the attempted price/quality position is indicative of the promotional and image elements of strategy. It indicates the broad set of appeals the firm is attempting to build into its products and services to make them appeal to its target customers [18].

In addition, the price/quality positioning adopted can be taken as an indication of differentiation (further explored below in relation to competitive edge or advantage created). Quality and/or price levels other than the same as major competitors are indicative of a differentiation strategy. While WALKER and RUEKERT [3] discuss differentiated defenders as one strategic type, and Porter [1] refers to industry-wide and focused differentiation, neither scheme distinguishes between price-based differentiation and quality-based differentiation. Our conceptualization, therefore, extends the concept of differentiation into these two fundamentally different approaches.

METHODOLOGY

The research commenced in summer 1992 with a series of in-depth interviews with 40 senior managers responsible for marketing in a range of Hungarian companies. The managers were selected to give a broad spread of opinions and approaches. The sample was structured to provide data from manufacturing companies, services and trade companies (retailers, wholesalers and agents), in business-to-business and consumer markets, and in small, medium and large categories. In addition, representation was sought from Hungarian state-owned and private companies, and those in joint ventures with foreign companies. At this preliminary stage, it was not intended to draw a representative sample of Hungarian businesses, but rather to cover the broadest range of companies possible. Interviews were conducted by Hungarian nationals (academics and postgraduate students) in Hungarian.

The in-depth interviews explored four main areas of interest. First, the changing business environment was considered; in particular, the changes which have taken place over the last two years and those expected to take place in the near future. Second, attitudes towards marketing were investigated. In this part of the interview, the degree of marketing orientation was explored. Third, the organization of the marketing effort, through the adoption of formal and informal structures, was examined. Finally, marketing strategies adopted from objective setting through strategic focus, approach to market and positioning were considered.

On the basis of these in-depth interviews a mailed questionnaire was developed to be despatched to a larger, more representative sample. In October 1992, the mailed survey was despatched to a representative sample of 3,000 companies drawn from an official database containing around

80% of all Hungarian companies across all industrial categories and stratified by size (number of employees). The database also provided full address and name of CEO. The questionnaire was despatched in three waves, with two weeks separating waves. Three weeks after the final wave 911 replies had been received. This represents a response rate of 30% which was encouraging by international standards [19] and similar to the 27% obtained by HOOLEY et al. [7] in the UK.

Initial concern that responses may be inhibited in a culture recently freed from a high degree of central direction was unfounded. In fact, managerial changes in Hungary predate the 1986 political developments. Economic reforms began in 1968, with the commencement of the move from a direct command economy towards a liberalized socialist market. Thus, managers in Hungary are used to taking decisions themselves and taking responsibility for those decisions. In addition, it should be noted that the questionnaires were returned anonymously and did not require, or even invite, respondents to identify themselves or their companies. Finally, Hungarian managers are used to social and economic research of this type.

Responses were compared with known national statistics where possible, showing no systematic bias in the survey response.

The response to the mailed survey included companies operating both inside Hungary and engaged in exporting. For the purposes of this article the analyses reported are restricted to those operating primarily in Hungarian markets and reporting their activities to be in those markets. In total, 576 (64% of the usable sample) were operating primarily in the domestic (Hungarian) market.

DATA ANALYSIS

The first objective of the data analysis was to identify any strategic types evident in the sample of Hungarian firms. This was achieved through a cluster analysis of firms on the basis of the set of marketing strategy variables. The variables used were developed from the conceptual framework discussed above, adapted for the Hungarian environment. The depth interviews showed that the same questions used in the HOOLEY et al. [7] study were broadly applicable, but to each variable was added an "other" category to encapsulate local differences. Prior to clustering, the strategy variables were translated into 16 dummy (0, 1) variables to enable them to be treated as metric in the subsequent analysis.

The clustering was achieved in a two-stage process. The sample (576 companies) was too large for hierarchical clustering using SPSSPC (the package available for analysis of the full survey); however, the appropriate number of clusters to seek was not known, making QuickCluster, also available on SPSSPC, an inappropriate technique (the number of clusters must be specified in advance). A random sample of 30% of the full sample was drawn, therefore, and subjected to hierarchical clustering (WARD'S method). This analysis of 161 firms showed a clear "elbow" in the scree diagram at five clusters. Subsequent tabulation against original variables confirmed that the five-cluster solution was interpretable and held face validity. The process was repeated drawing a fresh random sample of 178 companies, again resulting in a five-cluster solution.

The full sample of 576 firms was then submitted to the QuickCluster routine, with a target five-cluster solution sought. The solution from the hierarchical clustering was used as the initial cluster centroids but relocation and updating of cluster centroids were allowed. Due to missing data, 32 companies were not clustered, resulting in a final usable sample of 543 companies (broadly comparable to the 616 companies used by HOOLEY in the UK).

The final five-cluster solution resulted in the strategy types presented below and in the tables. The clarity of the solution was tested in the traditional manner by randomly splitting the sample, creating a discriminant model based on the original strategy variables to predict cluster membership, and using that model to predict cluster membership of the second half of the sample not used in discriminant model formulation. The model correctly predicted cluster membership for 95% of cases used to create the model, and 91% of hold-out cases. A random solution would only have achieved around 20% correct classification. In addition, the clusters were tabulated against the original strategy variables *(Table 1)* where the differences were shown clearly by the use of chi-square tests.

RESULTS

Before examining the results of the cluster analysis, a number of general observations can be made based on the total sample responses in the tables and the further questions asked on the questionnaire. These are relevant to the strategies being adopted.

Table 1. Marketing strategies adopted

	Total sample $n = 537$ (%)	Clus 1 $n = 147$ (%)	Clus 2 $n = 113$ (%)	Clus 3 $n = 88$ (%)	Clus 4 $n = 79$ (%)	Clus 5 $n = 116$ (%)
Marketing objectives						
Maintain or defend position	56.8	85.3	67.9	88.5	12.7	17.2
Steady sales growth	38.9	13.3	26.8	11.5	75.9	77.6
Aggressive sales growth to dominate the market	4.3	1.4	5.4	0.0	11.4	5.2
		chi = 231.27	sig = 0.0001			
Strategic focus						
Expand the total market	8.4	12.7	12.7	6.9	6.4	1.7
Enter newly emerging market segments	34.0	9.9	37.3	24.1	17.9	78.4
Win market share from competitors	20.8	16.9	13.6	10.3	67.9	8.6
Focus on cost reduction and/or productivity improvement	36.8	60.6	36.4	58.6	7.7	11.2
		chi = 284.39	sig = 0.0001			
Approach to the market						
Attack the whole market	23.0	23.4	29.4	11.5	51.3	6.1
Attack selected market segments	35.3	13.5	30.3	24.1	18.4	86.8
Target specific, individual customers	41.7	63.1	40.4	64.4	30.3	7.0
		chi = 223.9	sig = 0.0001			
Relative quality positioning						
Higher than competitors	29.7	0.0	97.3	10.2	16.5	25.0
About the same	67.2	100.0	0.0	80.7	78.5	73.3
Lower than competitors	3.1	0.0	2.7	9.1	5.1	1.7
		chi = 355.21	sig = 0.0001			
Relative price positioning						
Higher than competitors	9.6	2.0	24.8	3.4	10.1	8.6
About the same	61.7	98.0	72.6	0.0	21.5	79.3
Lower than competitors	28.7	0.0	2.7	96.6	68.4	12.1
		chi = 418.33	sig = 0.0001			

MARKET ENVIRONMENT

The domestic (Hungarian) business environment facing the majority of the responding firms is "hostile" to say the least. Nearly half (49%) reported that their main market was mature but unstable, unpredictable and difficult to cope with. A further quarter (23%) reported their main market to be in decline. Relatively few companies (23%) reported that they were operating in newly-emerging or growing markets. In addition, the highest proportion (48%) believe their markets to be essentially commodity markets where there is little differentiation in what customers are looking for in the products and services they buy (*Tables* 2 and 5).

Customer change is taking place, with their requirements changing slowly (53%) or rapidly (38%), but technological change is thought to be generally slow (60%) or non existent (20%). Competition is reported as intense in many markets (69%) but fluid and constantly changing in two out of five markets (40%). In other markets, competition was believed to be changing slowly (36%) or was firmly entrenched (24%). Entry into (67%) and exit from (78%) the market was generally believed to be relatively free, making the possibilities for increased competition even greater.

In summary, the business environment in Hungary is, for many companies, an extremely challenging one where increased competitive pressures make the need for marketing skills and techniques highly relevant. Levels of competition, both domestic and from an ingress of international firms, have increased dramatically in the recent past and are expected to continue to rise in the foreseeable future.

MARKETING STRATEGY VARIABLES

The 40 in-depth interviews confirmed the use of the five basic strategy variables suggested by O'SHAUNESSY [11], DOYLE et al. [12] and HOOLEY et al. [7]. There were, however, some minor differences in categories for the variables.

To the marketing objectives question were added two further categories. On the basis of the depth interviews a category "exit from the market" was included as a possible strategy. It had been found that at least one company wished to leave the market in which it was currently operating. The second additional category was "other", to allow for any objectives not covered by the original question. In the mailed survey response,

Table 2. Areas of advantage over competitors

Percentage mentioning each type of advantage	Total sample n = 543 (%)	Clus 1 n = 147 (%)	Clus 2 n = 113 (%)	Clus 3 n = 88 (%)	Clus 4 n = 79 (%)	Clus 5 n = 116 (%)	chi sig
Close links with key customers	40.9	42.2	38.1	45.5	38.0	40.5	1.5 ns
Competitive pricing	40.7	37.4	28.3	58.0	51.9	36.2	23.8 0.0001
Product quality	35.0	23.8	50.4	28.4	32.9	40.5	23.3 0.0001
Speed of reaction to customer requirements	28.5	21.8	32.7	35.2	30.4	26.7	6.5 ns
Company/brand reputation	27.6	21.1	34.5	18.2	38.0	29.3	14.1 0.007
Personal selling	18.6	17.0	15.0	31.8	20.3	12.9	13.9 0.008
Product range offered	17.7	11.6	19.5	18.2	29.1	15.5	11.5 0.02
Finance and credit offered	16.9	19.7	12.4	17.0	20.3	15.5	3.3 ns
Close links with industry suppliers	16.8	17.0	12.4	18.2	20.3	17.2	2.4 ns
Contacts throughout the industry	14.2	15.0	12.4	10.2	17.7	15.5	2.5 ns
Distribution coverage/uniqueness	13.6	9.5	14.2	9.1	22.8	15.5	9.6 0.05
Prior market research	13.1	10.9	18.6	11.4	10.1	13.8	4.5 ns
Product performance	12.7	8.2	19.5	9.1	11.4	15.5	9.4 0.05
A cost advantage	9.9	11.6	4.4	18.2	6.3	9.5	12.1 0.02
Other promotions	8.1	5.4	8.0	9.1	15.2	6.0	7.5 ns
After-sales service	7.9	6.8	6.2	12.5	7.6	7.8	3.3 ns
Advertising	6.8	6.1	5.3	5.7	12.7	6.0	5.1 ns
Product design	3.7	1.4	5.3	3.4	6.3	3.4	4.7 ns
Superior marketing information systems	3.7	2.0	4.4	4.5	2.5	5.2	2.5 ns
Superior packaging	2.8	0.0	6.2	2.3	2.5	3.4	9.4 0.05

however, only eight companies reported exit as an objective and a further nine "other" strategies. Because of the small number and percentage (3%) these were omitted from the further analysis for more individual treatment. The remaining 97% of cases readily identified with one of the three objectives options presented in *Table 1*. "Other" categories were also added to the strategic focus question and the approach to market question. The numbers indicating "other" or no reply for each question were 20 and 31, respectively, again indicating that the range adopted was generally highly efficient in encapsulating the options open to Hungarian managers.

Marketing objectives: It was immediately striking from the total sample column in *Table 1* that the dominant objective pursued in the hostile, turbulent, mature and declining Hungarian marketplace was one of maintaining or defending position (this is in sharp contrast to the predominantly growth objectives reported in the HOOLEY study in the UK). Nearly three out of five (57%) reported defensive objectives. Indeed, as *Table 3* shows, the strategic priority for many firms (68%) over the last two years has simply been survival. Very few companies (4%) reported highly aggressive, market domination, objectives demonstrating a less aggressive approach to business than that seen in many Western companies.

Strategic focus: Commensurate with the defensive objectives prevalent in the market, the dominant focus was on cost reduction and productivity improvements (37%). This constitutes an essentially inward focus for the company, looking predominantly as operations, manufacturing and processes, in attempts to improve efficiency rather than an external focus on customers and markets. Few companies (8%) sought to expand their total market, reflecting again the difficult economic trading conditions and the expectation of many that this route is not a feasible option in the local market. There were, however, encouraging signs of market evolution, with one-third (34%) focusing their efforts on newly emerging segments. This suggests that the predominantly unsegmented markets of the past are beginning to make way for more fragmented and segmented markets, in turn opening up opportunities for firms with clear positioning strategies.

Table 3. Strategic and marketing planning

	Total sample *n* = 535 (%)	Clus 1 *n* = 145 (%)	Clus 2 *n* = 109 (%)	Clus 3 *n* = 88 (%)	Clus 4 *n* = 79 (%)	Clus 5 *n* = 114 (%)
Strategic priorities over the last two years						
Survival	67.7	78.6	57.8	72.7	55.7	67.5
Good short-term profits	9.2	11.0	7.3	9.1	8.9	8.8
Long-term market position gain	23.2	10.3	34.9	18.2	35.4	23.7
			chi = 29.9	sig = 0.0002		
Strategic priorities over the next two years	*n* = 535	*n* = 145	*n* = 109	*n* = 88	*n* = 79	*n* = 114
Survival	42.1	56.9	48.1	50.0	22.8	25.0
Good short-term profits	3.7	4.9	4.6	3.4	2.5	2.6
Long-term market position gain	54.2	38.2	47.1	46.6	74.7	72.4
			chi = 48.3	sig = 0.0001		
The role of marketing in the company's strategic planning	*n* = 446	*n* = 114	*n* = 94	*n* = 74	*n* = 65	*n* = 99
None	20.4	34.2	17.0	20.3	15.4	11.1
Limited support role	33.6	31.6	34.0	36.5	26.2	38.4
A major role	37.4	28.1	43.6	36.5	44.6	38.4
Marketing leads planning	8.5	6.1	5.3	6.8	13.8	12.1
			chi = 28.6	sig = 0.005		
Company approach to new product development	*n* = 516	*n* = 141	*n* = 108	*n* = 84	*n* = 71	*n* = 112
Don't do any	45.9	61.7	31.5	45.2	39.4	44.6
Imitate successful competitors	15.5	12.8	17.6	21.4	12.7	14.3
Actively lead the market with new products	38.6	25.5	50.9	33.3	47.9	41.1
			chi = 29.5	sig = 0.0003		
Position in the market	*n* = 534	*n* = 144	*n* = 111	*n* = 88	*n* = 77	*n* = 114
Overall market leader	16.7	9.7	22.5	11.4	24.7	18.4
Market challenger	20.4	10.4	24.3	17.0	29.9	25.4
Market follower	62.9	79.9	53.2	71.6	45.5	56.1
			chi = 38.1	sig = 0.0001		

One-fifth of companies (21%) see their focus as being essentially a competitive one – i.e. with a focus on gaining market share from competitors. For ambitious competitors in mature, stagnant or declining markets the only option for growth, aside from entry into other markets, is at the expense of competitors. In the UK study, cited above, the dominant focus was one of winning market share from major competitors, again indicating the more aggressive approach of Western companies.

Approach to the market: A wide variety of approaches to the market were encountered, ranging from industry-wide attack (23%), through attack of selected market segments (35%), to targeting specific individual customers (42%). Given the lack of segmentation in the markets faced, reported above (primarily commodity markets), it was perhaps surprising to see such an extensive degree of more focused targeting. In the UK, the most often adopted approach is to target selected market segments, indicating the more clearly segmented nature of the UK market.

Competitive positioning: Around two-thirds of companies claimed that their quality was similar to major competitors (67%) and a further two-thirds claimed that their prices were similar to major competitors (62%). Few companies (only 3%) were prepared to admit (despite the questionnaire being returned anonymously) that their quality was inferior. Lower prices were claimed by nearly three in ten companies (29%). Price quality combinations are explored below.

Competitive advantage pursued: The in-depth interviews generated a list of 20 types of competitive advantage claimed by respondents. In addition, the mailed survey allowed an "other" category for self write-in. A number of advantages were mentioned repeatedly across the larger sample. Most frequently mentioned were the creations of close links with key customers and being competitively priced (each mentioned by 41% of the sample). Also frequently mentioned were product/service quality (35%), speed of reaction to customer requirements (29%), company and/or brand reputation (28%), personal selling (19%), product range (18%) and the offering of finance and credit (17%). The key factors here appear to centre on pricing, service and quality.

Relatively little mention was made of competitive advantage through cost advantage (10%) despite the need to keep costs down to be able to offer competitive prices, after-sales service (8%) despite the close links with the customer, and product/service design (4%), an essential ingredient in good quality.

Table 4. Company ownership

Current status of the company	Total sample $n = 470$ (%)	Clus 1 $n = 116$ (%)	Clus 2 $n = 96$ (%)	Clus 3 $n = 78$ (%)	Clus 4 $n = 73$ (%)	Clus 5 $n = 107$ (%)
Hungarian state owned	30.2	37.1	24.0	33.3	24.7	29.9
Hungarian state-private company	12.6	13.8	10.4	16.7	15.1	8.4
Hungarian private company	37.7	41.4	38.5	39.7	35.6	32.7
Joint venture with a foreign company	19.6	7.8	27.1	10.3	24.7	29.0
			chi = 29.0	sig = 0.004		

Table 5. Market type

	Total sample $n = 541$ (%)	Clus 1 $n = 145$ (%)	Clus 2 $n = 113$ (%)	Clus 3 $n = 88$ (%)	Clus 4 $n = 79$ (%)	Clus 5 $n = 116$ (%)
Market growth rate						
A new emerging market	10.9	8.3	9.7	9.1	8.9	18.1
An established, growing market	11.6	10.3	11.5	9.1	20.3	9.5
A mature, relatively stable market	5.2	4.1	4.5	5.7	6.3	6.0
A mature but unstable, turbulent market	49.4	44.1	55.8	47.7	50.6	50.0
A declining market	22.9	33.1	18.6	28.4	13.9	16.4
			chi = 29.6	sig = 0.02		
Nature of customer wants	$n = 530$	$n = 141$	$n = 110$	$n = 86$	$n = 77$	$n = 116$
Many customers each wanting a different product or service	20.4	23.4	18.2	16.3	18.2	23.3
Several distinct market segments each wanting different products and services	30.8	19.9	27.3	33.7	36.4	41.4
All customers want essentially the same products and services	48.9	56.7	54.5	50.0	45.5	35.3
			chi = 20.5	sig = 0.01		

Strategic planning: The most significant difference between the strategic priorities reported by these firms and those in the UK was the prime priority given to survival, especially over the last two years (68%), but also expected over the next two (42%). Relatively few companies (9% in the last two years and 4% in the next two) reported short-run profits to be the priority, in sharp contrast to those found by DOYLE and HOOLEY [20] in the UK where this priority dominated. It could be, however, that in the UK survival is achieved through short-term profits.

Long-term market position gain is expected to take over during the next two years as the main priority of over half of the companies sampled (54%). This may reflect general optimism that the worst of the economic troubles of the period of transition are almost over.

Finally, it was striking how many firms (46%) reported that they carry out no new product development (NPD). A further one in seven (16%) reported imitative NPD following the successful introductions of competitors. Again, this relatively low level of NPD activity may be indicative of both market conditions (where survival objectives prevail) and the consequent desire to increase efficiency, NPD being often seen in the short-term as a user of cash resources rather than as a means of reducing costs.

STRATEGIC TYPES

Following the cluster analysis described above, five distinct strategy types were identified and are discussed below. *Table 1* details aspects of marketing strategy followed in each of the strategy clusters. Names have been suggested for the clusters based on the strategies being pursued.

Two underlying groupings emerged from the analysis. The first constituted an essentially defensive response to the market conditions the firms find themselves in. This defensive posture is approached through three distinctly different routes: efficiency focus; quality differentiation; and price leadership. The second broad approach is expansionist. This is achieved by two main routes: competitor confrontation, in an attempt to win market share; and growth, through exploiting organic, market growth. Each strategy is discussed below.

CLUSTER 1: EFFICIENCY FOCUS DEFENDERS
(27.4% OF THE SAMPLE)

The prime objective of this cluster is to defend position. This is most often pursued through an internal focus on efficiency and productivity gains, targeting individual customers with products of comparable quality and price to those of competitors. This type of strategy was often encountered in declining or unstable, mature markets where customer wants and needs appear relatively homogeneous.

Companies in this cluster are the most likely to cite "survival" as their top priority, both in the past two years and in the coming two. They see little or no role for marketing in strategic planning, are by far the least likely of any cluster to engage in new product development and most often class themselves as market followers.

A surprisingly high proportion are Hungarian state-owned firms, but a high proportion are also Hungarian privately-owned enterprises. The participation of foreign capital, or the absorption of management expertise through joint ventures is the least likely in this cluster.

This is essentially an introverted strategy that passes little reason to the customer to buy. A cost advantage is claimed marginally more frequently than the average as a means of competitive advantage. The cluster is most like the "low cost defenders" identified by WALKER and RUEKERT [3]. This cluster is also less likely than the other groups to have a separate marketing department. Such a department was only present in one in ten efficiency focus defenders while, in all other groups, it was present in one in five (20%) cases.

CLUSTER 2: QUALITY FOCUS DEFENDERS
(21% OF THE SAMPLE)

The second cluster enjoys some of the same characteristics as the first – a focus on defending position in unstable but mature, homogeneous markets. What singles them out, however, is their focus on quality as a means of differentiating. Their quality is uniformly above that of competitors – product performance and quality are built in as major means of differentiation – and the consequence is a strong product or brand reputation. In addition, this group is the most innovative of any of the clusters, often leading their markets in new product development and introduction to enable them to stay ahead in quality terms.

After survival, the main priority of this group, in the past, has been long-term market position gain. Despite a major swing for the sample as a whole, however, towards this longer-term goal, the quality focus defenders expect to change direction relatively little. In contrast to the efficiency focus defenders, this group sees a much more central role for marketing in strategic planning and are more likely to be market leaders or market challengers. Significantly, a high proportion (over a quarter, at 27%) are involved in a joint venture with a foreign firm.

This cluster resembles in many ways, the PORTER "focused differentiator" strategy, building their positions as they do on a clear quality superiority platform while targeting specific segments or individual customers. Adopting the strategy for defensive rather than expansionist objectives equates the cluster very closely with WALKER and RUEKERT'S "differentiated defenders".

CLUSTER 3: LOW PRICE DEFENDERS
(16.4% OF THE SAMPLE)

The final defender cluster focuses in the same way as cluster 1, on efficiency and productivity. The position those companies aim for in the market, however, concerns quality parity but at lower prices than competitors. Typically targeting individual customers, selling, competitive pricing and cost leadership are all-important ingredients in the strategy. Interestingly, when they do undertake new product development it is often in imitation of the successful products of competitors, a second to market strategy.

This cluster typically comprises market followers where marketing plays a limited or more major role in strategic planning. With the exception of the first cluster (the efficiency focus defenders) they are least likely to set their priorities in terms of long-term market position gain, their low price strategies being aimed more at survival than market development and growth. A disproportionate number are found in declining markets.

In terms of the PORTER [1] framework, this group appears to be adopting a highly focused "cost leadership" strategy while at the same time differentiating from competitors on the basis of low price (i.e. passing on the cost advantage by way of low, competitive prices). Low price (as opposed to low cost) defenders are not explicitly recognized in the WALKER and RUEKERT scheme [3], presumably being subsumed in their "differentiated defenders", the differentiation being achieved through pricing. Low price is more often seen as an aggressive, growth-oriented strategy, rather than a route to defend position.

CLUSTER 4: MARKET SHARE CHALLENGERS
(14.7% OF THE SAMPLE)

Of the final two clusters, this group was the most aggressive, often following growth or even market domination objectives. Typically, these goals were pursued through focusing on winning market share by attacking the whole market with similar quality products at low prices. Competitive advantage was often built on pricing, distribution, reputation and range.

The goals of this group have been, and will continue to be, more concerned with long-term market position building than merely survival. This group have the greatest importance to marketing in taking a leading, or leadership, role in marketing planning. Such companies undertake proactive NPD to lead their markets and are often market leaders or close challengers. As with cluster 2, a high proportion were joint ventures with foreign firms.

Unlike the above strategy groups, this group sits less easily within the PORTER framework. While these companies resemble across-the-market differentiators on the basis of price, they do not differentiate clearly on other characteristics. They are more closely related to the "prospectors" of MILES and SNOW [2] and of WALKER and RUEKERT [3], and the "aggressors" identified by HOOLEY et al. [7].

CLUSTER 5: ORGANIC GROWTH SEGMENTERS
(21.6% OF THE SAMPLE)

The final group to emerge from the analysis was also growth oriented, but through growing with the market as new segments emerge rather than through direct confrontation with competitors for market share. The most significant differentiator of this group was its clear focus on selected market segments indicating a highly developed positioning strategy. The route favoured to achieving that focus was through a claimed quality advantage. The positioning on quality, however, was less clear than for the second cluster of quality focus defenders.

Though this cluster was very likely to have pursued survival priorities in the past, the switch to gaining market position in the next two years was most dramatic. Marketing typically plays a major role in strategic planning but NPD is polarized between actively setting out to lead the market or not undertaking any.

Figure 2. Strategic typologies of Hungarian firms

This group appears close to PORTER'S "focused differentiators". The focus element is clear, but the means of differentiation less so.

The above strategic groups form a clear typology, as is presented in *Fig. 2*. Though such strategy typologies bear some resemblance to the PORTER strategies, they are more clearly a hybrid between those strategies which relate to positioning, and the MILES and SNOW strategies which relate to ambition. There is a degree of overlap with the WALKER and RUEKERT hybrid typology but sub-strategies of this have been clearly identified.

MARKET AND CORPORATE PERFORMANCE

A number of studies have attempted to relate strategy pursued to performance achieved [20–25].

Table 6 presents a number of performance indicators across the sample of Hungarian firms, broken down by cluster membership. Three performance measurement methods were used in recognition of the widely differing strategic objectives pursued. Further, five measures were used – two financial (ROI and profit), two market based (sales volume and market share) and one survival based (cash flow). The table shows the percentage of each cluster reporting "better" performance on each criterion variable measured in each way.

Table 6. Performance indicators

Performance indicators	Total sample $n = 543$ (%)	Clus 1 $n = 147$ (%)	Clus 2 $n = 113$ (%)	Clus 3 $n = 88$ (%)	Clus 4 $n = 79$ (%)	Clus 5 $n = 116$ (%)	chi sig
Performance relative to original objectives							
Better profit	16.9	11.6	19.5	20.5	16.5	19.0	4.66 ns
Better sales volume	19.0	10.2	17.7	20.5	29.1	23.3	14.28 0.006
Better market share	13.4	7.5	15.9	10.2	20.3	16.4	9.88 0.04
Better return on investment	9.4	4.1	9.7	12.5	11.4	12.1	7.23 ns
Better cash flow	9.8	4.8	11.5	8.0	8.9	16.4	10.72 0.03
Performance relative to last financial year							
Better profit	23.0	14.3	23.0	25.0	26.6	30.2	10.44 0.04
Better sales volume	26.2	15.6	23.9	22.7	35.4	37.9	21.10 0.0003
Better market share	21.2	12.2	16.8	18.2	32.9	31.0	22.06 0.0002
Better return on investment	14.5	10.9	11.5	10.2	20.3	21.6	10.40 0.03
Better cash flow	13.4	10.2	14.2	9.1	13.9	19.8	6.89 ns
Performance relative to major competitors							
Better profit	21.4	16.3	25.7	20.5	21.5	24.1	4.04 ns
Better sales volume	23.8	15.6	26.5	15.9	30.4	32.8	15.92 0.003
Better market share	22.8	14.3	24.8	14.8	31.6	31.9	18.47 0.001
Better return on investment	14.0	6.8	19.5	13.6	13.9	18.1	10.77 0.03
Better cash flow	14.4	10.2	20.4	8.0	13.9	19.0	10.31 0.04

PERFORMANCE RELATIVE TO ORIGINAL OBJECTIVES

It can be argued that the only realistic way to measure corporate performance is relative to the objectives that were set at the outset. In this way, management sets its own benchmark for success based on its knowledge of the market in which the company operates and the capabilities (strengths and weaknesses) of the company.

Across the sample, 17% reported better profit performance than the objectives that had been originally set, 19% better sales performance, 13% better market share performance, 9% better return on investment (ROI) and 10% better cash flow.

The most significant differences between strategy clusters were encountered on the market performance criteria. The most aggressive strategy group, market share challengers, were most likely to report better sales volume and better market share performance than their original objectives. The second highest performing group on these criteria was the last cluster of organic growth segmenters. It is, however, hardly surprising that the most expansionist groups (clusters 4 and 5) should outperform the essentially defensive groups on these market-based criteria.

An interesting difference emerged with regard to cash flow, where it became apparent that the fifth cluster, organic growth segmenters, reported the best performance regarding cash flow relative to objectives. It is possible that the cash flow of the market share challengers has been depressed by the generally low prices that they charge as a means of competitive differentiation and advantage.

PERFORMANCE RELATIVE TO LAST FINANCIAL YEAR

A drawback of measuring performance relative to objectives only lies in assessing the appropriateness or otherwise of those original objectives. Some managers might be more aggressive in setting their objectives, others more modest. Some might be better informed about their market, others less so. A more objective measure of performance, then, is to look at performance change over the previous financial year. This enables the identification of those firms, and subsequently their strategies, which have improved their performance over the time period.

Across the sample, about a quarter reported improved profit (23%), improved sales volume (26%), and improved market share (21%). A further 15% reported improved ROI and 13% improved cash flow. With the exception of cash flow, significant differences were observed between strategy groups. Again, the more growth-oriented strategies (clusters four and five) were most likely to result in better performance, both on market-based criteria and on financial criteria. There was, however, little to separate these two strategies.

Among the defensive strategies pursued it was clear that efficiency-focused defence was likely to lead to the poorest performance improvement, both in terms of financial criteria (profit) and market criteria (sales and share). Though sales and share were clearly not objectives pursued, it is interesting to note the poor financial performance of this introverted efficiency focus.

PERFORMANCE RELATIVE TO MAJOR COMPETITORS

DOYLE and HOOLEY [20] argue that performance relative to the last financial year as a performance measure suffers from the significant drawback in cross-industry studies that market conditions are not held constant. In some markets a growth in sales of 10% might be poor (if the market is growing faster) while, in others, a growth rate of –10% might be good (where the market is declining faster). A more useful comparator is, therefore, performance relative to major competitors. By taking measures in this way each firm is judged relative to what is possible in its own market. Such measures are particularly useful in identifying industry high fliers.

Again, across the sample, just over one-fifth of companies reported performance better than major competitors on profit (21%), sales volume (24%) and market share (23%). Further, 14% reported better ROI and 14% better cash flow. Profit differences were not significant across clusters but differences did emerge with respect to the other criteria.

Once again, it was clear that the two groups exhibiting expansionist objectives and strategies were more likely to report better performance across sales volume and market share criteria. On ROI and cash flow, however, marginally better performance was reported by the quality focus defender group. It does seem that this strategy is the most competitively successful of the defence approaches.

CONCLUSIONS

Five clear strategic types have been identified in the Hungarian market. These extend our understanding of strategic types in general, and of non-Western markets in particular, through further refinement of the WALKER and RUEKERT hybrid typology.

The dominance of defensive strategies (in over 50% of cases), though with different approaches to defence, can be related directly to the market environment in Hungary at the time of the study. This was in direct comparison to a similar study in the UK which found predominantly growth strategies of one type or another in the booming UK economy of the mid to late 1980s. Strategy is clearly highly dependent on economic conditions as well as market, industry and company considerations. To date, the literature in the West has, perhaps because of relatively stable economic conditions, tended to play down the importance of the economic environment.

A variety of performance measures were examined across the strategy clusters. Though it was not surprising to find superior market performance among the more externally-oriented market developer groups, it was less expected to find that their financial and cash flow performance was also generally better.

Of the three defensive strategies identified, the focus on quality differentiation appeared to be the most successful over all criteria where significant differences emerged. The least successful strategy, overall, was the internal focus on efficiency and productivity gains.

Overall, while the strategies to emerge did differ from those found in Western studies, the lessons are strikingly similar. The most successful strategies are based on an external, market focus, rather than an internal, efficiency focus, irrespective of whether the objectives are growth or defence oriented. These findings are in line with those by ANDERSON and ZEITHAML [23], DOUGLAS and RHEE [6] and DOYLE and HOOLEY [20].

The research is not without its limitations. It should be recognized that, in line with other similar studies, the responses came from one respondent in each company. These respondents were the most senior executive responsible or marketing. The answers to the questions are, therefore, their views of the orientation and approach of their company. They report the strategy as they see it. Other executives in the same company may have given a different response and an impartial observer may have a still different view. In addition, no attempt was made to identify whether the strategy adopted was that which was originally intended, or whether it had come about through default or dictate of circumstances.

Further research in the other emerging markets of Central and Eastern Europe would be appropriate to further explore the link identified above between economic conditions and marketing strategy.

REFERENCES

[1] PORTER, M. E.: *Competitive Strategy*, The Free Press, New York, NY (1980).

[2] MILES, R. E., SNOW, C. C.: *Organisational Strategy, Structure and Process*, McGraw-Hill, New York, NY (1978).

[3] WALKER, O. C., RUEKERT, R. W.: "Marketing's Role in the Implementation of Business Strategies: A Critical Review and Conceptual Framework", *Journal of Marketing*, Vol. 51, pp. 15–33 (1987).

[4] COOL, K. O., SCHENDEL, D.: "Strategic Group Formation and Performance: The Case of the US Pharmaceutical Industry", *Management Science*, Vol. 33, No. 9, pp. 1102–1124 (1987).

[5] MCKEE, D. O., VARADARAJAN, P. R., Pride, W. M.: "Strategic Adaptability and Firm Performance: A Market-Contingent Perspective", *Journal of Marketing*, Vol. 53, pp. 21–35 (1989).

[6] DOUGLAS, S. P., RHEE, D. K.: "Examining Generic Competitive Strategy Types in US and European Markets", *Journal of International Business Studies*, Vol. 50, pp. 437–463 (1989).

[7] HOOLEY, G. J., LYNCH, J. E., JOBBER, D.: "Generic Marketing Strategies", *International Journal of Research in Marketing*, Vol. 9, No. 1, pp. 75–89 (1992).

[8] PlanEcon: "Economic Recovery in Eastern Europe", *PlanEcon Report*, Vol. VIII, Nos 47/48/49, 2 December 1992.

[9] PlanEcon: "Hungarian Output Continues to Fall", *PlanEcon Business Report*, Vol. 3, No. 10, May, p. 3 (1993).

[10] MCDONALD, K. R.: "Why Privatisation is Not Enough", *Harvard Business Review*, Vol. 71, No. 3, May–June, pp. 49–59 (1993).

[11] O'SHAUNESSY, J.: *Competitive Marketing*, 2nd ed., Unwin Hyman, London (1988).

[12] DOYLE, P., SAUNDERS, J., WONG, V.: "A Comparative Investigation of Japanese Marketing Strategies in the British Market", *Journal of International Business Studies*, Vol. 46, pp. 27–46 (1986).

[13] HAMEL, G., PRAHALAD, C. K.: "Strategic Intent", *Harvard Business Review*, Vol. 67, No. 3, pp. 63–76 (1989).

[14] DOYLE, P.: "The Realities of the Product Life Cycle", *Quarterly Review of Marketing*, pp. 1–6 (1976).

[15] KOTLER, P. C., SINGH, R.: "Marketing Warfare in the 1980s", *Journal of Business Strategy*, Vol. 1, No. 3, pp. 30–41 (1981).

[16] HOOLEY, G. J., SAUNDERS, J.: *Competitive Positioning: The Key to Market Success*, Prentice-Hall, London (1993).

[17] RIES, A., TROUT, J.: *Positioning: The Battle for your Mind*, McGraw Hill, New York, NY (1981).

[18] PHILLIPS, L. W., CHANG, D. R., BUZZELL, R. D.: "Product Quality, Cost Position and Business Performance: A Test of Some Key Hypotheses", *Journal of Marketing*, Vol. 47, pp. 26–43 (1983).

[19] HART, S.: "The Use of the Mail Survey in Industrial Market Research", *Journal of Marketing Management*, Vol. 3, pp. 25–38 (1987).

[20] DOYLE, P., HOOLEY, G. J.: "Strategic Orientation and Corporate Performance", *International Journal of Research in Marketing*, Vol. 9, No. 1, pp. 59–74 (1992).

[21] GALBRAITH, C., SCHENDEL, D.: "An Empirical Analysis of Strategy Types", *Strategic Management Journal*, Vol. 4, pp. 153–173 (1983).

[22] HAMBRICK, D. C.: "Some Tests of the Effectiveness and Functional Attributes of Miles and SNOW's Strategic Types", *Academy of Management Journal*, Vol. 26, pp. 5–26 (1983).

[23] ANDERSON, C. R., ZEITHAML, C. P.: "Stage of the Product Life Cycle, Business Strategy and Business Performance", *Academy of Management Journal*, Vol. 27, pp. 5–24 (1984).

[24] DESS, G. G., DAVIES, P. S.: "PORTER'S 1980 Generic Strategies as Determinants of Strategic Group Membership and Organisational Performance", *Academy of Management Journal*, Vol. 27, pp. 467–488 (1984).

[25] MILLER, D.: "Configuration of Strategy and Structure: Towards a Synthesis", *Strategic Management Journal*, Vol. 7, pp. 233–249 (1986).

[26] MCGEE, J., THOMAS, H.: "Strategic Groups: Theory, Research and Taxonomy", *Strategic Management Journal*, Vol. 7, pp. 141–160 (1986).

[27] COOL, K. O., SCHENDEL, D.: "Performance Differences Among Strategic Group Members", *Strategic Management Journal*, Vol. 9, pp. 207–223 (1988).

[28] SNOW, C. C., HREBINIAK, L. G.: "Strategy, Distinctive Competence and Organisational Performance", *Administrative Science Quarterly*, Vol. 25, pp. 317–336 (1980).

12

MARKETING STRATEGIES
FOR THE 21st CENTURY: LESSONS FROM
THE TOP HUNGARIAN COMPANIES*

By

GRAHAM J. HOOLEY, JÓZSEF BERÁCS

The paper discusses changes taking place in the competitive markets of the late 1990s and predicts future directions for the development of marketing strategy. Empirical findings from a study recently completed in Hungary are presented and key factors in the strategies of the more successful firms identified. Drawing on this research and other studies the authors propose a number of fundamentals for strategy in a changing world. Specifically the paper calls for future strategies to be based around: (i) creating a learning organization; (ii) heightened market orientation and a focus on creating superior customer satisfaction; (iii) competitive positioning based on marketing assets, capabilities and competencies; (iv) establishing closer relationships with key customers; and (v) finally, rethinking the role of marketing in the organization.

> "If it is to achieve sustainable success in the demanding world marketplace, tomorrow's company must be able to learn fast and change fast. To do this a winning company must inspire its people to new levels of skill, efficiency and creativity, supported by a sense of shared destiny with customers, suppliers and investors" (RSA, 1994).

INTRODUCTION

This paper presents the preliminary results of a study of marketing approaches and activities in Central and Eastern Europe (CEE). Since the collapse of the Berlin Wall at the end of the 1980s, governments throughout the region have pursued the transition from centrally planned to market-led economies. There have been two main planks to the policies used. First, governments have sought to privatize once state-owned industries. Privatization has been pursued through the sale of state assets and the

* In *Journal of Strategic Marketing*, 1997, Vol. 5, No. 3, pp. 143–165.

encouragement of organic private enterprise. Second, foreign investment has been encouraged to inject both financial and managerial
resources.

The research project set out to identify the effects on marketing approaches, strategies and activities of the transition. Fieldwork was undertaken in Hungary, Poland, Bulgaria and Slovenia, representing various
stages on the road to market economies.

The paper is organized as follows. First, changes in the business environment in Central and Eastern Europe are discussed. These changes
are compared to changes taking place in other, more developed economies. Second, the impact of privatization and foreign investment on Hungarian firms is addressed, highlighting the main changes in assets and
resources brought about by those processes. Third, the better performing
Hungarian firms are identified and compared across a number of criteria
with their less successful counterparts. Finally, a number of conclusions
for strategy development in a rapidly changing environment are suggested. These conclusions draw both on this research and related work in
other economies.

THE CHANGING COMPETITIVE ARENA

To claim that "the only constant is change" is trite but true in today's business environment. The recent UK study by the Royal Society for the encouragement of Arts, Manufactures & Commerce (RSA) termed "Tomorrow's Company" identified a number of major changes taking place in
business markets:

- The pace of economic change is accelerating. During the Industrial
  Revolution it took 60 years for productivity per person to double.
  China and South Korea have done the same in 10 years.

- There is an explosion in innovation and new knowledge generation
  that is also accelerating. Every year as much new knowledge is generated through research and development as the total sum of all human
  knowledge up to the 1960s.

- Competitive pressures are intensifying. Computer manufacturers, for
  example, need to reduce costs and improve product performance by
  around 30% per annum to remain competitive.

- Manufacturing can now take place almost anywhere. Companies are constantly seeking more efficient manufacturing options and that typically means sourcing from wherever makes economic sense. 1993 figures show UK manufacturing labour costs at half those of Germany but twice those of Korea and Taiwan. Labour costs in Poland, Thailand, China and Indonesia are significantly lower still.

- New organizational structures are emerging as firms seek to make themselves more competitive. Firms have reorganized, reduced overheads, de-layered, merged, created alliances and partnership in attempts to create advantage in the market place.

- International trade is being liberalized through the GATT and World Trade Organization but there are still massive regional trading blocks within which regional, nationalistic, ethnic and religious groupings seek to retain individual identity.

- Company actions are becoming increasingly visible, especially their effects on the environment. Customers are demanding more both economically and environmentally.

At the macro-level these changes can be grouped into economic, technological, social, legal and political issues. Most macro-environmental factors are outside the control of individual firms. Few companies have the ability to significantly influence political, economic, social, and technological processes. Most need to ensure they understand and predict the changes going on.

A number of further trends can be seen in modern markets that are likely to continue into the future.

First, customers are becoming increasingly demanding of the products and services they buy. Customers demand and expect, reliable and durable products with quick efficient service at reasonable prices. They also expect the products and services they buy to meet their needs. Different customers have different wants and needs and hence companies have an opportunity to select segments where their offerings most closely align with those needs and where they can focus their activities to create a competitive advantage.

A second major trend, one that particularly differentiates the 90s from the 80s, is that customers are less prepared to pay a substantial premium for products or services that do not offer demonstrably greater value. While it is undeniable that well developed and managed brands can command higher prices than unbranded products in many markets, the differentials commanded are now much less than they were and customers are increasingly questioning the extra value they get for the extra expense. Marlboro cigarettes are a case in point. On 2 April 1993 (Marlboro Friday) Philip Morris announced a one fifth reduction in price of its market leading brand of cigarettes to defend market share against aggressive US rivals. The brand had lost substantial market share to lower priced competitors. Customers were simply not convinced that Marlboro was worth the premium price it had been charging. The implications are clear. Differentiation needs to be based on providing demonstrably superior value to customers.

A third major trend is in both the level and nature of competition. Competition is becoming more intense and more global in nature. As international trade becomes more liberalized under the aegis of the World Trade Organization (WTO), the successor to the General Agreement on Tariffs and Trade (GATT), so firms face tougher international competition at home and increased opportunities abroad. Time and distance are shrinking rapidly as communications become near instantaneous. When Deng Xiaoping, the Chinese Paramount Leader, died on 18 February 1997 news of his death reached London, Washington and Bonn before many in Beijing knew about is. Firms are increasingly thinking global in their strategies, especially as cross-national segments are beginning to emerge for products and services from fast foods through toys to computers and automobiles.

Not only are markets becoming more competitive through more players emerging in them. Those firms that survive and thrive in these more competitive conditions are, by their very nature, tougher competitors. Weak firms are being shaken out of markets where they do not have clear positionings and attendant capabilities. The implications of heightened, more aggressive competition, both domestic and international, are that firms will need to look even more closely at their scope of operations and targeting in the future.

The wider ACE project confirmed that these trends originally observed in Western markets are equally apparent in Central and Eastern Europe. *Table 1* shows some of the significant findings.

It is clear from *Table 1* that the trends experienced in Western markets are equally evident in CEE. Despite concerns over costs and prices customers do increasingly expect better quality and reliability in the products and services they buy. They have more choice, and because of that new market segments are starting to emerge. These offer great market opportunities for the firms that can spot them and lead them.

Also significant is the increasing concern for the environmental impact of business. This was particularly marked in Hungary where four out of five respondents agreed with the statement.

Table 1. Changing customer expectations[a]

Changing customer expectations	Total ($n = 2672$) (%)	Hungary ($n = 585$) (%)	Poland ($n = 386$) (%)	Bulgaria ($n = 1080$) (%)	Slovenia ($n = 621$) (%)
Customers are increasingly demanding better quality and reliability	96	93	98	96	98
Customers are becoming increasingly price sensitive	94	95	89	94	94
There is increasing customer choice	94	94	98	92	97
New market segments are emerging with different needs and expectations	85	81	77	90	86
Customers are becoming increasingly sensitive to the environmental impact of business	60	79	38	65	59

Note: [a] Figures show % of respondents from each country agreeing with the statement.

In addition to changes in customer requirements and expectations many of the key pressures on business from other quarters were also mirrored in the research. *Table 2* shows some of these.

Cost pressures dominate business worldwide. They are particularly apparent during times of economic depression such as that experienced over the last few years. It is unlikely, however, that as economies in the region begin to grow more strongly as Poland and (to a lesser extent) Hungary are now doing these pressures will subside. Tomorrow's company needs to be both effective (giving customers what they want) and efficient (doing it as cheaply as possible).

Technological change also affects all markets. The figures here were actually lower than might have been expected perhaps reflecting the current technological infrastructure in some older industries. We must anticipate for the future that technological change will gather momentum.

Unlike Western economies a further overlay in CEE is the transition from centrally planned to market-led economies being pursued by governments of different hues across the region, albeit at different speeds and through different measures. *Table 3* shows the progress made to date.

Table 2. Pressures on business

Changing business pressures	Total (*n* = 2672) (%)	Hungary (*n* = 585) (%)	Poland (*n* = 386) (%)	Bulgaria (*n* = 1080) (%)	Slovenia (*n* = 621) (%)
There is increased pressure to keep business costs down	93	93	89	90	99
New products & services are coming to market more quickly than in the past	85	86	94	77	93
Technology is changing rapidly	66	73	73	49	86

Table 3. Progress towards market-led economies

Progress towards market-led economies	Total (*n* = 2672) (%)	Hungary (*n* = 585) (%)	Poland (*n* = 386) (%)	Bulgaria (*n* = 1080) (%)	Slovenia (*n* = 621) (%)
The country is well advanced on the road towards a market-led economy	34	60	53	5	50
The move towards a market-led economy is irreversible	79	85	88	75	75
Foreign investment has been a major boost to creating a market-led economy	30	71	31	15	19

It is clear that progress in Hungary has outpaced other countries of the region studied (though the Czech Republic has also made significant progress). The most striking factor in the case of Hungary has been the positive role played by foreign direct investment (FDI) in this process. As we know the scale of FDI in Hungary has been by far the greatest in the region and its impact in helping the transition is well acknowledged.

Table 4 shows the impact of privatization and foreign direct investment on firms in Hungary. Firms that had been state owned but are now private were asked how their assets and resources had changed following privatization. Those with foreign investment were asked how their resources and assets had changed as a result of that investment.

It is noticeable that the prime impacts of privatization and FDI are different. The most significant effects of privatization have been in enhancing relationships with customers (68%), bringing in entrepreneurial skills that were lacking (64%), bringing in marketing skills that were lacking (58%), enhancing the company reputation (48%) and enhancing ability to research and understand the market (47%). Foreign investment, on the other hand, has been most effective in introducing greater financial resources (62%) and enhancing production and operations capability (45%) as well as enhancing the company reputation (45%), enhancing customer relationships (44%) and bringing in needed marketing expertise (42%). This reflects the view that state-owned enterprises were restricted in their entrepreneurial and marketing activities largely through a lack of capabilities that have now been infused through private investment, while the biggest single benefit of FDI has been to provide capital resources, ahead of managerial expertise or technological know how.

Table 4. Changes brought about by privatization
and foreign invesment in Hungarian firms

	Changes brought about by privatization (*n* = 119) (%)		Changes brought about by foreign investment (*n* = 91) (%)	
Our relationships with customers is enhanced	68	(1)	44	(4)
We have access to entrepreneurial skills that we didn't have previously	64	(2)	25	(10)
We have access to marketing skills that we didn't have previously	58	(3)	42	(5)
Our company reputation has been enhanced	48	(4)	45	(2)
Our ability to research and understand the market is enhanced	47	(5)	33	(9)
We now have greater credibility with our customers	46	(6)	42	(5)
Our relationships with suppliers are enhanced	41	(7)	24	(11)
We now have access to greater financial resources	35	(8)	62	(1)
Our production and operations capability is enhanced	34	(9)	45	(2)
We now have greater credibility with our financiers	30	(10)	36	(7)
Our relationships with other related companies are enhanced	29	(11)	17	(13)
Our new product development capability is enhanced	26	(12)	22	(12)
We have access to new brands that we can exploit domestically	17	(13)	34	(8)
Our relationships with distributors are enhanced	16	(14)	12	(14)
There has been no real change	18		11	

Concerns have been expressed, however, concerning the general infrastructure in which business is conducted in CEE in general. While these difficulties are not as apparent in Hungary as elsewhere they do need to be born in mind by policy makers as their impact on legitimate business and the transition itself is not insignificant. *Table 5* shows some of the main factors.

Clearly there is a role for governments in providing and encouraging the conditions under which enterprise can flourish. While on most dimensions Hungary comes out ahead of her neighbours the high percentage (75%) of respondents signaling the effects of the "black" or "grey" market on their businesses is a major concern.

Following the changes noted above in markets, the last decade has seen a number of changes in organizations in response.

Table 5. The infrastructure for business

The infrastructure for business	Total (n = 2672) (%)	Hungary (n = 585) (%)	Poland (n = 386) (%)	Bulgaria (n = 1080) (%)	Slovenia (n = 621) (%)
Over-taxation on enterprises is reducing the funds available for re-investment	96	94	92	99	96
The level of official bureaucracy is a deterrent to foreign investment	72	63	58	90	60
There is a high level of business uncertainty in the market	71	62	50	89	59
The "black market" is a deterrent to trade and legitimate enterprise	65	75	39	71	63
The political situation in the country is conductive to business activity	19	30	27	4	29
The legal framework in the country is conductive to business activity	10	25	20	2	5
The financial infrastructure is conductive to business activity	10	25	17	1	6

ORGANIZATIONAL CHANGE

The 1990s saw a major emphasis in many Western organizations on corporate "downsizing" or "restructuring". In attempts to deal with the difficult economic conditions of the early 1990s in Western, developed markets costs came under increasing pressure and layers of both workers and managers were removed. In CEE also the impact of deregulation and privatization has been to push unemployment levels to heights never (overtly) seen under the planned economies of the past.

While "downsizing" in the West is now less fashionable, as firms have realized that there is only so much fat that can be cut before you damage the muscle and too aggressive slimming can lead to "anorexia industrialis" (the excessive desire to be leaner and fitter leading to total emaciation and eventual death) its impact on organizational structures for the new millennium has been far broader. These are manifest in two main directions. First the impact within the firm, second the impact on inter-firm relations.

Within firms the boundaries between functional areas are becoming more blurred. Where firms were once organized with clear cut divisions between marketing, finance and operations it is now recognized that "functional silos" can result in myopic operations and sub-optimal strategies. In leading firms the functional boundaries have long since been replaced by process teams that can view the operations of the organization in holistic terms and will not be hampered by petty rivalries between functions.

At the same time the role of marketing *per se* in the organization has been challenged (BRADY and DAVIS 1993; DOYLE 1995). In 1994 Lever Brothers abolished the job of marketing director, merged sales and marketing departments into business groups focusing on consumer research and product development. They also created "customer development teams" responsible for relationship building with key retail customers (*The Economist*, 9 April 1994).

Marketing departments can get in the way of serving customers for two main reasons. The first is territorial. They may see dealing with customers as their preserve and wish to retain the power and influence that goes with that. Second, however, they may encourage others in the organization to off-load responsibility for customer building to the marketing department. This creates the dangerous view that others don't need to concern themselves with customers, someone else will take care of it.

Between firms the boundaries of where one finishes and the next starts are also increasingly blurred. Boundaries with suppliers, distributors and customers are changing as more businesses understand the need to manage the entire value chain from raw materials through to customers, and work more closely with partner firms to achieve added value through the chain. A number of authors now refer to the "virtual organization" (PIERCY and CRAVENS 1995) as networks and alliances create supra-organizational entities.

The above major trends and changes taking place both in markets and organizations lead to a need to reassess business strategy in general and marketing strategy in particular. The strategies that will be successful in the future will need to be responsive and adaptive rather than rigid and fixed. Key will be creating an organizational context in which learning can take place, market changes can be identified and capabilities can be fashioned to ensure a strategic fit between market and firm.

The research project sought to identify the strategies and approaches being adopted by the most successful firms in the Hungarian market in order to locate the sources of their success. The lessons drawn from these top performers are presented below.

COMPETITIVE STRATEGIES
OF THE TOP PERFORMERS IN HUNGARY

In light of the above discussion the study sought to identify the approaches and practices that differentiated the better performing companies in the Hungarian sample from their less successful counterparts.

There are many ways that "top performers" might be defined. These include use of hard financial data on the last accounting period (accepting the pitfalls of different accounting methods), assessment of performance relative to objectives (which may have been ambitious or cautious) or relative to the previous period (improvers). Factors can include financial (e.g. Profit, ROI, cash flow), productivity (costs), social (employment provision) or market (sales and market share).

For our purposes here, however, we chose to define top performers as those firms reporting both superior financial (profitability) and market (market share) performance compared to their main sector rivals in the last financial year. This definition covers both market and financial criteria (so that one is not being treated off for the other) and also ensures that differences by sector are controlled for (we take the better performers in each sector rather than all those who happen to be in the most dynamic or profitable markets sectors). The absolute performance of these firms was, however, also assessed. Two thirds of the top performers also reported ROI of 10% or higher in the last financial year (compared with 31% of the rest), and over half (56%) reported market shares greater than their biggest rivals compared with 45% of the rest. The categories of top performers are, therefore, considered to be robust.

This definition resulted in 57 firms of the 589 (10%) being defined as "Top Performers", the others being categorized as "The Rest". The tables that follow show the strategies adopted by top performers. Many, but not all, of the elements of strategy identified in Western firms as essential to success in the years to come are evident in these top performers today. Their peers can learn from their successes but all can build on the current failings.

MARKETING APPROACH

Of initial interest was the approach of the firms to doing business. A number of different orientations have been suggested in marketing and business strategy texts including a market orientation, a product orientation, an efficiency orientation and a social orientation. Following piloting in the in-depth case studies these were translated into a set of seven statements and respondents were asked which they most closely identified their company approaches with. The results are shown in *Table 6.*

Table 6. Marketing approach

Which of the following best describes your company's approach to doing business? You may identify with several of the statements below but please select the one you think BEST summarizes your overall approach	Total sample (n = 564) (%)	Top performers (n = 54) (%)	The rest (n = 510) (%)
Use selling and advertising to help sell our products and services	9	9	9
Endeavor to offer the best technical product in our industry	24	26	24
Identify the demands and requirements of customers and ensure our products and services meet them	23	46	20
Concentrate on manufacturing efficiency to achieve low unit costs to sell our products at lowest possible prices	12	2	14
Use our assets and resources to maximize short term profits or other financial measures	9	4	9
Organize our activities in such a way as to provide security and continuity of employment for our staff and employees	16	6	18
Provide the goods and services society in general needs rather than simply satisfying individual customers	7	7	7

Chi = 26.0
Sig.[a] = 0.001

Note: [a] Significance.

It is interesting to note the wide spread across the sample as a whole, and indeed within the top performer group itself, of approaches. This indicates that different approaches may be more suited to different markets. For example, in high tech markets customers may not know what is possible and hence we might anticipate companies leading rather than being led by customer requirements.

It is, however, clearly apparent that the single most significant difference between the groups is the propensity of top performers to adopt a market orientation. Nearly half (46%) profess to devoting themselves to satisfying customer needs compared with only one in five (20%) of their counterparts. Also significant are higher proportions of The Rest adopting employment and financial (short run profit and internal efficiency) orientations. While these are laudable in themselves the danger occurs when they are adopted at the expense of serving customers. Indeed, the performance data would suggest that those that adopt a market orientation actually perform better in terms of achieving employment and financial goals than their counterparts. In other words, market orientation delivers better employment stability and financial return than pursuing these as goals at the expense of the market.

MARKETING STRATEGY

The project also looked at differences in marketing strategy between top performers and the rest. These are shown in *Table 7.*

Again the differences in approach and strategy of the top performers are striking. While nearly two thirds of the rest (60%) set their priorities as survival a similar proportion (63%) of the top performers have clearly set out to build long term positions in their markets. While the focus of the rest is primarily (62%) on cost reduction and efficiency gain, two thirds (64%) of the top performers have a market growth or market share winning focus. While nearly half (46%) of the rest set their marketing objectives in terms of defending their current positions nearly three quarters(72%) of top performers are seeking growth or market domination.

When we consider the product and service positions adopted by the top performers again we see major differences compared with their counterparts. Over half (52%) position on superior product quality compared to one quarter (27%) of the rest. Over half (53%) emphasize superior service quality compared with only one third (33%) of the rest. Twice as

Table 7. Marketing strategy

	Total sample (%)	Top performers (%)	The rest (%)	
Strategic priorities	(n = 572)	(n = 57)	(n = 515)	
Survival	57	26	60	
Good short term financial returns or profit	7	10	7	Chi = 23.7
Long term building of market position	36	63	33	Sig.[a] = 0.001
Strategic focus	(n = 542)	(n = 52)	(n = 490)	
Focus on cost reduction and efficiency gains	59	37	62	
Focus on expanding the total market for our products	27	31	27	Chi = 20.1
Focus on winning market share from competitors	14	32	12	Sig. = 0.001
Marketing objectives	(n = 582)	(n = 56)	(n = 526)	
To maintain or defend our current position	44	29	46	
To achieve steady sales growth	49	59	48	Chi = 7.5
To achieve aggressive sales growth or to dominate the market	7	13	6	Sig. = 0.02
Relative product quality	(n = 582)	(n = 56)	(n = 526)	
Technical quality higher than main competitors	29	52	27	
About the same as main competitors	69	48	71	Chi = 16.4
Lower than main competitors	2	0	2	Sig. = 0.001
Relative service quality	(n = 582)	(n = 56)	(n = 526)	
Service quality higher than main competitors	34	53	32	
About the same as main competitors	63	46	65	Chi = 9.8
Lower than main competitors	3	2	3	Sig. = 0.01
Relative price	(n = 582)	(n = 56)	(n = 526)	
Price higher than main competitors	12	22	11	
About the same as main competitors	61	56	62	Chi = 5.7
Lower than main competitors	27	22	27	Sig. = 0.05

Note: [a] Significance.

many (22% versus 11%) charge higher prices commensurate with higher quality offerings, while fewer (22% versus 27%) attempt to build position or market power from lower prices than competitors.

These differences are also apparent in the competitive advantages they seek to build in their markets *(Table 8).*

Table 8. Competitive advantage

On which of the following factors do you believe your firm has an edge (competitive advantage) over your main competitors?	Total sample (n = 589) (%)	Top performers (n = 57) (%)	The rest (n = 532) (%)	Sig.[a]
Technical product quality	36	51	34	0.01
Competitive pricing	36	35	36	ns[b]
Close links with key customers	31	37	31	ns
Speed of reaction to customer requirements	24	19	24	ns
Company and/or brand reputation	22	44	19	0.001
Product and/or service performance	21	40	19	0.001
Thorough understanding of customer wants and needs	21	33	20	0.02
Product range offered	16	25	15	0.05
Personal selling	14	14	14	ns
Close links with industry suppliers	12	18	11	ns
Distribution coverage	9	25	7	0.001
After sales service	7	12	7	ns
Superior internal information systems	5	11	4	0.03

Note: [a] Significance; [b] ns, not significant.

Table 8 shows the competitive advantages claimed by each of the groups. Across all groups the most important factors identified were quality of product (36%), competitive pricing (36%), close links with key customers (31%), speed or reaction to customer requirements (24%), company and brand reputation (marketing asset) (22%), product performance (21%) and a thorough understanding of customer wants and needs (21%).

The factors which most clearly distinguish the top performers from their competitors are technical quality (51%), reputation (44%), product or service performance (40%), understanding of customer wants and needs (33%), product range offered (25%), distribution coverage (25%) and superior internal information systems (learning organization) (11%).

MARKETING IMPLEMENTATION

Finally, marketing implementation was considered through a series of questions concerning the marketing mix adopted. Where differences emerged between the top performers and the rest results are shown in *Table 9*.

Table 9 shows how the strategies are implemented in the top performer companies. Service is clearly used as a way to build closer customer relationships (84% of top performers versus 73% of the rest) as well as offering technically better products and innovating to lead the market (81% versus 49%). There is a clear determination to build further marketing assets such as strong brands (60% versus 26%) and direct to customer distribution (84% versus 62%) or direct marketing (51% versus 30%).

Drawing on the above differences between Top Performers and The Rest, and building on the experiences of firms in other countries a number of lessons for strategy development in the next millennium can be suggested.

Table 9. Marketing implementation

Marketing implementation	Total sample (*n* = 589) (%)	Top performers (*n* = 57) (%)	The rest (*n* = 532) (%)	Sig.[a]
We use superior service as a way to build closer relationships with our valued customers	74	84	73	0.05
We are investing in creating strong, well known brands in the minds of our customers	29	60	26	0.001
Company and brand reputation are less important to our customers than keeping prices down	40	25	42	0.01
We actively develop new products to lead the market	52	81	49	0.001
We can charge more for our products because they offer superior value compared to competitors	16	33	15	0.001
We distribute our products direct to our customers	64	84	62	0.001
We rely on trade shows and exhibitions for promoting our products	47	67	45	0.01
We use public relations (PR) to promote our company and its products more widely	30	46	28	0.01
We use direct marketing methods to promote our products	32	51	30	0.001

Note: [a] Significance.

FUNDAMENTALS OF STRATEGY IN A CHANGING WORLD

Figure 1 below shows a number of factors that are increasingly essential in dealing with the complex and changing circumstances that characterize today's and tomorrow's markets. Each of these main factors is discussed below.

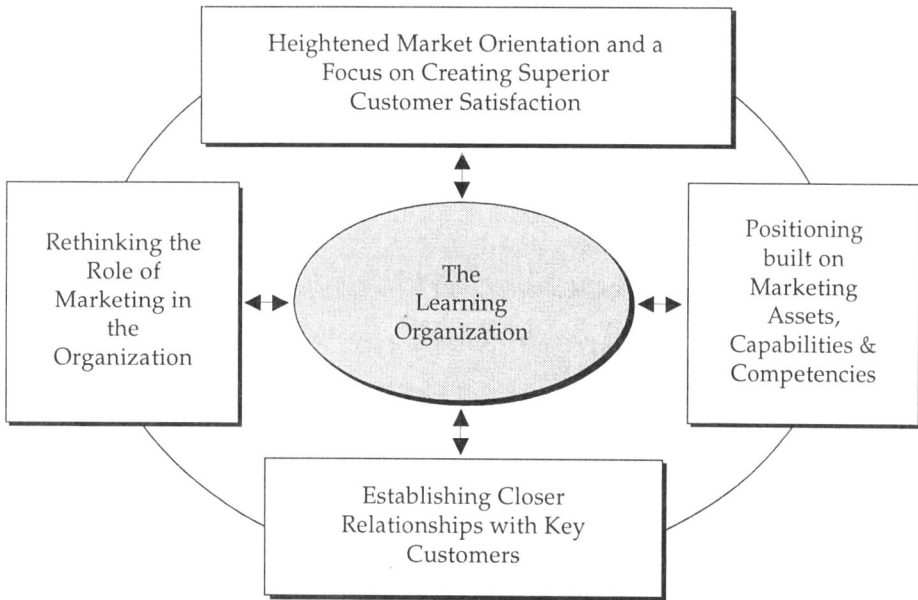

Figure 1. Fundamentals of strategy in a changing world

THE LEARNING ORGANIZATION

Central to developing a sustainable advantage in rapidly, and often unpredictably, changing circumstances, is the ability to learn and adapt. The competitive dynamics of markets with new entrants, substitute technologies and shifts in customer preferences can swiftly erode static advantages built on the "generic" strategies of cost leadership or product differentiation (MCKEE and VARADARAJAN 1995). Organizational learning, however, offers the potential to both respond to, and act on opportunities in the markets of the firm. Indeed, DICKSON (1992) suggests that ability to learn faster than competitors may be the only real source of sustainable competitive advantage.

Learning is manifest in the knowledge, experience and information held in an organization (MAHONEY 1995). It resides both in people and technical systems. Learning involves the acquisition, processing, storing and retrieval (dissemination) of knowledge. A major challenge for many organizations is to create the combination of culture and climate to maximize learning (SLATER and NARVER 1995). At the human level managerial systems need to be established to both create and control knowledge. At the technical level systems need to be established to facilitate the accumulation and storing of relevant information in a manner that makes it readily accessible to those who need to access it.

Much of an organization's knowledge base typically resides in the heads of managers and workers. When personnel leave through "downsizing" or recruitment by competitors that knowledge may be lost, or more damagingly, gained by a competitor. Employment contracts of key personnel are increasingly including "golden handcuffs" that prohibit critical managers from taking their knowledge to competitors. Organizations are also increasingly looking for ways of extracting the knowledge of their key people and transmitting it to others in the organization, through expert systems and training processes, so that the knowledge is more secure and embedded in the fabric of the organization.

Of particular importance in the context of marketing strategy is the development of knowledge and skills in how to create superior customer value. SLATER and NARVER (1995) show that a primary focus of market orientation is to create superior customer value, and that in turn needs to be based on knowledge derived from customer and competitor analysis, together with knowledge gleaned from suppliers, businesses in different industries, government sources, universities, consultants and other potential sources. They conclude that learning organizations continually acquire, process and disseminate knowledge about markets, products, technologies and business processes based on experience, experimentation, information from customers, suppliers, competitors and other sources. This learning enables them to anticipate and act on opportunities in turbulent and fragmented markets.

While the central requirement for competing in the future is learning, a number of other more specific building blocks can be suggested as important ingredients in fashioning competitive strategy.

HEIGHTENED MARKET ORIENTATION
AND FOCUS ON CREATING SUPERIOR CUSTOMER VALUE

In increasingly crowded and competitive markets there is no substitute for being market oriented. Put simply a market orientation focuses the firm's activities on meeting the needs and requirements of customers better than competitors. This is turn requires finding out what will give customers value and ensuring that the firm's energies are directed at providing that. Identifying ways of providing superior customer value is one of the central challenges of management for the new millennium.

A market orientation does not imply over-sophisticated marketing operation. Indeed it has been aruged by some that marketing departments can themselves get in the way of providing superior customer value.

As SIMON (1996) shows, German mid-sized "hidden champions" demonstrate a clear focus on providing solutions for their customers. These companies go deep rather than broad (they specialize in narrow niches of the market) but operate across global markets. Their success is based on understanding their customer needs and being highly responsive to delivering solutions to customer problems. They typically have dominant market shares of their chosen niches world-wide. For example, KRONES has 80% worldwide market share in bottle labelling machines, HAUNI is world market leader in cigarette machines with 90% share of high-speed machines, BRITA has 85% of the world market for point of use water filters and BAADER'S share of the world market for fish processing equipment is 90%. All have a narrow focus but operate across global markets.

Winterhalter Gastronom make dishwashers for commercial use. There are many markets for these products including hospitals, schools, companies, hotels, military institutions etc. each with different product requirements. Many products are on the market and Winterhalter found that, globally, they only commanded 2% of the market. This led to a re-focusing of the firm's strategy. First they decided to focus solely on hotels and restaurants (the second part of the company name was added after this decision to focus was made). The business was re-defined as the supplier of clean glasses and dishes for hotels and restaurants. In addition to designing the dishwashers to meet the specific requirements of the hotels and restaurants the company extended its product line to include water-conditioning devices, an own brand of detergent and round the clock service. Thus they were taking full responsibility for the provision of the clean glasses and dishes, going into depth with the chosen segment, rather than simply offering dishwashers across the market and leaving the provision of services and detergent to others. The company now has a world market share of its chosen segment of 20% and climbing (SIMON 1996).

In the quest to provide superior customer value no firm can stand still. What offers better value than competitors today will be standard tomorrow. Innovation, the constant improving of the offering to customers, is essential for sustained competitive advantage. Again SIMON's hidden champions demonstrate this clearly. Many of these firms created their own markets through technological breakthroughs but then continued to innovate to stay ahead of further industry entrants. They typically hold relatively large numbers of patents and derive disproportionate amounts of profits from new products. Critically, however, they achieve a balance between being technology driven and market led. While they are determined to exploit their technological advantages they also ensure that these are aligned with changing market requirements. W. L. Gore Inc., for example, an American "hidden champion", maker of semi-permeable Gore-Tex fabrics has exploited its technological lead in fabric manufacture to develop products suitable for its customers in the garment and shoe industries (SIMON 1996).

The focus of activities in firms that are truly market oriented and intent on creating superior value for their customers is on finding solutions to those customers' problems. Rather than a focus on selling the firm's own existing products it sets out first to identify current and future customer problems and then to find solutions to them. Solutions may involve creating new products and services, integrating the offerings of other providers (through alliances), and even in some instances accepting that customers cannot be well served and recommending alternative suppliers. After exhausting all other options a truly market oriented firm can gain more customer goodwill (and ultimately more long term business) by admitting that it cannot provide exactly what the customer wants rather than trying to persuade the customer to accept second best, or even pretending that the solution offered is appropriate.

POSITIONING BUILT ON MARKETING ASSETS, CAPABILITIES AND COMPETENCIES

Much of the emphasis in the strategy literature in the early 1990s focused on the "resource based theory" of the firm [see GRANT (1995) for a summary]. The theory emphasizes the need for strategies to be based on the resources and capabilities of the firm, rather than merely chasing customers irrespective of the ability of the firm to serve them. Resource based theorists, however, are in danger of losing sight of the fact that resources are only valuable when they are translated into providing something that customers want. This is the essence of the "asset based marketing" approach (see HOOLEY and SAUNDERS 1993).

Markets change and so too must assets and competencies. They need to be constantly improved and developed if the firm is to thrive. An essential task for strategic management is to identify the competencies and assets that will be needed in the future, as well as those that are needed today, so that they can be built or acquired in advance.

Marketing assets are any properties that can be exploited in the market place to create or sustain a competitive advantage. They range from recognized brand names, through unique use of distribution channels, to information and quality control system. These assets are the resource endowments the business has created or acquired over time and now has available to deploy in the market. Competencies are the skills that are used to deploy the assets to best effect in the market. DAY (1994) refers to them as the glue that binds the assets together and enables them to be deployed advantageously. He also offers a formal definition of capabilities:

> Capabilities are complex bundles of skills and collective learning, exercised through organizational processes, that ensure superior co-ordination of functional activities (DAY 1994: 38).

This definition is in line with BARNEY (1991) who suggest that it is management that is important in the resource based view of the firm because it is the managers who make use of the assets and other resources available to them based on their knowledge of the market acquired through their previous learning.

Competencies and Capabilities

DAY (1994) goes on to identify three main types of competencies: outside-in; inside-out; and spanning/integrating competencies. Outside-in competencies are those skills and abilities which enable a business to understand its customers and create closer linkages with them. They include market sensing skills, or the abilities of the firm to assess and judge changes in its markets. Specific skills include the ability to conduct and interpret marketing research, and the capability of disseminating that information to those who need to know within the firm. Also relevant are customer bonding and linking skills which help build closer links with key customers.

Inside-out competencies are the internal capabilities of the firm and its employees that might be deployed in the market place to provide better products and services to customers. They include financial management, cost controlling skills, technological skills, logistics management, manufacturing processes, and human resource management.

Spanning and integrating competencies bring together the inside-out and the outside-in to ensure delivery of appropriate products and services to customers. They include customer order fulfillment which is achieved through understanding customer wants and needs (outside-in) and using internal systems and procedures to ensure delivery (inside-out). Perhaps the most significant spanning and integrating capabilities are the ability to set competitive, yet profitable, prices and the development of new products. Both require a clear understanding of market needs coupled with internal, technical capabilities.

Alliance based assets and competencies

Not all assets and capabilities may be vested in the focal firm. Increasingly companies are creating alliances and networks with others that enable them to leverage further assets and competencies of partner firms. Alliances can offer four main sets of assets and competencies: and economic benefits.

Access to new markets might be provided through the networks and reputation of the partner firm. Western firms entering the newly emerging markets of central and Eastern Europe, for example, have typically done so through alliances, joint ventures or acquisitions with local firms that know the market, have some existing market presence on which to build and, perhaps most crucially, understand how to do business in that very different market environment. In essence the local firm provides market knowledge and existing relationships that can add to the fund of assets and competencies of the foreign partner (see HOOLEY et al. 1996). The local firm gains the financial and capital injection that the foreign investing firm can bring to bear (see *Table 4* where access to greater financial resources is seen as the single most significant change brought about by foreign investment into Hungarian firms).

Alliances may provide further managerial competencies above access to markets. These can include technical skills in dealing with local technologies, and human resource skills in dealing with local staff.

In strategic alliances technological competence can be gained through technology transfer and the sharing of core skills and processes. Alliances may be created to allow all partners to share in the enhanced technical abilities of the partnership. Economic benefits of alliances include the sharing of risks and costs (such as with new product development), taking advantage of locational assets such as cheap labour or availability of raw materials, volume and scale opportunities and access to funds.

Taken together marketing assets and competencies/capabilities are the basis on which any competitive positioning is built. Ideally firms are seeking to build their positions on the basis of assets and competencies which are superior to those of their competitors and difficult to duplicate. They are also seeking to create or acquire assets and competencies that can be exploited in many other situations (e.g. extend their brand name into new markets, exploit their technology in new industries, use their networks in different ways). A critical issue for the future is how different assets and competencies can be combined to create new products and services (HAMEL and PRAHALAD 1994).

ESTABLISHING CLOSER RELATIONSHIPS WITH KEY CUSTOMERS

Relationship marketing (PAYNE 1995) has been one of the most significant developments in marketing thought of recent years. While it has been recognized as important in some markets for some time (e.g. financial services) it is now generally agreed that customer retention, through superior service and relationship building is applicable in far wider markets.

In consumer markets relationships may be built initially through branding and reputation creation, while in business markets relationships are more generally built at an individual level. SIMON (1996), however, stresses that the relationships which endure in business markets are those based on sound economic and business grounds rather than perhaps ephemeral, personal/social bases. Relationships and reputations can be far harder for competitors to copy than possibly transitory product features, special offers or deals. As *Table 4* shows, reputation enhancement and relationship building with customers are seen as significant benefits both of privatization and foreign investment in Hungary.

ZEILKE and POHL (1996) show that key factors for success in the machine tool industry have changed since the start of the 1990s. In 1990 the keys to success were cross-functional teams, single sourcing and group working. These factors were seen to differentiate the better performing firms from the weaker ones. By 1996, however, these operational characteristics had become standard in the industry and no longer differentiated winners from losers. What now differentiates the more successful companies is their relationships with customers and suppliers. The market leaders are now managing the complete value chain with suppliers becoming increasingly concerned with new product development and quality improvement. They are also linking pay and other rewards with customer related performance targets. While efficiency has been the focus at the start of the decade, the emphasis has now shifted to customer and supplier relationship management.

RETHINKING THE ROLE OF MARKETING IN THE ORGANIZATION

The above leads to the inevitable conclusion that the role and function of marketing within the organization (or within the "virtual network") needs to be redefined and reasserted.

Basic to that rethinking is to escape from the notion that marketing is essentially a business function, a department on the organization chart. Increasingly marketing is being seen as a process within the value chain, a process responsible for ensuring the creation of value for customer in both the short and long term. This requires a focus more on marketing skills rather than marketing titles (BROWN 1995). Structures need to be created that facilitate rapid response and flexibility rather than hinder it. Indeed, it is interesting to note that some of the best Western firms such as VIRGIN, MARKS & SPENCER and BODYSHOP don't even have marketing departments yet few would dispute that they are close to their customers and responsive to their needs (DOYLE 1995).

SIMON (1996) also notes that many of the firms in his sample of "hidden champions" do not have marketing departments. They share, however, two main traits. First they are extremely close to their customers and ensure that all employees recognize their role in serving them. Second, they focus on solving customers' problems through innovation to constantly improve on their offerings to customers, continuously providing additional customer value. These two traits are the essence of a market orientation but are achieved without the trappings of a marketing department.

It is important in defining the role of marketing for the future to recognize that marketing operates at two main levels: strategic and operational. At the operational level brand managers and marketing managers deal with day to day marketing tasks such as liaison with market research companies, advertising and public relations agencies and so on. In FMCG companies they also spend much of their time organizing trade and consumer promotions, special deals, competitions etc.

At the strategic level, however, marketing is more concerned with decisions as to which markets to operate in and how to compete successfully in them. At this level marketing is not a functional activity but requires input from across the organization of alternative perspectives and skills.

Marketing needs to become and remain flexible and responsive to change. That entails distinguishing the philosophy from the trappings. At a strategic level everyone in the organization should place customers at the forefront of their minds because, as the CEO of XEROX says in the firm's mission statement, at the end of the day it is customers who will decide whether the firm survives and whether employees and managers have a job or not in the future.

In the highly competitive markets envisaged for the foreseeable future ability to assimilate and act on knowledge, to create strategies based on assets and competencies, to establish close, deep relationships with chosen customers in clearly defined market segments, and finally the ability to re-define the scope and role of marketing within the organization will be the bases for creating competitive advantage.

CONCLUSION

The above analysis has sought to profile the top performers amongst the sample of Hungarian enterprises sampled. The top performers demonstrate superior financial and market performance, not trading one off for the other.

A number of traits emerge that distinguish these top performers from their competitors. No one company, however, shares all these characteristics indicating that there is still a job for management to do in deciding what emphasis is more effective in any one industry. Nevertheless, it is clear that the firms that are being successful today in Hungary share many of the characteristics of successful firms in other parts of the world. While the Hungarian market has its own difficulties which need to be addressed the top performers in it closely follow the fundamentals of strategy outlined above. As exemplars it is hoped that they will encourage their counterparts to adopt similar market winning approaches. As individual companies, however, they know they cannot rest on their laurels and are constantly seeking ways of enhancing their competitive advantages. It is hoped that this study has provided some pointers for their future as well as for their competitors!

APPENDIX: METHODOLOGY

The research reported here was part of a wider study of the effects of privatization and foreign direct investment on the marketing approaches, practices and performance of enterprises in Hungary, Poland, Bulgaria and Slovenia. The study was supported by the European Union under its ACE-PHARE initiative and the work was conducted between March 1995 and January 1997.

The first phase of the research consisted of a series of 11 in-depth case studies of Hungarian companies and foreign companies investing in Hungary. The cases were researched by Hungarian academics and were used as exploratory research to identify issues for further research and to ensure respondent language was used in subsequent research instruments. The case studies were used to identify the main motivations for foreign direct investment in Hungary.

The results presented here are from the second phase, quantitative study. Questionnaires were developed first in English for use in the four countries under investigation. They were translated into Hungarian by the Hungarian academics and then tested on six independent executive directors of Hungarian companies. These respondents completed the questionnaires in advance of a personal interview which was designed to assess their comprehension of the questions. Following the personal interviews a number of minor modifications were made to the questionnaires to correct misinterpretation.

It has been estimated that there are around 150 000 enterprises in Hungary (Hungarian Central Statistical Agency). Of these, however, the vast majority (90%) are small business employing less than 20 people. This study focused on enterprises employing 20 people or more. In 1995 there were 14 999 officially registered legal entities employing 20 or more people in Hungary (Hungarian Central Statistical Agency). A sample of 3000 enterprises was constructed (20% of the target population) to be broadly representative of known industry sectors and firm sizes. The sample was constructed from commercially available mailing lists (through the business information company Céginfo SZÜV Rt.) supplemented by the Ministry of Finance and Compalmanach.

The survey was conducted by mail in two waves. The first was conducted in late October 1996, the second wave (to the same 3000 companies) in mid November 1996. Follow up telephone interviews were conducted with non-respondent companies during December 1996. By 20 January 1997, the agreed cut-off point for the study, 804 questionnaires had been returned. Of these 123 were returned as undeliverable (4.1% of the original sample) and 72 because the company was no longer trading (2.4% of the original sample) making an effective sample size of 2805. A further 20 were returned incomplete. The final usable sample was, therefore, 589 cases (a 21% response rate from the effective sample of 2805).

The achieved sample was compared to known population statistics for firm size and industry sector. Analysis showed a slight bias towards larger firms responding than small firms. This bas is to be expected, but caution is necessary when projecting results to the population of firms as a whole. With regard to industry sector similar proportions of firms were found in all categories except "production" and "other". The production category of the official figures was higher than the achieved sample, while the sample showed a large "other" category not evident in official statistics. Further analysis of written industry descriptions on returned questionnaires revealed a large proportion of "other" firms were indeed in the production and manufacturing sectors but had given more detailed descriptions of their sectors to help the research. From this further analysis it was concluded that there are no significant differences by industry sector.

ACKNOWLEDGEMENTS

The research reported in this paper was funded by the European Union under its ACE94 initiative (Project ACE-940766-R). Fieldwork was conducted in Hungary, Poland, Bulgaria and Slovenia. This paper focuses on results from Hungary only. The contributions of PROFESSORS DAVID SHIPLEY, JOHN FAHY, KRISZTINA KOLOS, IRMA AGÁRDI, TONY COX, KRZYSZTOF FONFARA, MARIN MARINOV, SVETLA MARINOVA, BORIS SNOJ and VLADIMIR GABRIJAN to the wider four country study are gratefully acknowledged.

REFERENCES

BARNEY, J. B.: Firm resources and sustained competitive advantage. *Journal of Management*, **17** (1), pp. 99–120 (1991).

BRADY, J., DAVIS, I.: Marketing's mid-life crisis. *The McKinsey Quarterly*, **2** (2), pp. 17–28 (1993).

BROWN, A.: The fall and rise of marketing. *Marketing Business*, February 37, pp. 25–28 (1995).

DAY, G. S.: The capabilities of market-driven organizations. *Journal of Marketing*, **58** (3), pp. 37–52 (1994).

DICKSON, P. R.: Towards a general theory of competitive rationality. *Journal of Marketing*, **56** (1), pp. 69–83 (1992).

DOYLE, P.: Marketing in the new millennium. *European Journal of Marketing*, **29** (13), pp. 23–41 (1995).

Economist: Death of the brand manager. *The Economist*, 9 April, pp. 79–80 (1994).

GRANT, R. M.: *Contemporary Strategy Analysis*, 2nd Edn, Cambridge Mass: Blackwell Business (1995).

HAMEL, G., PRAHALAD, C. K.: *Competing for the Future*, Boston: Harvard Business School Press (1994).

HOOLEY, G., SAUNDERS, J.: *Competitive Positioning*, London: Prentice Hall International (1993).

HOOLEY, G., COX, T., SHIPLEY, D., FAHY, J., BERÁCS, J., KOLOS, K.: Foreign direct investment in Hungary: resource acquisition and domestic competitive advantage. *Journal of International Business Studies*, **27** (4), pp. 683–709 (1996).

MCKEE, D., VARADARJAN, P. R.: Introduction: special issue on sustainable competitive advantage. *Journal of Business Research*, **33** (2), pp. 77–79 (1995).

MAHONEY, J. T.: The management of resources and the resource of management. *Journal of Business Research*, **33** (2), pp. 91–101 (1995).

PAYNE, ADRIAN (ed.): *Advances in Relationship Marketing*, London: Kogan Page (1995).

PIERCY, N., CRAVENS, D.: The network paradigm and the marketing organization. *European Journal of Marketing*, **29** (3), pp. 7–34 (1995).

RSA: *Tomorrow's Company: The Role of Business in a Changing World*, London: RSA (Royal Society for the Encouragement of Arts, Manufactures and Commerce) (1994).

SIMON, H.: *Hidden Champions*, Boston: Harvard Business School Press (1996).

SLATER, S., NARVER, J.: Market orientation and the learning organization. *Journal of Marketing*, **59** (7), pp. 63–74 (1995).

ZEILKE, A., POHL, M.: Virtual vertical integration: the key to success. *McKinsey Quarterly* (3), pp. 160–163 (1996).

FURTHER READING

ABRAHAMS, B.: Life after downsizing. *Marketing*, 30 May, pp. 26–27 (1996).

ARMISTEAD, C. G., CLARK, G.: *Customer Service and Support*, London: Financial Times Pitman Publishing (1992).

BERRY, L. L., PARASURAMAN, A.: *Marketing Services: Competing through quality*, New York: The Free Press (1991).

COOPER, R., KLEINSCHMIDT, E.: New product performance: keys to success, profitability and cycle time reduction. *Journal of Marketing Management*, **11** (4), pp. 315–337 (1995).

DOYLE, P., WONG, V.: Marketing and international competitiveness: an empirical study, Proceedings of 25th EMAC Conference. Eds: J. BERÁCS, A. BAUER and J. SIMON. *Marketing for an expanding Europe*, May 1996, pp. 351–370, European Marketing Academy: Budapest (1996).

HAMEL, G., PRAHALAD, C. K.: Corporate imagination and expeditionary marketing. *Harvard Business Review* (July–August), **69**, pp. 81–92 (1991).

KOTLER, P., ARMSTRONG, G., SAUNDERS, J., WONG, V.: *Principles of Marketing: the European Edition*, London: Prentice Hall International (1996).

MOORE, G. A.: *Crossing the Chasm*, New York: Harper Collins (1991).

PINE, B. J. II: *Mass Customization*, Boston: Harvard Business School Press (1993).

SAUNDERS, J., SAKER, J.: The changing consumer in the UK. *International Journal of Research in Marketing*, **11** (5), pp. 477–489 (1994).

TELLIS, G., GOLDER, P.: First to market, first to fail: real causes of enduring market leadership. *Sloan Management Review*, **37** (2), pp. 65–75 (1996).

13

FOREIGN CAPITAL IS WELCOME HERE*

By

MIHÁLY GÁLIK

Once upon a time... One feels tempted to begin an essay on the transformation of the media in Central and Eastern Europe this way, even though it started only a few years ago. The old command press of communism looks so strange right now, like part of a tired ghost story, because the media landscape of Central and Eastern Europe is being remade. And a significant part of its transformation is due to the arrival of international media conglomerates from Western Europe and the United States.

For half a century after World War II, Central and Eastern European media systems were frozen in a certain political, institutional, economic and legal structure that was broken during the revolutionary changes of 1989–1990. The legal and institutional structure that governed the media in Hungary was typical of that found in other communist countries. All newspapers and periodicals and all radio and television programs were controlled directly or indirectly by the ruling Hungarian Socialist Workers' Party. Although freedom of the press was guaranteed in the constitution, and a separate press law was passed by Parliament in 1986 (at the very end of the regime), the law was a mere facade. The infamous Hungarian press law of 1986 not only denied citizens the right to found any publishing organization but also required them to obtain a license from existing state- or party-owned publishing houses to publish new titles. The license was formally granted or denied by a state authority. The informal control exercised by the ruling party and the formal state control over entering the industry were accompanied by carefully designed direc-

* In *Media Studies Journal*, 1996, Spring/Summer, Vol. 10, Nos 2–3, pp. 139–146.

© SMIRNOV/CARTOONISTS & WRITERS SYNDICATE

tives related to the day-to-day operations of publishing houses: All strategic decisions were made by party or state authorities.

The collapse of the ruling party's dominance over the media was a clear sign of the decline of the old regime. In autumn of 1988 in Hungary, a few independent weeklies and fortnightlies were licensed as a political concession to the opposition forces. In June of 1989, the licensing system was abolished, and this event, together with the provisions of the Act on Business Associations enacted six months earlier, cleared the way for foreign investors to enter the media industries.

Magazine publishing was an especially appealing target. State and party authorities did not believe that consumer magazines were essential reading for citizens, so there were few such titles on the market. Unsatisfied demand on a large scale, supported by a booming advertising market and then-low newsprint prices, made room for rapid market expansion. New magazines devoted to fashion, sex, television programs, automobiles, women's issues, the home, youth and hobbies appeared on the market in short order.

Hungary's economy, like the other command economies of the region, suffered from a built-in shortage of capital. Consequently, investments required to publish these new titles were financed mostly by foreign investors. They knew how real media markets function and almost took it for granted that the same features would prevail in Hungary. They were right. Multinational companies, like AXEL SPRINGER of Germany and BONNIER from Sweden, entered the market. Smaller firms, mainly German and American, also founded or bought publishing houses and tried to get a share in the Hungarian market.

For the press, the most dramatic institutional changes occurred in the daily newspaper industry. The large old publishing houses that had been dominant for decades could not defend themselves against market forces. Due to the chaos created by the collapse of the old regime, they practically lost the titles they had published earlier. Foreign investors – multinational media empires like BERTELSMANN and AXEL SPRINGER, RUPERT MURDOCH'S News Corp., ROBERT MAXWELL'S Mirror Group, ROBERT HERSANT'S Socpresse from France and some smaller Austrian groups as well – took over. Taking advantage of the loopholes built into legal regulation left over from the old regime, these groups transferred into private ownership most of the national dailies and all but one regional daily in just a couple of months during 1990.

In many cases, Hungarian journalists supported these efforts. While journalists had played an important role in hastening the change from "goulash communism" to democracy, as elections approached the opposition parties made public statements about purges at state-owned publishers. Journalists who worked in such enterprises felt little choice but to support foreign companies in taking over.

Yet the role of media multinationals in Hungary must be understood in its proper context. By their own standards the new arrivals didn't invest too much capital, just a couple of million dollars. It was only in 1995 that Hebdo International from Canada paid about $20 million for the right to publish a Hungarian daily composed of classified advertisements, *Express,* the most profitable title on the market and the flagship of the only surviving state-owned publishing house. And these sums look like peanuts if you consider the privatization of telecoms in the region: Deutsche Telecom and Ameritech, for example, paid nearly $2 billion to buy a two-thirds share in MATÁV, the Hungarian telephone company. They planned to invest the same amount of money from 1994 to 1997. However, foreign investments in publishing, while relatively small, do hasten the transition from a command economy to a market economy.

The foreign investors typically promised in writing to fulfill certain conditions for editorial staff members, who felt threatened by the emerging political regime and calls for purges at state publishers. Standard concerns included computerization of editorial processes, investment in printing, job security for one or two years, editorial and political independence, and higher salaries. Looking back, these promises by and large were kept.

Of course, the entry of foreign capital was not limited to the privatization of existing firms or titles. Foreign investors, working mainly in joint ventures with Hungarian capital, launched tabloid and middlebrow newspapers – the kind that were in short supply. Not surprisingly the share of these two submarkets is growing continuously at the expense of "quality" national dailies. Publishing a quality daily costs a lot of money, and the Hungarian market does not support this. People are not willing to pay much more for a quality daily, and publishers are not willing to invest too much to improve quality enough to ultimately convince readers that their newspaper is worth the high price. The market is small, readership is rather general, and, at least in the short run, advertising revenues could not balance the increased costs. It is a vicious circle that is very hard to break out of – not only in Hungary but throughout Central and Eastern Europe.

In Hungary the share of foreign ownership in the press is extremely high. (In the rest of Central and Eastern Europe this share is not as high but still significant.) The two submarkets, national and regional/local dailies, show a slightly different picture. In 1996, among national dailies, 60% of the total daily newspaper market belongs to companies with a foreign majority interest.

Among regional (county) dailies, some 75% of the total daily newspaper market belongs to companies with a foreign majority interest. The comparable market share in Poland and the Czech Republic is about 50%. (The main difference between the two countries is that in the Polish national market foreign publishers have a weak position.) Otherwise, newspaper market concentration is not higher than elsewhere in Western Europe.

The dynamics of the national dailies' market in Hungary are characterized in the preceding graph. After ROBERT MAXWELL's death in 1992, the Mirror Group's interest was bought by a Swiss publisher, JURG MARQUARD of Ost Presse. MURDOCH's News Corp. pulled out in the same year; HERSANT's Socpresse in the next one. Their interests were sold to companies with a state majority, and the titles in question got privatized again only in 1995. (The commercial bank that bought these titles is partly owned by

Share of Publishing Houses with a Foreign Majority Interest
on the Market of National dailies in Hungary, 1991–96

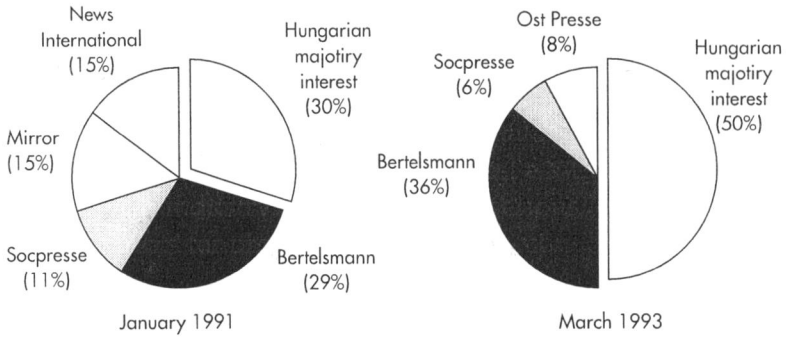

January 1991

March 1993

Source: Juhász, G. „Changes on the Press Market, 1990–1993." *Political Yearbook of Hungary*, 1994. Budapest: The Center for Hungarian Democracy Studies Foundation

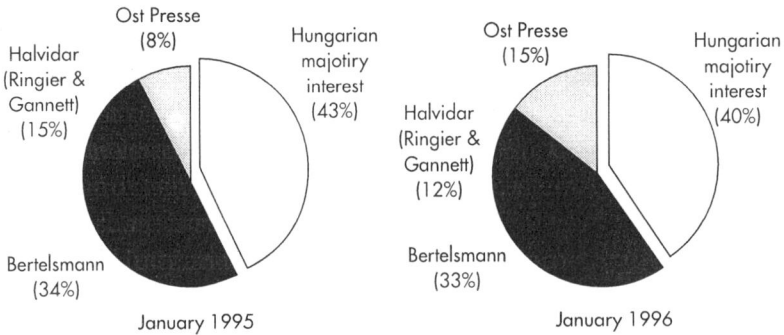

January 1995

January 1996

Source: Data gathered by G. Juhász and M. Gálik.

Austrian investors, but they do not have majority interest.) The Swiss RINGIER and the American GANNETT publishers launched *Blikk,* the first Hungarian color tabloid, in 1994 as a joint venture.

The magazine market in Hungary is highly concentrated and more segmented than the newspaper market. The share of the largest publisher, AXEL SPRINGER-Budapest Ltd., might amount to one-third of total sales turnover. German magazine publishers play a very active role in other Central and Eastern European countries, too, but the level of concentration there is less than in Hungary. Everywhere, the boom of the early '90s is over, competition is very strong and, in many cases, titles and their publishers fight for survival.

Foreign newspaper publishers who ventured into Central and Eastern Europe, with their firsthand experience in the relative stability and profitability of markets, invested first in printing and later in distribution. They built up vertical integration and followed the trends of mature newspaper markets. Compared to the bargain prices they paid for taking over the titles that had been on the market earlier, they had to invest a lot of money to modernize the newspaper industry. There were also serious investments in privatized printing plants for producing high-quality consumer magazines.

In broadcasting, the transition from communist control to the new era of international media conglomerates is another story. The new regimes in Central and Eastern Europe have been far from eager to give up their control of radio and television. Allowing private radio and television has not been a question of utmost urgency in the region, and the reason behind it seems quite clear: Governments fear losing influence over society's most influential media. Hungary has just passed a broadcasting bill, and two national terrestrial television channels are to be auctioned in late 1996. In the absence of the bill only a couple dozen local and regional broadcasters could get licenses, so their market share is still marginal.

While the American presence in Hungarian broadcasting is more pronounced than the American influence in print media, the strength of state broadcasting has tended to limit the influence of American firms. Nevertheless, the largest regional radio broadcaster has been under American control since 1994. And the largest investment in the Hungarian private sector went into cable when United Holding International Co., a joint venture of Time Warner, US West and TCI, spent $30 million during the '90s via its subsidiary, Kabelkom Ltd., on the distribution of HBO cable television programs in Hungary.

The Hungarian broadcasting bill itself has a 49% upper limit of interest to any individual or business group in terrestrial television broadcasting on the national market. It requires that at least 26% of the shares be owned by Hungarian citizens or business groups registered in the country, and the majority of board members must have Hungarian citizenship and permanent residency in the country. In spite of these limitations, it appears certain that foreign investors will play the lead in this field as well. Some $100 million will be needed to pay for these two licenses and to cover the losses of the first years in business. Leaving aside the financial risk involved, this is too much capital to raise in Hungary alone. Due to the strict rules against cross-ownership built into the bill, the multinational media conglomerates already present in the country have a small chance to expand their activities and dominate national broadcasting markets. Nevertheless, investors will surely appear.

The Czech Republic, however, provides an example of relevant and profitable privatization in television broadcasting. Nova Television, the private Czech broadcaster with American majority interest – cosmetics giant Estee Lauder Co.'s money can be found in the background – enjoys a monopoly status in the commercial sphere and has become a market leader, getting about 70% of the audience. Nova has capitalized on its singular position under the law and has been able to make money from the very beginning. This is good news for the shareholders of Nova Television, but the peculiarity of Czechs dismantling a state television monopoly only to create one in the private sector has confounded neutral observers. A private monopoly in commercial television broadcasting is hardly a situation that fits with democracy and a market economy. In Poland, by contrast, even though a broadcasting bill was passed years ago, a legal stalemate has allowed the state broadcaster to keep its *de facto* monopoly in television.

We are all aware nowadays that the transition out of communism is a long and controversial process. In 1989–1990 everything seemed possible. Right now the limits to change are more evident. Waiting for years to privatize broadcasting has done a lot of political harm and wasted resources throughout Central and Eastern Europe. And the successful Czech case has so many side effects that you can raise the question of whose success it is anyway.

Central and Eastern Europeans can't just jump into the realm of ideal democratic media. They also have to reconcile themselves with the less shiny parts of the media market, including relations with international media conglomerates. Looking back, it is apparent that there was a special trade-off between the share of foreign ownership and the privatization of the press in 1989–1990: If foreign conglomerates and foreign capital had not entered Hungary and other countries in the region, we might still be living with state-run press systems.

14

THE BUSINESS INFORMATION MARKET
IN HUNGARY*

By

HEDVIG HUSZÁR, ZSUZSANNA NAGY

Aims to map the Hungarian business information market emerging in the wake of the deep structural changes in the country's economy. Uses the results of a questionnaire survey conducted among business information providers in 1992–1993 in outlining the actors of the market and their behavioural patterns. States that the demand side of the market consists mainly of small and medium-sized enterprises (SMEs), and big, private companies with foreign interests. Notes that large, state-owned enterprises rarely use business information, and the supply side is represented by government institutions, by chambers, associations and foundations, and by private enterprises providing business information. Observes that many SMEs do not consider business information important and others are unaware of providers and sources. Explains that the type of business information services most in demand is consulting on legal, tax and accounting matters, followed by market and company information. Notes an increasing number of Hungarian business databases, some of them up to standard, and some needing improvement in quality and coverage. Argues that because of their resources and information skills, libraries should play an important role in the Hungarian business information market, not only as service providers, but as intermediaries as well, directing customers to the appropriate suppliers.

ECONOMIC SITUATION,
STATE OF THE BUSINESS SECTOR

Six years ago, with the collapse of socialism as a political system, radical changes began to unfold in the Hungarian economy and society. The transition from a centrally planned command economy to a Western-type economy, where market forces prevail, is a long and difficult process, and it has not been completed yet. After the change in the political system, the

* In *New Library World*, 1996, Vol. 97, No. 1131, pp. 5–10.

economy fell into recession – a transformational recession inevitably occurring when economic transformation takes place.

From 1989 to 1993, external and internal developments caused a 21% decline in GDP and considerable drops in incomes and in central revenues. The ratio of the central budget deficit increased to 5.2% in 1993 and 5.8% in 1994, and exceeded 10% in the first half of 1995. Unemployment reached a record 14% in 1993. starting from the second quarter of 1993, however, the economy has overcome the recession. Growth has been based on double-digit rates of investments. GDP started to recover with 2% growth in 1994 and a probable 2.5% in 1995. Exports have grown 20% in 1994. Labour productivity also increased.

Because of a deteriorating current account deficit and the enormous external and domestic debt, in March 1995 an austerity package was adopted, devaluing the forint, exposing extra import tariffs, and drastically cutting public, mainly welfare expenditure. Ownership changes started early owing to progressive legal regulation. Some of the most important acts, the Company Act and the Act on Company Transformation, were adopted in 1988 and 1989, providing the legal base for founding new enterprises, starting new businesses.

Privatization in Hungary took place in several phases: first the so-called spontaneous privatization, allowing employees of small state companies to buy the assets and transform the legal status; then came restitution, giving property nationalized in 1948, mainly land and buildings, back to proprietors and descendants. In the next phase, medium and large enterprises were offered to domestic and international investors, followed by the partial or total sell-off strategic industries (energy, telecommunication). The privatization of the financial sector has just begun.

These developments mean that the socio-economic environment of economic agents, in which individuals, entrepreneurs, organizations and government bodies live and work, changed dramatically. This environment is not a mirror-image of Western economies, but it progressed towards market-type conditions. With the multiplying number of economic actors and the expanding role of market relations, information, business information in particular, becomes more important for the survival and success of those involved in business activity. The formation of a business information market is both a prerequisite of the smooth operation of a market economy and one of the means of promoting small and medium-sized enterprises. The actors of the emerging business information market in Hungary struggle with serious problems.

Before overviewing the actors of the business information market, it should be made clear what is meant by business information. All kinds of data and information are considered business information which, either in themselves or arranged by specific aspects, are necessary for short- or long-term decision making on any level of economic or business activity. Types of business information are:

(1) *Factographic information:*
   • company information;
   • news and advertisements;
   • statistics;
   • patents and standards;
   • financial information.

(2) *Rules of law:*
   • Hungarian and international, with special regard to those of the European Union.

(3) *Analyses, studies:*
   • market reports;
   • economic surveys and forecasts;
   • methodological studies.

ACTORS OF THE HUNGARIAN BUSINESS INFORMATION MARKET

CLIENTS: THE BUSINESS SECTOR, COMPANIES AND ENTREPRENEURS

The number of economic organizations increased significantly in the past five years. The situation in December 1994 is shown in *Table 1* [1].

In 1995 the number of incorporated organizations continued to increase, but there are fewer unincorporated enterprises than last year. Of the incorporated enterprises 87% operate as limited liability companies and deposit partnerships (kft.-s and bt.-s), 7% as co-operatives and 3% as joint stock companies. The proportion of small enterprises grew, the percentage of enterprises with fewer than ten employees reached 74. Thirty-five % of enterprises are engaged in trade and repairing services, 19% in industry, 19% are involved in property transactions, 9% in construction and 6% in agriculture.

Concerning bankruptcies and liquidations, available data are somewhat contradictory. The Bankruptcy and Accounting Act adjusted to European standards was introduced ahead of the actual Hungarian conditions, amid a corporate liquidity crisis. As a consequence, the bankruptcy wave climaxed in 1992 and 1993. There were more than 4,000 bankruptcies reported in 1992 and more than 5,000 in 1993. Liquidations reached nearly 10,000 in 1992 and 17,000 in 1993. Although fewer in number, we are still not past the wave of bankruptcies and liquidations.

Table 1. Number of economic organizations in 1994

Denomination	December 1993 (thousands)	December 1994 (thousands)	November 1994 as a percentage of December	December 1994 (thousands)
Incorporated business organizations	85.6	99.7	116.5	101.2
Unincorporated business organizations	98.0	120.0	121.7	121.1
Government and social security organizations	14.9	15.1	100.7	15.1
Other non-profit organizations	38.5	44.4	115.3	44.8
Private enterprises	688.8	775.0	112.5	778.0

Source: [1, p. 8]

In this turbulent environment the information needs of enterprises and the actual demand for information services are rather varied. A survey was conducted by Budapest University of Economic Sciences (BUES) Central Library in 1992–1993 investigating the actors of business information market and their behavioural patterns. However, as the survey was targeted at information providers, we have only some indirectly gathered notion about the opinion and habits of business enterprises.

Although mainly small and medium-sized enterprises (SMEs) represent the demand side of the information market, it seems that quite a lot of small entrepreneurs either do not consider business information important or simply do not know where and how to find it. In the last two or three years, entrepreneurs and companies have become more active in their demand and use of external information sources, especially SMEs. They still have very limited knowledge about possible providers and sources, and many of them are dissatisfied with information services already used by them.

Entrepreneurs who use business information services mainly seek advice on specific practical problems, particularly on tax and accounting issues, and on how to start new ventures. It is usually larger companies with a more differentiated organizational structure which ask for different types of market and company information.

The information needs of different segments of the market vary according to industrial sector, to size and to ownership relations. Big, state-owned companies (there are ever fewer of them) are not really interested in market information. Either they are to be privatized or not. Informally obtainable information about power relations and government intentions is more important for them than market-related information. Large, already privatized companies, mostly with foreign interests in them, mainly rely on the information sources used by the foreign parent company and/or have their own information and intelligence department within the organization.

THE SUPPLY SIDE:
PROVIDERS OF BUSINESS INFORMATION SERVICES

Results of the questionnaire survey give an overview of the major suppliers of business information in Hungary, their characteristics and services. Libraries were not included in the survey; their role and possible path of development is a question to be tackled separately.

Organizations providing business information can be divided into three categories: there are government organizations (13%), association, chambers and foundations (44%) and private enterprises (43%).

Government institutions and government-backed organizations

These play an important role in the information market. Most of them are non-profit, but some operate or have separate units that operate as profit-seeking entities. The following are examples of the most important ones:

- the Courts of Registration making data on registered companies available to the public;
- the Ministry of Justice providing company data electronically;
- the National Office of Inventions (Országos Találmányi Hivatal) giving information about patents, trademarks and other forms of industrial property;

- the Institute for Small Business Development (Kisvállalkozásfejlesztési Intézet) belonging to the Ministry of Industry and Trade which, besides preparing analyses and recommendations to the government, provides business information services, such as online access to the company database of the State Property Agency, to the World Bank Info database on tenders, etc.;
- the State Privatization and Property Holding Co. Ltd. (Állami Privatizációs és Vagyonkezelő Rt.) which provides information about state assets to be privatized and about tenders.

Foundations, chambers and associations

These have a significant task in promoting SMEs, supporting existing ones and facilitating the establishment of new enterprises. Part of their activities is supplying business information.

Last year, the system of chambers was reformed and new industrial and commercial, agricultural, and handicraft chambers were created with obligatory membership and membership fee. Owing to these changes, the information activities of the new and reformed chambers are just now being established or reorganized.

The Hungarian Foundation for Enterprise Promotion was founded by the government in co-operation with major banks and business associations with the aim of promoting SMEs and assisting in the development of business culture. It was selected by the Commission of the European Union to implement the PHARE SME Development Programme and it has placed 59 million ECU to date through a nationwide network of Local Enterprise Agencies (LEAs). LEAs operate at county level against a business plan based on a comprehensive county study and provide free or subsidized service for entrepreneurs in the following areas:

- advice and counselling;
- business information;
- training and development;
- financial assistance through a Micro Credit Scheme.

Private enterprises

Hungarian enterprises supplying business information usually have other interests as well and information service is only part of their activities. They are mainly on the small side with the exception of a few large companies, such as Kopint-Datorg. Their technical equipment and expertise are rather varied.

Foreign business information companies have also opened their offices in Hungary or set up joint ventures with a Hungarian partner. They supply mainly "big business", i.e. international corporations, already privatized companies with some foreign stake in them, the financial sector, etc. Some well-known examples are:

- Dun & Bradstreet Hungary Ltd.;
- Creditreform Interinfo Ltd.;
- Kompass Hungaria Ltd.;
- Hoppenstedt Bonnier and Co. Ltd.;
- Intercredit Budapest;
- Transeurope Ltd. – Information Bank.

INFORMATION PRODUCTS AND SERVICES

According to the survey, the most heavily demanded form of service is consulting. Entrepreneurs seek advice on legal, tax and accounting matters and on how to set up new ventures. There is a slight difference in the service structure of non-profit and for-profit information suppliers: non-profits provide consulting as the first and training as the second most important function, whereas for-profits most frequently give market information followed by consulting.

As for market information, product information and advertising are the most popular types, followed by export-import and price information.

Concerning company information, there have been some new developments lately. According to an amendment to the law on company registration passed in June, data on companies under registration will be public. It is hoped that the amended law will streamline the procedures of courts of registration and the availability of data. Public data on companies, including from now on a company's balance sheet and other financial reports, may be requested from any regional court of registration. Since May, company information has also been available at the Ministry of Justice from an electronic database. The service is fee-based. Small users get the information in printed form, large users may join the system online. Within company information, the most commonly offered service is partner searching and matching, then comes financial and accounting information.

Training and education is also an important activity, particularly for non-profit organizations. Many of the information providers produce databases themselves. The Hungarian Chamber of Database Suppliers annually compiles a database of databases produced and distributed in Hungary, called Metadatabase. Of the 200 databases in it, about a quarter can be considered as business or business-related databases. Most of them gather company information, other subjects include financial information, business offers, legal information, products, etc. The majority of these databases have been established in recent years, and the picture is promising if the increase in number is accompanied by improvement in quality, reliability and coverage.

To illustrate the supply of Hungarian business databases, a few of them can be mentioned:

(1) The Press Database of the Hungarian News Agency (MTI Sajtóadatbázis) contains the full-text news reports published by MTI since 1988. MTI's English language service, EcoNews, provides daily economic and business news bulletins, including stock and bond listings of the Budapest Stock Exchange. It can be accessed either through a real-time telecommunication service or through local online access.

(2) The Company Data electronic database, produced by an Austrian–Hungarian joint venture, Company Data Informatics Ltd. (Company Data Informatikai Szolgáltató Kft.), aims to provide up-to-date information on all registered companies, based on official registration data. In contains the usual key data of companies. It can be accessed online via Videotext or can be installed for in-house use.

(3) Kerszöv "CD Company News" (Kerszöv "CD Céghírek") contains data on all the companies registered in Hungary, plus company news from 45 newspapers and journals. The database is distributed on CD-ROM with monthly updates but can be accessed online as well.

(4) Hoppenstedt Bonnier produces three online databases:
   • large and medium-sized Hungarian companies (Magyarország nagy- és középvállalatai);
   • Hungarian managers (Magyarország menedzserei);
   • institutions and organizations (Intézmények és szervezetek).

(5) HUCO, a directory database of Hungarian companies and HUNTECH, a database of Hungarian technologies and industries, offering co-operation to international partners, are both produced by the Institute of

International Technology (Nemzetközi Technológiai Intézet = NETI). Both databases are available on the GBI (German Business Information) host.

(6) HUNPATÉKA is a bibliographic database of Hungarian patent documents on CD-ROM. HUNPADOC is a PC-based database listing bibliographic data of Hungarian patents since 1975. PRECES contains patent documents from six East-European countries on CD-ROM. All three are produced by the National Office of Inventions (Országos Találmányi Hivatal).

HOW INFORMATION PROVIDERS WORK

About half of the information sources on which services are based are purchased. The other half are collected and processed by service organizations themselves. Among purchased media, traditional types (books, journals, etc.) are more frequent than CD-ROM or online databases. Many firms build their own databases, and quite a lot of them compile directories, indexes and bibliographies, and publish newsletters and circulars. Profit-oriented information firms turn slightly more frequently to libraries when seeking information than do non-profit organizations, although they do not consider libraries a primary source.

It is very difficult to assess qualitative characteristics of information providers, although there is common understanding that reliability is the most important factor for success. Speed of service and price are also significant. Pricing conditions of information services are chaotic in Hungary, although more and more organizations have started charging for previously free services. This is because operating budgets in the non-profit sector have been severely cut and other sources of funding (grants from domestic and foreign organizations, foundations, project tenders, etc.) have decreased.

THE ROLE OF LIBRARIES

Libraries in Hungary should play an important role in the information market as they have large collections of relevant documents, they have the necessary communication technology and expertise to use it, they have professional staff trained in information enquiry and they are obvious places to which people can turn when seeking information.

In 1992, a business information project was started by the Hungarian Association of Librarians, supported by the Ministry of Education and Culture and it has paved the way to establishing business-related services in some of the libraries. It was in its framework that the above-mentioned questionnaire survey on business information providers was conducted, and two databases were created. One is called VIP: TIPP-TÁR, produced by BUES Central Library, containing the data of organizations that provide business information, excluding libraries; the other is VIP:VIA by OMIKK (the National Technical Information Centre and Library), featuring main libraries' business-related holdings.

There are libraries already providing business information. BUES Central Library has a significant collection of CD-ROM databases relevant to business (e.g. ABI, Business Periodicals Ondisc full text, International Statistical Yearbook, SEC Online, WISO (Wirtschafts- und Sozialwissenschaftliche Literatur – CD-ROM edition), IBFD (International Bureau of Fiscal Documentation, European Taxation, UK Corporations, etc.). It is mounted on a local area network (LAN), and can be accessed online as well. The library's own catalogue, also available on the Internet, to some extent serves as a bibliographic database of books and periodical articles. Services include searching international commercial databases, news clippings, subject monitoring, etc.

OMIKK also provides business information, mainly related to technical fields, through its library service which also provides access to many CD-ROMs via its LAN (European Kompass, Wer liefert was?, F&S Index plus Text, etc.), and to foreign databases via different international hosts. OMIKK established a comprehensive service sponsored by UNIDO, called "BIS for SMEs in Hungary".

More and more county and city libraries engage in business information services, e.g. Veszprém, Zalaegerszeg, Békéscsaba. Some of them offer not only general but tailor-made services as well, owing to their knowledge of local conditions and the needs of the local business community.

Libraries wanting to establish business-related services face a lot of problems. Apart from the obvious lack of funds which makes it ever harder even to maintain the level of acquisitions, there are problems with library routine, with the organizational structure and the organization of work. All these do not support fast and flexible service which is essential for business clients. New methods of activity and new organizational solutions should be worked out to able to match services to the needs of the business community.

Besides providing business information services directly to clients, libraries could play a role as intermediaries, directing customers to the appropriate supplier. They have the necessary sources and knowledge to match customers with specific information needs to the providers that are able to serve them.

Monitoring developments in the information market and strengthening international co-operation are also tasks that can be undertaken by libraries. In 1995, BUES Central Library took part in a joint project with ISTEI, Warsaw (Institute for Scientific, Technical and Economic Information) in the framework of Assistance, an international association for scientific communication and co-operation, sponsored by the Austrian Government. The aim of the project was to work out a comparative study on the information needs of SMEs in Poland and Hungary. A questionnaire survey was conducted and the results summarized and presented to the sponsor organization.

The specialized training of librarians is essential for creating a business information infrastructure. The first business information courses were organized in 1992 by the Hungarian Library Association with the help of foreign BI professionals. From 1993–1994, both the Berzsenyi Dániel Teachers' Training College at Szombathely and the Bessenyei György Teachers' Training College in Nyíregyháza have been offering business information services (BIS) courses for their students of librarianship. In 1994 a 120-hour training course was held by Berzsenyi Dániel College in the framework of the business information project of libraries where some 15 librarians participated.

The LISTEN TEMPUS Joint European Project, in the framework of which BIS courses are held, aims to train business information professionals who will be able, in turn, to train Hungarian librarians in this field.

REFERENCE

[1] National Bank of Hungary Monthly Report, Vol. 2 (1995).

FURTHER READING

DEMMLER, Á., ALFÖLDI DÁN, G.: "A könyvtárak és az üzleti információ" ("Libraries and business information"). Manuscript, Budapest (1994).

HUSZÁR, H.: "Vállalkozási információs projekt: helyzet és kiindulás" ("Business information project: present state and beginnings"). Manuscript, Budapest (1992).

HUSZÁR, H.: "Vállalkozási információs projekt (VIP)" ("Business information project"). *Könyv, könyvtár, könyvtáros.* April, pp. 29–30 (1993).

HUSZÁR, H.: "Üzlet-e az üzleti információ?" ("Business information – is it good business?"). *Tudományos és Műszaki Tájékoztatás.* Vol. 1, pp. 3–6 (1994).

"Kevesebb az egyéni vállalkozó" ("Fewer individual entrepreneurs"). *Magyar Nemzet,* 17 October, p. 8 (1995).

SZÁNTÓ, P.: "Business information in Hungary." Manuscript, Budapest (1995).

SZÁNTÓ, P., HUSZÁR, H.: "Business information in Hungary." *FID News Bulletin.* No. 6, pp. 127–129 (1993).

III

ORGANIZATIONAL CHANGE: MANAGEMENT LEARNING AND BUSINESS EDUCATION

INTRODUCTION TO PART THREE

Undoubtedly the most critical and dramatic change of the economic transition period has taken place in company organizational life. Companies and branches of industry with decades, even centuries of tradition have found themselves uprooted from one year to the next. Behind the unprecedented figure of over 10% unemployment lie the individual tragedies of hundreds of thousands of people, their search for a new life, and efforts to struggle out of their difficulties. The "Eureka-sensation" of gaining democratic rights has often been thrust into the background by the demoralizing effect of the hopelessness felt at the individual level and the experience of sinking into the grip of poverty.

In view of the well-known pessimism of the Hungarian people, there is ample scope for sociologically motivated research. In this part we have selected articles that attempt to shed light on the origins of the successful survival strategy that can be observed at the level both of individuals and of organizations. Hungary's 1100 years of history are full of events that reflect survival skills. (It is enough just to mention the last two world wars and their consequences: the country lost two-thirds of its territory, and this was followed by 40 years of Soviet occupation.) In the 90s, for half of all company executives survival was the top strategic priority (though to a decreasing extent). In this part we approach from three directions the ability to react positively to change: first from the organization learning side, secondly from the angle of the value of work and creativity, and thirdly from the point of view of business education.

The first three articles (Chapters 15, 16 and 17) apply three differently-oriented organization theory approaches to describe organizational changes. The PEARCE–BRANYICZKI–BAKACSI article examines person-based reward systems and their transformation in the period immediately before and after the change in the régime. Company cases are analyzed and tests are made to see to what extent theoretical hypotheses are validated. As a control group, use is made of examples of companies with a non-person-based reward system. The authors assert, for example, that the somewhat romanticized version of the clan theory associated with the name of OUCHI (Markets, Bureaucracies and Clans. *Administrative Science Quarterly*, Vol. 25) is given a more realistic basis by the Hungarian data.

The PEARCE–BRANYICZKI article focusses specifically on change management. Its self-contradictory title, claiming that bureaucracy can and must be revolutionized, symbolizes the difficulty of transforming state companies. The process of dismantling state socialism is illustrated by presenting the story of a successful and an unsuccessful company. Through the survival of a large state advertising agency the management tasks involved in organizational survival are demonstrated.

The evolution of organizational forms from the 1980s up to 1995 is shown by the DOBÁK–TARI study. They adopt a contextual approach, according to which from the economic and social changes in the country it is possible to comprehend the alterations that have occurred in the organizational structure. They illustrate with vivid examples why in the period before 1989 it was not possible for modern attempts at organizational transformation such as the matrix or divisional forms of organization to succeed. After the change in the régime, the dramatic increase in the number of small and medium-sized companies determined the trend of organizational development. At the same time, however, large companies underwent a transformation to conform to the market, and this is still going on. One tendency within this process is the emergence of group concerns and holding organizations, which serve to consolidate private enterprises.

In the international specialized literature there is increasing mention of intercultural surveys aimed at demonstrating cultural differences. ELIZUR–BORG–HUNT–MAGYARI-BECK examined the structure of the value of work in eight countries. Their data collection was carried out in 1988, before the change in the system, thus it was possible to compare two socialist countries (Hungary and China) with advanced and moderately developed countries. The surprising result of this research was that the structure of the value of work showed a remarkable degree of constancy, regardless of a country's political and economic set-up or its geographical situation.

MAGYARI-BECK has undertaken to demonstrate the creativity rooted in Hungarian culture. Using the method of the JONES Inventory and EKVALL's Creativity Climate Questionnaire, the author found some unexpected results. For example, women lag behind men in creativity, but Hungary's enterprise culture also leaves something to be desired from this point of view.

The last two articles (Chapters 20 and 21) deal with business training. From the operation of U.S. business schools Czakó draws conclusions about what needs to be done to develop Hungarian higher education. She summarizes how certain topic areas (e.g. the competitive situation) cause difficulties (e.g. conflict between academic requirements and practical training) and suggests the measures necessary to overcome them. In the last chapter of Part Three, the GROSS–HARTLEY–BERÁCS–GÁSPÁR article analyzes East Central Europe's business training from a historical perspective. Starting with the difference in the structure of education in America and in Europe, the authors examine, as part of the latter, the experience of Hungary and Poland. It may be attributable to the survival of traditions that the barriers to admission to the education sector (the gaining of appropriate accreditation) are high, and the whole system faces opportunities for further development and improvement.

15

PERSON-BASED REWARD SYSTEMS: A THEORY OF ORGANIZATIONAL REWARD PRACTICES IN REFORM-COMMUNIST ORGANIZATIONS*

By

JONE L. PEARCE, IMRE BRANYICZKI, GYULA BAKACSI

A type of organizational reward system based on personal power is described and partially tested. The theory, developed from observations of Hungarian organizations, is grounded in theories of procedural justice and learned helplessness. Person-based organizational reward systems are characterized by highly valued rewards combined with personalistic criteria for reward distribution. Such organizational reward systems were hypothesized to lead to employee perceptions of organizational unfairness; negative evaluations of others; anxiety; and perceptions of self, collegial and organizational inefficacy. These hypotheses were supported in tests in a sample of three Hungarian state-owned organizations classified as having person-based systems and five non-person-based organizations (two Hungarian privately-owned companies, one American state-owned and two American privately-owned organizations). In addition, several behavioral effects of person-based reward systems were proposed: they foster bargaining behavior, withholding of information, avoidance of collaborative tasks, ingratiation and noncompliance with rules.

INTRODUCTION

This paper presents and partially tests a theory of the affective and behavioral effects of the organizational reward system in Hungarian state-owned organizations in the early period of economic transformation. While there are excellent sociological and economic studies of state-socialist enterprises, there has been less attention to the development of theoretically grounded analyses of these organizations' incentive systems. Below,

* In *Journal of Organizational Behavior*, 1994, Vol. 15, pp. 261–282.
Acknowledgement. This research has been supported by the Vállalatgazdasági Tudományos Egyesület (Hungarian Business Economics Scientific Society and an Irvine Faculty Fellowship. An earlier version of the paper was presented at the Second Annual Western Academy of Management International Conference. Katholieke Universiteit, June 21–24, 1992. The authors wish to thank ANNE TSUI, LYMAN PORTER, DAN MCALLISTER, ROCHELLE KLEIN, and MARCIA FRIDEGER for their comments on earlier drafts.

we develop and test several hypotheses regarding what we term "person-based organizational reward systems". Although personal influence is present in all organizations (PFEFFER 1981), we will argue that these organizations were dominated by a particularly powerful form of personal power. Furthermore, these person-based reward systems were part of a conscious strategy designed to obtain specific employee behaviors. We prefer the term "person-based" because similar terms, such as "unfair" or "arbitrary", emphasize evaluative judgement about such systems or imply that they are inadvertent.

Research and theory on the psychology of organizational reward systems has been dominated by cognitive utilitarian approaches pioneered by VROOM (1964). This early work has been enriched by attention to equity (ADAMS 1965) and to justice (FOLGER and GREENBERG 1985) in employee responses to incentives, as well as to the placement of incentive systems in social (WHYTE 1955; PEARCE 1987), political (STAW 1977), and institutional contexts (EISENHARDT 1988). We hope to contribute to the development of this literature through this analysis of Hungarian organizational incentives during the period "reform communism" (late 1980s until the Spring 1990 election of a non-communist government). This form of person-based reward system is less familiar to organizational psychologists and, therefore, provides a fruitful basis for the development of general theories.

EISENHARDT (1989) suggested that empirically grounded theory creation, which arises from the juxtaposition of data and theory, leads to divergent thinking and to truly novel theories. We believe that the theory of person-based reward systems presented here is an example of the new ways of thinking that can arise in an inductive theory-building process. Our understanding of employee reward systems under reform-communism provides insights into a type of reward system that can appear in organizations throughout the world. Although sometimes more muted in other economies, these systems are not unique. Rather, their stark character in these organizations helps to illuminate psychological features of reward systems that have been difficult to study.

The theoretical arguments are based on a systematic contrast of observational and interview data collected in the late 1980s in Hungary (the American author taught in the International Management Center in Budapest in 1989) with paradigmatic theoretical work in procedural justice and learned helplessness. This grounded theory is then partially tested using questionnaire self-reports collected in a *different* sample of Hungarian organizations in early 1990 and a comparable American sample.

The paper is organized as follows. First, person-based reward systems as they existed in Hungarian state-owned organizations are described. Second, we contrast our , person-based reward concept with the extant literature on employee rewards, especially with the well-known performance-based theory of organizational rewards. Next, hypotheses about the affective and behavioral effects of person-based reward systems are developed from related literatures on procedural justice and learned helplessness. Following this, the methods and results of the hypothesis testing are reported. The paper concludes with comments on both the possible generalizability of these ideas to other settings and their functional autonomy from their political origins.

Before beginning, it is important to note that state-socialist enterprises have had substantially different task environments than either private or publicly-owned enterprises in capitalist countries. These differing environmental pressures set the contexts within which enterprise managers used the person-based reward systems to obtain the organizational behavior they needed to meet organizational objectives. Although we will briefly refer to this context throughout, space does not permit a political or an economic analysis of these systems. For a more detailed analysis of Hungary after the 1968 economic reforms, the interested reader is directed to KORNAI (1986), LAUTER (1972), and STARK (1990); additional material on enterprises in the Soviet Union is available from GREGORY (1989), GRANCELLI (1987), and LAWRENCE and VLACHOUTSICOS (1990); and, on the recent economic reforms in the People's Republic of China, from BOISOT and CHILD (1988) and NEE (1989).

PERSON-BASED ORGANIZATIONAL REWARD SYSTEMS

A person-based reward system contains two components: (1) highly valued rewards and (2) personal criteria for reward distribution. Each of these two components will be described in detail.

HIGHLY VALUED ORGANIZATIONAL REWARDS

Because it had been virtually impossible to fire employees, many Westerns have mistakenly extrapolated that under state-socialism managers controlled few powerful rewards and punishment for employees. In fact, government planners in these economies quickly recognized the unworkability of organizations without material incentives: "When workers recognised in Cuba that their labour was ineffective because of disorganization – spare parts were unavailable, inputs did not arrive on schedule, finished goods awaited transportation – whatever commitment they had was substantially undermined... Also, some workers were less motivated than others and either stayed away from work or did not exert themselves, and with low morale there is less commitment and consequently less work accomplished: a classic vicious circle. Since 1970 in Cuba more and more stress has been given to the use of traditional material incentives' (WOOD 1987).

By the 1970s, the use of powerful material incentives was adopted in state-socialist societies except in the People's Republic of China where it was delayed until 1978 because of MAO's ideologically-based Cultural Revolution. That is, in practice, managers in state-socialist economies controlled powerful material incentives which they have not hesitated to administer to obtain desired actions. The three most important organizational rewards distributed to employees at all organizational levels in Hungary were (1) promotions and perquisites, (2) bonuses, and (3) access to resources.

(1) Promotions in all organizations are one of the most valuable rewards that can be bestowed, since they are accompanied by higher salaries, more autonomous work, perquisites, enhanced status, and feelings of power (LOCKE 1976). However, promotions may be even more important in state-socialist societies than in the capitalist ones. This is because, for ideological reasons, opportunities for independent wealth creation have been limited. This has meant that most of the attractive forms of consumption (comfortable housing, foreign travel, cars, vacations in the countryside) were controlled by employers, and virtually all of these attractions became more accessible as one rose in hierarchical rank.

Foreign travel is particularly attractive in a small country such as Hungary, yet even under post-communism, foreign travel has been extremely difficult. For example, in 1990, Hungarian citizens were allowed only the equivalent of US$280 in foreign exchange every three years (which bought a very short stay in western Europe). Even after the new market freedoms brought foreign currency earnings, private persons were allowed to buy only one plane ticket per year (as a policy to build foreign currency balances). Yet, one could have unlimited travel through employers. Of course, the situation in fully state-socialist societies is even more severe: for example, private car ownership was forbidden in People's Republic of China, but cars-and-drivers come with ranking managerial positions. Now, there is widespread knowledge of the special stores, apartments, hospitals, and other privileges reserved for the elite (see SIMIS 1982; VOS-LENSKY 1984).

In these economies, promotions retained all of the capitalist advantages of increased power and income with the additional attractions of providing desirable goods and services for oneself and one's family.

(2) The use of material organizational rewards in state-socialist societies is most visible in the use of financial bonuses. Yearly bonuses play a much larger role in employee compensation in state-socialist societies than they do in capitalist ones, since a substantially larger proportion of the pay of *all* employees at all levels is "at risk" in these enterprises than in capitalist ones. In Hungary, as in other state-socialist countries, it has been normal compensation practice to provide yearly bonuses ranging from 0% to 200% of base pay. In contrast, highly variable pay is confined to only a relatively narrow range of jobs in the West. Western "merit pay" increases typically have ranged between 5% and 7% (GREELEY and OCHSNER 1986). As is the practice in all variable pay systems, relatively few employees in Hungary received no bonus at all. Nevertheless, the variation in actual take-home pay has been substantially wider for Hungarian employees than for employees in developed countries holding comparable positions.

The amount of pay at risk is even more important in these enterprises because base pay was set at bare subsistence levels. The following statistics give a flavor of how little purchasing power base wages provide: in Hungary, it took 927 hours of work to purchase a color television (versus 88 hours in the Federal Republic of Germany) or 404 hours of labor to buy an automatic washing machine (versus 83 hours in Germany) (*Heti Világ-gazdaság*, 431, September 5, 1987). In the study period, the base pay of a Hungarian employee of a state-owned enterprise usually did not cover his or her rent or mortgage payment. Although it is true that food and other necessities were subsidized, the perennial shortages often meant that, in practice, extra payments (bribes) were necessary to secure many services, such as health care. Thus, Hungarians depended on supplemental income: large bonuses and second (and even third) jobs. Such supplemental income was a vital necessity to virtually all families.

(3) The other valuable reward that organizations could administer was illicit access to organizational resources, including time off. As is common

in the organizations of the West, many managers find they can expand their available incentives by allowing favored employees to "break the rules". For example, SAYLES (1989, p. 45) suggested that successful supervisors learn to protect their subordinates, sometimes even "covering up for them". Although these practices are common in capitalist organizations (particularly in certain occupations – see MARS, 1982), such practice in Hungary were quite open and widespread. Common examples of illicit rewards in Hungary included letting certain employees leave early or allowing them to take company supplies for their own use. While most of these practices were not officially sanctioned (or formally acknowledged) by managers, neither were they aggressively prosecuted.

While these kinds of rewards may be minor to more affluent Western employees, the supply shortages can make them very valuable in state-socialist countries. An example from an interview conducted by the American researcher in November 1989:

"W": There's a rule in the company, if you build a house you can go to the main plant and buy things.

Interviewer: If you're an employee? You can buy it at a cheap price?

"W": It's not much cheaper. The thing is it's not always available in Hungary. As a company everything is available, whatever you want. If you want [-], it's available there. Their task is to have everything. It doesn't matter how much.

Interviewer: These inventories must be quite...

"W": Fantastic! Hundreds of meters...

Interviewer: This is horrible. It is horrible. It costs a lot of money...

"W": In the shops you can't get anything... OK, so I went and asked the person [warehouse foreman]. I've never seen that man before. I gave him my name. Why is he so friendly? He said, "You could get a much better type of pipe, a [-] pipe". What he offered me is much better quality. "When do I get it?" Then he says, "Tomorrow morning when you wake up go outside, you'll have it next to your house". The next morning I went out and I found this huge heap of pipe. A huge heap. A coach load of eight meters long... I was able to sell to five other [building cooperatives].*

* In Hungary at the time of data collection, the waiting list for subsidized state apartments was many years long, and in 1989 the price of a modest apartment was 20 to 30 times annual earnings. Therefore, an individual seeking an apartment often joined with others in a cooperative that collectively would build an apartment building in which individual members would then own their own apartments. Prices were so high that most cooperatives just built the outer shells and individuals had to finish their own apartments using their own supplies and labor. This process often lasted several years because of high supply costs and the difficulty of finding additional free time after working at the necessary second and third jobs.

Interviewer: These are hard pipes to get that you couldn't get in the store?

"W": You can't get them anywhere.

Interviewer: The other cooperative people must have loved you when you walked up with these pipes.

"W": In the afternoon I had no pipe left... Everybody just rushed, took it and paid and went away. I didn't want the [extra] pipe.

In summary, state-socialist organizations wield rewards that are highly valued by many employees. Managers found that they needed material rewards to prevent a vicious circle of demoralization and performance shirking. These rewards were all the more attractive because the endemic shortages and restrictive economic and public policies meant that organizations retained virtual monopolies over access to certain attractive goods and services.

PERSONAL CRITERIA FOR REWARD DISTRIBUTION

Before discussing the criteria, the processes by which these organizational rewards were distributed need to be described. For promotions, the process was much like that in capitalist countries: executives decided behind closed doors. The only difference (until late 1989 in Hungary) was a legally mandated role fort the communist party. However, by 1990, by all reports, the communist party as an institution no longer wielded significant decision influence.

Bonuses were determined by a formal "quadrangle" committee composed of supervisors (or higher ranking managers, if they preferred not to delegate these decisions) at one corner, the [communist] party representative at the second, the labor union representatives at the third, and the communist youth organization at the fourth. The deliberations (and relative influence of the parties) were kept in strict secrecy, and no formal measures of employee performance or productivity were used in these decisions. With the waning influence of the party, supervisors have assumed control of bonus decisions.

Access to resources was informal and could be given by supervisors, higher ranking managers, peers, and even lower-ranking employees. Certainly, the higher an individual's hierarchical rank, the more resources that person was likely to control, but even individuals of formally low rank (such as the warehouseman in the above quotation) might hold positions allowing valued access.

With such powerful rewards at a management's command, who was rewarded and why? Persistent questioning of middle managers and employees yielded two distinct views: (1) there is no reason at all; and (2) those who have good personal relationships with distributors received the rewards. The prevalence of the belief in no criteria at all is reflected in the following passage describing a discussion during training for executives (heads or deputy heads of the regional offices) in a large state-owned company in September 1989:

> In their organization, the central office collects all of the revenue and then makes decisions about the allocation of funds to the regional offices. They said that one of the problems was that "central" did not make its decisions based on "the best economic sense". They offered anecdotes about the recent allocation of a "big machine" to illustrate... I aggressively tried to push them to use the [resource dependence] model to analyze central's criteria. If not economic criteria, then it must be something else... what? "M" said that it is the "big mouths" who get the machines. So I said, does that mean that central is trying to obtain a peaceful existence? No response. Another said that at meetings managers try to sit next to the general manager, because if they can get his ear they may get a bigger allocation. Many repeatedly mentioned the importance of keeping "good relations" with central. I kept trying to push them to explain what they meant by "good relations". They seem to mean simple friendliness, having coffee with someone. An older manager, who had been drinking heavily during the day, said, "Central depends on itself". There was only one person there from central and he was not providing any concrete answers to my pressing for central's criteria for resource allocation. Later, over dinner, I asked one of the other managers about the central manager's nonresponse and he said that he thought that this manager from central was too junior and so really did not know central's criteria.

There is substantial evidence that these top executives do, indeed, "depend on themselves" more than executives do in market-driven organizations and that they are comparatively less dependent on the performance of their employees. With virtually all resources coming from governmental allocation, power was much more centralized than in market-driven organizations (BIHARI 1980; MARKÓCZY 1990). Managers in market-driven organizations depend on their employees for new product ideas, for service quality, and to take the initiative, in numerous small ways, in solving problems and improving customer and client responsiveness (GALBRAITH 1978; THOMPSON 1967). They also need to maintain the flexibility to respond rapidly to changing markets. In state-socialist economies, virtually all revenue, as well as permissions and regulations, came from centralized governmental decisions, so executives learned to focus their attention up, rather than down or laterally.

This uncertainty in the criteria used by top management in its allocation decisions was exacerbated by the practice of many top executives (or top party officials) to receive complaints and problems of all sorts and then magnanimously help some supplicants. In this process, all appeals are personal and all assistance is given personally, as favors. Although middle managers are bypassed for these favors, they might be more important in some allocations, such as for bonuses. Therefore, everyone believed that the "the top" had power, but who else had what other powers was unclear. This illustration is from an interview in October 1989 with a politician involved in writing the government's new democratic constitution:

> Last week the parliament passed a bill removing the [communist] party from the workplace. I again asked my question: what difference does it make if the party no longer runs the government and the enterprises are privatized? He said that for the past two years it [the formal involvement of party officials in personnel decisions] hasn't made much difference to the general manager, since the party no longer instils fear or monopolizes resource distribution... However, for those at the very bottom the party is still seen as significant in decision making. Non-managerial employees do not have detailed information about the party's power loss, since decisions are made behind closed doors. He said that party officials would certainly try to hide their loss of power with the general manager, since then they would lose the influence they have over employees.

This conspiracy of silence about reward allocation processes is pervasive, as illustrated by this excerpt from HARASZTI's participant observer's study of factory millers (1977, pp. 98–102): "Supplementary wages are our most frequent topic of conversation with the foremen. They have at their disposal a relatively large sum for the adjustment of individual wages. No one knows exactly how much, nor whether all or part of it is used up. The foremen's accounts never mention 'deficits' or 'outgoings' or in the 'official bulletin of results'... The foremen, setters and inspectors never once mentioned the existence of supplements, and it was only some time after my arrival that I heard about it from old M... Only one thing is certain: the foremen resist paying supplementary wages. Each worker therefore concludes that if there are two many demands less will be left for him... So each worker treats what he gets as a supplemental wage as a secret... Information I got from other millers slipped out unawares in a moment of anger."

Of course, as LANGER (1975) has demonstrated, people have a difficult time accepting that the rationale for the way important rewards are allocated is unknown and, therefore, genuinely uncontrollable. Furthermore, allocators ultimately had to use some method, however, arbitrary, to distribute limited resources. As is indicated by the above passages, the most common view was that "personal relationship" were the basis of reward distribution decisions. That is, distributors will reward their friends and punish their enemies. Of course, friendships can be based on productivity or the performance of useful services; still, the belief in the importance of proximity and "friendliness" among interviewees remained strong and unshaken. This reward system is much like traditional systems of personal patronage (WEBER 1947).

Although the criterion of personal relations for reward distribution may seem less ambiguous than "no reason at all", in practice, it too could be highly uncertain. In these centralized and complex industrial societies, one's "good connections" may or may not deliver, and the supplicant often does not know why. Further, the opportunities to develop personal relationships with the truly powerful top executives were limited for most employees. While social scientists can trace the dependencies that actually may account for the flow of rewards (for example, see KORNAI and MATITS 1987), participants in organizations act on what they believe to be the criteria for reward distribution (VROOM 1964). In Hungary during this period, everyone believed in the value of personal relationships; unfortunately, for most people they were difficult to obtain.

This description can be summarized by comparing person-based reward systems to one type of reward system that has received substantial research attention, "performance-based systems". The ideal performance-based system provides valued rewards for clear, controllable job behaviors (LAWLER 1981). Employees should be clear about what behaviors are to be rewarded, and much of the motivation literature in (Western) organizational behavior emphasized the importance of clarity. For example, KERR (1975) chided managers for a lack of clarity in the behaviors that would be rewarded, and LAWLER (1971) emphasized the importance of unambiguously attaching truly valued rewards to desired workplace behaviors. From this perspective, person-based reward systems could be seen as a familiar kind of "failure to reward performance".

However, we suggest that person-based reward systems should not be seen as inadvertent incompetence but rather as systems designed to obtain the behaviors desired – specifically, tractability. Allocators making personal judgements centralize power in their own hands. If subordinates "caused trouble", even if the trouble was unrelated to job performance, they might jeopardize their bonuses (and their travel and their apartments, as well). We suggest that arbitrary personal criteria, rather than being "mistakes", were the result of a strategy to foster compliance and dependence by a government/employer not interested in testing its mandate in contested elections. While disingenuousness about what is rewarded really is well-known in nominally performance-based reward systems (e.g. KERR 1975), person-based systems have two distinctive characteristics: (1) the high value of the rewards to employees, and (2) the absence of formal criteria and rules. Further, isolating these two distinguishing features helps to illuminate several important affective and behavioral reactions of person-based system participants.

AFFECTIVE EFFECTS
OF PERSON-BASED REWARDS

Although these person-based organizational reward systems were largely successful in producing relatively tractable employees, they entailed substantial costs. These workplaces were characterized by several affective and behavioral "dysfunctions" that we propose were a direct consequence of the use of person-based reward systems. Drawing on the research on procedural justice and learned helplessness, as well as the field interviews and observations, hypotheses regarding the effects of this type organizational reward system have been developed.

UNFAIR ORGANIZATIONS

Procedural justice theory focuses on the reactions of individuals to just or unjust procedures (THIBAUT and WALKER 1975; FOLGER and GREENBERG 1985). LEVENTHAL (1980) argued that just procedures serve to suppress bias, create consistent allocations, rely on accurate information, are correctable, and consider the concerns of all participants. Focusing specifically on procedural justice in organizational allocations, FOLGER and GREENBERG (1985) emphasized the importance of openness or publicness of criteria in the perceptions that pay systems will be perceived as fair. With their characteristic secrecy and use of personalistic criteria, we believe that person-based systems can be characterized as procedurally unjust.

The substantial experimental evidence on reactions to procedural (in)justice suggests possible reactions to person-based reward systems that we found mirrored in our observations. In a comprehensive review of research on procedural justice, LIND and TYLER (1988) drew conclusions about the affective effects of injustice: it results in a perception of system unfairness and in a lowered evaluation of authorities and institutions. Therefore,

> *H1: Employees will perceive their person-based organizational reward systems as more unfair than will employees with other types of reward systems.*

NEGATIVE EVALUATIONS OF OTHERS

Consistent with , LIND and TYLER, there is also evidence that those in authority often were negatively evaluated under person-based systems. However, in these highly centralized and secretive organizations, the responsibility of those below the very top was unclear. Hostility was not focused invariably on managers (who could represent expertise and efficiency) but more often on party representatives. In an extension of procedural justice research, managers in these organizations sometimes held negative evaluations of those below them. The American investigator's notes from a managerial training seminar in April 1989 provide an illustration of these "downward", negative evaluations:

> One manager said he withheld information from his subordinates "because they couldn't handle it", and several other managers chimed in their agreement... I don't yet fully understand these man-

agers' discussion of their "paid enemies", "spies", and "black-mailers" among their subordinates. [Detailed description of how managers must cheat to meet their production targets in a shortage economy.] Once a manager has cheated, he or she is subject to black-mail... How can managers exercise "authority" over someone willing and able to expose him or her? It increases the general level of secrecy and restricted communication. As one manager said, "Because of these paid enemies among my subordinates, I need to distrust even the good ones".

In, LIND and TYLER'S experiments, authority figures were negatively evaluated because they were seen as responsible for procedural injustices. These observational and interview data reflect additional lateral and downward negative evaluations, because it was difficult in these organizations to identify clearly who caused an injustice. Authority was split between management and the party, and accountability was avoided by those who felt they had no possible control. The combination of a desire to blame and uncertainty about who was clearly responsible leads to the choice of different targets in different settings, depending on the actions or personal characteristics of the particular individuals involved. However, we expect that, on average,

> *H2: Person-based organizational reward systems will be associated with relatively more negative employee evaluations of supervisors and coworkers than will other types of organizational reward systems.*

Further, person-based organizational reward systems provided conditions much like those in the learned helplessness experiments. The literature on learned helplessness focuses on reactions to negative sanctions over which the recipients believe they have no control (HIROTO and SELIGMAN 1975; WORTMAN and BREHM 1976). While research on the effects of learned helplessness appears in a wide range of subdisciplines, the work focusing on task performance evaluation provides several insights applicable to person-based organizational rewards CARVER, BLANEY and SCHEIER (1979), COYNE, METALSKY and LAVELLE (1980), and KUHL (1981) concluded that task-based learned helplessness provoked anxiety and self-inefficacy.

ANXIETY

Employees in these person-based systems lacked the security imparted by clear rules and procedures. They had difficulty knowing whether they had done enough or if additional efforts might be worthwhile. One might have had a good connection but could never be sure whether that connection would (or could) deliver when needed. Such uncertainty is palpable in the above quotation from HARASZTI describing the behavior of machinists who were dubious about whether or not they had received their "due" supplemental wages. Therefore,

> H3: *Under person-based reward systems, employees report relatively more anxiety than is reported by employees working under other organizational reward systems.*

INEFFICACY

A sense of self-inefficacy was also observed in these person-based systems. Employees often were unsure which actions would be effective and which would not, and even high-ranking managers would complain that "they could do nothing". With the distribution of valuable rewards based on secretive personal criteria in these complex systems, all of the participants felt powerless. When employees did receive rewards, they did not know exactly why, and when they did not achieve a desired reward, they could never be sure whether it was the result of some ineffective action on their part or of some unknownable series of events. This response seemed to generalize to their assumptions about their colleagues and their organizations. Employees not only doubted that they would be able to succeed, they also believed their colleagues, supervisors and organizations to be ineffective. Research on learned helplessness suggest that these person-based reward systems may be a major reason for the pervasive Hungarian self-denigration described by LÖVEY (1986),

> H4: *Employees in person-based systems will report less efficacy for themselves, their colleagues, and their organizations than will be reported by employees in other systems.*

Thus, it is hypothesized that person-based reward systems lead to the affective reactions of system distrust, negative evaluations of others, anxiety, and low perceptions of efficacy. The tests of these hypotheses are reported in the next section.

BEHAVIORAL EFFECTS OF PERSON-BASED SYSTEMS

Several of the behavioral reactions observed in these state-owned enterprises are consistent with what would be predicted from research on procedural justice and learned helplessness. In addition, these interview and observational data suggest other effects consistent with their theoretical perspectives but not tested by these psychologists. Unfortunately, our existing comparative data do not allow us to test these ideas systematically. However, their discussion here in propositional form provides a more complete theory grounded in the qualitative data and literatures on procedural justice and learned helplessness. LIND and TYLER (1988) concluded their literature review of procedural justice research by noting that perceived injustice leads to more dispute and protest behavior, greater interpersonal conflict, and lowered compliance with laws.

DISPUTATIONS

Dispute and protest behaviors were common in face-to-face encounters and in collective settings, such as trade union meetings. However, one of the most distinctive forms in which these behaviors were manifest was pervasive bargaining. To illustrate, it was widely assumed that employees viewed their "base pay" as pay for "just showing up" and their bonus money as potential payment for any work they might perform. This led supervisors and subordinates to haggle continually over job assignments and payments. Subordinates believed that aggressive bargaining was the only way to get their "fair shares" of the bonus money that they suspected the supervisor was retaining. For example, one personnel director of a large state-owned industrial organization described how he wanted to establish a performance appraisal system. He asked one of his professional staff members to head the cross-functional task force to design the system. She would not agree until he told her "how much she would be paid". She knew that the director retained some bonus money "in his desk drawer", and she expected to be paid for this extra task. This sort of task-based financial negotiation is relatively rare among professionals in western organizations, yet it is all too familiar to state enterprise managers in Hungary,

> *P1: Under person-based reward systems, employees initiate more bargaining for rewards than do employees working under other reward systems.*

WITHHOLD INFORMATION

The protest behavior predicted from learned helplessness research often took an indirect form in many Hungarian state-owned organizations. With powerful rewards and punishments at the command of bosses, often, overt disputes were risky. Rather, employees would sometimes withhold information from coworkers and supervisors. Partly, this was an aid in bargaining (as for HARASZTI's foremen described above). But it also became a form of protest behavior: the plans and directives could be "shown" to be wrong if employees let others go ahead using faulty data and assumption.

> P2: Under person-based reward systems, employees withhold more information from one another than do employees working under other systems.

AVOID COMPLEX COLLABORATIVE TASKS

Additional behavioral effects more particular to the managerial job were observed. In an environment in which most interchanges became bargaining sessions, managers learned to avoid asking for assistance. Each time managers must begin unexpected projects or solve new problems, they must "use" their bargaining resources. Since managers must hoard their scarce resources, it is easy to understand that they may be unwilling to "spend" their precious resources to help one another unless the exchange is part of some larger bargain between them.

The implications of this practice for organizational coordination and flexibility in response to changing environments are clear. In rapidly changing environments, managers would soon deplete their resources, and the complexity of the deals would overhwhelm their bargaining and resource capacity. Thus, organizational work that was complex and required collaboration across units was avoided,

> P3: Those working under person-based reward systems tend to avoid complex, collaborative tasks to a greater extent than do those working under other reward systems.

INGRATIATION

Those working under person-based reward systems believed that good relations with the high ranking would be rewarded. Thus, it is not surprising that many would try to develop good connections with people at the top. Yet, because power so centralized, access to the truly powerful for many employees usually was limited. The following passage describes the American investigator's reaction to one manager's seizing a rare opportunity:

> At the training for "T" managers, I was surprised to see one of the regional managers toadying to the human resources director who visited on the last day. This regional manager hung around the director whenever he could, his heretofore aggressive demeanor turned sweet and mild. I had admired him as an aggressive fighter (even if he did step on a few toes). Yet now he followed the director around like a fawning puppy, literally waiting to be the last to see him at the end of the training.

Of course, all reward systems are designed to encourage certain employee behaviors and to discourage others, and toadying hardly is unknown in the West. However, in systems with clearer allocation criteria, employees can "ingratiate" themselves through performance on those criteria. In person-based systems, the only reliable method to obtain the desired rewards is through personal ingratiation tactics, such as charm, wit or toadying. If employees believe that good connections with the high ranking, based on nothing more substantial than friendship, are the routes to rewards, they will invest their energy in such personal ingratiation,

> *P4: Those working under person-based reward systems tend to engage in relatively more personal ingratiation with potential reward allocators than will those in other types of reward systems.*

RULE COMPLIANCE

LIND and TYLER (1988) reported that there was more rule breaking and less law compliance among those who felt that their systems were not procedurally just. Law breaking in state-socialist societies has been well-documented (e.g. SIMIS 1982). GREGORY (1989) analyzed why Soviet managers needed to violate rules in order to solve the problems created by supply breakdowns and incompatible directives. The quotations provided throughout this paper reflect insubordination, theft and blackmail. Although anger at an unjust system was not the only reason for rule breaking, nevertheless, research in procedural justice suggests person-based reward systems may make a significant contribution to the problem,

> *P5: Person-based organizational reward systems foster relatively more rule noncompliance than do other types of organizational reward systems.*

METHOD

SAMPLE AND PROCEDURES

The sample used to test the hypotheses about the affective effects of person-based reward systems consists of the employees and managers in eight organizations: three state-owned Hungarian enterprises, two private Hungarian companies, a state-owned American university, and two large American corporations. The Hungarian organizations were different from the ones used to develop the theory, and no managers or employees had undergone "Western-style training" prior to data collection. An attempt was made to survey the entire population of Hungarian employees; however, poor records and a low response rate limited the samples.

Hungarian state-owned enterprises

The porcelain factory was founded in 1777 by a count on his estate in remote wooded mountains in what is today just inside the border with Slovakia. It produces china goods, figurines and porcelain fancy goods, with about 80% of its products sold in Hungary through the state retail distribution network and a small number of their own shops. At the time of data collection in early 1990, it had 1045 employees, many of whom were grandchildren and great grandchildren of former porcelain factory employees. One-hundred and eighty-four questionnaires were received from a sample of 780 managers and employees who received them through company internal mail (19% response rate).

The sheet glass manufacturer, located in a northern industrial city, was established in 1893 and was controlled by non-Hungarian owners until its nationalization in 1949. Its primary customers were domestic construction companies, with about 15% of sales from Western exports. At the time of data collection the company produced four major types of glass (drawn sheet glass, safety glass, security glass, and insulating glass) and had over

2000 employees. Company psychologists distributed surveys to 1760 employees, and 271 usable surveys were returned to the researchers (14% response rate).

The advertising agency was one of the two advertising agencies in Hungary until the reforms of the 1980s permitted the formation of small partnerships. It was founded in 1968 as part of the New Economic mechanism reforms and focused on developing advertising for state-owned organizations conducting foreign trade. In early 1990 the agency had 118 employees, and surveys were received from 30 of the 94 agency employees and managers surveyed (32% response rate).

Hungarian privately-owned companies

The business machines manufacturer was founded in the early 1980s as a "cooperative" by four engineers who left their jobs in the national postal service because they felt their employer was not adequately developing their ideas for coin- and bill-counting machines. (In Hungary the postal service is also the major institution for small savers.) The Hungarian postal service soon became the first customer for this cooperative's lines of coin- and bill-counting and other small business machines. Their reliable machines were sold in the CMEA countries where the business machine manufacturer had become adept in the complex arrangements necessary to receive payments for their products. At the time of data collection, the cooperative had become a "share-holding company" and had two primary manufacturing facilities in two small towns. At the time questionnaires were distributed, it had 72 employees, with 32 usable surveys returned to the researchers from a sample of 60 (53% response rate).

The speciality lamps manufacturer, which also began as a "cooperative", was started in 1983 by a man who had owned and operated his own company until he was forced out of business during the communist nationalizations of the late 1940s. It produced specialty lamps and chandeliers, primarily for hotels and other large corporate customers. In addition, at the time of data collection, it was serving as a subcontracting manufacturer for robotic parts for a (then) West German company. It had 40 employees in early 1990 when 14 usable surveys were mailed to the researchers from 36 distributed to employees (39% response rate).

American organizations

Questionnaires containing some of the same scales as those distributed in the Hungarian organizations were distributed in three American organizations, one state-owned and two privately-owned corporations. The first is a large state-owned research university. Questionnaires were distributed in early 1989, in group settings, to a random sample of the non-academic professional and managerial employees. One hundred and eighty-five employees returned completed questionnaires (a 60% response rate). The second is a regional office of one of the largest international public accounting firms. All of the non-partner professional accountants received questionnaires in late 1985. The questionnaires were distributed and returned by mail, with 62 usable responses (a 67% response rate). The third American organization was an aerospace division of one the largest American manufacturing corporations. All of the 284 engineers and engineering technicians in three "groups" in the aerospace division received questionnaires late in 1988. Two hundred and twenty-three usable questionnaires were obtained (a 79% response rate). In all Hungarian and American organizations, the respondents were promised anonymity, and they and their managers received summary feedback of the results.

MEASURES

All of the measures reported here appeared in the Hungarian surveys; however, three of these measures were not available from the earlier American instruments. The scale construction, reliabilities, construct and discriminant validity of the scales used in both the American and Hungarian organizations is reported in PEARCE, SOMMER, MORRIS and FRIDEGER (1993). Two scales used only in the Hungarian sample, Non-Merit Criteria and Nepotism, were developed in a Saudi Arabian sample with the scale development reported in AL-AIBAN and PEARCE (1993). Only the Organizational Innovation scale was developed for the Hungarian data collection.

All of the questions were originally developed in English. For the Hungarian data collection, these questions were translated into Hungarian and then back-translated into English to check translation accuracy (BRISLIN 1986). Because ADLER, CAMPBELL and LAURENT (1989) reported that the factor structure of their scales was not replicated in their sample of managers from the People's Republic of China, all of these scales were factor analyzed again on this Hungarian sample. Using a rotated varimax procedure, items were retained for a factor if they loaded at least 0.40 on the target factor and at least 0.10 greater on any other factors. Using this conservative procedure, none of the items on scales developed in the American and Saudi samples cross-loaded onto any other scale in the Hungarian sample (although a few original items were dropped from the scales). Thus our confidence in the comparability of the scales was strengthened when this factor analysis in the Hungarian sample repro-duced the same scales as had the analyses on the American and Saudi samples. We believe the surprisingly strong corredspondence between the factor structures in these different countries can be accounted for by the following: (1) these scales had originally been developed in large multi-organizational public and private sector samples; (2) questionnaires were administered in contexts where respondents did not feel intimidated; and (3) the careful correspondence of the translations. The Appendix contains the items for all of the scales used in hypothesis testing. The means, stan-dard deviations, internal consistency reliabilities and intercorrelations among these scales appear in *Table 1*.

Table 1. Means, standard deviations,
internal consistency reliabilities, and intercorrelations
among self-report scales

Variable	X̄	S.D.	1	2	3	4	5	6	7	8	9	10
1. Non-merit criteria	3.75†	0.76	(79)									
2. Nepotism practiced	3.29†	1.00	54	(61)								
3. Job performance rewarded	2.89	0.93	–60	–33	(86)							
4. Organizational trust-worthiness	3.11	0.67	–60	–50	47	(86)						
5. Supervisory favoritism	2.86	0.89	32	25	–19	–34	(63)					
6. Exploitive coworkers	2.73	0.77	18	22	–14	–39	51	(73)				
7. Job security anxiety	3.15	0.94	–44	–26	46	52	–24	–18	(57)			
8. Coworker effort	3.25	0.76	–45	–22	32	39	–26	–27	41	(77)		
9. Organizational innova-tion	2.81†	0.78	–43	–18	29	17	–14	–00‡	38	35	(72)	
10. Own quality standards	3.94	0.68	16	10	–08	–17	10	08	–04‡	–04‡	–07‡	(63)

* All scales five-point LIKERT-type with 1 = strongly disagree to 5 = strongly agree.
† *n* = 351; rest *n* = 851.
‡ *Not* statistically significant (*p* ≤ 0.05).

SYSTEM CLASSIFICATION

While it was expected that the Hungarian state-owned organizations would have person-based systems and that the private Hungarian and American organizations would use more performance-based systems, it was necessary to test the validity of this classification. While both person-based and performance-based reward systems can have highly valued rewards, the criteria for administration should differ.

In *Table 2*, the employees report that the Hungarian state-owned organizations were significantly more likely to use non-merit criteria and nepotism than were the Hungarian privately-owned companies. In addition, employees in the Hungarian state-owned organizations reported significantly less likelihood that job performance would be rewarded than was reported in Hungarian privately-owned or in their type of American organization. Therefore, although the Hungarian private organizations also controlled powerful rewards (and the economic reforms had weakened the monopoly position of all Hungarian employers in 1990), the employees' percpeitons of the criteria for reward allocation led us to classify the three Hungarian state-owned enterprises as "person-based systems" and the two Hungarian private companies and the American state-owned university and two businesses as "performance-based systems".

Table 2. Employee perceptions of reward system criteria
in state-owned and private companies

| | Hungarian | | American | | | | | |
	State-owned*	Privately-owned	State-owned	Privately-owned	df	SS	F	Eta
Non-merit criteria	3.89	2.80	–	–	1	43.23	97.25†	0.48
Error					319	141.79		
Nepotism practice	3.41	2.48	–	–	1	31.74	35.47†	0.32
Error					319	285.40		
Job performance rewarded	2.38‡	2.96	2.92	3.37	3	136.40	64.66†	0.30
Error					838	587.13		
n	293	43	234	281				

* All scales five-point LIKERT-type with 1 = strongly disagree to 5 = strongly agree.
†$p < 0.01$.
‡Hungarian state-owned significantly lower than all others; American privately-owned significantly higher than all others.

RESULTS

HYPOTHESIS 1

Employees working under person-based systems were expected to perceive their systems as more unfair than would employees working under non-person-based systems. *Table 3* reports the employees' perceptions of the fairness of their organizational rewards systems ("Organizational trustworthiness"). Consistent with the hypothesis, the employees of the Hungarian state-owned organization were significantly more likely to report that their organization's personnel system was unfair than were the employees in the non-person-based reward systems perceive their systems as less fair than the Hungarians and Americans working under performance-based organizational reward systems.

Table 3. Employee evaluation of organizational trustworthiness, their supervisors, coworkers, job security and efficacy

	Hungarian		American					
	State-owned*	Privately-owned	State-owned	Privately-owned	df	SS	F	Eta
Organizational trustworthiness	2.78†	3.46	3.00	3.29	3	22.96	18.83‡	0.30
Error					560	227.58		
Supervisory favoritism	2.98§	2.49	2.74	2.86	3	12.45	5.29‡	0.14
Error					793	622.24		
Exploitive coworkers	2.80 ‖	2.40	2.70	2.74	3	6.22	3.53‡	0.11
Error					822	483.11		
Job security anxiety	2.49[1]	3.63	3.48	3.49	3	196.15	100.22‡	0.51
Error					847	552.59		
Coworker effort	2.93[1]	3.52	3.41	3.45	3	46.66	30.12‡	0.32
Error					769	397.06		
Organizational innovation	2.72	3.40	–	–	1	16.56	30.04‡	0.30
Error					298	164.33		
Own quality standards	3.82[2]	3.74	4.05	4.02	3	9.52	6.94‡	0.16
Error					783	358.36		
n	293	43	234	281				

* All scales five-point LIKERT-type, with 1 = strongly disagree and 5 = strongly agree.
‡ $p < 0.01$.
† Hungarian state-owned significantly lower than all others; American state-owned significantly lower than American privately-owned.
§ Hungarian state-owned significantly higher than Hungarian privately-owned and American state-owned; American privately-owned higher than Hungarian privately-owned and American state-owned.
‖ Hungarian state-owned and American privately-owned significantly higher than Hungarian privately-owned.
[1] Hungarian state-owned significantly lower than all others.
[2] Both Hungarian types significantly lower than both American types.

HYPOTHESIS 2

Employees in organizations with person-based organizational reward systems were expected to report more negative evaluations of their supervisors and coworkers than would be reported by employees in organizations with other kinds of reward systems. Negative evaluations are assessed with the scales "Supervisory favoritism" and "Exploitive coworkers". As can be seen in *Table 3*, this hypothesis was largely supported. The employees in the person-based Hungarian state-owned organizations were significantly more likely to report that their supervisors engaged in favortism than were their counterparts in the organizations. However, the employees in both the Hungarian state-owned organizations and the two American privately-owned organizations were significantly more likely to perceive their coworkers as exploitive than were the employees in the private Hungarian organization or in the American state-owned university. Although this pattern of results is largely consistent with the expectations for more negative evaluation in person-based systems, the results do suggest that factors other than reward systems can also contribute to negative evaluations.

HYPOTHESIS 3

Person-based system employees were expected to report greater workplace anxiety than would employees working under other organizational reward systems. The closest measure to workplace anxiety is employees' reported anxiety about their job security. Of course, the Hungarian state-owned sector was expected to have to reorganize at the time of questionnaire administration in early 1990 (although no layoffs had been conducted in these organizations). However, this needs to be compared to the very real job insecurity of the employees in the American privately-owned organizations who were public accountants facing stringent "up-or-out" promotion policies and aerospace engineers in a highly cyclical industry, as well as the uncertain future of the Hungarian entrepreneurial companies. In *Table 3*, it can be seen that the person-based system employees reported significantly more anxiety about their job security than did the employees in any of the other organizations. Thus, for this one measure, person-based system employees did report greater workplace anxiety than was reported by non-person-based system employees.

HYPOTHESIS 4

Finally, employees working under person-based reward systems were expected to perceive themselves, their coworkers and their organizations as less efficacious than would employees under non- person-based reward systems. This hypothesis was tested using reports of employees' "Own quality standards", "Coworker effort", and "Organizational innovation". In *Table 3*, it can be seen that the Hungarian employees in both sectors reported themselves as having significantly lower quality standards than the America employees in both sectors reported for themselves. However, reports of coworker effort and organizational innovation are consistent with the hypothesis that employees working under person-based organizational reward systems will perceive their colleagues and organizations as less efficacious than will employees in non-person-based systems.

To summarize, the results of the hypothesis testing are consistent with the hypothesized affective effects of person-based reward systems. Thus, the generalization of the paradigmatic theories of procedural justice and learned helplessness to predict the affective reactions of employees in person-based reward systems has been supported. Each of these tests is imperfect, for they lack the inability to control all of the possible unmeasured variables (for examples, the occupations and skills across organizational types) and are cross-sectional rather than causal, which limits our confidence that type, and only type, caused the difference. Nevertheless, they do, when taken as a whole, provide an independent confirmation of the hypotheses developed from the observations grounded in theories of procedural justice and learned helplessness.

CONCLUSION

This study provides a theory derived from the paradigmatic work on procedural justice and learned helplessness, which has been grounded in observations of Hungarian state-owned organizational reward practices during the period of "reform-communism". It was argued that person-based systems lead to employee perceptions that their organizations were unfair, to negative evaluations of others at work, to anxiety, and to feelings that they, their colleagues and their organizations were inefficacious. Self-report perceptions of employees in the three Hungarian state-owned organizations categorized as having person-based systems and in the five more performance-based organizations in Hungary and the United States were consistent with these hypotheses. In addition, several behavioral effects of person-based reward systems were suggested which could not be tested with these data, such as, person-based systems lead employees to more frequent bargaining with one another, to withhold information, to avoid collaborative tasks, to engage in more personal ingratiation behaviors, and to avoid rule compliance. Although this research is preliminary and incomplete, nevertheless, the movement between field observation linked to paradigmatic theories and hypothesis testing in a separate sample, when possible, provides the basis for a comprehensive theory of a very complex (and timely) phenomenon.

The affective and behavioral dysfunctions resulting from the person-based organizational reward systems documented here are not trivial ones for organizational performance. Employee distrust has been shown to lead to individual performance shirking, lying and cheating (ROTTER 1980), and serious systemic malfunction (GAMBETTA 1988). Negative evaluations of coworkers and supervisors have been shown to lead to turnover (STEERS and MOWDAY 1981) and absenteesim (STEERS and RHODES 1978). Although there has not been comparable research documenting the effects of bargaining, behaviors such as withholding information, avoidance of collaboration, and rule-breaking would seem to be cause for serious concern.

In state-socialist societies, it is traditional for authorities to respond to criticism with a declaration that the proper measures have been taken and the problem no longer exists. For example, in the transcript of HARASZTI'S trial (for the participant observer's account which we have quoted), the judge sought to dismiss his portrayal of factory life as no longer accurate because the factory he described had been absorbed into a conglomerate (HARASZTI 1977, p. 164). While this work is not intended as a criticism, clearly it is not a flattering portrait of reward systems in the earliest period of economic transition. It is particularly tempting, since there has been an epochal change with a freely elected non-communist government assuming power in Hungary in 1990, to conclude that this is a description of a system that was unique to a particular set of historical circumstances that now have passed. Yet, we are cautious about unilateral declarations that these dysfunctions no longer exist. A valuable area for future research would be the tracking of changes in affect and behavior as the transformation unfolds.

For the formerly communist countries seeking to transform their economies, this question is compelling. While the political conditions in

Hungary that created these organizational reward systems have changed, many of the structural features have not (for example, state ownership still dominates the economy). The feelings of unfairness and distrust that pervaded these workplaces have not disappeared overnight. There is every reason to believe that these affective and behavioral effects will have considerable functional autonomy from their originating conditions. Individuals who feel that others are getting unfair advantages are not going to respond to the calls by newly non-communist managers for commitment to productivity and self-sacrifice.

Certainly, we expect there to be important boundary conditions to the phenomenon, but we cannot be certain what they might be. For example, an important research question is whether partially person-based systems may have similar effects. Is there a certain "threshold" beyond which these affective and behavioral effects would be found? Or, do some of the affective and behavioral effects appear in partial or weaker forms? Future research is needed to test hypotheses about person-based systems, as well as what the boundary conditions are to establish these affective and behavioral effects.

We expect that versions of person-based organizational reward systems are probably more common in the capitalist countries than is generally acknowledged. For example, OUCHI'S (1980) "clans" and BOISOT and CHILD'S (1988) "fiefs" may have person-based reward systems for their individual participants. The Hungarian organizations studied here did have many of the characteristics of such clans and fiefs, and, therefore, some of these dysfunctional affective and behavioral effects may also appear in clans, fiefdoms, and similar types of organizations. Attention to such non-bureaucratic organizational forms in the Western organization behavior literature is in its infancy, and we hope this unflattering account may serve as a counterbalance to the somewhat romanticized portraits of clans offered by OUCHI (1980). While it may have been unintended, OUCHI'S use of terms that emphasize the warm, familial aspects of such organizations may not accurately portray the actual affective and behavioral reactions of all employees, particularly those at the lowest levels. After all, employees traditionally have attempted to protect themselves by fostering greater "bureaucratization" through clearer procedures and due-process protections from arbitrary treatment (JACOBY 1985). This work suggests that research on employee reactions in these and other "non-bureaucratic" organizations may provide a broader perspective on the role of alternative organizational forms.

REFERENCES

ADAMS, J. S.: "Inequity in social exchange." In: BERKOWITZ, L. (ed.): *Advances in Experimental Social Psychology*, Vol. 2, Academic Press, New York, pp. 267–299 (1965).

ADLER, N. J., CAMPBELL, N., LAURENT, A.: "In search of appropriate methodology: From outside the People's Republic of China looking in", *Journal of International Business Studies,*20, pp. 61–74 (1989).

AL-AIBAN, K., PEARCE, J. L.: "The influence of values on management practices: A test in Saudi Arabia and the United States", *International Studies of Management and Organization,* 23 (3), pp. 35–52 (1993).

BIHARI, M.: "A döntésmechanizmus szervezeti, hatalmi és érdekkörnyezete" (The organizational, power, and interests framework for decision making). In: BIHARI, M. (ed.): *Közigazgatás és Politika (Public Administration and Politics)*, Kossuth Könyvkiadó, Budapest (1980).

BOISOT, M., CHILD, J.: "The iron law of fiefs: Bureaucratic failure and the problem of governance in the Chinese economic reforms", *Administrative Science Quarterly,* 33, pp. 507–527 (1988).

BRISLIN, R. W.: "The wording and translation of research instruments." In: LONNER, WALTER J., BERRY, JOHN W. (eds): *Field Methods in Cross Cultural Research,* Sage, Beverly Hills, CA (1986).

CARVER, C. S., BLANEY, P. H., SCHEIER, M. F.: "Reassertion and giving up: The interactive role of self-directed attention and outcome expectancy", *Journal of Personality and Social Psychology,* 37, pp. 859–870 (1979).

COYNE, J. C., METALSKY, G. I., LAVELLE, T. L.: "Learned helplessness as experimenter-induced failure and its alleviation with attentional redeployment", *Journal of Abnormal Psychology,* 89, pp. 350–357 (1980).

EISENHARDT, K. M.: "Agency and institutional-theory explanations: The case of retail sales compensation", *Academy of Management Journal,* 31, pp. 488–511 (1988).

EISENHARDT, K. M.: "Building theories from case study research", *Academy of Management Review,* 14, pp. 532–550.

FOLGER, R., GREENBERG, J.: "Procedural justice: An interpretive analysis of personnel systems." In: ROWLAND, K. M., FERRIS, G. R. (eds): *Research in Personnel and Human Resources Management,* Vol. 3, JAI Press, Greenwich, CT (1985).

GALBRAITH, J.: *Organization Design*, Addison-Wesley. Reading, MA (1978).

GAMBETTA, D.: "Mafia: The price of distrust." In: GAMBETTA, D. (ed.): *Trust,* Basil Blackwell, New York (1988).

GRANCELLI, B.: "Managerial practices and patterns of employee behaviour in the Soviet enterprise." In: CHILD, J., BATE, P. (eds): *Organization of Innovation: East–West Perspectives,* Walter de Gruyter, New York, pp. 205–220 (1987).

GREELEY, T. P., OCHSNER, R. C.: "Putting merit pay back into salary administration." In: OCHSNER, R. C. (ed.): *Topics in Total Compensation,* A Panel Publication, Greenvale, New York (1986).

GREGORY, P. R.: "Soviet bureaucratic behavior: Khozyastvenniki and Apparatchiki", *Soviet Studies,* 41, pp. 511–525 (1989).

HARASZTI, M.: *A Worker in a Worker's State*, Penguin Books, New York (1977).

HIROTO, D. S., SELIGMAN, M. E. P.: "Generality of learned helplessness in man", *Journal of Personality and Social Psychology*, **31**, pp. 311–327 (1975).

JACOBY, S. M.: *Employing Bureaucracy*, Columbia University Press, New York (1985).

KERR, S.: "On the folly of rewarding A while hoping for B", *Academy of Management Journal*, **18**, pp. 769–783 (1975).

KORNAI, J.: "The Hungarian reform process: Visions, hopes, and reality", *Journal of Economic Literature*, **24**, pp. 1687–1737 (1986).

KORNAI, J., MATITS, A.: *A vállalatok nyereségének bürokratikus újraelosztása (The bureaucratic redistribution of company profit)*, Közgazdasági és Jogi Könyvkiadó, Budapest (1987).

KUHL, J.: "Motivational and functional helplessness: The moderating effect of state vs. action-orientation", *Journal of Personality and Social Psychology*, **31**, pp. 155–170 (1981).

LANGER, E. J.: "The illusion of control", *Journal of Personality and Social Psychology*, **32**, pp. 311–328 (1975).

LAUTER, G. P.: *The Manager and Economic Reform in Hungary*, Praeger, New York (1972).

LAWLER, E. E.: *Pay and Organizational Effectiveness: A Psychological View*, McGraw-Hill, New York (1971).

LAWLER, E. E III: *Pay and Organization Development*, Addison-Wesley, Reading, MA (1981).

LAWRENCE, P. R., VLACHOUTSICOS, C. A. (eds): *Behind the Factory Walls: Decision Making in Soviet and U.S. Enterprises*, Harvard Business School Press, Boston (1990).

LEVENTHAL, G. S.: "What should be done with equity theory?" In: GERGEN, K. J., GREENBERG, M. S., WILLIS, R. H. (eds): *Social Exchange: Advances in Theory and Research*, Plenum, New York, pp. 27–55 (1980).

LIND, E. A., TYLER, T. R.: *The Social Psychology of Procedural Justice*, Plenum, New York (1988).

LOCKE, E. A.: "The nature and causes of job satisfaction." In: DUNNETTE, M. D. (ed.): *Handbook of Industrial Organizational Psychology*, Rand McNally, Chicago, pp. 1297–1349 (1976).

LÖVEY, I.: "The whole nation is complaining", *Mozgó Világ*, **12**, Panaszkodik az ország (1986).

MARKÓCZY, L.: "State-directed profit motive and resource dependency." Working paper, Department of Business Economics, Budapest University of Economics (1990).

MARS, G.: *Cheats at Work*, Allen Unwin, London (1982).

NEE, V.: "Theory of market transition: From redistribution to markets in state socialism", *American Sociological Review*, **54**, pp. 663–681 (1989).

OUCHI, W. G.: "Markets, bureaucracies, and clans", *Administrative Science Quarterly*, **25**, pp. 129–141 (1980).

PEARCE, J. L.: "Why merit pay doesn't work: Implications from organizational theory." In: BALKIN, D. B., GOMEZ-MEIJA, L. R. (eds): *New Perspectives on Compensation*, Prentice-Hall, Englewood Cliffs, NJ, pp. 169–178 (1987).

PEARCE, J. L., SOMMER, S. M., MORRIS, A., FRIDEGER, M.: "A configurational approach to interpersonal relations: Profiles of workplace social relations and task interdependence." Working paper #OB92015: Graduate School of Management, University of California, Irvine (1993).

PFEFFER, J.: *Power in Organizations,* Pitman, Marshfield, MA (1981).

ROTTER, J. B.: "Interpersonal trust, trustworthiness, and gullibility", *American Psychologist,* **35,** pp. 1–7 (1980).

SAYLES. L. R.: *Leadership: Managing in Real Organizations,* (2nd edn) McGraw-Hill, New York (1989).

SIMIS, K. M.: *USSR: The Corrupt Society,* Simon & Schuster, New York (1982).

STARK, D.: "Privatization in Hungary: From plan to market or from plan to clan?" *East European Politics and Societies,* **4,** pp. 351–392 (1990).

STAW, B. M.: "Motivation in organizations: Toward synthesis and redirection." In: STAW, B. M., SALANCIK, G. R. (eds): *New Directions in Organizational Behavior,* St. Clair Press, Chicago, pp. 55–96 (1977).

STEERS, R. M., MOWDAY, R. T.: "Employee turnover and post-decision accommodation process." In: CUMMINGS, L. L., STAW, B. M. (eds): *Research in Organizational Behavior,* Vol. 3, JAI Press, Greenwich, CN, pp. 237–249 (1981).

STEERS, R. M., RHODES, S. R.: "Major influences on employee attendance: A process model", *Journal of Applied Psychology,* **63,** pp. 391–407 (1978).

THIBAUT, J., WALKER, L.: *Procedural Justice: A Psychological Analysis,* Lawrence Erlbaum Associates, Hillsdale, NJ (1975).

THOMPSON, J. D.: *Organizations in Action,* McGraw-Hill, New York (1967).

VOSLENSKY, M.: *Nomenklatura,* Doubleday, Garden City, NY (1984).

VROOM, V. H.: *Work and Motivation,* Wiley, New York (1964).

WEBER, M.: *The Theory of Social and Economic Organization,* Free Press, New York (1947).

WHYTE, W. F.: *Money and Motivation,* Harper and Brothers, New York (1955).

WOOD, S.: "Toward socialist–capitalist comparisons of the organizational problem." In: CHILD, J., BATE, P. (eds): *Organization of Innovation: East–West Perspectives,* Walter de Gruyter, New York, pp. 52–71 (1987).

16

REVOLUTIONIZING BUREAUCRACIES: MANAGING CHANGE IN HUNGARIAN STATE-OWNED ENTERPRISES*

By

JONE L. PEARCE, IMRE BRANYICZKI

Massive political and economic transformations in formerly state-socialist countries have captured the world's attention. Yet, while the world cheers greater political freedom in these countries and voices growing concern about the economic hardships in them, organizational scientists have a particular reason to attend to events there. These revolutionary changes provide an historically unprecedented opportunity to learn about revolutionary organizational change in highly industrialized countries with complex institutions and developed, organizationally sophisticated societies. Here, case studies of change in two large Hungarian state-owned enterprises provide the basis for a discussion of the initial stages of revolutionary change.

The phrase "revolutionizing bureaucracies" is self-contradictory: Bureaucracies are designed to do the same things over and over again, and once a bureaucratic organization has found a strategic focus, powerful forces seek to assure that the rest of the organization converges to support this strategic direction. There is a large literature documenting many of these forces – technological, structural, selection and socialization systems – that tend to lead organizations towards "inertia" (see TUSHMAN and ROMANELLI 1985, for an excellent review). Of course, bureaucratic organizations do change, but in the normal course of events they make slow, marginal adjustments, because exceptions of such magnitude must wind their way through the hierarchical levels and various committees until changes can be developed and communicated.

* In *Journal of Organizational Change Management*, 1993, Vol. 6, No. 2, pp. 53–64

The members of organizations quite rightly abhor revolutionary changes. Abrupt changes may disrupt ongoing relationships on which long-term payoffs depend (ABERNATHY 1978). They can make individuals' specialized skills obsolete (CROZIER 1964). Stability in bureaucracies encourages individuals to make long-term investments (THUROW 1975) and to plan for "careers" in their organizations. Individuals who have been socialized into organizational norms and values will resist radical changes that threaten those values (Van MAANEN 1976).

How do bureaucratic organizations and their members react to revolutionary change? Organizational scientists have long been interested in change, but little empirical research has been done on truly revolutionary organizational transformations. There is a rich literature in organizational innovating (e.g. JELINEK and SCHOONHOVEN 1990), but it is focused on developing knowledge about the regularization of the production of "innovative products", not on the revolutionary transformation of organizations themselves. Similarly, research and practice in "planned change" seeks to assist organizations in regularizing more open communication in the organization or in introducing a new technology or procedure which is intended to become part of the organization's predictable practice (FRENCH et al. 1983; MOCH and BARTUNEK 1990). As valuable as this literature is in helping us to understand how to assist organizations in needed adjustments, it tells us little about reactions to revolutionary change.

What we do know about revolutionary organizational change comes from organizational theorists. TUSHMAN and ROMANELLI (1985) provide a "punctuated equilibrium model" of organizational change that contains numerous insights relevant to understanding the revolutionary changes in transforming state-socialist organizations. They suggest that the inherent pressures towards inertia can be and are disrupted by external and internal pressures for what they call reorientations. TUSHMAN et al. (1986) contrast the different processes involved in the incremental adjustments of "converging change" with "frame-breaking" revolutionary change:

> The usual process of making [incremental changes] is well known: wide acceptance of the need for change, openness to possible alternatives, objective examination of the pros and cons of each plausible alternative, participation of those directly affected in the preceding analysis, a market test or pilot operation where feasible (p. 6).

In contrast they characterized "frame-breaking change" as requiring a rapid, simultaneous implementation because a piecemeal approach can get bogged down by members' resistance to change. Their research suggests that successful frame-breaking change is characterized by:

(1) executive leadership which is personally involved in planning and in implementing the changes;

(2) executive succession; and

(3) executive attention to overcoming internal resistance to change.

However, TUSHMAN et al. (1986) studied western corporations which have not undergone the level of revolutionary change now occurring in formerly state-socialist organizations. Because TUSHMAN and ROMANELLI assume a market economy, their discussion of precipitating pressures focuses on drops in firm economic performance arising from legal or product changes. In Hungarian state-owned organizations, the external pressures for change are massive, actually "revolutionary". The managers of these organizations face not only a severe drop in revenue (from the collapse of the CMEA trading system) and pressures for product innovation now that they must sell their products (without government subsidies) in capitalist markets but a complete revolution in the sources of and methods to obtain revenue. These organizations are being forced to shift from being agents of production and political control to being profit-oriented market-driven enterprises. Further, each organization's traditional suppliers, customers, and bankers are also seeking to adjust. These two cases provide an opportunity to examine whether TUSHMAN and ROMANELLI'S (1985) characterization of successfully managed frame-breaking changes also applies to the more fundamentally revolutionary changes required of these Hungarian organizations.

The other important theoretical source on revolutionary organizational change is GERSICK (1991), whose research on such change in small groups provides insights about individual reactions to revolutionary change. GERSICK emphasizes the cognitive confusion which occurs as old patterns of behaviour are seen to be ineffective but new ones have yet to emerge, and she has documented the severe emotional distress that participants experience under these circumstances. Interestingly, her groups rapidly developed a "pivotal insight" which formed the basis for their reorientation, and GERSICK suggested that a "nucleus" within the organization develops the pivotal insight first and then organizational change spreads from this group. Data from these revolutionizing Hungarian organizations can be compared with her data to examine the extent to which the development of an insightful "cadre" is reflected in revolutionary organizational change.

ORGANIZATIONS UNDER STATE-SOCIALISM

This article focuses on changes taking place in two state-owned Hungarian organizations. Because Hungary began its economic and political transformation earlier and more gradually than its state-socialist neighbours, organizational transformation has moved farther and in 1991 was much more variable than in many of the others. In Hungary, unlike its formerly communist and reform communist neighbours, the ruling élite knew they would lose power about two years before they actually lost control of the law-making and economic institutions. During that period, they had powerful incentives (and the means) to move into managerial positions in state-owned businesses and then to secure their autonomy from the next government's interference through legislation and joint ventures with foreign business partners. By 1991, Hungary thus had a significantly larger proportion of foreign joint-ventures and foreign investment than its formerly state-socialist neighbours. This variety and Hungary's earlier experience with market-socialist experiments make it an ideal setting in which to study how organizations form and recreate themselves in the transition from state-socialism, to capitalism. Each country has a unique culture, history and governmental policies governing economic transformation, but the headstart many of these Hungarian managers' have had with revolutionary organizational change will probably foreshadow some of the experiences of other formerly state-socialist organizations.

There can be little doubt about the revolutionary nature of the changes demanded of organizations in the formerly state-socialist countries. The basic outlines of state-socialism are well known to readers. To summarize briefly, although the enterprises of Hungary had not had a true command economy for many years, for complex reasons (KORNAI 1986) managers in its state-controlled enterprises have faced an environment more similar to their command economy than to their capitalist neighbours. Under state-socialism Hungarian enterprises were significantly dependent on the state for numerous credits and "permissions" (KORNAI 1986; MARKÓCZY 1990). Further, state-dominated economies are "scarcity economies" (KORNAI 1980). This means that all components of organized activity are difficult to obtain – raw material, labour, replacement parts, capital. In practice, this has meant that managers' chief operational objective has been to secure reliable supplies of needed credits, material and labour.

In addition, the Hungarian economy, like that of its state-socialist neighbours, was dominated by monopolies. The reasons for this were partly ideological (it reduced the "inefficiency" of numerous suppliers of nearly identical products), partly practical (it was easier for government planners to monitor fewer big combines than numerous small companies), and partly strategic (managers found that their bargaining power with government planners was greater if their large size and monopoly position made their threats of collapse more fearsome to officials). Thus managers in state-socialist enterprises focused substantial attention "upwards" towards the officials who determined their revenue and investments and, in thousands of other ways, controlled the "success" of the enterprises. It is important to note that most enterprise managers were not the passive underlings of government officials but could use their monopoly positions and large size to drive hard bargains. Of course, these brief descriptions cannot do justice to the complexity of managerial relationships or to the elaborate web of "private contracts" that evolved within and between state-owned organizations and "private associations" as the restrictions on private enterprise were gradually loosened in Hungary in the past decades. The interested reader is directed to KORNAI (1986) and STARK (1990a; 1990b) for excellent description of Hungarian state-socialist enterprises before political change escalated in 1989.

CHANGING STATE-SOCIALISM

The very scale of the necessary economic transformation puts pressure on organizations to transform themselves radically. In capitalist societies, individual organizations which fail (usually) are allowed to go bankrupt, their participants go to work for other organizations, and their suppliers and customers, to find alternatives. In these settings, it is individuals who must learn radically new behaviours, not the organizations as such. However, two features of the transformation in former state-socialist economies work against this form of "natural" organizational death.

First, these economies have several structural features which made their economies very interdependent and inflexible. As noted, state-socialist economies are composed of numerous bilateral monopolies. If one company collapses, vital supplies cannot reach other organizations which have been wholly dependent on them. Often, for highly-specialized technology, there may be no alternative available "on the market". Thus, the collapse of a large company has a greater "multiplier effect" than in capitalist economies. Second, another rigidity built into these economies is the tight housing market which makes relocating to another city to find work literally impossible for many. Third, this (mostly failing) state-owned sector comprises a significantly larger proportion of the entire economy than in capitalist societies. The Hungarian government, which employs 80% (or more) of the country's workforce, cannot just standby and watch all "failed" state-owned companies declare bankruptcy. In the West, writers characterize some organizations as "too big to fail", and this statement certainly has great appeal to the elected governments in formerly state-socialist countries. Governmental officials feel forced to take actions to maintain their existing organizations and to encourage the organizations to make the revolutionary transformations necessary to survive in a market-driven economy.

The scope and depth of change that is being demanded of these organizations cannot be overstated. For example, these organizations are seeking (simultaneously) to:

- open new markets for existing products;
- add new functions such as marketing and financial analysis that previously did not exist;
- improve existing products to meet international standards;
- purchase and install upgraded technologies;
- reconfigure personnel departments from agencies of political control to sources of professional guidance on human resources management;
- improve and adhere to management information and control systems;
- learn how to obtain capital from capital markets rather than from governmental officials; and in their spare time
- redecorate the buildings so they look "more professional" to foreigners from rich capitalist countries.

Even employees at the lowest organizational levels must:

- determine which old skills and approaches are still appropriate and which new skills must be acquired;
- conform to strictly enforced performance standards;
- try to analyse who has what power as old comrades retire and organizations fragment into complicated forms;
- face what is for some a crippling blow to their professional pride as they learn how poorly their products compare with Western ones;
- live with uncertainty about whether they will be laid off next week or next month.

As the following cases will illustrate, this disintegration of the old system before the new ones have solidified (during which most organizations continue) has created a broad scope for individual initiative and creativity, as well as paralysis.

LONGITUDINAL RESEARCH PROJECT

The following two cases are drawn from a longitudinal research project of the transformation of Hungarian state-owned enterprises begun by authors and their colleague, Professor GYULA BAKACSI of Budapest University of Economic Sciences, in 1989 (when the first author was a visiting professor in Budapest at the International Management Centre). The study consists of a sample of four state-owned enterprises (one had signed a joint-venture agreement with a West European partner at the start of data collection) and two entrepreneurial companies. The study is designed to track organizational change through the collection of company archival information, structured and unstructured interviews, and questionnaires conducted yearly in these organizations. The two organizations which are the focus of this report were selected because both were still controlled by Hungarians (versus the West European partner in the joint-venture) and represented the extremes of successful and unsuccessful adaptation to revolutionary change by late 1991. The present report draws on structured interviews with managers and employees conducted in 1990 and 1991.

The terms "successful" and "unsuccessful change", as we are using them in this context, need to be defined. By successful change we mean that the organization has succeeded both in introducing new market-oriented procedures and structures and in obtaining revenue from the sales of its products on an open market (usually, but not necessarily, to Western customers who are able to pay). That is, a successful company has reorganized itself, changed employees' jobs through training, new hires, or both, and has made market sales. An unsuccessful company is one which has not changed its structures, procedures, or jobs and has not obtained new customers. Note that the collapse of the trading system in Hungary in 1991 and the deep depression in the national economy has meant that unsuccessful firms are faced with a precipitous drop in income (50% was not uncommon) as their plan-directed customers of the past cannot pay their bills. In this context, there is a sharp and unambigious distinction between successful and unsuccessful companies.

SUCCESSFUL CHANGE:
THE ADVERTISING AGENCY

The Advertising Agency was one of the two advertising agencies in Hungary until the reforms of the 1980s permitted the formation of small partnerships. At the end of 1990, the Advertising Agency had 110 employees. It was founded in 1968 as part of the New Economic Mechanism reforms of that period and focused on advertising the products of Hungarian state-owned enterprises. It was a component of a large state-owned organization which also had interests in domestic and international trade shows and the major fairgrounds in Budapest. Traditionally, the agency had handled the advertising accounts of all companies participating in trade shows and fairs.

In early 1990 it was facing numerous crises:

- Unaccustomed competition from private advertising companies (approximately 2,000 advertising companies had been established by 1990).
- Loss of many of their most talented employees to these private competitors who were not burdened, as was the state-owned agency, by regulations governing maximum pay to employees.
- A managing director under investigation by the new non-communist government for taking kickbacks for the placement of advertisement.
- A reduction in the agency's attractiveness to many clients (who retained the Advertising Agency to maintain influence with the fair organizers to ensure favourable booth placement and other advantages) due to the pending privatization programme which would separate the advertising agency from the fairgrounds.
- Troubled state-owned clients were not paying their bills.

In early 1990 it appeared that this company, an "artificial creation of the old system", was soon to be replaced by numerous competing private advertisers. However, 18 months later, the Advertising Agency had secured a partnership (on very favourable terms) with one of the largest Western multinational advertising agencies, attracted back one of the most dynamic creative people from a private partnership to head its creative department, had begun a comprehensive programme involving restructuring and extensive training by professionals from the Western partner, and had begun to secure "Western accounts" through the multinational partner. The managers felt they were building a solid foundation for future growth and were only waiting for the long-delayed privatization to give them the flexibility to make the remaining changes.

This turnaround was accomplished, first by the early retirement of the former managing director as part of the settlement of his legal case with the government (CEO succession, TUSHMAN et al. 1986). The deputy director was then appointed managing director, and she had developed a plan for the rescue of the agency. She immediately called the creative professional to try to attract him to work with her on the transformation of the agency. She knew that the multinational company which was to become their partner was one of the few major international advertising agencies that did not already have a presence in Hungary. She believed they would be interested in developing the capability of advertising in Hungary for their international consumer-products clients and that her agency, as one of the largest agencies in Hungary, might be attractive as a partner.

Consistent with GERSICK, she worked first to build a group dedicated to the change. She developed a small cadre of professionals and managers in their thirties who worked to effect the change:

> There are two camps. One contains those who may be laid off. They know they don't have as much work and in three months may be out of a job. They are setting and waiting. In the other camp are those who have to work 12 hours a day and who take their work home at night. They are struggling to learn Western systems, working all day in English. Because they don't have expertise they feel they have to work twice as hard, because that is what they can give, their effort.
>
> Aren't you worried about these people burning out?
>
> Yes... that's true. Recently [managing director] was sick. Before, in 20 years she had never been sick, but she become exhausted and was sick at home for ten days. While she was gone everything fell apart (Creative Deputy Director, 9 April 1991).

As is reflected in the above quotation, the managing director of the agency was deeply involved in day-to-day implementation of the changes, as suggested by TUSHMAN and ROMANELLI.

One feature of TUSHMAN and ROMANELLI'S experience with frame-breaking change in Western organizations did not apply – their description of massive resistance to change. Within the agency, there was relatively little resistance to change. While those in the cadre may have spent a great deal of time cajoling and encouraging other employees, they did not have to fight active resistance. Although probably there were many who preferred to avoid change, few thought that resistance was feasible. Rather, as reflected in the above quotation, employees either worked hard to change themselves and the organization or were passive.

The strength of the motivation to change required an openness to feedback that was as painfully difficult for these professionals as it would be for Westerners. From the new Creative Deputy Director:

> Now we [the Western partner and the agency] have got to know each other and we have real problems. They sent us accounts from [company major international consumer products company who wishes to sell its products in Hungary]. We had prepared a presentation for [company] and they were very unhappy. We received a fax from [West European capital] saying [managing director]. WILL be in here for a day long meeting this Thursday... They were very honet and a little bit rude. They said "We were confused. Media should not be talking about that. The managing director spoke too long. Market research didn't know it was talking about. The conference room must be changed. You must have Western equipment. The creative people should not be handling products, the account handlers should do that." And on and on. When the managing director returned she reported all of this to the departments.

> Weren't you upset at this rudeness? They aren't your bosses.

> Yes... but they send us the accounts and they do not want to ruin their own reputations with these accounts. We need them... In many things they are right and we need to be trained; everyone is happy to have the training. But in others they don't understand that we cannot produce the information they are used to. For example, in media planning in the West you just call up the television station and ask for the rates and viewer demographics for certain shows. Our television stations don't provide this information, nothing. They don't understand the East European situation (9 April 1991).

This case suggests that the other features of TUSHMAN and ROMANELLI'S (1985) description of frame-breaking change did apply in this Hungarian company. The managing director and several other key top executives were replaced by managers with a vision of how to change the organization. The top management was deeply involved in the transition, working at self-sacrificial levels for the survival of this state-owned company. However, the top management had not needed to overcome resistance to change, as TUSHMAN and ROMANELLI had found in their Western organizations, most worked hard to learn the thousands of new things necessary to adapt to their new demands. The reasons why there seemed to be less resistance to change in this organization (and the unsuccessful one) are discussed in the concluding section.

UNSUCCESSFUL CHANGE:
THE PORCELAIN FACTORY

One of the organizations in our study illustrates how dependent these organizations are on the dynamic, far-sighted cadre who assume responsibility when the old managing directors leave.

The Porcelain Factory was founded in 1777 by a count on his estate in remote wooded mountains in what is today just inside the border with Slovakia. It produces china-goods, figurines and porcelain fancy goods, with about 80% of its product sold in Hungary through the state retail distribution network and a handful of its own shops. Because of its prior role as a production facility working to plan, its marketing and sales functions were very undeveloped. As the major employer in the region, it owned and managed apartments, workmen's hostels, a grocery store, as well as its own museum. It had just over 900 employees in 1990, most of them the grandchildren and great grandchildren of former Porcelain Factory employees. The factory was governed by a company council (established in 1985 as the official governing bodies for companies). In Hungary the managing directors appointed 49% of the council members (usually their dependent middle managers) with the rest elected directly by employees.

By early 1990, despite having a product which wins international competitions and sells for one-tenth the price of comparable products from Western Europe, the Porcelain Factory faced insolvency:

- Energy costs had increased four-fold, and this energy-intensive business had old, energy-inefficient equipment.
- Sales had plummeted as depression-ravaged Hungarian consumers stopped purchasing these luxury goods.
- The tastes of its largest customers (transport companies and upscale restaurants) had shifted to plain white porcelain, yet the company felt bound to retain its élite "hand painters".

In contrast to the Advertising Agency, the Porcelain Factory had made no effort by the end of 1991 to develop markets for its products. Rather, its company council voted a 30% salary increase to the employees. By October 1991 the government succeeded in replacing the company council with a government-appointed governing board. In November 1991 this new board insisted that the company begin advertising for a new trade (sales) director. Believing the factory may still be viable despite several unprofitable years requiring subsidy, the government had not shut the factory down. At the end of 1991, the only foreign partner which had expressed interest in the factory was a foreign porcelain company which may purchase it to manufacture its own historical line of porcelain. Every observer would agree that the Porcelain Factory had not yet begun to make the changes needed to be successful in a market economy.

Certainly, the Porcelain Factory never developed a cadre with a vision of the future, as GERSICK suggested. However, it did experience management succession, but the purpose of the change was an attempt by the managers and employees to prevent radical restructuring:

> In June (1990) the managing director was fired by the company council. In Spring 1990 the Porcelain Factory managing director had completed a Western management education programme and had decided to streamline the company by removing several administrators which he considered to be non-performing party hacks. The threatened managers and employees were able to convince enough colleagues on the company council that this managing director was dangerous, so a majority voted to fire him in June. One of the three deputy directors was appointed acting managing director and the council undertook a search for a replacement.

> On December 15, 1990 the secretary to the technical deputy director reported as follows: "All of the changes have been negative. The trade deputy director left after the managing director so we only have one deputy now for the trade, technical and production departments. The council still has not selected a managing director. The products is piling up in the warehouse, our energy prices have skyrocketed and all they talk about is the gate keeper's hours, instead of what really should be done. They are putting in time-card machines and not dealing with the important issues."

This organization had made some technical changes to improve energy efficiency but had not been able to undertake the strategic reorientations that would be necessary for the organization to survive. Managers and employees were passively resigned to wait for a foreigner to take over the company (in the promised, but long delayed, government privatization programme) and make the needed changes.

ANALYSIS

GERICK'S and TUSHMAN and ROMANELLI'S descriptions of the ingredients for successful revolutionary change were largely reflected in the successful organization, the Advertising Agency. In this organization the old managers were replaced by a cadre of top managers with a vision of how they would need to change the organization. These managers worked very long hours, with the managing director taking direct personal responsibility for changing the organization. However, these managers did not need to spend substantial time trying to overcome resistance within the organization to change. The resistance that did appear in these organizations was of a different form than usually observed in the West.

In the Porcelain Factory the managing director sought first to remove middle managers he thought were incompetent rather than to articulate a vision of how the organization should reorient itself. At that time, employees had real governing power over the organization and in this organization they used the small time frame, between the collapse of party control and the assumption of control by the government through "business-like" governing boards, to remove this threatening manager. This was simply a defensive action taken by managers and employees to remove an immediate threat. They solidified their defenses by appointing a passive manager who would not threaten their jobs. There was no sense that they were resisting change, as such. In fact, the above quotation from the secretary reflects the general frustration with the factory's inability to develop new markets. Rather, these employees used their power to protect their jobs (in the short run) and did not consider the reorientation of the company to be their responsibility. They were as passive towards revolutionary organizational change as were the majority of employees of the Advertising Agency.

The different levels of success in implementing changes in these two companies seemed to result from a combination of luck (no dynamic visionary deputy was available in the Porcelain Factory) and power structure: the Advertising Agency was controlled by a large state-owned combine which did not want to subsidize losses, while the Porcelain Factory was legally controlled by a company council which found that it did not have to be a rubber stamp after the collapse of the communist party.

The lack in these organizations of active resistance to change deserves attention. One factor, no doubt, was the very scale and scope of the political, societal and economic changes these individuals faced. These companies unambiguously were facing immediate collapse, and the only ones who had any vision at all of a possible way out were the Advertising Agency managing director and her team. It may be that resistance to change occurs only when the crisis is less visible to employees and is less relevant personally. When truly revolutionary change in the face of unambiguous crisis is undertaken, the active resistance of employees may simply evaporate of its own accord.

Another feature of these organizations may contribute to lower resistance to change – the participants' experiences under state-socialism. Decision making was highly centralized under Hungarian state-socialism (BAKACSI 1989; MARKÓCZY 1990; PEARCE 1991). Top managers were personally involved in many more decisions than were their counterparts in Western organizations. In addition, the former régime encouraged employee passivity, since this would facilitate achieving planned production targets (PEARCE 1991). In planned economies, many more decisions were made at the top and any initiative from below would interfere with the system's "smooth functioning". Thus most employees would not expect, based on their experience, to be consulted on organizational changes. Middle managers, particularly, were less powerful than their western counterparts, and this would preclude the establishment of powerful "baronies" which could mount effective resistance to change.

Therefore, the absence of resistance to change in the Advertising Agency may be a characteristic of truly revolutionary change, or it may be the traditional pattern of employee reaction in these organizations, or both. Further research on revolutionary changes in other settings can help to isolate the roles of these factors in muting resistance to organizational change.

The key difference between these two organizations seems attributable to the presence of deputy directors with very different visions (GERWICK'S "pivotal insight"). In the Advertising Agency, a deputy was available who had formulated a plan for rescuing the company. In the Porcelain Factory no such deputy was available. This difference may result from the different tasks and histories of the companies. The agency works in a dynamic and creative field in the country's capital, and the factory is staffed by employees from an isolated rural labour market which was virtually preindustrial.

We conclude by noting that the change process in the successfully changing Advertising Agency is still very fragile. It is excessively dependent on the sacrifice of one or a few individuals. The example of the near collapse of the Advertising Agency during the few days that the managing director was away reflects the fragility of her still-centralized approach. In addition, this change process appears to be costly to the executive cadre. They assume the pressures and long hours of entrepreneurs. They hope for rewards similar to those of entrepreneurs: to buy undervalued shares in a privatizing company (and to retain their privileged positions). Yet, like many entrepreneurs, they may find that their new (and probably foreign) owners can become dissatisfied with their tight personal control, with the way that these executive "can't seem to let go". However, the Western entrepreneur's dismissal is usually softened with a generous golden handshake. Not so for these Hungarian managers who, after all, are sacrificing themselves for state-owned companies.

REFERENCES

ABERNATHY, W: J.: *The Productivity Dilemma: Roadblock to Innovation in the Automobile Industry,* Johns Hopkins University Press, Baltimore, MD (1978).

BAKACSI, G.: *Fiedler's Contingency Model: Survey and Theoretical Thoughts,* working paper, Department of Management and Organization, Budapest University of Economic Sciences (1989).

CROZIER, M.: *The Bureaucratic Phenomenon,* University of Chicago Press, Chicago, IL (1964).

FRENCH, W. L., BELL, C. H. JR., ZAWACKI, R. A.: *Organization Development: Theory, Practice and Research* (rev. ed.), Business Publications, Plano, TX (1983).

GERSICK, C. J. G.: "Revolutionary Change Theories: A Multilevel Exploration of the Punctuated Equilibrium Paradigm", *Academy of Management Review,* Vol. 16, No. 1, pp. 10–36 (1991).

JELINEK, M., SCHOONHOVEN, C. B.: *Innovation Marathon: Lessons from High Technology Firms,* Basil Blackwell, Cambridge, MA (1990).

KORNAI, J.: *Economics of Shortage,* North-Holland, Amsterdam (1980).

KORNAI, J.: "The Hungarian Reform Process: Visions, Hopes and Reality", *Journal of Economic Literature,* Vol. 24, December, pp. 1687–1737 (1986).

MARKÓCZY, L.: *State Directed Profit Motive and Resource Dependence,* working paper, Department of Business Economics, Budapest University of Economic Sciences (1990).

MOCH, M. K., BARTUNEK, J. M.: *Creating Alternative Realities at Work,* Harper & Row, New York, NY (1990).

PEARCE, J. L.: "Socialism to Capitalism: Organizational Behavior in the Period of Hungarian Economic Reform", *The Academy of Management Executive,* Vol. 5, No. 4, pp. 75–88 (1991).

STARK, D.: "Privatization in Hungary: From Plan to Market or from Plan to Clan?", *East European Politics and Societies,* Vol. 4, No. 3, pp. 351–392 (1990a).

STARK, D.: *Work Worth and Justice in a Socialist Mixed Economy,* working paper, Department of Sociology, Cornell University (published in French translation in 1990, *Actes de la Recherche en Sciences Sociales,* Vol. 85, pp. 3–19 (1990b).

THUROW, L. C.: *Generating Inequality,* Basic Books, New York, NY (1975).

TUSHMAN, M. L., ROMANELLI, E.: "Organizational Evolution: A Metamorphosis Model of Convergence and Reorientation", *Research in Organizational Behavior,* Vol. 7, pp. 171–222 (1985).

TUSHMAN, M. L., NEWMAN, W. H., ROMANELLI, E.: "Convergence and Upheaval: Managing the Unsteady Pace of Organizational Evolution", *California Management Review,* Vol. 29, No. 1, pp. 1–16 (1986).

VAN MAANEN, J: "Breaking In: Socialization to Work", in DUBLIN, R. (ed.), *Handbook of Work, Organization and Society,* Rand-McNally, Chicago, IL, pp. 67–130 (1976).

17

EVOLUTION OF ORGANIZATIONAL FORMS IN THE TRANSITION PERIOD OF HUNGARY*

By

MIKLÓS DOBÁK, ERNŐ TARI

PREFACE

Advances in Hungarian companies' organizational structures show a slightly different trend compared to experiences in most Central-Eastern European and ex-Soviet countries. The most important differences are felt in the development of Hungarian companies, which – unlike the Central-Eastern European standard – bear several elements (for instance establishing legally independent affiliates, or matrix and product management system, divisions) resembling corporate practice in the market economies as early as in the 80's (preceding the "big switch"). Reasons are found in relatively liberal and open economic policies (roots of which are traced back to 1968, the time of the "new economic mechanism" with the main objective to combine planned economy elements with those of market economies). On the other hand, in the 80's, there were political pressures advocating independent company management and decision making with an increasing urgency.

Thus we believe it is important to introduce the development of Hungarian companies' organizational structures in their historic context. The radical political changes in 1990 themselves would not provide sufficient explanation to understand the structural changes of Hungarian organizations.

One of the bases of our analysis was the research performed from the early 1970's until the mid 80's by the Faculty of Management and Organization at the Budapest University of Economic Sciences, concerning the

* In *Journal of East European Management Studies*, 1996, Vol. 1, No. 2, pp. 7–35.

study of the organizational and structural properties of the sixty biggest industrial enterprises. The study of these enterprises – which are responsible for about 50% of the Hungarian industrial production – was conducted by the colleagues of the Faculty, using mainly top management interviews and on site observation.

We used information from several empirical sources for the description of organizational development of the enterprises after the mid 80's. We examined the internal documents of numerous enterprises and enterprise-groups, conducted personal interviews with executives, used company case studies and theses dealing with organizational analysis (prepared during the classes and specialized seminars under the guidance of our Faculty), and we also relied on the practical experiences gathered during the consultancy activity performed by the Faculty. Of the other sources, we analyzed professional articles, books dealing with certain aspects of the subject, and the informative articles of Figyelő, Heti Világgazdaság and other Hungarian economic periodicals and daily papers.

In the study we differentiate among the examined organizational forms (structures) based on the following *structural dimensions:*

- specialization;
- centralization–decentralization;
- coordination;
- configuration.

Under *specialization,* we mean the method of diving a task-complex into subtasks and the installing of it to each of the organizational units (persons). *Centralization–decentralization* deals with the regulation of the competency (decision and direction sphere of authority) of the organizational units (persons) in the hierarchy. With *coordination* – in our understanding – the activity of the organizational units (persons) with different tasks and spheres of authority is harmonized, in order to achieve the organization's goals. *Configuration* refers to the span of control and the vertical hierarchical levels of the organization.

So the focuses of our study are the structural dimensions of the enterprises (companies) and the developmental characteristics of internal organizational independence; thus we do not deal with the analysis of operations, for example the production process. The examined organizations are within the state enterprise sphere, and its *successor organizations* joined by the self-supported *domestic private capital organizations.*

I. HISTORICAL BACKGROUND (1945–1980)

The development of Hungarian organizational structures during 1945 to 1980 – compared to organizational structural changes in the evolution of American or West European companies – is characterized by an epochal lagging behind by several decades. In order to explain the reasons for delay, the time period following the nationalization after 1945–1948 should be recalled when company structures were transformed according to the Soviet model. Essentially, the centralized functional organization representing the early first stage of Western company development served as the scheme to be followed. In consequence, by Western standards, out of date organizational formation – represented the initial point for organizing the new "socialist" Hungarian enterprise. Later on, the centralized functional structures of organizations were preserved. What is more, these were strengthened by the enterprise mergers in the sixties (see *Table 1*). In those days the cooperation between newly formed large enterprises and developing, the integrated "cooperative" relations of production units became established and gained ground. In the seventies, increase in the verticality of production of large Hungarian enterprises continues, even though their number was already disproportionate compared to small and medium enterprises. In the early eighties, centralized functional organization was still regarded as the almost exclusive organizational structure in Hungary (see *Fig. 1*). This way, the Hungarian development of organizational forms between 1945 and 1980 has achieved the first stage of the US and Western European companies (which was completed by the fifties and sixties)! (MÁRIÁS et al. 1981.)

Table 1. Comparison of Danish and Hungarian breakdown on enterprises size (% of total enterprises)

Number of employees	Denmark			Hungary
over 500		1	37	
200–499		4	25	
100–199		7	22	
50–99		12	12	
20–49		29	3	
5–19		47	1	

Source: SCHWEITZER 1982.

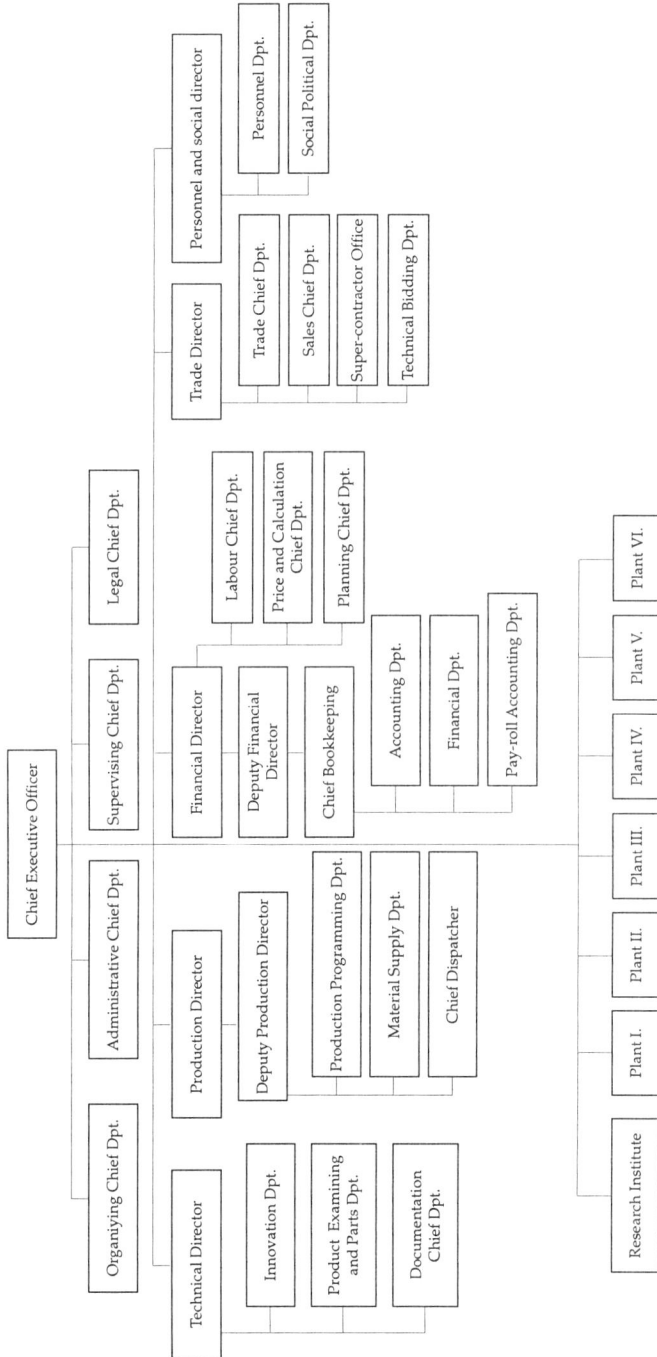

Figure 1. The organization chart of a typical, linear-functional machinery large enterprise

II. SEEKING WAYS AND MEANS IN THE 80'S
(1981–1987)

By the early eighties, most of the external resources ensuring profitable corporate running or simply "surviving" were used up or exhausted, and the partial actions made under the slogan of "structural modernization" proved to be largely ineffective. It was clear that the exports expansion, particularly prompted by the central economic authorities and later on by gaining World Bank credits (the latter appearing as a new facility) could be achieved only by changes penetrating and renewing the organizational structure of state enterprises. Following this recognition, certain experts on innovation in the central and corporate economic management started to seek after opportunities for applying the organizational formations that had proved to be viable in developed industrial states. Seeking ways and means started in two directions. On one hand, experiments for (1) establishing new organizational formations – essentially connected with small enterprises – were effected and, on the other, theoretical and practical steps for (2) changing organizational structures of conventional – centralized, linear-functional – large state enterprises were made.

1. NEW ORGANIZATIONAL AND LEGAL FORMS
OF SMALL BUSINESS

It is worth pointing out the essentially more flexible, smaller organizations found in the frame of these new organizational formations. Such were, first of all, the so-called "economic working pools", "small cooperatives" and "civil legal partnerships" operating independently from large organizations (while it has been allowed for some time to found the "civil legal partnership" in certain fields). It is considered that the biggest advantage of these organizations of private enterprise initiative is the motivation and interest of their management and personnel, which was generally much stronger than of those in conventional organizations. In the majority of cases this meant a higher requirement for performance. Drawing on the experience of small scale family enterprises in capitalist countries, it was found that signs of linear formations could be well perceived at these small enterprises. However, what is more significant was that the project type structural solutions could be found as a major part of these small organizations. Of course, this development was not deliberate in most cases, but resulted from the fact that there were small power distances in these organizations, without costly central apparatus, and the distribution of responsibilities among their employees could be amended flexibly, depending upon the current tasks. This provided for those working is small enterprises to have a qualification and mobility much higher than the national average.

The leaders of the Hungarian economy believed at this time that these small, private initiative organizations – besides filling the market gaps – would work their way into the national economic division of labour between companies. They were expected to be better connected to large enterprises through contractual relations and coordinated system of home-working. However, this remained mainly a mere wish, since, de facto, handling the small enterprises as "stepchildren" was not eliminated even as late as the end of the 80's: No regulation providing equal conditions was introduced; the dominance of state property was maintained. And also, the organizational weakness of large state enterprises undermined the performance of these small enterprises, cutting back on their potential opportunities (MAKAI 1991).

2. FIRST ORGANIZATIONAL MODIFICATIONS OF LARGE STATE ENTERPRISES

2.1 Efforts and Failures of Establishing Matrix Structure

Initially, the intention to alter the organizational structures of the linear-functional, conventional large state enterprises turned towards matrix organization and product management systems (introduced as a pioneer initiative in Hungary by the Taurus Rubber Works at the end of the 1970's).

The matrix structure for organizations seemed to be suitable for gaining ground and adopting competitive products more quickly, without having to break down the internal cooperation built up in large enterprises, or making major readjustments in decision-making authorities. Applying matrix management, the leaders of large enterprises – referring to the "impressed economy" and the frequent amendment of regulations – could invariably maintain the connection between organization and environment in the old manner, through the corporate centre (headquarter).

Drawing on experiences up to now, the appearance of the matrix organization has represented some advances in mediating market effects and

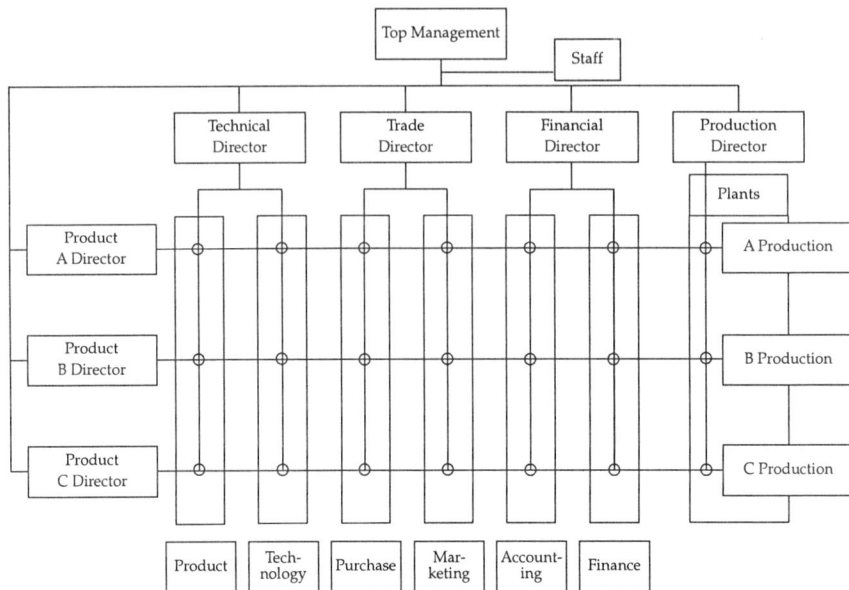

Figure 2. The direction of functional based matrix organization in the early 80's

in establishing agreement between corporate functional areas and productive departments. At the same time, the principle of functional division of labour continued to be dominant in large enterprises implanting
the matrix management, sometimes almost "putting down" the product
line. This was because in most cases the newly appointed product managers were not assigned with the right to give directions, but only with a
reconciling and coordinating function provided by their formal role, or
with the right to agree/disagree (see *Fig. 2* for a matrix structure based on
a functional organization).

In the absence of balance between functional and product management, latent conflicts could not come to the surface and be "institutionalized". The different interests could not confront to each other openly. Consequently, effective compromises or properly reconciled decisions for
evolving the market sensibility, and regrouping resources rapidly and
flexibly could not be made, either. In turn, the concentration on partial
responsibility – so peculiar to the functional point of view – survived. The
excessive written regulation remained in force, and as for functional bodies, they jealously watched over their resources, questioning from time to
time the product management system as a whole.

The partial, or in some cases, total failure of Hungarian experiments
aimed at introducing the matrix organization underlay the idea that the

obsolete centralized functional organization was intended to transform directly into matrix type. In this way, the coordination was directed not to genuine independent units (e.g. divisions), but the organizational units – bedded in the conventional linear-functional hierarchy and left untouched in their authorities. These were drawn into the matrix network through the product managers. The consequence could not be other than the survival of the fundamental structure of the functional organization, since the functional (and line) managers could have an "effective hold" on the product line from their previous position. This proved to be successful particularly when the product manager reported not directly to the enterprise's top manager but for example was posted under the direction of the head of a functional department (TARI 1988).

2.2 Affiliates as Units of Responsibility and Accounting

Affiliates – daughter company – as the internal company of the parent company, having a specific legal status, are considered to be an organizational formation applied and known in Western economies for a long time. These affiliates – assigned with considerable independence and a legal entity – have been operating as profit-oriented divisions (profit centers) in the organizational and proprietary frame of American and West European countries decades.

The appearance of the formation of affiliates in Hungary was connected to the organizational measures of partial central reforms initiated in 1981–1982. Nevertheless, executive of large enterprises have not regarded these affiliates as potential divisional profit centres. They took a views on the newly permitted organizational formation, rather as a "station" leading towards the total independence of the plant division. This is why initially they listed numerous arguments against the establishing of affiliates of legal entity.

But later, they found the form of affiliates suitable for saving the important internal producing units, for upsetting the efforts to become totally independent, as well as for utilizing other financial and taxation benefits.

Among the large enterprises "indisposed" or longer periods, it was no secret that operation of the parent company is intended to be "straightened up" by means of the affiliates. Large organizations battling against everyday financial troubles established affiliates from all (or almost all) the plant sections. Taking these considerations into account, it is not surprising that in many cases the elements of direction – reminiscent of the traditional relationship between the corporate centre and the plants – and the unilateral relations of dependence survived.

Therefore, to operate the affiliates as a unit of responsibility and accounting (for instance as a profit centre) was hindered by numerous limitations, provisions, and prohibitions by preemptory order on behalf of the parent enterprise. In contrast, it can be stated that affiliate formation – whilst breaking the privilege for ministries to found enterprise – triggered a sort of dynamic move in the field of independence. Numerous affiliates "became conscious" in the meanwhile and learned to make use the authority they had obtained and increased freedom of movement. Conversely, other affiliates, could acquire only a formal set of rights and there was almost no difference in their position from the period of former "existence": as a plant without legal entity (DEÁK 1987).

2.3 Ideas and Initial Steps for Developing the Divisional Organizations

In the second half of the eighties, the projects for modernizing organization in order to increase their competitiveness and to adjust themselves flexibly were promoted by World Bank experts, American and West European consulting firms, and Hungarian organization designers. On the basis of their suggestions, the divisional formation of organization came to the fore gradually, offering good opportunities for creating genuine internal independence of large enterprises, for decentralizing responsibilities, and for developing the initiative of communities in plant divisions.

Both favourable and unfavourable experiences were gained in the course of operating the divisions within the large companies whilst having no legal entity (self-accounting units, centres of responsibility, strategic business units, business branches, etc.). At some large enterprises, the flexibility and the entrepreneurial spirit of internal divisions and plant units undoubtedly increased. In the possession of capacities put at their disposal, they were able to "switch over" to manufacture products requested by the market, within a relative short period of time. For certain enterprises, a venture project function under the direct supervision of head of division, was set up, endeavouring to exploit the opportunities disclosed by market survey's as soon as possible.

It is said, in general, that the division managers' proprietary view improved remarkably where these units learned to "think in money".

Turning to the unfavourable phenomena, it should be pointed out that proposals for establishing divisions were not carried out to the full. Certain developments were in vain e.g. sales as a decentralized function by restructuring consultants, if the commercial apparatuses – left untouched in certain large enterprises – continued to "coordinate" the sales pursuit of divisions (profit centres). It occurred that Participation for a head of division in concluding the contracts concerning his own range of products or in discussions made with external partners, was not allowed. At another location, the division was allowed only to keep contact with the home market, while the enterprise centre continued to negotiate directly with foreign business partners.

Another basic principle of divisional organizations was violated when such requirements were imposed for plant unit divisions, the performance of which their managers could not influence in part or full. Similarly, the principle of divisional organizations was questioned by large enterprise centres which – referring to the frequent regulatory amendments and the governmental "manual control" developing between 1985 and 1988 – limited divisional manoeuvring by reallocating the resources and not even gave full scope for heads of profit (or cost) centres in distributing the resources within the division.

Generally speaking, it is said that the system of divisions not assigned with legal independence has left the centres of large enterprises untouched. (At a large chemical enterprise for instance, while functions were installed to newly organized divisions the central apparatus of several hundred, directed by seven Deputy General Manager invariably remained). In these large enterprises, said to be "divisional", the cutting back of headquarters did not take place to an extent, that only coordination and strategic link functions were retained at the central management level (Dobák 1988).

III. ECONOMIC AND LEGAL REGULATIONS TOWARDS A MARKET ECONOMY AND THEIR EFFECTS ON ORGANIZATIONAL STRUCTURE OF STATE ENTERPRISES AND PRIVATE FIRMS (1988–1993)

1. COMPREHENSIVE LEGAL REGULATIONS AND THE CONCEPTION OF PRIVATIZATION

The period starting in 1988 is practically the overture for breaking down the centralized system of "socialist" political and economic control. One of the most essential elements – having special importance on organizational structures – was the commencement of modification of economic and politic regulation. During these activities, elaboration of laws and legal rules has started which, through their codification in the period of 1988–1991:

- ensured the diversity of corporate or venture formations, the freedom of joining relieved the branch, sub-branch classification;
- altered the order of accounting and statistic provisions;
- allowed free venture for enterprises, and external and internal market movements;
- created the conditions for new labour and wages management as well as for restructuring the internal corporate systems of accounting and responsibility.

Legal regulations provided for diversity of company and venture formations. Freedom in joining – with regard to arrangement of organizational structures – conform with market principles so that they offered a principal opportunity for establishing, terminating and permanently rearranging the company and partnership formations, developing in an organic manner, both in the small and large entrepreneurial spheres. The crucial law from this standpoint is, beyond doubt, the Act VI of 1988 on Business Organizations. This ensures the establishment and operation of company formations in Hungary, compare with organizations operating in the Western market economies. This law ensured, inter alia, secure frameworks for small enterprises and also offered possibilities for business done in trade-houses and for the creation of large organization operating as a holding or concern.

Legislation of major importance was also launched in relation to changes to the accounting rules. This is because the former accounting system had – for its approach – a registration, accounting-oriented character. Supplying information speedily for preparing management decisions was difficult to achieve. Again, to create correct records on real expenses of cost-locations and cost-bearer was also difficult. It was difficult to achieve the separation of single units of accounting and responsibility, based on the obsolete accounting order, though all these are indispensable conditions for developing divisional organizations. The new accounting law came into force in 1991 (No. 1991/XVIII).

To provide enterprise, it is essential that – for instance in case of realizing the divisional form of organizations – single divisions (especially if these are to operate like profit centres) will be in contact with the purchase and sales market. This also means that customers, suppliers, the home and foreign trade companies, etc. should accept these divisions as partners having equal rights – independently from the legal status of the division.

Finally, it should be mentioned that the legislation provided independent labour and wages management for companies. One of the bases of sound operation of divisional organizations is the development of units of accounting and responsibility, as well as creating an internal system of interests serving the purposes of both the division and the company. It is therefore unavoidable for the company management to be independent in developing and operating systems of labour wages and management incentives. There is another reason for its importance, namely the wage differentiation within the company which may have an important – person-oriented – coordinating role. Wages and incomes can be effective means for the company management to select the heads of every single division and to "keep them in hand" (just in order to effect the total company interests).

The new government formed after the free elections released its privatization concept in the autumn of 1990. The government program outlined three methods of privatization, i.e. when the ownership changes is initiated centrally, by the enterprise itself, and externally. The government intended a prime role for centrally initialized privatization from these methods and shortly afterwards, launched privatizing actions through the State Property Agency established in 1990. The so-called first privatization program concerned, in particular, large organizations operating divisions and self-accounting units without legal entity. (This is because state enterprises in a relatively favourable financial position – seeming to be attractive for private investors – were found among the organizations.) And for the smaller companies (maximum 300 persons) the government allowed the so-called self-privatization to start initiated by themselves (MÓRA 1991).

At the end of 1992 the government elaborated, once again, a new privatization strategy and precisely stated the strengthening of a wide home proprietary circle. Practically the government desired to break with the former budget-income orientation of centrally initiated privatization, which lead to the slowing down of privatization actions due to centrally directed transactions and favourable deals of foreign capital investment.

2. RESULTS OF COMPREHENSIVE LEGAL REGULATIONS ON THE APPEARANCE OF CORPORATE GROUPS (CONCERNS AND HOLDINGS)

2.1 PRELIMINARY CONCEPTUAL REMARKS

Concerns and holdings in developed industrial countries go back several decades. A company group jointly competing in an industry common market appearance, utilising development resources, optimum capital allocation as well as coordinated product and technology policy, is referred to as a concern. Accordingly, a concern is the form of appearance of capital concentration in which solutions are both built upon lateral or horizontal principles and those preferring vertical connections. That is, there are structures in which contracts or other horizontal type system of relations control the common uniform appearance, and there are concerns (characteristics in practice) in which a sub/superordinate relationship is developed between the enterprises. This is why managing and managed companies and business units are mentioned (THEISSEN 1992).

The expression of holding, both in its theoretical and practical guise in Hungary is mixed with the concern concept very often. The relationship between a holding and a concern is not expressly made clear in the special literature or in practice.

Recently, perspectives were clarified up, or got nearer to each other, and there is a compromise shown in the following interpretation: the holding is partly a special case of the concern where the managing company as a holding, influences the managed company, basically with the means of "property handling" alone. This means that the managing company (holding) intervenes into the life of the managed business organization through the forums which are deemed suitable be the different corporate rights (General Assembly, Owners' Meeting) and making it possible to enforce the effect of external assessment (e.g. purchasing of shares through share sale). The holding, at the same time, can not be considered simply as a special case, since the holding, in the case of an activity of mixed profile, can combine investments or capital property, between which the above mentioned relations do not exist in the case of a concern (HUNGENBERG 1992).

Developing a concern or a holding has, of course set prerequisites both in building up a system of legal institutes and in proprietary structures.

Regarding this issue, studying the internal organizational and structural matters of the company is also very important, in connection with the "historic preliminaries" of Hungarian large enterprises.

The overall spread of concerns and holding organizations in the developed industrial countries is the result of an organic development. Formation of divisional organizations fostered this development to a great extent. There is a principle being established in classical divisional organizations, that units of accounting and responsibility exist, these render operative service related to a particular product group, to a particular region, and the role of the centre of divisional organization. These refer predominantly to dealing with strategic issues, to finance, investment and development issues, and to operating the coordinating mechanisms. The development of divisional structures has let the division operate in legally independent business organization formations, pursuing their activities more or less independently from each other whilst the managing centre organization has been transformed in the framework of the legal regulation into a managing company, according to proprietary structure.

To summarize, it can be stated that concerns and holdings show a structure solution similar in many regards to divisional organizations. Otherwise, this means that developing the concern and holding organization is unthinkable without operating a divisional type of structure. The market economies, and particularly the experiences gained in the developed industrial countries, serve to offer a number of lessons in relation to bringing about the domestic concern and holding structures.

One of the most important lessons in the course of studying the concern and holding structure in Western countries is that chronology, continuity and succession are effective from these structures. This means first of all that operative management conceptions and means of strategy finance and property handling indicate a specific order for organization transformation and organization development. This is especially to be considered for the Hungarian organization transformation, since the former structure of large state enterprises (including organization structures of trusts) might present the basis of a concern structure operating in a highly dictatorial way. In most cases, a concern coordinated through strategic or financial means can be the first station of the move from this base. It was hardly to be expected that transforming a large enterprise showing an operative concern structure of "zero status" into a holding performing classical property handling tasks could happen in one step. However, it should be added that the types of concern management not imply automatically subsequent phases. The place taken by a certain concern in the national economy, its market determination, proprietary structure and technological peculiarities (with special attention to verticality) largely determine what type of philosophy of concern management can be realized. In this context, it is clearly shown that a concern having an intense verticality (e.g. in metallurgy) could never achieve, to all probability, a concern or holding structure operating with classical property handling functions. Otherwise formulated: this structure would be inadequate for the activity and technology run in this organization. In connection with concern and holding management in the developed industrial countries mixed solution are found very frequently. This means that in the course of managing a concern various types of concepts may coexist. The concern might have parts for which the centre exercises property handling functions of holding type, and in the case of the managed business organization, except for units closely belonging to the central concern core (core business), operative management can also take place. All these are inevitable, since the activities belonging to a concern or holding can be in several markets or can be diverse and the organization can be operated through various technologies (BÜHNER 1992).

For a significant portion of domestic efforts for organization transformation seeking after mixed solutions is unavoidable, as when transforming the organization of large companies it is reasonable to separate some pursuits closely belonging to the core business from those connected to the company primarily via capital functions. Ultimately there is the phenomenon of the so-called superposition related to concern and holding management. This is seen mainly at major multinational organizations where the operative, strategic, financial and property handling management are separated at superimposed organizational levels. This has the concrete meaning that holdings exercising a strategic and operative type management belong to a holding providing the financial and property handling function. With respect to the Hungarian enterprise and trust structures, this solution was expected to materialise only at the largest companies and trusts.

2.2 Concerns and Holdings on the Basis of State Enterprises

With the Act of Business Organizations (No. 1988/VI) coming come into force, establishing legal forms of company by existing enterprises was accelerated. Up to March of 1990, more than 100 large organizations took a smaller or higher portion of enterprise assets into business units of legal entity (shareholder companies and limited liability companies).

Often those among Hungarian large enterprises, who had financial difficulties, found the organizational form of a corporate group appropriate and, according to this, started to operate former plants (producing units) and certain departments of the enterprise centre in the form of a shareholder company or a limited liability company (MATOLCSY 1991).

Simultaneously, the remaining part of enterprise centres, cut back in their functions and staff number, were transformed into so-called "state property handling centres" or "managing companies". In the course of the "metamorphosis" into business units of legal entity, the majority of the restructured large enterprises substituted the strictly centralized, functional organization with the formation of a number of business units (shareholder companies and limited liabilities companies) directed by the property handler.

Beyond the enactment of Companies' Act of 1988, this spontaneous organizational metamorphosis could be accomplished within the meaning of the Act of Enterprise (1984). The latter law authorized organs of self-government of state enterprises (so-called enterprise committees) to decide about essential organizational changes (SÁRKÖZY 1986).

In fact, organizational (and legal) transformations of large state enterprises into concerns and holdings were incorrectly referred to as "spontaneous privatization" by Hungarian public opinion, while at first no effective privatization was realized (VOSZKA 1991a).

After the transformation, the same persons, who formerly sat in the top positions of large enterprises became the heads of the property handling centres. These "old-new" top managers, controlling the majority of shares in the business units, declared and provided in advance at the transformation, and succeeded at least for a temporary period – in saving their influence and power, and the major part of their decision competence. In order to retain their position, they were willing to agree and to make a compromise with plant managers who required complete independence. This compromise took place peacefully for the most part, since finally, plants were satisfied with the independence from the higher level, promised by the legally separated business unit formation. Moreover, the willingness of plant managers to make a compromise was supported by the condition that directors, managers, deputy directors and some in other positions in a shareolder company or limited liability company – exempted from the limitations imposed by wage regulations – could reckon to have much higher income than the actual salaries belonging to posts in the former plant.

When applying the business unit formations as legal entities – contrary to preliminary assumptions – the independence of internal units at large companies did not increase automatically. Much depended upon what freedom plant sections had gained earlier. Where plant divisions dropped into the business unit formation with legal entities to form the state of "feudal" defenselessness (almost overnight), the managing company – independently from possessing the majority of shares – gained a wider ground for realizing their intention to intervene. The property handling centre (holding) could prescribe for instance to its business units (companies) to contact with foreign business parties only indirectly, through the central trade division or to evaluate the common supplies between each other at old, internal accounting prices. Also, responding to old reflexes, the managing company (holding) could supervise the activity of their business units as well.

Nevertheless, the corporate group-model provided a relatively wider range to manoeuvre for the ex-plant divisions which were allowed, more or less, to decide on their own development, production and sales policy and to form their independent market and financial relations – in the frame of legal independence. With an increase in independence, modernizing the internal organization and management of the ex-plant division became possible, too. For instance, the role of the commercial sphere (including marketing) increased and production dominance was driven back. New functions (strategic planning, controlling) appeared at the level of new business units of legal entity, some Business units restructured their production sections into "mini" divisions which did not do business, but were allowed to decide over the operative production management, the technical parameters of materials to be purchased, and to report on offers, orders, and to make proposals for prices to be developed (DOBÁK et al. 1992).

Notwithstanding the positive movements, initially a good number of business units, managed with a deficit, operated within the corporate group. For business units of legal entity cancelling the East European export and shrinking the domestic market was often accompanied by oppressive obligations of credit installment inherited from the past. (It is to be noted that in certain parts of corporate groups the plant departments transformed into business units could start with a "new page", since the property handling centres assumed their debts). However, the operational difficulties could be attributed not only to external reasons: among others, modernizing the product range, rationalizing the working procedures, providing adequate quality standards did not manage to work out everywhere. Just then, when establishing the companies, inventories were reevaluated to an artificially low level several times, and the cash assets "adjusted to this", resulted in liquidity difficulties at an early stage. In addition, business units were charged by high rentals where the assets (real estates, machinery) remained in state property, because the cash percentage specified for the transformation in the Act of Business Organizations was not available for disposal. Last but not at least, a serious problem in operating business units of legal entities was raised by failing initially to change management. In the majority of cases the old directors of plant divisions became operative managers. This also occures in the new business units which, due to their former situation were usually proficient in managing the production but proved ill-suited for finding up new markets, for marketing tasks or financial management (VOSZKA 1991b).

All in all, the formation of corporate groups made the first massive breakthrough in the centralized, functional organization of large state enterprises. This specific organizational/legal formation which appeared in the last period of the party-state regime, partially succeeded in clearing the air from tensions emanating from the differences of efficiency between the plants (factories) of large enterprises. (Otherwise, the possibility of total independence of plant divisions was ensured by a newly enacted law only as of 1990, offering a way of retirement for "separate internal economic units" of large enterprises.) Similarly, the "closed", hierarchical organization of large enterprises was partly "opened" to new owners (banks, suppliers, clients) converting debts for shares. However, the appearance of new owners (beside the state) in the corporate groups did not mean privatization, because "external proprietors" were from the circle of state owned banking institutions and state enterprises. (Foreign capital investment was not too significant at the time.)

2.3 Transformations into Legal Forms of Company Without Establishing Concern or Holding Structure

Critical remarks concerning "spontaneous privatisation" or the process of transforming the large, state owned enterprises into organizational/legal form of company group grew considerably more frequent around 1989, during the first period of changing the political system. Critical voices stated among others that managing companies (property handling centres) were not subject to any formal control of performance and that right from the beginning "they get the owner's right for the shares or the founding capital as a free grant, and then as final proprietors they can do with the assets whatever they want" (AUTH/KROKOS 1989).

However, spontaneous privatisation was not blocked officially by the government, although there had been some steps made to establish a "superholding" to manage the assets of the state owned enterprises, despite protests by managers of large state owned firms.

The fact that the State Property Agency was founded in the spring of next year signalled that there was already some kind of consensus between certain political forces and different groups representing various economic interests which stated that "an effective control over managing the state property is necessary" (SZALAY 1992).

This change in the official evaluation of spontaneous privatisation resulted in the fact that the corporate group model lost on popularity and a number of state owned enterprises were transformed into new entities as a whole. The transition law that was passed by parliament and that came into effect in mid-1989 provided the legal framework for this process. This concept means that firms keep their former organisational unity after the transformation into company form and can later be sold this way as well.

Very few companies transformed themselves according to this latter model before the formation of the State Property Agency, which showed that enterprise leaders preferred the spontaneous way of privatisation (concern-type organisational and legal structures) that had been enabled by the Act on business organisations which had been passed earlier.

Although spontaneous privatisation did actually occur on a much smaller scale, fewer and fewer managers decided not to apply the law of transition after 1990. Spontaneous privatizations that took place after this were already controlled by the State Property Agency and it was limited to some factories of large organisations.

There was suddenly a huge increase in the number of state enterprises starting to transform themselves as "one intact entity" (160 enterprises during the period between March 1990 and mid-1991). There are several factors explaining this phenomenon. No doubt, since the government had a different perspective to spontaneous privatization, politics must have played a role in the back of managers' mind. Firm leaders, eager to keep their positions and to avoid possible accusations thought twice before "organising the companies out of the social control" by deciding to apply the corporate group-model. Intending to keep the company organisation as one entity did also play an important role. Advantages of maintaining one single and intact company organization include aspects such as owning only one seat where the firm would have to continue working, or intensive co-operation in the production phase between different plants of the company (see *Fig. 3* as a printing firm transformed into a one level company forms as a whole).

Managers also had to keep in mind the long term outlooks of the company as well as strategic interests: There was reason to believe that should the firm keep on working without any change in its organisational structure it would take no more than one or two years until serious problems would emerge, thanks to worsening economic conditions, the traditional markets getting scarcer, and the lack of resources to develop.

A further driving force was the fact that a new law was being prepared and later passed that forced nearly all state owned enterprises to transform into some new legal form of company by the middle of 1993. Consequently, it did not come as a surprise that the data base of the State Property Agency registered nearly 190 whole transformations during the year 1991, and 155 only during the first part of 1992.

2.4 Development of Private Organisations After Act on Business Organisations Came Into Effect – From Small Business to Private Holding

After the Act on Business Organizations came into effect, private initiative organizations adopting a direction of growth and transformed themselves wholly into legal forms of company (shareolder company or limited lia-

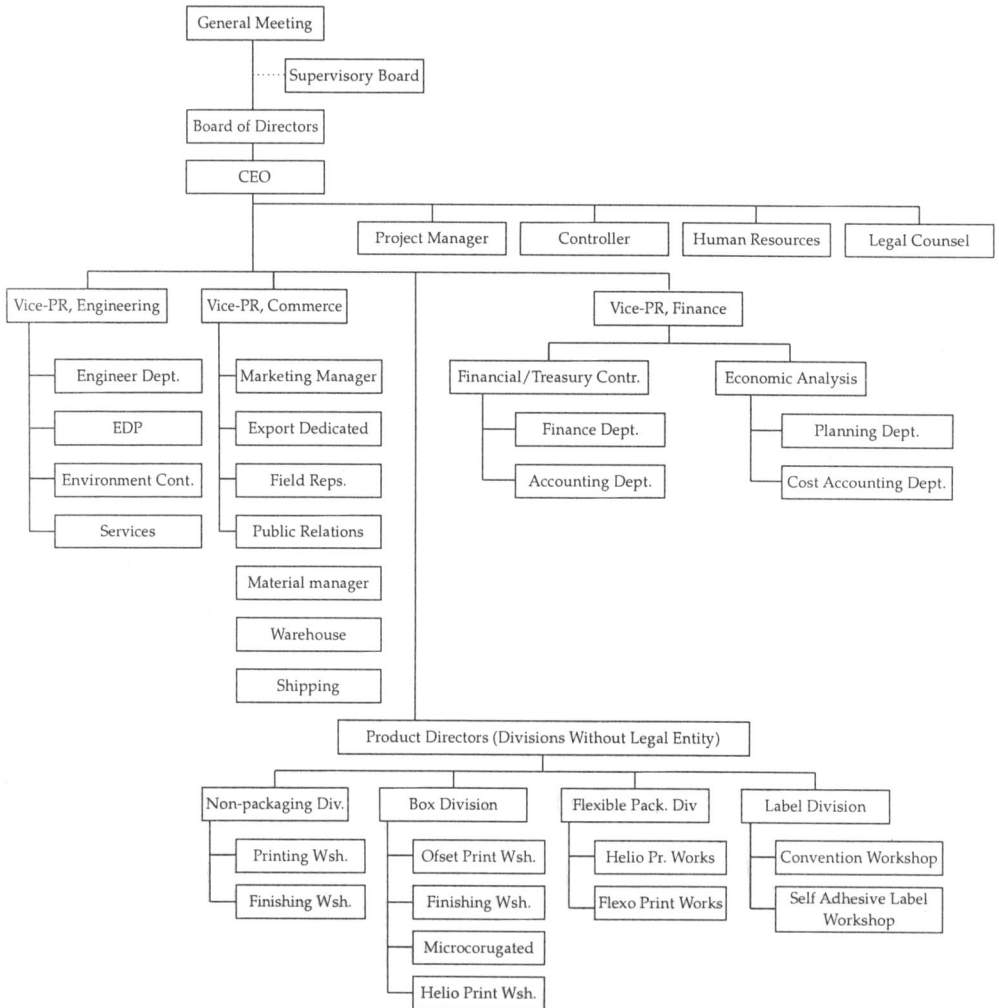

Figure 3. Organization chart of Petőfi Printing
and Packaging Co. Ltd. by Shares (1994)

bility company). But the growth was not exclusively continuing in the framework of a single level company structure.

In reality, small "satellite" firms were also founded (with or without other, foreign or Hungarian investors) in parallel to the growth and transformation of the "mother entrepreneurship". To be quite exact, this "quiet growth" had started earlier: even before the Act on business organisations was passed small private initiative enterprises such as small co-operatives began to buy interests in a number of fields of activities. Some experts explain this by stating that it would have been a political risk to "grow too large" in one field at all costs, particularly between 1986 and 1988, that is, before political changes started to happen. This might be the reason why private capital was divided among several small scale firms (MEIXNER 1991).

This resulted in the fact that, on the turn of the decade, a number of expanding private initiative enterprises were transformed into limited or shareholders' companies while owning minority or majority shares parallel in several different firms. Business successes after the "flagship" enterprise had been legally transformed then drove private entrepreneurs to found additional companies. Consequently, the transition from a single level company structure into a two level structure (holding) took place within a relatively short time with these dynamic private enterprises (one or two years altogether).

There was a *"de facto"* and *"de jure"* way to transform a private firm (with single company organization) into a holding. In the first case, the legal control of the group was not taken over by a holding centre, but the "flagship" enterprise (or its leader) did have informal ways to control all functions of the group members. The second case meant that a holding structure was created officially as well, and all branches and divisions of the former one level company were transformed into separate legal entities, whereas the "rest" that remained of the single company organisational structure took over the control functions of the holding centre.

The most frequent reason why growing private companies chose to apply a two level holding structure was that, due to the increase in market share and the number of employees, the activities of different divisions were about to get out of control. Also, shares owned in other companies could no longer be controlled without the supervision of a legally separated entity. Most private groups applied the methods of operative or strategic holding control, which means that control is not purely financial. This is quite similar to the case of the concerns emerging on the basis of state enterprises (FIÁTH/KISS 1994).

There are two ways in which the private companies or groups of companies developed further. A part of them continued to invest too heavily – they built for example new headquarters – acquired shares in peripheral fields of activity, borrowed high-interest loans only to get into the trap of growth and then went bankrupt (VARGA 1993).

Another part of expanding private companies and company groups realised the dangers in growing too quickly and succeeded in slowing down and consolidating their spheres of activities. We will return to what happened afterwards with these two kinds of expanded private enterprises and holdings in the next section.

IV. TENDENCIES IN THE DEVELOPMENT
OF ORGANISATIONAL FORMS (STRUCTURES)
IN THE MID-NINETIES

1. SUCCESSOR ORGANISATIONS OF LARGE STATE
ENTERPRISES – THE "TURN" EVENTS OF CORPORATE
GROUPS AND OF ONE LEVEL COMPANIES

All that we can hope to describe when writing about the tendencies of organisational changes in the recent past is to broadly discuss the main directions and characteristics of these changes. In doing so, we will keep on following the previous structure of our analysis: on one hand we will shortly summarise recent experience of the successor organisations of state owned companies, whereas on the other hand we will also provide (without claiming that we give an in-depth analysis), an overview of organisational issues of the Hungarian private sector with special regard to the difficulties that emerged during the last couple of years.

A. There are basically two directions in which formerly state owned companies, transformed into concerns (holdings) developed further. A part of them acted in a very responsible and conscious way and involved professional (meaning: not purely financial) foreign investors while selling them a share in the concern. These concerns (holdings) were capable of further building the corporate group and maintaining a large organisational structure (some of them by succeeding in persuading the state to write off debts of the concern) and these are currently either making a profit, or, at any rate, maintaining operations at an acceptable level. Concerns (holdings) in this category include Pannonplast Holding (plastic), Medicor (medical equipment), Dunaferr (steel) and Ganz Gépgyár Holding (machinery, see *Fig. 4*) (HUSZTY 1995).

Another part of concerns based in state enterprises proved unable to maintain operating profitably, and have thus "fallen apart". A part of these concerns (holdings) were either sold or went bankrupt, and large scale operations ceased to exist. Due to the fact that inland and East European markets had mostly been lost, some of these concerns could not be sold to investors any more so their assets were liquidated. (An example to this was Csavaripari Vállalat, once producing screws.) In case of other

Holding Rt.

91%

Holding Kft.

91% 91% 91% 91%

| Producers | Energetics Machinery Kft. | Motor Kft. | Logker Kft. | Ganz David Brown Kft. |

50% 91%

| Service Plants | Ganz Services Kft. | Maintenance Kft. |

50% 51% 100%

| New Products | Ganz Hydro Kft. | Ganz Automatika Kft. | Ganz AVIA Kft. |

50% 26% 50% 50%

| Foreign Trade, engineering | Ganz Nikma-simpex Kft. | Ganz Egypt Kft. | Ganz Sema Kft. | Ganz Technip Kft. |

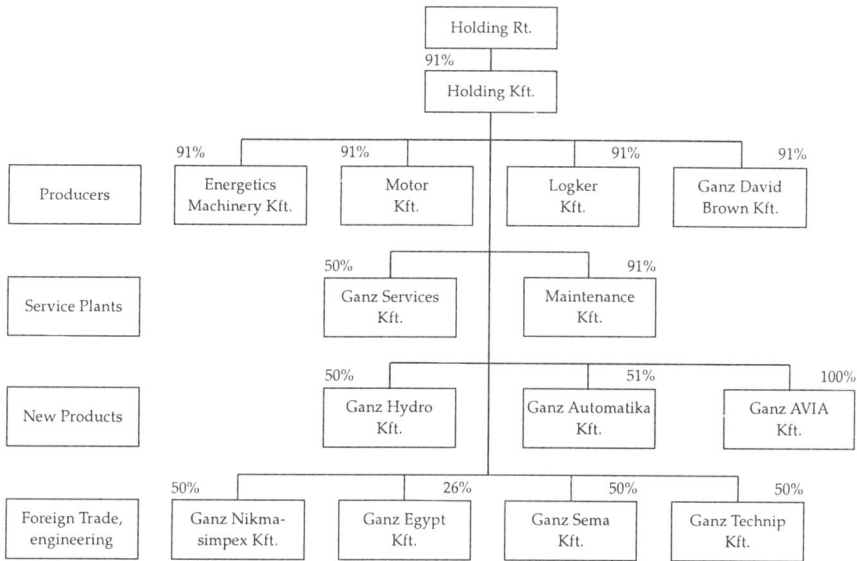

Rt.: a company limited by shares. Kft.: a company of limited liabilities.

Figure 4. The Organizational structure of Ganz Holding as of January 1996

concerns (holdings), some companies of the corporate group were sold to private investors, the rest of the (inner) companies went bankrupt (or had to pass through a difficult period) and the property handling centre of the corporate group was liquidated. (See example of the shipyard Ganz Danubius.) (VOSZKA 1994.) In some other instances the company members of the corporate group split into smaller companies that are currently working independently, all by themselves (Magyar Optikai Művek).

B. Our view is that if we have a look at companies that had been earlier transformed into a new legal entity as a whole there are also two main directions of development to be examined. A proportion of the companies that used to have a one level structure have transformed (or are about to transform) themselves and applied (or start to apply) a two level concern structure. The reason for that could either be to operate more effectively or to encourage investors to privatise the new inner companies. Another group of companies still stock to a one level structure. This can be the case where the privatisation strategy was successful and an "organic" structure could be developed. (A small portion of companies applied a die-hard strategy instead of privatisation and are constantly consuming their assets while heading for bankruptcy.)

A company with a share of less than 100% is a joint venture (the number above the box represents the share of Ganz Holding in the company).

The most general reason why companies take further steps into the direction of a concern structure is that managers think the company group will be more ready to react to market challenges if the legal entities are smaller and have a clearer profile. Also, foreign capital is more likely to be invested in these smaller entities (inner companies). Two recent and typical examples for the transition of large shareholders' companies with one level organisational structures are Rába (a well known vehicle maker), and IBUSZ (a traditional travel agency). These organisations hope to combine the advantage of both large and small organisations within the concern structure (similarly to the intentions of the age of spontaneous privatisation). The experiences of the last one or two years seem to justify these expectations of effectiveness (H. L. 1994).

Quite a few firms were able to find an investor (either professional or financial) among those companies that have kept the one level company structure all the time until now. (The privatisation strategy of these firms at the beginning was aimed at finding a professional investor to buy a minority stake, with an option to buy a majority share in the future, or to find a financial investor that would initially obtain a minority share which it would later sell to a foreign professional partner, thus enabling it to acquire a majority stake.) These companies developed a less rigid, "looser" version of a linear-functional structure (as a result of the initiative of either the foreign partner or the Hungarian management). This inner structure seems to provide the necessary organisational and management framework for effective operations. Examples for this are, among others, Hungarian pharmaceutical companies (with an outstandingly high income/profit ratio of 20 to 25%). It is worth noting here that these companies are mostly working at only "one seat" where vertical connections between the phases of production do not force (or enable) the company to apply a divisional structure that would otherwise be considered to be "more advanced". Examples for companies that have kept a one level structure and were successful in carrying out the kind of privatisation they had in mind include the two pharmaceutical "success stories" Chinoin and Egis (TARI 1994).

2. PRIVATE HOLDINGS IN THE GROWTH TRAP
AND THE SUCCESSFUL CONSOLIDATIONS

There were different things to happen to private groups after bankruptcy. Microsystem, once a computer seller "empire" simply ceased to exist after its shareholders decided to liquidate the company in November, 1994. The prestigious private firm could only maintain rapid growth by acquiring high interest loans, and although the capital assets were raised two years before the collapse, these extra resources were also used to finance a forced speed of growth. What is even worse, these resources were concentrated to markets where Microsystem had weak positions in the first place. After a lengthy period of considering what decision to make the proprietors explained: "we thought even if we had created a number of entirely independent, small limited companies they would only have produced profit for our creditors, and even afterwards it would have remained an open question whether Microsystem is ever to recover. The period of time after which recovery could be hoped for seemed to be too long" (Új Dunkerque 1994).

On the other hand, the case of Controll-group, another huge (but largely diversified) private holding represents another type of a company group after bankruptcy. The structure of Controll-group looked similar to what we described previously as a *"de facto"* holding. This enabled the companies of the group to abandon Controll Rt., the holding centre. It is true that the flagship firm failed but smaller companies succeeded in buying themselves out and start a life of their own. Examples include Controll Quality Consulting and "head-hunter" Hill International, as newly independent companies.

A manager of one of the former satellite firms explains: "This was possible thanks to the fact that Controll-group was not built up entirely based on profit reasons. Controll used to be a real incubator, where reasonable propositions of good experts could come to reality. Naturally, these firms were also in contact with the mother company, but not only and mainly with the mother company. This is why these firms are still alive today." (MEIXNER 1993.)

Private companies that were able to avoid falling into the growth trap realised the danger of growing too quickly as early as in 1991 or 1992. Firms where the management noticed the warning signs of increased debts started paying back a large part of them without hesitation: they sold entire branches, raised the assets, had their debtors pay the invoices (even via court, if necessary). They introduced strict inventory control and made the organisation leaner. (In some cases this meant dismissing as much as several hundred people.)

A number of surviving private groups started to offer complex services instead of trading with goods in the traditional way. Others diversified operations, made it possible for separate branches to mutually support each other as well as integrating production and sales. The strategy aimed at finding market gaps "that had remained unseen before" which meant that operations could be built up from practically nothing, proved to be correct for selecting new markets: relatively huge sums of income could be collected relatively quickly.

Another major factor for success was when the system of incentives as well as the corporate group image, and management style were designed to fit the credo and strategy of the holding right from the very beginning (both in the case of companies that were privately founded or bought). A number of holdings realised it was also necessary to renew the management and carry out personal changes. Since a period of growth is followed by a period of stabilisation, entrepreneur type top managers should be substituted by people who are capable of consolidate operations. Examples for companies sharing the opinions described above include Rolitron-group (medical equipment), Fotex-group (photo services, furniture production and retail, cosmetics, glassware, etc., see *Table 2* on the growth of the Fotex-group) as well as Műszertechnika Holding (computers, information technologies, and other kinds of technical equipment) (DOBÁK et al. 1996).

V. CONCLUSIONS, SUMMARY STATEMENTS

As it has been shown in the previous chapters, *actual* organisational changes *have proven* suppositions about small organisational structures becoming more frequent. Also, a large number of concerns and holdings have appeared, and the way they work did not come as a surprise to experts, either; breaking up of monolith state enterprises and organic growth of private initiative entrepreneurships provided the possibility for the functioning of concern and holding forms.

On the other hand, expectations concerning the creation and development of horizontal interorganizational cooperations, hire work, integration of activities, R & D cooperations and strategic alliances did not, or only partly proved to be successful.

Table 2. Members of the Fotex-group,
the growth chronicle of four years

(In the brackets are the share capital and the share of Fotex Ltd.)

1989.

Fotex Ltd. (Limited Liability Company) (236 million HUF)
Europtic Ltd. (234 million HUF, 50.1%)
Multivízió Ltd. (1 million HUF, 50.1%)

1990.

Fotex Ltd. (Shareolder company) (September: 2601.6 million HUF;
November: 3101.6 million HUF)
Europtic Ltd. (234 million HUF, 50.1%)
Multivízió Ltd. (71 million HUF, 50.1%)
Proficolor Ltd. (1 million HUF, 30%)
Ajka Kristály Ltd. (August: 55.5 million HUF, 30%;
December: 317 million HUF, 50.1%)
Azurunio Ltd. (254 million HUF, 93%)
Azurinvest Ltd. (702 million HUF, 50% of the voting shares)
Kontúr Ltd. (268 million HUF, 15%)

1991.

Fotex Ltd. (4538.6 million HUF)
Multivízió Ltd. (73.5 million HUF, 53.6%)
Europic Ltd. (234 million HUF, 50.1%)
Ajka Kristály Ltd. (March: 705.5 million HUF, 50.1%)
Azurunio Ltd. (254 million HUF, 93%)
Azurinvest Ltd. (702 million HUF, 71.6% of the voting shares)
Kontúr Ltd. (853 million HUF, 50.8%)
Domus Ltd. (1633 million HUF, 6.1%)
Fotex Agent Ltd. (1 million HUF, 51%)
Interkristály Ltd. (48 million HUF, 50%)
Ingatlanfejlesztő Ltd. (1.3 million HUF, 90%)

1992. Changes compared to previous year:

Fotex Ltd. (4606.6 million HUF)
Europic Ltd. (234 million HUF, 100%)
Ajka Kristály Ltd. (705.5 million HUF, 100%)
Kontúr Ltd. (913 million HUF, 50.8%)
Domus Ltd. (1633 million HUF, 21.1%)
Ofotért Ltd. (1000 million HUF, 50%)
Ingatlanfejlesztő Ltd. (900 million HUF, 90%)
G. Pharma Ltd. (1 million HUF, 100%)
Számítástechnikai Ltd. (1 million HUF, 51%)

The growing share of small private organisations directed professional interest to the importance of less formalised and regulated management structures and spontaneous inner mechanisms of managing an organisation.

Two level concern and holding structures made it possible for a certain section of the producing plants of large state owned enterprises to survive for a little while, "to take a deep breath" while improving chances to convince outer capital to invest into the business unit. These production units were later developed into real divisions (profit centres) within the framework of the company group after a successful partial privatisation of the companies. Concern and holding structures could also be utilised to coordinate business units in private initiative companies as well as to create encourage profit-orientation in separate branches of the private groups.

Viewing things from a different angle, it is also a fact that organisational networks (e.g. subcontracting) are not as wide-spread as could reasonably be expected, based on the large number of small organisations. The overwhelming majority of small enterprises have remained economically independent meaning that no long-lasting interorganizational cooperation links have been formed to the present time.

Similarly, due to a number of factors inherited from the past, there are still very few cooperations with a strategic vision in R & D, marketing-sales, logistics-purchase between foreign and Hungarian (state owned or private) companies.

Nevertheless, some signs indicate that connections between companies are being reorganised. The disintegration of former interorganizational systems (as a result of market shocks, changes in the ownership and economic-political measures) seems to have come to an end. The volume of subcontractors' billings have increased considerably during the last two years, which means that the "trust crises", the lack of confidence in one's partners is decreasing. There are three centres of gravity for subcontractors: successful industrial concerns based on former state enterprises, private company groups and subsidiaries of multinational companies established in Hungary.*

* The authors are grateful to SOMA HORVÁTH, Assistant to the Department of Management and Organization for the finish up of the article.

REFERENCES

AUTH, H., KROKOS, J.: Kié az állami vállalat? Csodás átváltozások (Who is the owner of the state enterprise? Miraculous metamorphosis). Figyelő. 9 February (1989).

BÜHNER, R.: Management – Holding. Verlag Moderne Industrie (1992).

DEÁK, J.: Vállalkozás és szervezeti formák (Entrepreneurship and organizational forms). Vezetés. Szervezés. March (1987).

DOBÁK, M.: Szervezetátalakítás és szervezeti formák (Organizational design and organizational forms). Közgazdasági és Jogi Könyvkiadó. Budapest (1988).

DOBÁK, M. et al.: Szervezeti formák és koordináció (Organizational forms and coordination). Közgazdasági és Jogi Könyvkiadó. Budapest (1992).

DOBÁK, M. et al.: Szervezeti formák és vezetés (Organizational forms and management). Közgazdasági és Jogi Könyvkiadó. Budapest (1996).

FIÁTH, A./KISS, T.: Dicső múlt – a Kontrax vállalatcsoport története (Glorious past – history of the Kontrax-group). Vezetéstudomány. June (1994).

H. L.: Holdinggá szervezik a Rábát (Rába will be transformed into holding). Magyar Hírlap. 6 May (1994).

HUNGENBERG, H.: Die Aufgaben der Zentrale (Ansatzpunkte zur zeitgemäßen Organisation der Unternehmensführung in Konzernen). Zeitschrift für Organisation. Nr. 6 (1992).

HUSZTY, A.: A Pannonplast és a stratégia – a szellemi erők összpontosítása (The Pannonplast-group and the strategy – concentration of the rational forces). Menedzser Piac. January (1995).

MAKAI, L.: Rázós úton. A társas magánvállalkozások formaválasztásának folyamatai 1982-től 1989-ig (On rough way. Processes of choosing organizational and legal forms for private entrepreneurships from 1982 to 1989). Vezetéstudomány. January (1991).

MÁRIÁS, A. et al.: Organization of large industrial enterprises in Hungary: a comparative analysis. Acta Oeconomica. Vol. 27, Nr. 3/4 (1981).

MATOLCSY, G. (ed.): Lábadozásunk évei. A magyar privatizáció (Years of our reconvalescence. The Hungarian privatization). Privatizációs Kutatóintézet. Budapest (1991).

MEIXNER, Z.: Magánvállalati stratégiák (Strategies of private organizations). Figyelő. 15 August (1991).

MEIXNER, Z.: A holding holdudvara (Satellits of the holding). Figyelő. 7 December (1993).

MÓRA, M.: Az állami vállalatok (ál)privatizációja (Pseudo privatization of state enterprises). Közgazdasági Szemle. June (1991).

SÁRKÖZY, T.: Egy gazdasági szervezeti reform sodrában (In the drift of an organizational reform). Magvető Kiadó. Budapest (1986).

SCHWEITZER, I.: A vállalatnagyság (The company size). Közgazdasági és Jogi Könyvkiadó. Budapest (1982).

SZALAI, E.: Perpetuum mobile? Nagyvállalatok az államszocializmus után (Perpetuum mobile? Large enterprises after the period of state socialism). Valóság. April (1992).

TARI, E.: Iparvállalatok belső irányítási szervezete (Organizational structure of the industrial enterprises). Közgazdasági és Jogi Könyvkiadó. Budapest (1988).

Tari, E.: Stratégiai szövetség és privatizáció. A Chinoin–Sanofi "házasság" (Strategic alliance and privatization. The Chinoin–Sanofi "marriage"). Esettanulmány. BKE Vezetési és Szervezési Tanszék (1994).

Theissen, M. R.: Der Konzern. Poeschel Verlag. Stuttgart (1991).

Új Dunkerque: A Microsystem felszámolása (New Dunkerque: winding-up of Micro-system). Figyelő. 12 December (1994).

Varga, G.: Korszakváltás a Fotex Rt.-ben (Beginning a new era in the Fotex-group). Figyelő. 11 March (1993).

Varga, G.: Növekedési csapda (Pitfall of growth). Figyelő. 25 March (1993).

Voszka, É.: Ownership reforms or privatization. Eastern European Economics. Fall (1991a).

Voszka, É.: Tulajdonosok és menedzserek (Owners and managers). Európa Fórum. No. 2 (1991b).

Voszka, É.: An attempt at crisis management and failure of the spontaneous privatization. Industrial and Environmental Crisis Quarterly. Vol. 8, No. 1 (1994).

18

THE STRUCTURE OF WORK VALUES:
A CROSS CULTURAL COMPARISON*

By

DOV ELIZUR, INGWER BORG, RAYMOND HUNT,
ISTVÁN MAGYARI-BECK

Several years ago a research project on work values was originated. The study strived to examine the relative importance of work value items and to analyze the structure of the domain for samples from various cultural environments. A facet definition of work values was suggested that provided guidelines for constructing the Work Values Questionnaire and the formulation of hypotheses regarding the structure of relationships among components of work values. Based on data collected from 2280 respondents in eight countries the hypotheses were tested by means of GUTTMAN's Smallest Space Analysis. The results support the hypotheses. An empirical double-ordered conceptual system, a radex structure, was obtained in each of the samples reflecting the facets of the definition: modality of outcome – cognitive, affective and instrumental, and system – performance contingency – reward, resource.

In terms of the issue of cultural differences the results indicate the presence of cultural differences in the rating of a limited number of specific values. These differences are only minor variations within a much broader pattern of structural similarity. The fact that essentially the same structure was obtained in eight independent samples lends substantial support to the definitional framework of work values suggested.

INTRODUCTION

There has been growing interest in recent years in the analysis of value systems in general (ROKEACH 1979; BRAITHWAITE and LAW 1985; SCHWARTZ and BILSKY 1987), and of work values specifically (BORG 1986; ELIZUR 1984; ENGLAND 1967; FURNHAM 1984; HOFSTEDE 1980). Extensive changes in work values between populations (DICKSON and BUCHHOLZ 1977), subpopulations (RONEN 1978) and generations (CHERRINGTON 1980; LEVY-LE BOYER

* In *Journal of Organizational Behavior*, 1991, Vol. 12, pp. 21–38.

1986; YANKELOVICH 1979), have been reported. Some authors observed a decline in traditional work values and an increased concern with quality of work life, comfort and avoiding risks (ETZIONI 1979).

In view of the large number of studies, it is surprising to find that little attention has been devoted to the basic structure of the work values domain (CAMPBELL and PRITCHARD 1976). Better understanding of the concept structure of the work values domain would facilitate integration of theory and aid in developing items for research and evaluation (BILLINGS and CORNELIUS 1980).

Based on previous research and on data collected from samples in eight countries, the present study strives to find the basic concept structure of work values. Special emphasis was placed on defining the work values domain explicitly in terms of its component elements by means of facet analysis (ELIZUR 1970; ELIZUR and GUTTMAN 1976; GUTTMAN 1968). We then proceed to examine the extent to which the empirical data (i.e. subject's responses to questionnaire items) reflect the conceptual structure underlying the definition. A major objective of the present study was to examine differential levels of work values in various cultures. Data collected from 2280 respondents in eight countries, constituted an essential part of the study.

Any study of values or work values requires a clear conceptualization of these terms. Indeed the meaning of values and work values and the affinity between them and related concepts has been the subject of considerable deliberations in the literature. Authors usually consider values as affecting behavior. Values are important elements in an individual's frame of reference (PENNINGS 1970). They are considered as normative standards to judge and to choose among alternative modes of behavior (BECKER and McKLINTOCK 1967; KLUCKHOHN 1952). ALLPORT, VERNON and LINDSEY (1951) consider values as basic interests or motives and evaluative attitudes. Certain authors regard values as a particular class of motives (FEATHER 1982). FRENCH and KAHN (1962) describe both needs and values as having the basic conceptual property of the ability to motivate goal directed behavior in the person by inducing valence on certain environmental objects, behavior, or states of affair. Values constitute a basic component in cognitive theories of motivation (PORTER and LAWLER 1968; VROOM 1964).

Some authors suggest a distinction between values and attitudes (ROKEACH 1973), whereas GUTTMAN (1982) considers values a subset of attitudes with a special emphasis on the concept of importance. According to GUTTMAN an item belongs to the universe of value items if, and only if, its domain asks estimation of the degree of importance of a goal or behavior in life area (z) and the range is ordered from very important to obtain to very important to avoid the goal.

We propose that "value" of a given social group is any entity (object, behavior, situation) on which that group places a high worth or importance. Consequently work values are such entities in the work context.

The most widely used approach classifies work values as intrinsic or extrinsic, but the adequacy of the intrinsic–extrinsic dichotomy has been questioned. Researchers working within different paradigms have used different definitions of intrinsic and extrinsic (BILLINGS and CORNELIUS 1978). DYER and PARKER (1975) concluded that the entire intrinsic–extrinsic issue should be reexamined. Do they represent two separate constructs, as suggested by WERNIMONT (1972), are they facets of a single concept, or are they elements of a single facet?

There have been few comprehensive research attempts to define and sample systematically the domain. What is available has used some variants of the factor analytic procedure. Such procedures do not include, however, an *a priori* definition of the domain and testing it empirically. This is an area where classification is sorely needed as argued by FITZGERALD and HUBERT (1987) and a reframing of the basic research issue in a form amenable to a scaling analysis might prove helpful in resolving some of the confusion surrounding this area such as what the basic dimensions (structure) of work values are and whether there are differences in the emphasis placed on these dimensions in different populations.

The present study proposed and tested a general definitional framework for work values, and assessed its validity for samples from different cultural environments.

The formal approach of facet analysis (ELIZUR 1970, 1984; ELIZUR and GUTTMAN 1976; GUTTMAN 1959; SHAPIRA and ZEVULUN 1979; SHYE 1978) was the central tool used in the present study. Facet analysis attempts to formally define the universe of observations, and to test hypotheses about the relationship between the definitional framework and the structure of the empirical observations. A facet is a conceptional criterion for classifying observational items. More than one facet can be used in designing observations. Each additional domain facet defines a new classification and further differentiates among items. A multiple faceted design is composed of a set of profiles, or structuples, based on selecting one element of each of the facets.

DEFINING THE WORK VALUES DOMAIN

In order to analyze the work values domain systematically, an attempt was made to define its essential facets. Two basic facets were distinguished: modality of outcome and system performance contingency.

Facet A – Modality of outcome

Various work outcomes are of material nature. Some of them can be directly applied (such as pay), others have direct practical consequences (such as benefits, hours of work, work conditions, etc.). This class of outcomes can be defined as material, or *instrumental*, in a sense that they are concrete and of practical use. It should be noted that the term instrumental is applied here in a sense common to definitions of attitudes (ELIZUR 1970; ELIZUR and GUTTMAN 1976; FISCHBEIN and AJZEN 1975), rather than the meaning applied in theories of work motivation (e.g. GRAEN 1969; VROOM 1964 and others). The instrumentality of outcome refers here to the external nature of this class of outcomes rather than the internal nature of the other modalities.

Although material outcomes are more salient, there exist various other outcomes which are not of material nature. Most studies include items which ask about relations with people, including colleagues, supervisor, and others. These items deal with interpersonal relations, and they are *affective* rather than material.

An additional class of outcomes include items such as interest, achievement, responsibility, and independence. These items may be classified as *cognitive* rather than affective or instrumental.

Thus, facet A deals with the modality of the outcome. Its three elements specify whether the outcome is instrumental, affective, or cognitive. The various modalities may be considered as comprising a specific conceptual facet of work values and each of them appears in combination with elements of other facets. The generality of the modalities facet in social research may be advantageous for the study of work values in that it may facilitate wider comparison of research results and integration of theory.

Facet B – System-performance contingency

The second classification concerns system performance contingency, and can be considered to cut across that of modality. Management of organizations recognize the necessity of motivating individuals to join the organization and to attend to work. For that purpose they provide various incentives which are usually given before task performance and are not conditional upon its outcome. These include benefit plans, work conditions, various services, such as transplantation, subsidized meals, as well as other resources provided by the organizations. KATZ and KAHN (1966) refer to these as systems rewards, earned merely through membership in the system. The term *resources* is suggested to characterize this class of outcomes.

Certain other outcomes, however, are usually provided after task performance and in exchange for it, such as pay, recognition, achievement, and status. The term *rewards* may best characterize this class of work outcomes.

On the basis of these observations, a formal definition of work values by means of a mapping sentence was drafted, whose domain includes two facets, and the range of which expresses the degree of importance of the outcomes to the respondent. Application of the mapping sentence (see *Fig. 1*) to one of the work values, e.g. hours of work, may be illustrated by the following example: The extent to which employee x assess the importance to her or him of having convenient hours of work is of (very high to very low) importance to her or him for a sense of well-being at work.

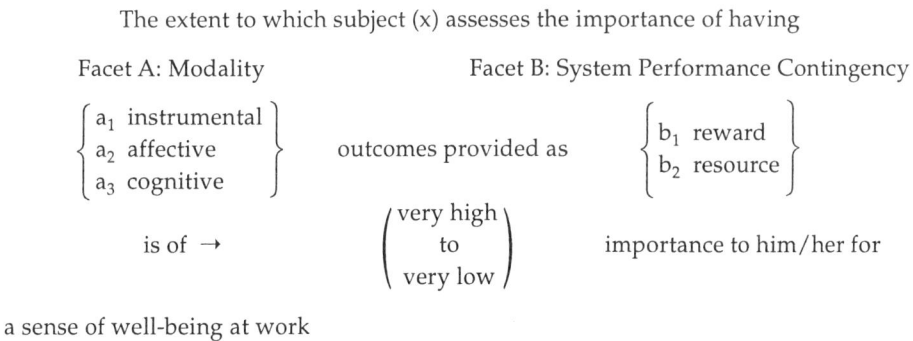

The extent to which subject (x) assesses the importance of having

Facet A: Modality   Facet B: System Performance Contingency

$$\begin{Bmatrix} a_1 \ \text{instrumental} \\ a_2 \ \text{affective} \\ a_3 \ \text{cognitive} \end{Bmatrix} \quad \text{outcomes provided as} \quad \begin{Bmatrix} b_1 \ \text{reward} \\ b_2 \ \text{resource} \end{Bmatrix}$$

$$\text{is of} \ \rightarrow \quad \begin{pmatrix} \text{very high} \\ \text{to} \\ \text{very low} \end{pmatrix} \quad \text{importance to him/her for}$$

a sense of well-being at work

Figure 1. Mapping sentence definition of work values

OBJECTIVES AND HYPOTHESES

The main objective of the present study was to examine the importance and structure of work values for respondents from different countries. It was expected that although differences in the relative importance of work outcomes might exist, the basic structure of the work values domain would be similar for respondents of the various samples.

It was hypothesized that with an appropriate structural analysis of empirical data, the two facets of the definition suggested would be reflected as two independent classifications in each of the samples.

For facet B an order based on the relationship to task performance was specified. Performance contingent rewards were expected to be nearer to the origin, while systems rewards were expected to be in the peripheral region of the map.

The modality facet (facet A) has no *a priori* ordering for this problem. Each of the modalities was expected to correspond to a different direction away from the origin. This does not imply that, for other problems, there can be no simple ordering of this facet. In certain other studies order specifications could be found for the elements of the modality facet (ELIZUR 1979; LEVY 1981).

The total structure hypothesized is that of a radex structure (GUTTMAN 1954). This is a radial distribution of the items as points where one facet corresponds to the axial direction from center to periphery and the second facet relates to the direction angles around the axis.

METHOD

Subjects

Data were collected from samples of managers, employees and students in eight countries: U.S.A., China, Korea, Taiwan, Germany, Holland, Hungary and Israel.

The U.S.A. sample was composed of 154 individuals enrolled in the graduate and undergraduate evening business programs at the School of Management, The State University of New York/Buffalo. Over 90% had full-time jobs, the remaining were employed on a part-time basis. Occupations span a very wide variety of classifications including professionals (engineers, pharmacists, lawyers, etc.), managers, and laborers. The majority of the sample were between 21–39 years of age and males constituted 54% of the sample.

The China sample consisted of 108 participants enrolled in the "Young Executive Program" at the National Center for Science and Technology, Management Development at Dalian, China, which is supported by PRC and U.S.A. funding. This is a 3 year program, the first year of which is devoted to learning English and general business courses. The last two years constitute an MBA program similar to the program at SUNY Buffalo. Demographically, this group is similar in most respects to the U.S.A. sample, except that the sample is about 90% male.

The Korea sample of 95 individuals were composed of two groups of students at Chung-Ang University and a group of workers in an automobile manufacturing company. One group of students were enrolled in the evening BA in Management program. All had full-time jobs, and about 95% were in their 20s. The second group of students were engineering majors also enrolled in the evening program. All had full-time jobs during they day. The third group represented employees who work in the head office of KAI, the third largest auto manufacturer in Korea. These were people who worked in various business functional units, not manufacturing line workers. 81% of the sample were males.

The Taiwan samples of 148 individuals were composed of groups of students at the National Tsing Ijua University. One group of undergraduates in the Department of Industrial Engineering, and other groups of graduate students. The majority of the sample were within the 20–29 age category. About 60% were males and the majority were full-time students.

The German sample consisted of 345 managers and employees of various small business organizations and students of business. The majority of the sample were between 20 and 29 years of age and about 60% were males.

The Dutch sample of 515 individuals included managers from various organizations and students of business and economies at the Haarlem School of Economics and graduate and undergraduate students at the Amsterdam University faculty of psychology. The majority of the sample were between 20 to 29 years of age and 73% were males.

The Hungary sample consisted of 540 managers and employees of a large industrial corporation. 69% were males. About half of the females and two thirds of the male respondents were responsible for the work of others.

The Israel sample of 378 respondents consisted of samples of private and public sector managers and of graduate students of business and economics at Tel Aviv, Jerusalem and Bar Ilan Universities. The majority of the sample were between 21 and 39 years of age and 70% of the sample were males.

Since the major objective of the study at the present stage of development was to examine the structure of work values in various cultural environments, opportunity samples were found suitable for this purpose. Comparison of the major characteristics of the various samples in *Table 1* shows that the majority of respondents in all samples were males. The modal age group was 21 to 29 years of age except of the Dutch sample who are younger and the Hungarian who are older. The U.S.A. and China samples consist of higher educated respondents while in the European and Israel samples only about one-third or less have completed their bachelor degree studies. Most samples contain about 30% of supervisory or managerial staff, while the Korea, Germany and Dutch samples include mainly non-supervisory personnel.

Table 1. Comparison of the samples

	China	Germany	Holland	Hungary	Israel	Korea	Taiwan	U.S.A.
Males (%)	90	61	73	69	70	81	60	55
Females (%)	10	39	27	31	30	19	40	40
Modal age group	21–29	21–29	19–20	30–39	21–29	21–29	21–29	21–29
BA or higher (%)	88	33	4	25	35	65	57	100
Supervise 10 or more workers	29	3	4	31	29	0	23	32
No. of respondents	108	345	515	540	378	95	148	154

Total n = 2280

THE QUESTIONNAIRE

Based on the extent literature on work values and motivation a structured 24 item Work Values Questionnaire (WVQ) has been systematically designed to represent the various aspects of work values. Items were selected to represent the major perspectives outlined by basic theories of motivation: Need theories such as MASLOW (1954), ALDERFER (1972) e.g. existence – pay security; relatedness – esteem, recognition; growth – personal growth; MCCLELLAND'S (1961) achievement; affiliation – co-workers; and power – influence; HERZBERG'S (1974) motivators (the cognitive items), and hygiene (material and social items). The job characteristics model of HACKMAN and OLDHAM (1980) is represented by items like: variety, use of ability, meaningful work, independence (autonomy), feedback, recognition. All items assess the importance of the various items which represent the valence of outcomes in terms of expectancy theory (VROOM 1964). Respondents were asked to indicate for each of the items to what extent it is important. There were six possible response categories ranging from "very important" to "very unimportant" (see list of items in *Table 2*).

Classification of the items according to the facets lead to the categorization of pay, hours of work, security, benefits, and work conditions as instrumental: relations with supervisor, co-workers, recognition, esteem, and opportunity to interact with people as affective; responsibility, advancement, achievement, influence, interest, feedback, meaningful work, use of abilities, independence, company, status, and contribution to society as cognitive. Pay, recognition, feedback advancement, and status were classified as rewards, and the remaining items as resources.

Table 2. List of work value items and key to variables
in *Figures* 2 to 9

1. Achievement in work
2. Advancement, changes for promotion
3. Benefits, vacation, sick leave, pension, insurance, etc.
4. Company, to be employed by a company for which you are proud to work
5. Contribution to society
6. Convenient hours of work
7. Co-workers, fellow workers who are pleasant and agreeable
8. Esteem, that you are valued as a person
9. Feedback concerning the results of your work
10. Independence in work
11. Influence in the organization
12. Influence in work
13. Job interest, to do work which is interesting to you
14. Job security, permanent job
15. Job status
16. Meaningful work
17. Opportunity for personal growth
18. Opportunity to meet people and interact with them
19. Pay, the amount of money you receive
20. Recognition for doing a good job
21. Responsibility
22. Supervisor, a fair and considerate boss
23. Use of ability and knowledge in your work
24. Work conditions, comfortable and clean

SMALLEST SPACE ANALYSIS

Smallest space analysis (SSA) was found suitable for analyzing the relations between the items and for testing the hypotheses concerning the structure of the domain. Smallest Space Analysis is one of a variety of nonmetric multidimensional scaling (MDS) analysis techniques for structural analysis of similarity data (ELIZUR 1970; ELIZUR and GUTTMAN 1976; GUTTMAN 1968; SCHLESINGER and GUTTMAN 1969). For a given matrix of pairwise similarity coefficients between items, the SSA-I computer program maps items into a space of prespecified dimensionality. Each item is represented by a point. The distances among the points are inversely related to the observed relationships among the items as defined by the similarity coefficients. When the similarity between two items is high, the distance between the points representing them is relatively small. Conversely, when the similarity between two items is low, the distance between their geometric points should be relatively large. When the SSA dimensionality is higher than 2.0, the program prints out a series of two-dimensional projections of the multidimensional configuration.

The structure of the relationships among items can readily be examined by considering the configuration of the points. When there is an *a priori* definitional framework suggested, it is possible to examine whether the space can be partitioned into regions that reflect the facets and their elements.

The division into regions is accomplished by introducing partition lines according to the facet definition of the items. Regions are in general not "clusters" that are discernible by "empty space" around them. The content universe is conceived as a geometrical space, where the specific items are but a sample of all conceivable items (of that universe) comprising the total space with points everywhere. This means that some items at the edge of one region may correlate less with other items of the same region than they do with certain items on the edge of neighboring regions.

Regional hypotheses relate to the roles that the facets of the items can play in partitioning the conceptual space of the empirical similarity coefficients matrix. Rationales for various kinds of partitioning come in part from considerations of order among the elements of the facet. An unordered facet can play a polar role: each element corresponding to a different direction in the space, emanating from a common origin. A simple ordered facet can play a modular role, namely, have a correspondence with distance from the origin.

Various laws of correspondence between regions of the SSA space and elements of the facets have been defined (ELIZUR and GUTTMAN 1976; LEVY 1981; SHYE 1978). Examples of such patterns are the duplex – the result of two modular roles in two linear orderings – and, as in the present case, the radex – the result of a linear ordering and a circular one.

RESULTS AND INTERPRETATION

The results of the SSA-I computer program in the form of a map are reproduced in *Figs 2* to *9*. Each point represents one of the work values. The distance between the points is based on the correlation between each item and the other items; the higher the correlation between two items, the closer they should be in the space.

Observing the maps in *Figs 2* to *9* which depict the structure of the variables for the eight samples, one sees that basically similar structures were obtained for the different samples. The structure of the empirical data for the eight independent samples thus reflects a division of the space into regions according to the facets defined. The modality facet, facet A, was found to be polarizing and, therefore, each modality corresponds to a

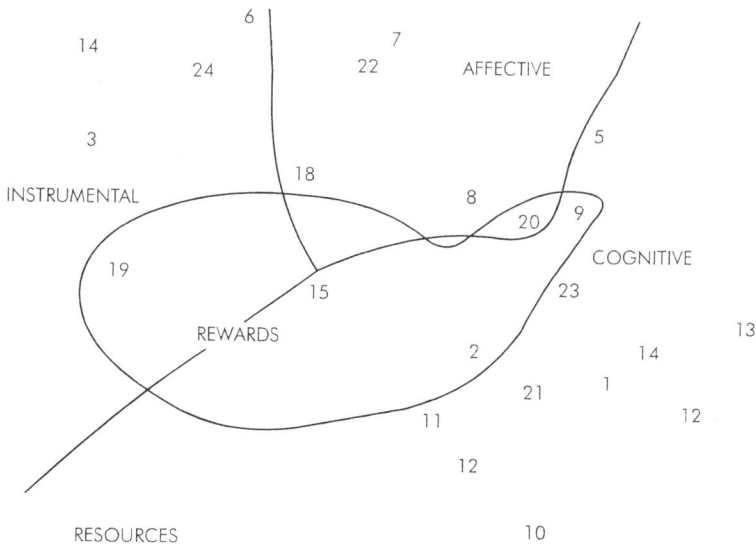

Figure 2. The structure of work values. The U.S.A. sample, 2 dimensional SSA
(coef. of alienation = 0.21)

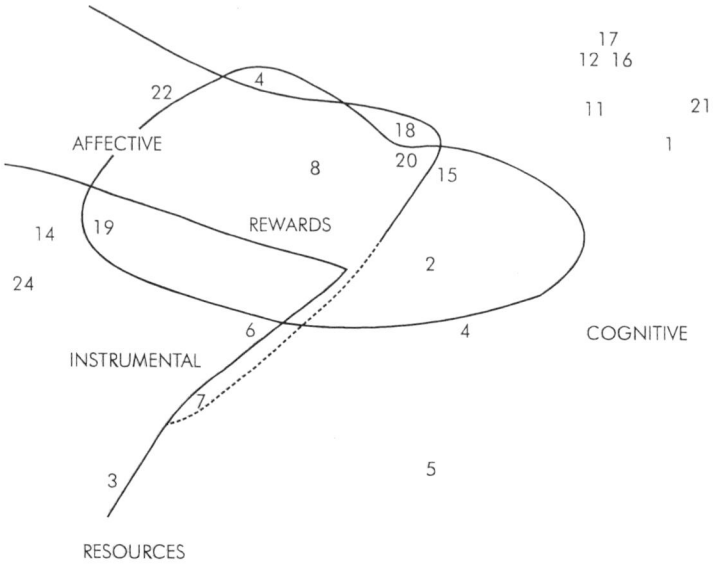

Figure 3. The structures of work values. The Taiwan sample. 2 out of 3 dim. SSA
(coef. of alienation = 0.19)

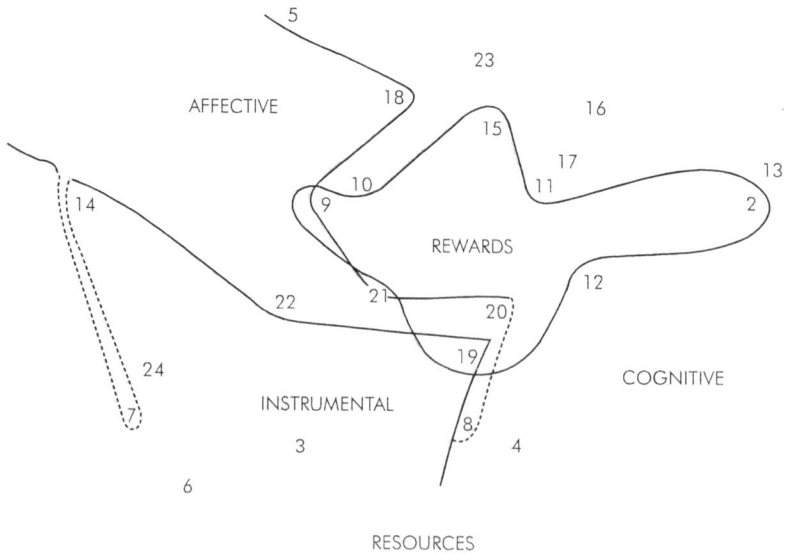

Figure 4. The structures of work values. The China sample. 2 out of 3 dim. SSA
(coef. of alienation = 0.20)

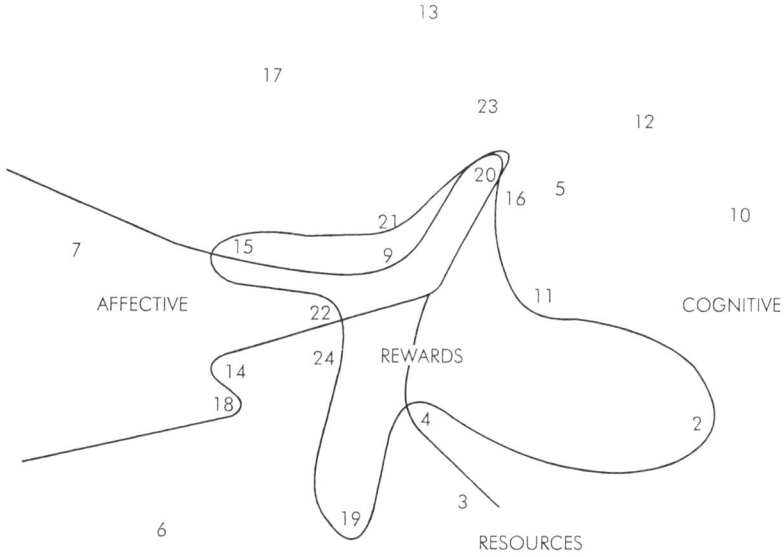

Figure 5. The structures of work values. The Korea sample. 2 dimensional SSA
(coef. of alienation = 0.31)

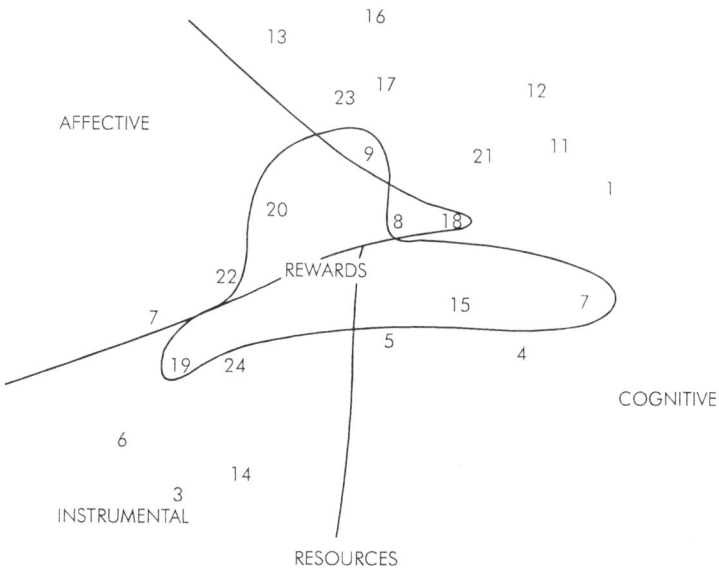

Figure 6. The structures of work values. The Hungarian sample. 2 dimensional SSA
(coef. of alienation = 0.22)

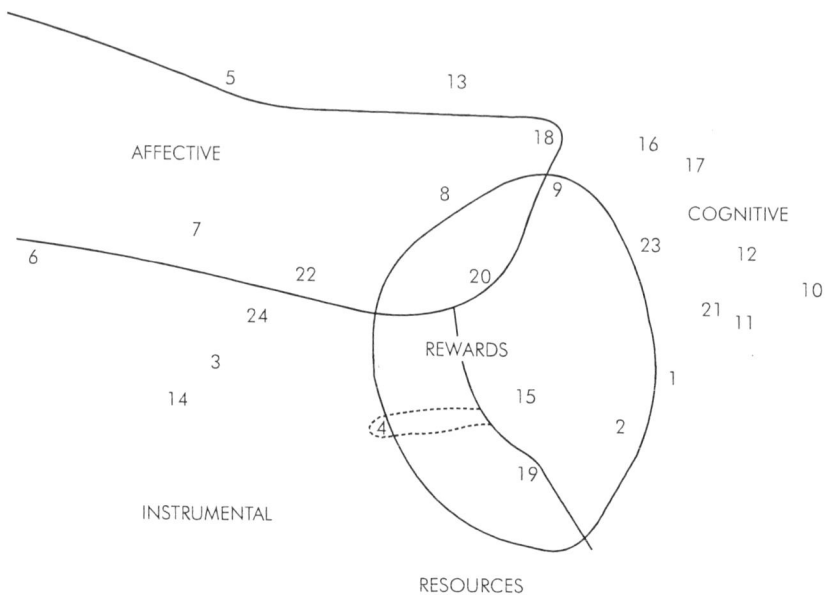

Figure 7. The structures of work values. The Dutch sample. 2 dimensional SSA
(coef. of alienation = 0.19)

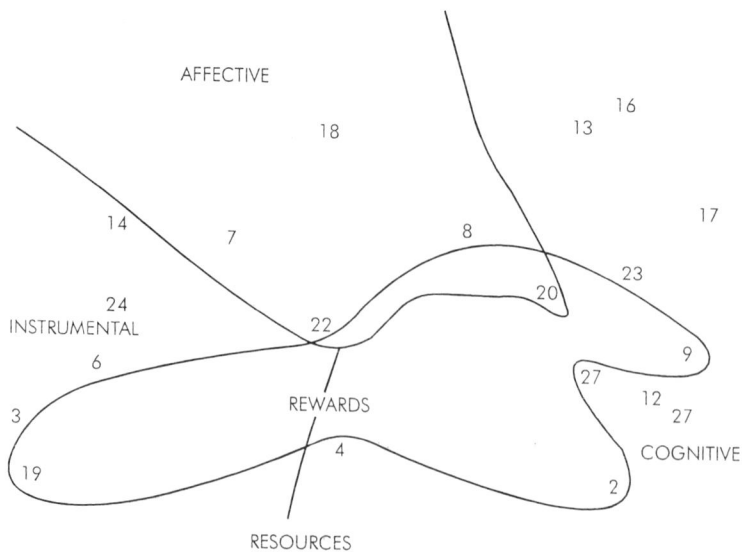

Figure 8. The structures of work values. The Israel sample. 2 dimensional SSA
(coef. of alienation = 0.26)

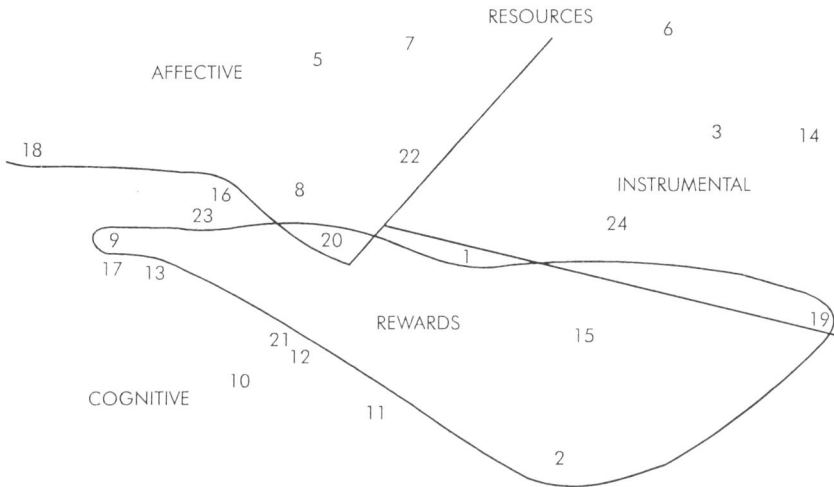

Figure 9. The structures of work values. The German sample. 2 dimensional SSA (coef. of alienation = 0.24)

different direction. Facet B, concerning system-performance contingency, orders the conceptual space from center to periphery. Rewards are in the central region of the map; resources available in the work environment and not directly related to job performance are located in the peripheral region of the map. In other words, the two facets together correspond to a radial partitioning of the space. The system-performance contingency corresponds to the direction of the radius from center to periphery, and the modality facet corresponds to the circumference of the structures, with the three modalities indicating three directions from the origin. Thus, the kind of lawfulness that relates the definitional system to the empirical structure is indeed a radex.

In light of the structural similarity of work values for samples from different cultural environments, it may be of interest to examine deviations in the location of specific items and to consider whether these deviations reflect qualitative cultural differences. In fact there are very few items which are dislocated, i.e. located in a region not in accordance with their classification. The item "co-workers" (item 7) for instance was classified as affective and is located in the instrumental region for the China and Taiwan samples, and the item "esteem" (item 8) classified as affective is located in the cognitive region for the Korean sample. The item "company" (item 4) classified as cognitive appears in the instrumental region for the Dutch sample. It may be that this deviation is due to the fact that the younger Dutch respondents consider the company only as a means to find a job without much commitment to a specific organization.

The item "supervisor" (item 22) classified as resource is located in the Hungary, Korea, Israel and Taiwan samples near the "rewards" region. Although these are no deviations, together with the high ranking of supervisor in these samples (see *Table 3*) it may indicate that supervisors in these cultures possess higher authority and reward power than in others.

The item "esteem as a person" (no. 8) classified as a resource is in most samples located nearby the rewards region. This may be due to the fact that in work organizations esteem as a person is mainly based on performance. Since most of the deviations appear in the smaller samples further research will be required to determine whether these deviations show real differences in the meaning of work value items in different cultures rather than errors resulting of the small samples.

The relative importance of work value items to respondents in the various cultural environments was also of interest. *Table 3* presents the percentage of extreme positive responses to each of the items. The major similarities and differences between the samples may be better comprehended by considering the rank order of the work values items based on the marginal distributions as presented in *Table 4*. Achievement was considered as the most important work value by respondents of four countries including China, Taiwan, Korea and Israel, it was regarded second in importance by respondents of the U.S.A., Dutch and Hungarian samples only ninth or tenth by the German respondents. Job interest was considered the most important in the U.S.A., Dutch and German samples, second in the Taiwan and Israel samples and third in the Korean sample. It was ranked, however, considerably lower by the China and Hungarian respondents. Personal growth, recognition, esteem, advancement and use of abilities were relatively highly ranked in most samples, but were quite low in specific samples (e.g. advancement and personal growth in the German and Hungarian samples; responsibility in the German sample and recognition in the China and German samples).

Table 3. Work values of samples from eight countries.
Percentage of extreme positive response

Content	Germany n = 345	Holland n = 515	Israel n = 378	U.S.A. n = 154	Korea n = 95	Taiwan n = 148	China n = 108	Hungary n = 540
Cognitive								
1. Advancement	19	32	61	54	36	47	30	3
2. Feedback	24	21	48	36	19	32	18	38
3. Status	3	4	41	16	16	19	10	3
4. Achievement	30	44	69	58	71	60	73	49
5. Job interest	61	75	67	62	42	53	32	41
6. Meaningful work	39	22	46	29	35	28	17	48
7. Personal growth	27	37	49	49	39	45	36	31
8. Use of ability	31	27	43	41	37	35	51	42
9. Responsibility	10	23	49	36	35	45	34	30
10. Contribution to society	5	6	25	10	20	16	44	13
11. Independence	33	33	52	36	24	37	34	25
12. Company	7	6	35	22	26	21	9	9
13. Work influence	28	29	36	29	28	25	11	15
14. Organizational influence	9	21	29	20	23	22	17	6
Affective								
15. Recognition	16	22	42	34	36	39	11	49
16. Co-workers	44	41	42	21	37	33	18	31
17. Esteem	22	21	55	49	25	47	44	37
18. Interaction	14	25	26	18	19	17	6	15
19. Supervisor	34	25	49	34	37	38	29	61
Instrumental								
20. Pay	24	20	43	27	33	28	7	46
21. Benefits	36	16	38	27	35	35	9	24
22. Security	34	22	34	36	43	45	7	35
23. Convenient hours	19	7	31	18	32	24	7	33
24. Work condition	15	15	43	19	36	27	6	34

Supervisor was ranked as the most important by the majority of the Hungarian sample and contribution to society was assessed as very important by members of the China sample while it is almost the last in most other samples. The instrumental items are very low for the China sample, are quite low for the Dutch, U.S.A. and Israeli samples, and they are high for the Korea and Hungary samples (except benefits). Pay was usually assessed to be between the tenth and twentieth rank. The Hungarian respondents, however, ranked pay considerably higher (the fifth

Table 4. Rank order of work values for samples
from eight countries

Content	Germany	Holland	U.S.A.	Israel	Korea	Taiwan	China	Hungary
Cognitive								
1. Advancement	15	6	3	3	8	4	9	24
2. Feedback	13	16	9	9	22	14	11	8
3. Status	24	24	23	15	24	22	17	23
4. Achievement	9	2	2	1	1	1	1	2
5. Job interest	1	1	1	2	3	2	8	7
6. Meaningful work	3	13	13	10	13	16	14	14
7. Personal growth	11	4	4	6	4	6	5	13
8. Use of ability	8	8	6	11	5	11	2	6
9. Responsibility	20	11	8	8	11	5	6	15
10. Contribution								
to society	23	23	24	24	21	24	4	20
11. Independence	7	5	7	5	19	10	7	16
12. Company	22	22	17	18	17	21	18	21
13. Work influence	10	7	14	17	16	18	15	18
14. Organizational								
influence	21	17	19	22	20	20	13	22
Affective								
15. Recognition	17	12	12	13	10	8	16	3
16. Co-workers	2	3	18	14	6	13	12	14
17. Esteem	14	15	5	4	18	3	3	9
18. Interaction	19	10	21	23	23	23	23	19
19. Supervisor	5	9	11	7	7	9	10	1
Instrumental								
20. Pay	12	18	15	12	14	15	20	5
21. Benefits	4	19	16	16	12	12	19	17
22. Security	6	14	10	19	2	7	22	10
23. Convenient hours	16	21	22	21	15	19	21	12
24. Work condition	18	20	20	20	9	17	24	11

rank). Security is high for the Korea, German and Taiwan samples and
benefits for the German sample. Thus, cultural differences appear to arise
in both the relative meaning and importance given to specific values.

DISCUSSION

The present study attempted to examine the importance and structure of
work value items for respondents in different cultural environments. It
was expected that considerable differences in the relative importance of

specific work value items will be found in the various samples. It could be expected that certain similarity of responses will be found between the Far Eastern cultures (China, Korea, Taiwan) and the Western countries or between countries with communist regimes versus western societies. Achievement for instance, is considered characteristic to the western culture and could be expected to be considered remarkably less important in Eastern cultures. Quite remarkably, however, achievement was ranked as very important by the Eastern samples and was ranked considerably lower by the German respondents only.

Job interest is ranked considerably lower by respondents in China and Hungary than in other samples. On several other items, however, there are considerable differences between these two samples. Supervisor, recognition, meaningful work and pay are ranked very high by the Hungarian respondents, but considerably lower by the Chinese respondents. These differences between the Hungary and China samples may be partly due to the specific samples. The China sample includes participants in a Young Executive Program, while the Hungarian samples consists of employees of a large industrial corporation. In order to examine cultural differences between East and West European cultures it will be necessary to have additional samples of East European countries in future research.

The major objective of the study at the present stage of development was to examine the structure of work values in samples from various cultural environments. Opportunity samples were found appropriate for that purpose. It was expected that the basic structure of work values at least for West European and North American samples would be similar. It was of special interest to examine the conceptual structure of work values in samples of workers in Western and Far Eastern cultures. Although advanced technology and work procedures are applied in the Far Eastern countries their specific culture may affect their view of work and the valuation of its outcomes. Thus it was expected that there may be certain changes due to cultural differences. Indeed the high importance ranking of "contribution to society" in the China sample may reflect the more collective culture in this society. Similarly the location of "co-workers" in the instrumental rather than the affective region in the China and Taiwan samples may be based on common cultural meaning. Most remarkably, however, these differences are far and away only minor deviations within a much broader pattern of structural similarity. Indeed the fact that in eight independent samples from various cultural environments an essentially similar structure was obtained lends strong support to the conceptual framework suggested for work values. Additional samples of East European and Far Eastern respondents will be required in future research to explore possible cultural differences in the structure and relative importance of work values in these cultures.

The concepts suggested in this study provide a more meaningful and generalizable framework for analyzing work values than those suggested in previous studies. Most of the concepts suggested previously for classifying work value items were typically from works concerned with occupational setups (Lofquist and Dawis 1978; Herzberg 1974; Rosenberg 1957) and usually they were developed with reference to work related context.

While the formulation or inference of specifically work-related facets for work values has its value, and, in fact constitutes an essential stage in the evolution of conceptual frameworks; ultimately a reliable and comprehensive framework would be grounded in generalized *facets*, those that have been validated in other contexts.

The modality facet with its three elements: cognitive, affective and instrumental is shared by work values and various other study areas in the behavioral sciences (Elizur 1970, 1979, 1984; Elizur and Guttman 1976; Levy 1981). The performance contingency facet, on the other hand, appears to be a more unique facet to work values, work motivation and similar work-related studies.

SUMMARY AND CONCLUSIONS

The aim of this study was to analyze the structure of work values for respondents from various cultural environments. Based on analysis of previous investigations, a faceted definition of work values was suggested which facilitated formulation of hypotheses regarding the relations between the definitional framework and the empirical observations.

Two basic facets of the work values domain were defined and tested. One facet specified the *modality* of the outcome (instrumental, affective, or cognitive). The other facet specified the *system performance contingency* (reward or resource).

The conceptual structure of work values presented here subsumes many of the distinctions currently made. For example, the intrinsic–extrinsic distinction may be considered to be covered by the modality facet. Intrinsic outcomes are cognitive, whereas extrinsic outcomes are either instrumental or affective. The modality facet, with its three elements, seems to provide a more detailed and generalizable classification than does the intrinsic–extrinsic dichotomy. The intrinsic–extrinsic dichotomy, however, relates to only one of the facets of the work values domain defined in this study.

The results support the definitional hypotheses of the study. A basically similar structure, a *radex* structure, was obtained in samples from eight countries, reflecting the facets of the definition. The fact that essentially the same structure was obtained in eight independent samples lends substantial support to the definitional framework suggested for work values and to the hypothesis that the structure of the domain is basically similar for respondents in different samples.

Review of the study results indicates the presence of cultural differences in relative importance for a limited range of work values. Hungarian respondents rated supervisor, recognition, meaningful work and pay considerably higher than respondents in other samples did. The China sample considered contribution to society as very important but pay and other material outcomes as quite unimportant. The German respondents rated co-workers, benefits and security very high but responsibility as quite unimportant.

Close examination of these differences evokes two comments. First, these differences are, far and away only minor variations within a much broader pattern of structural similarity. Second, these differences appear to reflect the broader socio-cultural and technological conditions in which individuals function in the different countries represented. These results suggest that in future cross-cultural comparisons of work values, it might be beneficial to obtain wider samples of respondents to explore the influence of these broader life conditions.

REFERENCES

ALDERFER, C. P.: *Existence, Relatedness and Growth: Human Needs in Organizational Settings,* Free Press (1972).

ALLPORT, G. W., VERNON, P. E., LINDSEY, G.: *Study of Values: Manual of Directions,* rev. edn, Houghton Mifflin, Boston (1951).

BECKER, G. M., McCLINTOCK, G. G.: "Value: Behavioral decision theory", *Annual Review of Psychology,* **18,** pp. 239–286 (1967).

BILLINGS, R. S., CORNELIUS, E. T.: "Dimensions underlying the intrinsic/extrinsic dichotomy: A literature review and conceptional analysis." (Industrial/Organizational Psychology Working Paper, No. 78–1). Department of Psychology, Ohio State University, Columbus (1978).

BILLINGS, R. S., CORNELIUS, E. T.: "Dimensions of work outcomes: A multi-dimensional scaling approach", *Personnel Psychology*, **33**, pp. 151–162 (1980).

BORG, I.: "A cross culture replication on ELIZUR'S facets of work values", *Multivariante Behavioral Research*, **21**, pp. 401–410 (1986).

BRAITHWAITE, V. A., LAW, H. G.: "Structure of human values: Testing the adequacy of the ROKEACH Value survey", *Journal of Personality and Social Psychology*, **49**, pp. 250–263 (1985).

CAMPBELL, J. P., PRITCHARD, R. D.: "Motivation theory in industrial and organizational psychology." In: DUNNETTE, M. D. (ed.): *Handbook of Industrial and Organizational Psychology*, Rand McNally, Chicago (1975).

CHERRINGTON, D: J.: *The Work Ethic: Working Values and Values that Work*, Amacom, New York (1980).

DICKSON, J., BUCHHOLZ, R.: "Managerial beliefs about work in Scotland and the U.S.A.", *Journal of Management Studies*, **14**, pp. 80–101 (1977).

DYER, L., PARKER, D. F.: "Classifying outcomes in work motivation research: An examination of the intrinsic–extrinsic dichotomy", *Journal of Applied Psychology*, **60**, pp. 455–458 (1975).

ELIZUR, D.: *Adapting to Innovation: A Facet Analysis of the Case of the Computer*, Jerusalem Academic Press, Jerusalem (1970).

ELIZUR, D.: "Assessing achievement motive of American and Israeli managers: Design and application of a three-facet measure", *Applied Psychological Measurement*, **3**, pp. 210–212 (1979).

ELIZUR, D.: "Facets of work values: A structural analysis of work outcomes", *Journal of Applied Psychology*, **69**, pp. 379–389 (1984).

ELIZUR, D., GUTTMAN, L.: "The structure of the attitudes toward work and technological change within an organization", *Administrative Science Quarterly*, **21**, pp. 611–622 (1976).

ELIZUR, D., SHYE, S.: "The inclination to re-immigrate: A structural analysis of the case of Israelis residing in France and in the U.S.A.", *Human Relations*, **29**, pp. 73–84 (1976).

ENGLAND, G. W.: "Organizational goals and expected behavior of American managers", *Academy of Management Journal*, **10**, pp. 107–117 (1967).

ETZIONI, A.: "Work in the American future: Reindustrialization or quality of life." In: KERR, C., ROSOW, J. M. (eds): *Work in America: The Decade Ahead*, Van Nostrand, New York, pp. 27–34 (1979).

FEATHER, N. T.: *Expectations and Actions: Expectancy–Value models in Psychology*, Erlbaum, Hillsdale, N. J. (1982).

FISHBEIN, M., AJZEN, I.: *Belief, Attitude and Behavior*, Addison-Wesley, Reading, Mass. (1975).

FITZGERALD, L. F., HUBERT, L. J.: "Multidimensional scaling: Some possibilities for counseling psychology", *Journal of Counseling Psychology*, **34**, pp. 469–480 (1987).

FRENCH, J. R. P. JR., KAHN, R. L.: "A programmatic approach to studying the industrial environment and mental health", *Journal of Social Issues*, **18**, pp. 1–47 (1962).

FURNHAM, A.: "Work values and beliefs in Britain", *Journal of Occupational Behavior*, **5**, pp. 281–291 (1984).

GRAEN, G.: "Instrumentality theory of work motivation: Some experimental results and suggested modifications", *Journal of Applied Psychology* (Monograph), **53**, pp. 1–25 (1969).

GUTTMAN, L.: "A new approach to factor analysis: The radex." In: LAZARSFELD, P. (ed.): *Mathematical Thinking in the Social Sciences*, Free Press, Glencoe, IL (1954).

GUTTMAN, L.: "A structural theory of intergroup beliefs and action", *American Sociological, Review,* **24,** pp. 318–328 (1959).

GUTTMAN, L.: "A general nonmetric technique for finding the smallest coordinate space for a configuration of points", *Psychometrika,* **33,** pp. 469–506 (1968).

GUTTMAN, L.: "What is not what in theory construction." In: HAUSER, R. M., MECHANIC, D., HALLER, A. (eds): *Social Structure and Behavior,* Academic Press, New York, pp. 331–348 (1982).

HACKMAN, J. R., OLDHAM, G. R.: *Work Redesign,* Addison-Wesley, Reading, Mass. (1980).

HERZBERG, F.: "New perspectives on the will to work", *Management Review.* November, pp. 52–54 (1974).

HOFSTEDE, G.: *Culture's Consequences: International Differences in Work Related Values,* Sage, Beverly Hills (1980).

KATZ, D., KAHN, R. L.: *The Social Psychology of Organizations,* Wiley, New York (1966).

KLUCKHOHN, C.: "Values and value orientations in the theory of action." In: PARSONS, T., SHILS, E. A. (eds): *Towards a General Theory of Action,* Harvard University Press, Cambridge, pp. 338–433 (1952).

LEVY-LE BOYER, C.: "A psychologist's analysis of the work value crisis", *International Review of Applied Psychology,* **35,** pp. 53–62 (1986).

LEVY, S.: "Lawful roles of facets in social theories." In: BORG, I. (ed): *Multidimensional Data Representation: When and Why,* Mathesis Press, Ann Arbor, MI (1981).

LOFQUIST, J. H., DAWIS, R. V.: "Values as a second-order needs in the theory of work adjustment", *Journal of Vocational Behavior,* **12,** pp.12–19 (1978).

McCLELLAND, D. C.: *The Achieving Society,* Van Nostrand, Princeton (1961).

MASLOW, A. H.: *Motivation and Personality,* Harper, New York (1954).

PENNINGS, I. M.: "Work value systems of white-collar workers", *Administrative Science Quarterly,* **15,** pp. 397–405 (1970).

PORTER, L. W., LAWLER, E. E.: *Managerial Attitudes and Performance,* Dorsey Press, Homewood, IL (1968).

ROKEACH, M.: *The Nature of Human Values,* The Free Press, New York (1973).

RONEN, S.: "Personal values: A basis for work motivation set and work attitude", *Organizational Behavior and Human Performance,* **21,** pp. 80–107 (1978).

ROSENBERG, M. W.: *Occupations and Values,* The Free Press, Glenco, IL (1957).

SCHLESINGER, I. M., GUTTMAN, L.: "Smallest space analysis of intelligence and achievement tests", *Psychological Bulletin,* **71,** pp. 95–100 (1969).

SCHWARTZ, S. H., BILSKY, W.: "Toward a universal psychological structure of human values", *Journal of Personality and Social Psychology,* **53,** pp. 550–562 (1987).

SHAPIRA, A., ZEVULUN, E.: "On the use of facet analysis in organizational behavior research: Some conceptual considerations and an example", *Organizational Behavior and Human Performance,* **23,** pp. 411–428 (1979).

SHYE, S. (ed.): *Theory Construction and Data Analysis in the Behavioral Sciences,* Jossey-Bass, San Francisco (1978).

VROOM, V. H.: *Work and Motivation,* Wiley, New York (1964).

WERNIMONT, P. F.: "A systems view of job satisfaction", *Journal of Applied Psychology,* **56,** pp. 173–176 (1972).

YANKELOVICH, D.: "Work values, and the newbreed." In: KERR, C., ROSOW, J. M. (eds): *Work in America: the Decade Ahead,* Van Nostrand, New York (1976).

19

IDENTIFYING THE BLOCKS TO CREATIVITY IN HUNGARIAN CULTURE*

By

ISTVÁN MAGYARI-BECK

One of the main topics of creatology is the identification of the degree and type of creativeness of different cultures. The point is that individuals can successfully practice their creativity if and only if there are no substantial obstacles in the society preventing them from their creative work. Otherwise creativity tests are unable to make good acceptable predictions. This theoretical and practical question is especially important for Central Europe in the current period of transition. The Jones Inventory was used to identify the type of obstacles (blocks) of creativity in Hungarian culture. That this culture (and perhaps the whole Central Europe) tries to follow the examples of the most flourishing cultures and turns much less attention to its specific problems which can make this strategy of a follower not really successful.

The new discipline of creativity, or *creatology* as I called it elsewhere (MAGYARI-BECK 1990), deals not only with psychological affairs. It also studies cultures, organizations, and groups. There are at least three subtopics within each of the above mentioned foci. These are product, process, and ability. Naturally the scholars of this domain are working not merely to understand what is going on at different levels and in the various subtopics; they also intend to initiate the necessary changes and develop cultures, organizations, groups, and people to obtain better products, more effective creative problem-solving processes, and to raise the level of abilities.

A huge number of philosophical and axiological questions are involved in such statements as those just made. However, this article will not touch on any of them. The aim of this work is simply to give a static empirical picture of contemporary Hungarian culture. Why is this important? It is relevant for the following three reasons:

* In *Creativity Research Journal*, 1992, Vol. 5, No. 4, pp. 419–427.

(1) Any culture (as any organization, team, or person) deserves the identification of its level and type of creativeness in and by the independent discipline of creativity (i.e. creatology).
(2) At this historical moment, Hungary is an especially interesting culture as the whole movement in Central and Eastern Europe was started and influenced by Hungary. Although the real beginning of this recent movement can be found in the early 1980s, the role of Hungary as a model for the surrounding countries dates back to the revolution of 1956.
(3) The well-elaborated picture of the geographical, political, and cultural area in question helps not only with the understanding of the very complex Central European situation, but with the handling of this situation as well. One must not forget that two World Wars broke out in Central Europe (recall Sarajevo and Gdansk!) because of the inability to solve the difficult problems of this region by the celebrated, illustrious politicians of those times. Creative studies are important in this context, for they can point at those potentials and blocks of a culture (organization, team, and person) which could be relevant in the course of further development of culture.

THE PROBLEM OF STUDY

There are at least three forms in which any culture exists. The first, and perhaps the most *visible* form is the wide set of its products, including books, buildings, pieces of music, scientific achievements, factories, roads, and different social events. All are typical and represent that particular culture to which they belong. The second and mostly semivisible form is the process by which the products of a culture are created. Thus, the processes of publication, building, organizing, exchanging of information, thinking, imagination, and so on are parts of this important concept. The third and usually invisible form is the ability to create. This is of great importance for the studies in creativity because the visible and semivisible part of the world is dependent first on its invisible background.

In the creatological framework the ability to create is not limited to personal creativity. The explicit and hidden structure of a culture, its traditions, the formal and informal patterns of an organization, and the various types of groups can all be interpreted in terms of ability (MAGYARI-BECK 1990). In a strict sense, each of the categories (product, process, abilities) contains the other two as well. For example, products must be regarded as obligatory parts of any creative processes running from product to product through another product. Or creativity as an ability on any level of society is always brought up in and by the creative processes which are in their essence the manifestations of creativity.

Another type of approach distinguishes the holistic versus the atomist way of thinking. According to this distinction any culture can be described both as a whole, comprehensible in itself, or as a set of parts, for example, individuals. This article applies the ability and atomist approach to the contemporary Hungarian culture so as to grasp its present state of affairs from the creative point of view. In brief, the creative ability of a sample of individuals and the creative climate surrounding them were studied. However, hypothetical inferences will be drawn concerning the state of affairs in the culture in question.

METHOD

MEASURES

The JONES Inventory (JONES 1990; JONES & RICKARDS 1991) and the Creativity Climate Questionnaire (EKVALL, ARVONEN & WALDENSTROM-LIND-BLAD 1983) were administered in the course of the present survey. The JONES Inventory was designed to measure the blocks to creativity on the following four dimensions: strategy, values, perceptions, and self-image. This inventory also identifies a number of personality features (see *Table 1* and *Table 2*) which are important from the point of view of the creative behavior. EKVALL'S Creativity Climate Questionnaire can measure the creativeness of an organizational climate on such dimensions as challenge, motivation, freedom, idea support by the social environment, trust and openness, dynamism, playfulness and humor, debates, conflicts, risk-taking, and finally time pressure. Each of these is described by two figures: One of them characterizes the innovative level of this dimension whereas the other characterizes its stagnated level. The average level of any of these dimensions can also be calculated.

SUBJECTS AND PROCEDURE

The JONES Inventory was administered to 217 people. One group of them studied at the Budapest University of Economics as either undergraduate ($n = 53$) or postgraduate ($n = 98$) students. Another group ($n = 66$) worked in the Hungarian transport service. Some members of this group ($n = 50$) graduated from colleges and universities, whereas the rest ($n = 16$) only finished high school. The average age of the 217 people was 33 years. The sample contained 137 men and 80 women, with the average ages of 33.2 and 32.7 years, respectively.

The Creative Climate Questionnaire was administered only to 94 people. All of them were either undergraduate ($n = 23$), or postgraduate ($n = 71$) students of the Budapest University of Economics. All 217 completed the JONES Inventory. The average age of the 94 people was 38.8; 55 of the 94 persons were men, and the remaining 39 women. The average age of men was 40.1 and the average of women was 39.3

A statistically important remark should be added at this point because not all of these persons were undergraduate students of the Budapest University of Economics. A large part of the sample filled in the questionnaires keeping their personalities and *jobs* in mind. Consequently there was no need to limit the interpretations of the results of this survey merely to the Budapest University of Economics.

RESULTS

JONES INVENTORY

The strength or the levels of various blocks to creativity in the sample of 217 people can be characterized by the following mean scores: strategic barriers 37, value barriers 27, perceptual barriers 29, and self-image barriers 37.

Table 1 presents the frequencies of different personality features identified by the JONES Inventory. To understand these figures the reader should take into consideration that the maximum frequencies in the second column can be either 651 (217×3) or 434 (217×2). This occurs only if all the people measured by this inventory have their own profile – that is, if there are no nonprofile persons in the sample.

The next Table shows the rank order of these features in our sample in accordance with the frequencies of their occurrence indicated already in *Table 2*.

Table 1. The frequencies of personality features identified by the Jones Inventory in the sample of 217 individuals

Dimensions	Qualifications	Personality features	Frequencies	
Strategic Blocks	High	Likes the familiar	31	200
		Likes structure	86	
		Serious	83	
	Low	Open to new ideas	100	164
		Tolerates uncertainty	26	
		Imaginative	38	
Value Blocks	High	Strong principles	10	47
		Conservative	30	
		Tends to use stereotypes	7	
	Low	Broadminded	129	397
		Open to change	74	
		Unprejudiced	194	
Perceptual Blocks	High	Unperceptive	12	31
		Unaware of others	19	
	Low	Perceptive	110	188
		Aware of others	78	
Self-Image Blocks	High	Unassertive	42	270
		Undemonstrative	109	
		Independent	119	
	Low	Assertive	94	207
		Open	100	
		Prepared to involve others	13	

Table 2. The rank order of personality features according
to the frequency of their occurrence

Personality Features	Rank Order	Code	
Unprejudiced	197	lv	
Broadminded	129	lv	
Independent	119	hsi	
Perceptive	110	lp	
Undemonstrative	109	hsi	7 out of 11
Open	100	lsi	belong to the
Open to new ideas	100	ls	low barriers
Assertive	94	lsi	
Likes structure	86	hs	
Serious	83	hs	
Aware of others	78	lp	
Open to change	74	lv	
Unassertive	42	hsi	
Imaginative	38	ls	
Likes the familiar	31	hs	7 out of 11
Conservative	30	hv	belong to the
Tolerates uncertainty	26	ls	high barriers
Unaware of others	19	hp	
Prepared to involve others	13	lsi	
Unperceptive	12	hp	
Strong principles	10	hv	
Tends to use stereotypes	7	hv	

Note: h = high, l = low, s = strategic, v = values, p = perceptual, and si = self-image.

Perhaps the most interesting fact in this Table is that the whole set of 22 features identified by the JONES Inventory can be divided into two subsets, with 11 features in each, in such a way that in the first subset of the more frequent features, 7 out of 11 belong to the low barriers. In the second subset of the less frequent features, a directly symmetrical situation can be observed; 7 out of 11 features belong to the high barriers.

The whole sample was divided according to gender. The mean scores of the levels of men's strategic and self-image barriers each reached 37. These figures equal those of the whole sample. However, the levels of the mean scores of the value and perceptual barriers were 25 and 30, respectively. In comparison, women's results were 37 (strategic barriers), 29 (value barriers), 28 (perceptual barriers), and 40 (self-image barriers).

The question of differences between the group of people graduated from colleges and universities and the group of people having only a high school degree is also of a great interest in the context of the blocks to creativity. The 66 people from the Hungarian transport service were divided into two groups; 16 of those 66 people had only a high school certificate. The mean scores in this subsample of 16 people were: 35 (strategic barriers), 26 (value barriers), 26 (perceptual barriers), and 41 (self-image barriers). The figures in the subsample of 50 college or university graduates were 42, 29, 27, and 38, respectively.

EKVALL'S CREATIVE CLIMATE QUESTIONNAIRE

Table 3 shows the results of the climate survey in the sample of 94 people. The most striking fact in this Table is that, except for the dimensions of "debates" and "conflicts", the results given by this population were well below even the level of the stagnated climate. The population's mean score of "debates" was lower than the standard characterizing innovative climate but is higher than the average computed by EKVALL, ARVONEN, and WALDENSTROM-LINDBLAD (1983) (1.28). The population's mean score of "conflicts" was higher than both the mean score of the average (0.88) and that of the innovative climate.

A part of the sample of 94 people included future innovation managers, all of them postgraduate students attending the Budapest University of Economics. Their climate background is of an especially great interest *(Table 4)*.

The level of idea support in this group of person is equal to the level of idea support in a stagnated climate. In regard to the levels of playfulness and humor, debates, conflict, and risk-taking, they were between the innovative and stagnated climate.

The climate background of the women in this group was somewhat different. Indeed, the future women innovation managers gave judgments which in any dimension surpassed the figures of stagnated climate.

Table 3. The results of climate survey
in the sample of 94 individuals

Dimensions	Empirical data			Standards		
	Men	Women	All	Innovative	Average	Stagnated
Challenge/Motivation	1.45	1.48	1.46	2.35	1.90	1.64
Freedom	1.20	1.04	1.13	2.17	1.74	1.52
Idea Support	1.17	1.12	1.15	2.09	1.64	1.31
Trust/Openness	0.92	0.87	0.89	1.82	1.60	1.37
Dynamism	0.99	1.16	1.06	2.31	1.55	1.30
Playfulness/Humor	1.12	1.04	1.09	2.16	1.69	1.29
Debates	1.45	1.36	1.41	1.54	1.28	0.92
Conflicts	1.10	1.16	1.12	0.71	0.88	0.85
Risk-taking	0.91	0.93	0.92	2.34	1.12	0.94
Time	1.34	1.14	1.26		1.11	
Averages	1.16	1.13	1.14	1.94	1.45	1.23

Table 4. The results from the subsample of the future
innovation managers

Dimensions	Empirical data			Standards		
	Men	Women	All	Innovative	Average	Stagnated
Challenge/Motivation	1.30	2.10	1.43	2.35	1.90	1.64
Freedom	1.14	1.80	1.25	2.17	1.74	1.52
Idea Support	1.27	1.50	1.31	2.09	1.64	1.31
Trust/Openness	1.11	1.70	1.21	1.82	1.60	1.37
Dynamism	0.99	2.15	1.19	2.31	1.55	1.30
Playfulness/Humor	1.09	1.85	1.39	2.16	1.69	1.29
Debates	1.27	1.95	1.14	1.54	1.28	0.92
Conflicts	1.18	0.95	1.04	0.71	0.88	0.85
Risk-taking	0.95	1.50	1.08	2.34	1.12	0.94
Time	1.01	1.45	1.22		1.11	
Averages	1.13	1.69	1.22	1.94	1.45	1.23

GENERAL DISCUSSION

JONES INVENTORY

As we presently have no international standards of blocks to creativity, the only possibility in the course of interpretation would involve taking the median points from the JONES scales to determine how our results compared to the median points. With the minimum possible scores on JONES scales equaling 12 and the maximum possible scores equaling 60, the median points of these scales can be found at their figures of 36. In this case the sample of 217 people studied is considerably blocked concerning the strategic and self-image barriers of their members. On the other hand, the value barriers and the perceptual barriers found in the sample in question are much weaker. The obvious fact that the people of this population are a little bit more open concerning their values and perceptions than with their strategic readiness and self-image suggests that *the kind of creativity identified in this sample is not an active but a receptive one.* These people (perhaps in this historical situation) are much more eager to accept models and ideas coming from outside than to work out their own. It is true that openness is an important part of creativity (McCRAE 1987), but it is only a part of it.

The proportions presented in *Table 2* suggest that the active creative behavior is nevertheless not alien to this population despite the considerable strength or levels of blocks to creativity in the domains of strategy and self-image. The *exact* meaning of this needs further research.

The men and women in our samples had exactly the same levels of strategic barriers. The men were more open concerning the universe of values. Women, on the other hand, can be described as the supporters of (perhaps some particular) values. Regarding the perceptual dimension, men were a little more closed, and women slightly more open. One of the most likely explanations for the higher fixation in the values and the more perceptive character *is that Hungarian women are likely to be more stressful than men.* Using an everyday common sense expression, these women can both see, and at the same time judge, things on a more intense level. If we add the aforesaid that the women of this sample had a higher self-image barrier than the men, which prevented them from being really very active in order to solve the problems they confront, the above conclusion will have an even firmer basis.

In the comparisons of the more educated (graduated from colleges and universities) with the less educated persons (graduated only from high schools), some interesting findings were detected. Except for the self-image barriers, all blocks to creativity were higher and stronger in the population of more educated people. It is as if *they have acquired not only knowledge but the blocks and barriers to creativity as well in the colleges and universities.* The exception, which was the lower level of self-image barriers among college and university graduates, unfortunately does not improve the picture. On the contrary, it becomes even worse. Although we can only speak of the tendencies on the basis of these mean scores, this tendency is more or less clear: We have on the one hand a little more self-confident and a little more venturesome actors who are more severely blocked in other aspects of their creativity, and, on the other hand, individuals who are a little more creative in almost all of the aspects measured by the JONES Inventory, but lacking appropriate self-respect. Unfortunately these tendencies are not unusual for Central Europe in general and for Hungary in particular.

EKVALL'S CREATIVE CLIMATE QUESTIONNAIRE

Recall that according to the findings of this survey, the levels of motivation, freedom, idea support, trust, dynamism, playfulness, humor, and risk-taking were low, whereas the levels of conflicts and debates were high. It seems that *in the course of this research a new, third type of climate was discovered for which a new term of "destructive" had to be coined. Thus in the future it will be possible to identify altogether three sorts of organizational climate: innovative, stagnated, and destructive.* Taking the averages of averages in *Table 3*, the figure 1.94 reflects the innovative climate; 1.23 reflects the stagnated climate; and 1.14 the destructive climate. However, these figures must be regarded as only three isolated points on a future climate scale to be further developed in its details.

At this point, an intriguing question should be raised. Is it useful for the contemporary Hungarian (and perhaps Central European) changes to have a directly destructive climate in places of work? An important part of the answer can be that a *destructive climate beyond a doubt has its own useful functions in the historical period when the old and bad political and economic structure has to be destroyed in order to build a new and more advanced one.*

The picture is almost the same for the future innovation managers as that of the whole sample of 94 people. Some small favorable differences were nevertheless found: The climate measured in the sample of the future innovation managers was not destructive in any respect. This was especially true for the subsample of women. Now, the question is, *Have these women a generally better climate background than other persons in our sample? Or do they perhaps create a much better creative climate around themselves on their own basis?* (Consider the role of, for example, French women informally organizing the artistic and scientific life in France from the XVII Century on.) These questions require further investigation.

Two weaknesses of this research should be mentioned. First, the sample was small and almost homogeneous. It would be very risky to draw general inferences on the basis of this research. But despite it, we shall go beyond our empirical data because a countless quantity of everyday observations confirm the inferences we have drawn in various sections of contemporary Hungarian life. It is an important aspect of these kinds of investigations when somebody investigates into his or her culture, that the investigator himself or herself can also be regarded as a participant observer.

The second and perhaps the main weakness of this study mentioned already was the lack of necessary international standards for the questionnaires we applied. Artificial points of references had to be used. EKVALL et al.'s (1983) Creative Climate Questionnaire also needs further development. The figures describing both the creative and the stagnated climate were established by EKVALL on an extremely narrow empirical basis. It would be very important to have an internationally reliable and valid scale of organizational climate which could identify innovative, stagnated, and destructive climates.

Having these shortcomings in mind, the results can be reframed for a hypothetical picture of the contemporary Hungarian culture from the point of view of its creativeness. As the Hungarian people now are mostly blocked in terms of their strategic ability and self-confidence, and are more open in values and perceptions, the Hungarian creativity today is perhaps first of all a passive and receptive one. The most widespread personality features (see *Table 2*) seem to be consonant with this hypothesis. In the present historical period Hungarians are largely unprejudiced, broad minded, perceptive, and open. It should also be added that *the readiness to follow different models outside of the culture is always a starting point of a new cultural flourishing.* Renaissance Italy began by following the social and artistic model of ancient Greek and Rome. Japan has taken many lessons from the West before jumping on the scene as its strong competitor.

Another interesting finding is that in all likelihood Hungarian women are more tense and problematic than Hungarian men. It also seems likely that *the women of this nation should be regarded as a kind of "gold reserve" of Hungarian creativity.* It would be possible to confirm this hypothesis by countless numbers of everyday observations. There is a growing interest among Hungarian women in the jobs which need a high level of education. The proportion of women graduated from colleges and universities is high and growing in the long run. Theoretically, it would be very easy to compare Hungarian men and women from the point of view of their creativeness.

The present study also contains a serious criticism of the present Hungarian school system. Results indicated that Hungarian colleges and universities tend to raise the level of self-respect of their students, but this excellent part of Hungarian people acquires not only knowledge in these institutions, but numerous blocks to creativity as well.

The "creative" climate in Hungarian corporate cultures is mostly destructive. But on the other hand, the types of people can be distinguished in this respect: First are the innovation managers, and second are the women. These two types of people can hypothetically be taken as starting forces of the constructive and innovative period of our history standing presumably before this small, but influential (in Central Europe) country.

REFERENCES

EKVALL, G., ARVONEN, J., WALDENSTROM-LINDBLAD, I.: *Creative organization climate: Construction and validation of a measuring instrument.* Report 2, Swedish Council of Management and Organization Behavior, Stockholm (1983).

JONES, L.: *Barriers to creativity and their relationship to individual, group and organizational behavior.* Paper presented at the International Creativity Conference, Buffalo, NY (August 1990).

JONES, L., RICKARDS, T.: Towards the identification of situational barriers to creative behaviors: The development of a self-report inventory. *Creativity Research Journal, 4,* pp. 303–315 (1991).

MAGYARI-BECK, I.: An introduction to the framework of creatology. *Journal of Creative Behavior* (1990).

MCCRAE, R. R.: Creativity, divergent thinking, and openness to experience. *Journal of Personality and Social Psychology, 52,* pp. 1258–1265 (1987).

20

LESSONS OF THE US BUSINESS SCHOOLS
FOR HUNGARY: A COMPARISON*

By

ERZSÉBET CZAKÓ

This article concentrates on business and management education at university level, focusing on that which is provided at universities in Hungary compared with that in the United States, and suggesting some possible approaches to developing and implementing lessons learned from the US in Hungary.

ROAD TO THE POSSIBILITIES

The idea of business and management education at university level is not new in Hungary. It arose in the middle of the nineteenth century, at approximately the same time as it arose in the United States [1, 2]. The practical movement towards establishing business and management higher schools, however, began at the beginning of the twentieth century. Developing schools that were faculties of universities was not without trouble. The results of the First and the Second World Wars taught these institutions and the whole Hungarian society that the key factor in survival is adaptation. The German root of business and management education was influenced a little by Anglo-Saxon theory and practice between the two World Wars and then it was deformed by the practical consequences and Soviet ideology of communism.

A separate University of Economics was created in 1948, the year which used to be called the "turning year" in Hungarian history because of the coming to power of the communist party. Theoretically it was a higher

* In *Journal of Management Development*, 1993, Vol. 11, No. 3, pp 48–55.

school of economics and business but practically it was only higher school of political economics with a strong emphasis on ideology. Until the end of the 1960s, it provided as many political economists as were required by the economy.

At the end of the 1960s, in parallel with the new economic mechanism that aimed to oppose the rigid centrally planned economy and to improve economic efficiency, three colleges were set up which emphasized professional training. A new faculty at the university in Pécs was also created with the same profile [3]. The first institutions for management training were also formed with the responsibility of developing and training managers. This institutional change led to a three-level system in business and management higher education: undergraduate training belonged to colleges; undergraduate education to the universities; and managers to the training institutions. The logic behind this system is the ideology. The main criterion for becoming a manager was political reliability and that is why only those chosen to be managers received management training. The new economic mechanism brought changes in the curricula of the higher schools and more professional subjects were introduced in the fields of business and management while ideology lost strength. This tendency became stronger in parallel with decreasing efficiency in the economy.

In theory these changes were good news for the community of Hungarian business but bad news for the University of Economics, since possible competitors were both created and strengthened. Fortunately the university, which is called the Budapest University of Economic Sciences today, has played an initiating role in changes in Hungarian business and management higher education. Its Soviet orientation was gradually replaced by a more Anglo-Saxon (and less German) one, since the dominant language of economics, business and management sciences is English. But before we turn our attention to what this institution has learnt from the American business schools, let us turn our attention to a comparison of the two systems.

COMPARING THE HUNGARIAN AND US SYSTEMS

As *Figs 1* and 2 show, entry to business and management higher education is at the same age in both countries. The criteria of application are similar for students from different types of high school in each country but it is said that the Hungarian high schools provide a stronger general

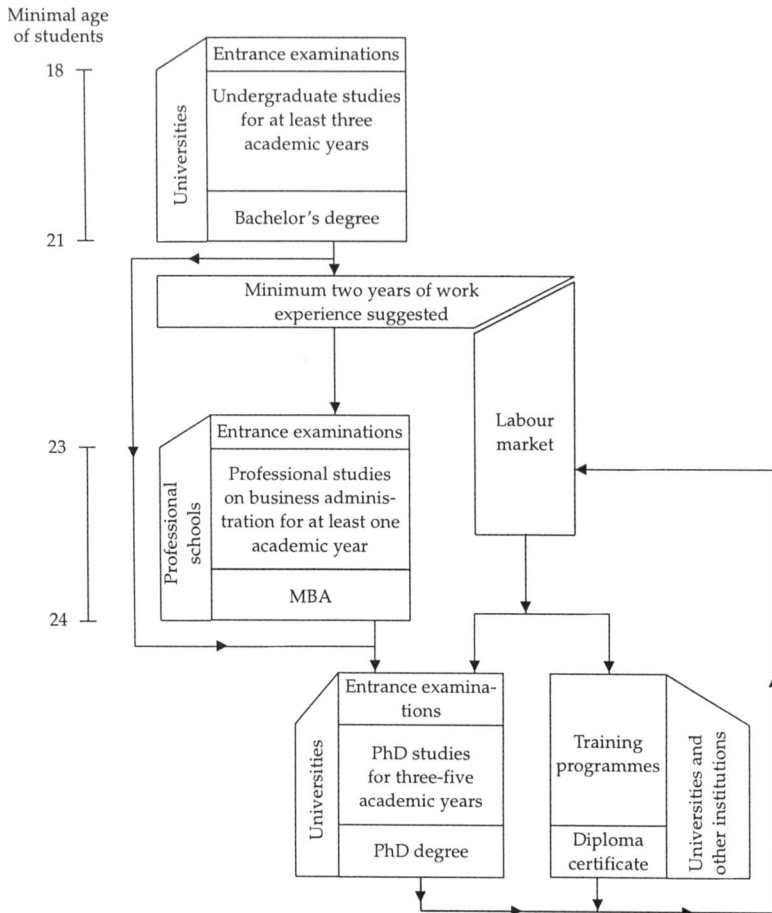

Figure 1. Business and management education in the USA

education than their counterparts in the USA. The difference is that in the United States students applying to a university or a college are not required to choose a profession, while in Hungary students should choose their future profession when applying to a professional university or a college. The dominant selection criterion for students in the USA is the prestige of the university or college, in Hungary it is the choice of profession.

After three to four years of education, students obtain their first university degree in the USA. During their studies they have great freedom in selecting subjects, and they have to choose major(s) after prerequisites. The credit system does not exist in Hungary. There are compulsory and

Minimal age
of students

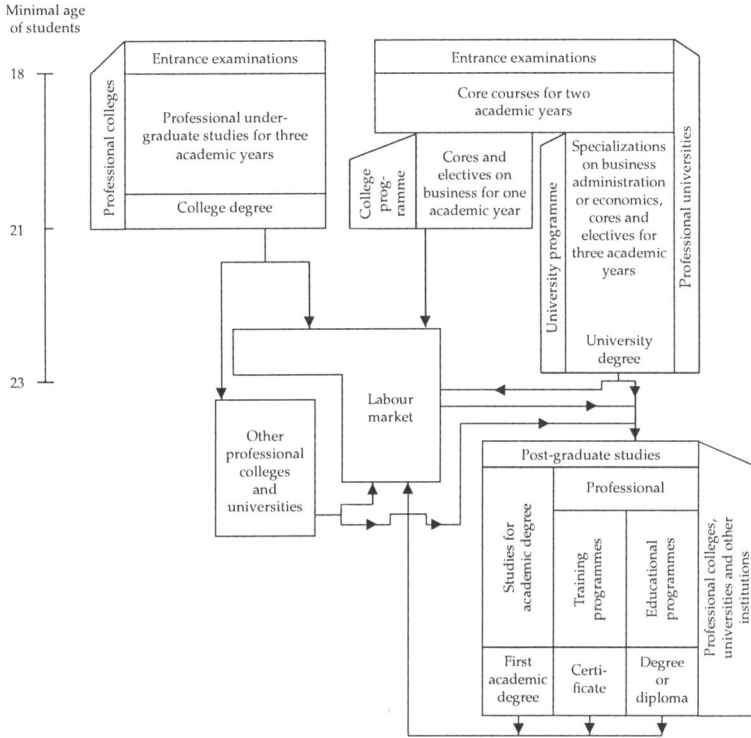

Figure 2. Business and management education in Hungary

elective subjects. In the first part of the course the compulsory are dominant, but later on the elective courses take the dominant role. The compulsory courses are general introductory classes in economics, social
sciences and business and management, and are intended to be the basis
for further studies. The Hungarian majors are subspecializations within a
field of a profession.

After finishing their studies, USA students can enter the labour market
or can continue in professional schools if they fulfil entrance prerequisites.
The number of students is smaller at the second level than it is at the previous level. In Hungary there is no possibility for interruption of studies
at colleges. After finishing college studies students enter the labour market but they also have the possibility of continuing their studies at universities after meeting university entrance requirements. They can choose
between full-time and part-time education but they prefer part-time education for their second degree. Completing university studies is the end of
formal full-time higher education. Graduates can continue their studies in
part-time education or can apply for training programmes. To obtain their

Table 1. Comparison of US and Hungarian business
and management education

Features	USA	Hungary
High school backgrounds	Relatively weak	Strong
Criterion for selection of schools	Prestige	Profession
Duration of education for first degree	Three or four academic years	Three or five academic years
Liberty in choosing subjects	Great	Restricted
Character of the education	General	Professional
Tuition cost	Substantial	Free
Placement option with first degree	Wide, independent from studies	Determined by professions
Postgraduate studies	Full-time programmes in both professional and academic fields	Part-time programmes
Professional control	AACSB and the business community	Ministry of Education

first postgraduate (academic) degree they have to pass examinations without formal courses and complete and defend a thesis based on their own research work.

The USA students have greater liberty in choosing their field of work with a bachelor's degree, but less with an MBA degree. A degree from a Hungarian college or university gives similar possibilities for students to an MBA degree in the USA.

Education is not free in the United States, but it is free in Hungary. There are both state and private universities in the USA, whereas there are only state colleges and universities in Hungary. *Table 1* gives an overview of the comparison of the two systems.

LESSONS IN PRACTICE:
THE BUDAPEST UNIVERSITY OF ECONOMIC SCIENCES

The Budapest University of Economic Sciences pioneered Hungarian business and management education at university level over the last two decades. It introduced subspecializations and new subjects to try to keep up with Western universities as much as possible. It was the first institution to change its curriculum. The latest curriculum reform started in 1985

– to move the university closer to international standards [4]. The result of that reform was a new educational system, introduced at the university in 1989. The education became two-tiered, and resembles the division of undergraduate and graduate schools in the USA. There is an opportunity to interrupt studies with a bachelor's (college) degree after three years of education or to continue them for a master's (university) degree, having obtained work experience and met entrance requirements. This possibility is open to other college graduates, too.

Students study compulsory introductory subjects (economics, business, social sciences and quantitative fields) for two academic years. At the end of the second academic year they have to pass examinations in economics, business and quantitative subjects. The results decide whether students can continue the studies they began at the university or on the college programme. At the university, they can now choose between three schools or specializations, namely social sciences, economics and business administration. Most students choose business administration. Every specialization is built on a few compulsory courses, majors and electives.

The curriculum has changed a lot. Macro- and microeconomics, business economics, marketing, management and organizational behaviour have become compulsory for every student. In addition to new subjects there are changes in the contents of the courses. The main weak point of the curriculum is that the management approach is missing from the business courses. It arises from the fact that management sciences was considered an individual discipline and was not taught to every student and it takes time to synthesize pure functional knowledge and its management. The other area for improvement is teaching methods [5]. The case-study method is known in Hungary. I learnt it in its essence when I took part in case discussion at Harvard Business School. In spite of my theoretical knowledge I was impressed. I envied the professors: they put forth questions, asked this or that student to give his/her opinion and made some notes on the blackboard. It seemed very easy and the students were highly motivated. When we introduced a course on the basis of case-method I realized that in practice it is much more difficult to have good questions and students working on them than it is to give a lecture on a special topic and test their knowledge.

Experience suggests that a two-level system *within* the university is strange, since the prestige of education at a university and in college is different. The university students do not like the college programme since they applied for a university and they want a university degree. The students from colleges of business and management appreciate this system since it is easier to meet the entrance requirements of a college than a university.

The newcomers' basic motivation has changed. They want to get practical knowledge. It is quite frequent that they make use of their brand new theoretical knowledge in practice. A student may earn money as a book-keeper for an entrepreneur, or take part in entrepreneurship as an owner or as an employee. This mentality is also true for potential employers who want to have usable manpower and consider in-house training a time- and money-wasting process in the short run.

On the other hand, the large role of business administration arouses fear of becoming a big business school instead of a great university. There are concerns about preserving the university character of the institution and providing students with education and not training. The Hungarian headhunter joint ventures also consider it to be useful and profitable in the long run, and international tendencies seem to strengthen this tendency. Though curriculum reform was once far ahead of social and economic changes, because of time pressure, the economy is now ahead of education in Hungary because of the need for professionals armed with knowledge of business and management techniques.

These facts are forcing the university to revise its curriculum and to work out a new strategy.

In principle, the university does not want to give up its academic character, and its purpose is to combine teaching and research activities in the fields of economics, business and management, and social sciences, and to provide students with basic knowledge of these fields in the first part of their education. A modified two-tier system is recommended: students can leave the university with a bachelor's degree after meeting the requirements of further studies at the end of the third academic year, but the main objective is to give a master's degree after five years of education. In business and management education this will mean an MBA without practical experience. The presumption behind this solution is that the task of the university is to provide students with a wide spectrum and solid basis of knowledge in order to prepare them for lifelong learning in the field of business and management. This seems to be quite different from US practice.

DILEMMAS AND POSSIBLE APPROACHES
FOR HUNGARIAN BUSINESS AND MANAGEMENT
HIGHER EDUCATION

As Hungary wants to belong to the community of market economies, and since it is in Europe, it is important to follow a European model, if it exists at all, and to take international tendencies into consideration. It is quite difficult to find an adaptable model, but we can learn from the example of those countries which have learned from the American business schools.

Table 2. Key issues in adaptation of business
and management education in Hungary

Issues	Difficulties	Course of action needed
Competition of schools	Academic education versus training institutions	Revision of the system of business and management education
	Laissez-faire versus regulated competition	Specialized schools
	Specialized managers	In-house training programmes
Professional, functional and management knowledge and skills	Lack of management approaches in professional education	Revision of curriculum and courses
		Post-graduate programmes for managers
		Teaching professors and trainers
Relevance to the Hungarian situation	Missing fields of knowledge (e.g. managerial accounting, corporate finance)	Adapting to supply missing knowledge
		Giving more courses on these key subjects
	Bridging the gap between Hungarian and Western business	Understanding the similar or dissimilar character of foreign business
Teaching methods	Lack of experience	Learning from foreign experience
	Poorness of teaching facilities	Developing the teaching infrastructure
	Relevance of cases used in Western education	Developing Hungarian cases
Transition of the economy	Urgent practical requirements in management and business education	Teaching special subjects on privatization
		Short training programmes on hot topics
		In-house training programmes
		Consultancy

The British example teaches us that it is hard to adapt the American business and management education system when universities resist and business and management sciences are not regarded as academic.

The French learned a great deal about American business and management education and adapted them into their own educational system while preserving their cultural heritage.

The Germans adapted less of the American model, since they had their own excellent business and management theory and practice [6, 7].

The Hungarian situation is similar to the British and the German in having a two-level higher educational system: colleges which are practice-oriented, and universities rather science-oriented on professional bases. There are increasing scholarship opportunities for Hungarian professors to go to the USA to obtain deeper knowledge and understanding of business and management sciences and practice; this is similar to the French situation. At the moment Hungarian business and managerial practice and theory are not based on the market economy and the country is open for adapting other systems. But there is a question of how things will change in the near future.

As European unification comes closer and the world markets become more similar, there are converging tendencies in business and management education the root of which is American business and management education [8].

There is great demand in Hungary for business and management training and education and the number of management training and development institutions is increasing. Some of them are close to European standards, like the International Management Center, but some of them are poor. The universities of other professions are working on launching faculties of business and management. Competitors have appeared in the field of management and business education and training. This tendency may be strengthened by the forthcoming higher education regulation that will allow private schools and universities to be created. Such competition must change the behaviour of the old universities and colleges of business and management. They will have to answer several questions and the answers will depend on the transitional process in Hungary – especially on the changing structure of the economy. The property structure of the economy must change first the private sector of the economy becoming more dominant than it was in the age of "socialism". This will have consequences for the structure of businesses. Owners, managers and employees will have to learn their own changed roles within organizations; they will require new knowledge and techniques of business operation. At this moment these roles are mixed [9].

The world market is expanding and international tendencies should not be neglected. The success of the US economy is still attractive and culturally it stands closer to Hungary than does Japan; the identification of successes and failures in the market economies in the field of management is very important. The heritage of the previous Hungarian system could be of great importance: its advantages should be preserved and a new market economy built on them. However, there seems to bed time pressure and the transition requires practical solutions to practical problems.

CONCLUSIONS

Business and management education in Hungary has begun to change in response to the transition to a new economic order. In Hungary, we are looking to the very different American business and management higher education system – Hungary can learn from the US business schools especially about the curriculum and the teaching methods. It is of great importance to create business schools and/or to strengthen those that have operated for several years in Hungary. However, the adaptation of the system seems to be difficult, as *Table 2* shows.

In spite of the difficulties there is good basis for adaptation in Hungary. The urgent need for transition in the field of business and management education requires help from foreign countries with knowledge, and the training of professors and teachers abroad. However, the success or failure of these efforts depends on the Hungarian institutions themselves and especially on their professors.

REFERENCES

[1] HELLER, F.: The Hungarian Academy of Sciences and the Economic Sciences. Franklin társulat (in Hungarian) (1930).
[2] JAMES, E. J.: "Commercial Education." In: N. M. BUTLER (ed.): *Monographs on Education in the United States.* J. B. Lyon Co. (1899).
[3] BEREND, T. I., STARK, A., TORDAI, I.: "Our Economic Higher Education. Its History and Solutions and Dissolutions of the Present." *Gazdaság*, No. 2 (in Hungarian) (1978).
[4] CSÁKI, Cs., ZALAI, E.: "Concept for the Curriculum Reform of the Karl Marx University of Economics." *Gazdaság*, No. 2 (in Hungarian) (1987).

[5] KINDLER, J., KISS, I., MÁRIÁS, A.: "On Management Education." *Közgazdasági Szemle*, No. 11 (in Hungarian) (1982).

[6] ALBACH, H.: "Business Administration: History in German Speaking Countries." In: E. GROCHLA, E. GAUGLER (eds): *Handbook of German Business Management*. C. E. Poechal Verlag, Stuttgart, and Springer-Verlag, Berlin (1990).

[7] LOCKE, R. R.: *Management and Higher Education since 1940: The Influence of America and Japon on West Germany, Great Britain and France*. Cambridge University Press, Cambridge (1989).

[8] PORTER, L. W., McKIBBIN, L. E.: *Management Education and Development: Drift or Thrust into the 21st Century?* McGraw-Hill, New York (1988).

[9] VECSENYI, J.: "Selection and Development of Young Managers", paper presented at the 2nd Congress of Human Resource Managers (in Hungarian) (1990).

FURTHER READING

CRUIKSHANK, J. L.: *A Delicate Experiment. The Harvard Business School 1908–1945*. Harvard Business School Press, Boston, MA (1987).

RHEDER, R. R.: "Education and Training: Have the Japanese Beaten US Again?" *Personnel Journal*, January (1983).

21

BUSINESS EDUCATION AND MANAGEMENT TRAINING IN THE OLD AND NEW EAST CENTRAL EUROPE*

By

ANDREW GROSS, ROBERT HARTLEY, JÓZSEF BERÁCS,
PÁL PÉTER GÁSPÁR

This paper focuses on business education and management training in the old and new East Central Europe – that is, in a historical perspective. Emphasis is given to social and cultural settings in which such learning and teaching take place. The paper investigates the structure, the conduct, and the performance of the business education "industry" in the region. We conclude the essay with a series of specific recommendations. *[Article copies available from The Haworth Document Delivery Service: 1-800-342-9678.]*

INTRODUCTION

When the historians of the 21st century look back on the 20th, they will identify certain landmarks; one of these is bound to be the 1989 political and economic upheaval in Eastern Europe. The underlying causes of the changes will prove to be numerous, ranging from those within to those outside the region. Major domestic factors include repressive regimes, economic failures, and a yearning for freedom and more consumer goods. Key leaders played major roles (in the region: Gorbachev, Walesa, Havel, and others), but thousands of ordinary citizens also showed much courage under tremendous pressure. Foreign influences range from political threats or promises to satellites beaming in news of a better way of life.

As the reform processes now unfold, there is much change, but also much disillusionment. Bringing capitalism to historically planned economies is no easy task; governing democratically in former dictatorships is a risky undertaking. Unemployment and inflation are both up sharply from previous levels; the gap between haves and have-nots has

* In *Journal of Teaching in International Business*, 1995, Vol. 7, No. 2, pp. 35–60.

widened. Advisers, doers, dreamers, and schemers flock in from abroad; for each humanitarian step, one can cite an act of greed. How can the old structure be dismantled; how can established practices change? Slogans have changed, but the underlying culture and values are hard to alter.

The educational system of each nation in the region is in the throes of change, with emphasis on rethinking the curriculum, the methods of teaching and learning, as well as most administrative practices. Institutions of higher education can hasten the transformation toward political pluralism, market economy, and technical progress. At the same time, as we know too well, these institutions have much inertia and indeed can pose barriers to reforms. There is a fundamental faith, however, that by opening many windows and doors – that is by becoming part of the global educational milieu institutes can change themselves and act as agents of change for the societies in which they exist. In Eastern Europe, political/economic leaders often come from (and return) to universities.

In this paper we analyze business education in East Central Europe (defined as: Poland, Czech Republic, Slovakia, Hungary, Romania, and the former Yugoslavia), with emphasis on what is right, what is wrong, and what needs changing. To delineate these points, we sought answers to three major questions. First, what are some of the fundamental social, economic and other values in their region and in each nation? Second, what are the characteristics of management education and training, past and present, and how do these differ from others around the globe? Third, what is the structure, the content, and the performance of business education at universities and at new management centers?

The central theme which runs through the essay is this: Business education is indeed changing and does act as a change agent in the new East Central Europe. The more specific topic of teaching international business is in the vanguard of this movement. However, it is crucial to delineate clearly what needs changing, what can be changed and what facets can be retained. Of equal importance is the time dimension; a few facets can be changed in weeks, but most undergo transformations after years. While some new policies, and technical apparatus are quickly put into place, the values of individuals and the cultures of organizations alter very slowly. To use a legal analogy – enacting laws is one thing; implementing and enforcing them is quite another.

LITERATURE REVIEW

Our review yielded four categories of publications. First, we found many "newsy" articles which can be labelled as timely and optimistic. These are one to three-page long in popular news magazines and business weeklies (BALTKI 1989; GRIEVES 1988, etc.). As a general rule, the authors – often reporters – extol the virtues of bringing Western (North American or West European) business education to Eastern Europe. A more thorough treatment is found in the academic newspaper, the *Chronicle of Higher Education* (e.g. BOLLAG 1992; MASSEY 1990; WOODWARD 1990). These contributions show what programs are aimed at what audiences, and at what cost; in short, they present an up-to-date, comparative picture, but one which can change rapidly. Still, these items are useful to actual and potential students, faculty administrators, and even policy-makers.

The second category consists of longer, more academic articles usually written by faculty members who seek to analyze the nature of business education in Poland, Hungary, or one of the other nations. Three sub-categories can be distinguished, depending on the writer's perspective:

(1) faculty members at an East European university reporting from "the home front" (KASPERSON 1992; NICOLESCU 1992; TIMÁR 1992);
(2) Western educators focusing on comparative aspects (BOYATZIS 1992; NEHRT 1987; SARATHY 1990); and
(3) writers of various origins, emphasizing the actual transfer of the "best of the West" to the East (CZAKÓ 1992; MADHAVAN and FOGEL 1992; VECSENYI 1992. The three sets yield a useful perspective.

The third category consists of articles which veer away from the academic or educational view and move to a managerial or corporate one. The authors of these articles (BEAMISH and CALOF 1989; CELLICH 1990; MCNULTY 1992) are able to step back and deliver an applied perspective, often from a user's point of view. Included here are evaluations of programs and institutes – with frank comments on what seems to work and what does not – and how those who enroll in them now are likely to benefit.

In the fourth and final category, contributions focus on long-range views of how business education evolved and how it is changing, both East and West. These articles, special journal issues, and books usually encompass findings from surveys conducted in various countries and regions. The focus is on a combination of academic and administrative aspects, but usually emphasizing the former. In the past these contributions usually had limited information about Eastern Europe (BYRT 1989; KUBR 1987; PORTER and McKIBBIN 1988; THANOPOULOS and VERNON 1987). But more recently, several new books and proceedings came to light, or are in progress, offering useful insights and analysis (AACSB 1993; FOGEL 1991; HASKINS 1993; MINISTRY 1990; and TESAR 1994). These volumes take a long time to develop, but the treatment is much more in-depth.

METHODOLOGY

During the past year and a half we reviewed the literature cited above (for the full set of sources, see the references at the end). In addition, we have conducted over 50 informal interviews with selected business school faculty members and administrators in Hungary, the Czech Republic, Poland, and the former Yugoslavia. Their ranks ranged from lecturers to full professors, from assistants to chairpersons, deans, and rectors. Next, we talked informally with many recent and older graduates now employed both in the public and private sectors of the various countries. Our goal in this regard was to focus both in their education and the utilization of the same in their current positions.

Of course, we made observations of our own as a result of teaching both at established universities and newly founded management schools in two of the countries as well as guest-lecturing or visiting at institutes in other nations of the region. Two of us carried out administrative assignments at various locations and all of us served on a wide variety of committees at several institutes as regular or visiting faculty members. At all times we interacted with numerous graduate and undergraduate students, seeking their frank comments after the completion of a course. Two of the four authors have taught extensively in the East, two in the West; but all four have visited for several months or half-year periods in the opposite region during the period 1989–1993 (and even before).

In the sections which follow, we look at certain historical highlights and cultural values as well as at policies affecting institutes of higher education. Then we analyze business education in East Central Europe in terms of structure, conduct and performance. Finally, we delineate the duality we see–namely what is worth retaining and what needs major transformation, including "installation of the new".

STEEPED IN HISTORY, BOUND IN TRADITION

While some universities in the region trace their roots to the 14th or 17th century, the majority of the institutes of higher education came into being during the 19th and 20th centuries. Regardless of founding dates, we find wide diversity; some patterned themselves along classical lines emulating West European universities; others followed their own unique paths as national laws governing them were not always clear cut. There was practically no formal education for managers; as for technical workers, they entered schools of engineering or entered vocational programs. Managers as such came from the ranks of scientists, engineers and even liberal arts majors.

The end of World War II represented a sea-change in East Central Europe as these nations came under Soviet domination. The educational system reflected this. Communist ideology became a topic not only to be taught, but was designed to permeate the social fabric of each nation. At the universities, such ideology invaded the social sciences, especially classical economics. It was in this kind of atmosphere that new universities of economics were formed. They did offer a sprinkling of accounting, finance, and labor courses, but hardly a modern management curriculum. Nevertheless, the graduates found attractive jobs as line managers and staff officials in large state organizations. To be sure, they did have to complete against those who came from the old-liberal arts and engineering institutes.

Four decades of Communist ideology could not wipe out centuries of tradition. Thus, whether we speak of professional, technical, or liberal arts training – or apprenticeship and vocational education – many of the traditional values and skills have been retained. Graduates of programs from many universities and colleges in the region continued to display language and mathematical skills; some of the entrepreneurial attitudes and drives have also survived. But a the same time, in part due to isolation from the West and the lack of advanced equipment, there was a loss of self-confidence. Many came to realize that political connections (known as nomenklatura) counted more than knowledge and skills.

Thus, what we find in Hungary, Poland, the Czech Republic and elsewhere now is a vast mixture of century-old habits, overlaid with four decades of ideology, and a few years (1989–1993) of sudden reforms. The mantle of the old is streaked with the shock of the new fibers and this results in attitudes that are quite different from those in the West. This sit-

Table 1. Selected socio-cultural patterns and values:
comparison of Hungarian and U.S. workers
(managerial, technical, skilled factory) similarities
and differences as of 1989–1991

HUNGARY	U.S.A.
PART 1	
50% introvert, 50% extrovert	majority extrovert
less intuitive, more sensing	more intuitive
too cerebral	more feeling, emotion
quick to judge	more likely to postpone judgment
speak after deliberation	speak almost immediately
certain lack of confidence	have much confidence
more adapting to situation, boss	more used to open debate
limited use of hi-tech equipment	wide-use of hi-tech equipment
PART 2	
good technical skills	good technical skills
relatively warm and cordial	relatively warm and cordial
can implement with relative ease	can implement with relative ease
good personal interaction	good personal interaction
troubled with leadership role	not reluctant to take leader role
troubled with concept of profit, etc.	familiar with profit, margin, etc.
problem integrating functions	little problem integrating functions
thinks managers are in place due to nomenklatura, politics, etc.	thinks managers hold positions due to merit and networking
will rely more and/or prefer written instructions	comfortable with oral instructions and/or brief memoranda
tech. equip. for communication in workplace and outside: very poor	tech. equip. for communication in workplace and outside: very good

Note:

Part 1 based on a survey of 300 Hungarian and 700 U.S. managers.
Part 2 based on a survey of General Electric (USA) and Tungsram (Hungary) workers.
Shortened, revised and adapted from the original.

Source:

Concordia, a management consulting firm in Budapest, Hungary 1990.

uation is illustrated in *Table 1* for a group of managerial, technical and skilled workers in Hungary and in the USA as of the early 1990s. This is just one illustration; many journal articles are bringing additional evidence that there are still vast cultural differences between East and West.

In short, we find that prevailing values, existing practices, and established institutions reflect the "baggage of tradition", some of which is a century old, some of which is decades-old. In such a setting, as one author put it, "believing that all East Europe needs is American-style management is a myth. It is probably the last kind of management that could be directly transferred without careful adaption" (MᴄNᴜʟᴛʏ 1992, 80). The same holds true for management education.

BUSINESS EDUCATION IN THE REGION, 1945–1993

After World War II, the structure of higher education in Western Europe was reorganized along lines practiced in the dominant political power, the USSR. Essentially, university autonomy gave way to control by the central government in Poland, Hungary, Czechoslovakia, and elsewhere. To please rural and urban populations, new institutes, two-year colleges, and specialized universities were established (but central control still prevailed). Evening programs and correspondence courses proliferated. Financing higher education generally consumed about 0.7 to 0.9% of the state budget in each nation, because expensive academic research was cut back.

Advanced research was reserved for centers which were affiliated with Academies of Science. Such academies were also given the right to award degrees and membership which were of higher rank than the diplomas, certificates, and degrees of the colleges and universities. In most countries of the region, this "academization" of degrees has been at odds with older traditions. To this day (1994), the power struggle between the academies and the faculties of universities is ongoing; it involves questions of degrees and research. There are some indications that the governments in Hungary, Poland, and the Czech Republic will rule in favor of the universities, while encouraging the academies to seek funds for their research centers from the domestic private sector and from abroad.

Management or business education did not escape the heavy hand of Communist ideology or practice as noted above. The education of future managers, however, did not become the sole domain of the relatively new universities of economics. Yes, they became the training ground for a vast cadre of state officials. Still, it was possible to get an engineering degree or a liberal arts training, with a few courses on administration and individual operations, and assume the post of a factory manager or state bureaucrat. Yet another avenue for advancement (albeit for lower ranks) came via the two-year colleges which offered specialized training in such fields as: foreign trade; hospitality management; accounting and finance.

After the grand transformation of 1989, three distinct institutes emerged which are able and willing to provide "modern" business education and management training. These are national universities of economics, with new programs; locally developed, new private schools, with limited scope and funding; and new Western-sponsored centers. Until recently, the national governments were reluctant to give full accreditation to the last two categories, but this situation may be changing and they may be able to give "state certified diplomas", bachelor's or even master of business administration degrees. All three types of institutes offer a wide variety of short executive development programs as well. Among old schools with new programs are the Budapest University of Economic Sciences in Hungary, the Universities of Łódź and Poznan in Poland, and the Institute of Social Management in Bulgaria. Examples of locally developed schools are the Executive Training Center at Kranj, Slovenia (former Yugoslavia) and the International Business School in Warsaw. Western-sponsored schools include the International Management Center near Budapest and the Czech Management Center in a suburb of Prague, both aided by the University of Pittsburgh. All three types co-exist in all capital cities of the region and beyond (Baltic Republics, Russia, etc.).

Regardless of which category was established first in the euphoria of 1989–1990, today there is much jockeying among the categories for sources of funds, faculty and students. Ministries of education appear to favor the first group in terms of accreditation and funding, but it is likely that tuition fees, often unheard of until now, will be charged. Meanwhile the local or foreign-assisted schools are charging upwards of $2,000 per semester and yet still seek financial aid from companies, near and far.

There is much debate about various dimensions of higher education, especially about the way in which power or control will be shared and about how scarce funds will be allocated. Yet another topic is: Where will the students come from? Traditionally, in the region, only 10% of the 18- to 24-year-olds entered institutes of higher education; now, some of them are attracted by entrepreneurial (legal and illegal) opportunities, while still others cannot afford tuition. Room and board expenses are on the rise, even if living at home. A related topic is: Where will the faculty come from? Faculty members often toil at several institutes in order to survive, leaving little time for class preparation and research. Despite travel to the West, they often have meager knowledge of market systems.

The central question, however, is how to shape the curriculum, what to offer. Ministry officials, rectors, provosts, and others are giving much

Table 2. Differences and similarities in business education
on two continents, 1990–1993

North America	Western and Eastern Europe
Emphasis on quantitative skill	Emphasis on mix of theory and practice
Limited emphasis on language skills but some schools are changing	Emphasis on language skills (but many students acquired them)
Limited field work, limited but changing emphasis on co-op program	Emphasis on internships, co-op programs, action learning, field work
Emphasis on case studies as useful learning tools	Case studies used but only for purpose of illustration, simulation
Growing emphasis on team work, largely neglected until now	Emphasis on teams and groups, on and off campus
Cross-disciplinary studies, neglected until now, receive emphasis	Growing emphasis on cross-disciplinary studies neglected in some places, emphasized elsewhere (variety)
Programs, schools have lost sight of customers; companies claim they now seek generalists (but they still hire specialists)	Programs, schools have lost sight of customers; companies are seeking graduates with managerial, not political skills (but contacts count)
Growing emphasis on good teaching, largely neglected till now	Some leading schools do emphasize the importance of good teaching, not many
Limited use of outside speakers, restrict use of part-timers	Wider use of outside speakers, part-time lecturers
Large role for accrediting body, e.g. AACSB in USA	Limited role for accrediting agencies accrediting procedures
Limited use of seeking approval from selected outside bodies	Some use of seeking approval or working with trade associations
Chambers of Commerce not used in/for continuing education	Chambers of Commerce are non-political, offer contin. educ. courses
Professors seldom allowed to offer special course at last minute	Some schools allow professors to offer course at last minute
No close relationship with centers of contin. educ. on campus	Some schools will coordinate closely contin. educ. centers
New buildings, up-to-date facilities, modern equipment emphasized	Less emphasis on new facilities, equipment but this is changing
Libraries well-equipped, some have campus electronic network ability to tap distant databases	Encourage use of other public libraries; some have modern electronic network capability
Growing mix of age, gender, and nationality among students	Growing mix of age, gender, nationality among students

Source:

Primary research by the authors

thought to executing reforms. In regard to business education, a gulf exists not so much between East and West as between North America and Europe. (Japan presents yet a third model, not dealt with here.) The key differences and some similarities are illustrated in *Table 2*. It would be foolish to think that the North American model is appropriate for either Western or Eastern Europe. More likely, each region and each nation will have to define and then refine the dimensions of management education. In our view, the European paradigm is fortunately already more global in character than those in the USA and Canada.

There appears to be cross-fertilization going on, with concepts and practices traded across the Atlantic. Thus, North American schools are internationalizing the curriculum, re-emphasizing good teaching, looking at distance learning and at paperback (or even customized) textbooks. Meanwhile, their European counterparts are adopting the case method (up to a point), replacing subjective oral exams with both written essay and multiple choice tests and considering accreditation. They are also eager to equip their students with personal computers, but this will take some time. On both sides we note the growth of short, executive development programs in intensive day, evening, or weekend settings. These are designed to capture working managers who wish to renew themselves.

In the remaining sections we take a look at management education in the region in a manner analogous to looking at an industry, namely its (1) structure, (2) conduct, and (3) performance. Structure refers to the number of universities or schools, the organization of such institutes, and facilities. Conduct is the manner in which the tasks are carried out; just what is being taught and how. In short this means a look at the curriculum, at implementation. Performance refers to an evaluation of the institutes, the programs, and, ultimately, the faculty and student bodies.

STRUCTURE

An exact count of public universities and private schools offering business education in the region is not meaningful, as the numbers fluctuate; the expansionary phase is ending and consolidation is expected by the mid-1990s. Entry barriers are defined by availability or lack of funding. The SOROS Foundation has been especially generous in the region, to private and even public institutes; others have contributed too, ranging from West European governments to individual banks and companies. However, funding sources suddenly seem more scarce and we expect that several of the private institutes may fold or merge with others, while the public ones will be forced to enact or raise tuition fees (and demand payment in Western currencies from Western and Third World students).

In Poland, as of 1992, there were 12 public universities and higher institutes plus the Catholic university of Lublin offering management education. In addition, 12 management schools or centers have sprung up, mostly foundation supported or as joint stock companies. In Hungary, the corresponding numbers are about 5 and 5; in the Czech Republic 3 and 3. The numbers reflect the population and urban base in each country, government policies, and public/private sector budgets.

Competition between public and private schools is becoming more intense. As a general rule, a Western-sponsored management institute was established in the capital city of each nation in 1989–1990; this was then followed by reforms and a partial switch – from classical economics to business education – at the leading public university. Other universities and private schools then entered and – like their predecessors – began offering programs and courses in both the native tongue and English. The physical facilities seldom consist of newly-built edifices; but old castles and office buildings are being refurnished, often with modern equipment. Some schools now boast modern copiers, computers, and telecom links.

The number and type of constituent units (colleges, departments, etc.) can range from many to a few. In *Table 3* we see how the Budapest and Prague universities of economics have organized themselves. We note that in addition to traditional business topics, these schools will stress economics, social sciences, and general studies. There are numerous departments within units; for example, the Budapest University of Economic Sciences (BUES) has a total of 36 departments in 6 units. As for degrees awarded, these include the bachelor's degree, master's degrees (which can be an M.A., an M. Sc. or an M.B.A.), and a doctoral degree.

Both public and private institutions in the region now offer degrees in their native tongue (to the vast majority of students), but they also embarked on offering bachelor and/or master degrees in English (to anywhere from 5% to 25% of the student body). The latter usually commands a premium, meaning a hefty tuition. Faculties are recruited at home and abroad; students include wealthy citizens and those recruited from both within and outside Europe. At BUES, master's level programs in English consist of 60 credit hours over four semesters, with 12 hours devoted to a common core, the rest to specialized and other elective courses. Three

Table 3. Organization and degree offered at major economics/business universities in Eastern Europe as of 1993

Budapest University of Economics, Hungary

Units:
College of Social Sciences
College of Economics
College of General Studies and Languages
College of Graduate Studies
Institute of Continuing Education

Degrees:
Bachelor of Science (comprehensive exams)
Master of Business Admin.; Mester of Science
Ph.D. (comprehensive exams; thesis; oral defense)

The Prague School of Economics, Czech Republic

Units:
College of Finance and Accounting
College of International Relations
College of Industrial Engineering
College of Information Science and Statistics
College of General Economy

Degrees:
Bachelor of Science (comprehensive exams)
Engineer (approx. Master of Science) (thesis)
Ph.D. (comprehensive exams, thesis, defense)

Source:
for Budapest: authors' primary research
for Prague: M. PRIBOVA, "Manager or Amateur?" (GEORGE TESAR, ed.)

Reprinted with permission: TESAR, *Management Education and Training: Understanding Eastern European Perspectives*, 1994, Krieger Publishing Company, Malabar, Florida.

areas of specialization are offered: international economics; social and political studies; and business administration.

The competition among public and private institutes to attract students for short seminars and executive development courses is even more intense than is the case for degree programs. The short courses cover the usual functional areas, that is accounting, business law, finance, information, management, marketing, strategy, etc. Many course titles are the same as in the West, but some are different, e.g. Privatizing the Firm or Negotiating with Western Partners. The courses are often team taught by a local lecturer and a visitor from the West. The fees are generally high ($50 to $300), but attendance has been solid until now (from 10 to 100, though some specify a maximum of 30). In-house seminars are becoming popular.

What is the right model for a business school – university-based, private/independent, or possibly company-based? All three varieties are now in place in East Central Europe, as is the case in the West, but which will endure and which will fail remains to be seen. Those with longer tradition have an edge, but newcomers can carve out special niches, e.g. a group from France is emphasizing the teaching of banking practices in Budapest. There is agreement that all institutes have a major task ahead of them – educating their students, while trying to market themselves to sponsors (be they private or public), potential faculty, and the population at large.

CONDUCT (BEHAVIOR)

Higher education is a partnership among many: students, alumni, faculty members, administrators, funding agencies, and others. Equally important in the past have been the non-human gate-keepers-written rules and the unwritten policies which determined who (and how many) can be admitted. Now the selection is changing, albeit slowly. Admission is still highly selective, early career choice-going back to junior high school is still the rule. But there are little or no preferential quotas for children of factory workers or farmers. Instead, there is a notable trend toward the admission of children of high-level professionals, managers, and public officials, who received better early training and hence do better in high school and on entrance examinations.

Once admitted, university students in Eastern Europe, including those in business schools, tend to relax at first. Their attitude is one of nonchalance, similar to their counterparts in Japan. But then reality sets in, since they normally must carry over 20 or even 25 credit hours at the undergraduate level. Course requirements are becoming tighter. A final source of pressure is that many students work part-time, two-thirds out of necessity to make ends meet, one-third to earn money for luxuries. Business school students are now concerned about jobs; finding a well-paid position upon graduation used to be easier in the pre-1989 era. Placement offices simply do not exist on most campuses.

The faculty members in the business schools of state universities are a mix of young and old. While many express willingness to adapt to the new era, incrementalism is the order of the day. Younger faculty are more likely to be computer-literate, to have travel opportunities, and to teach in English. But older faculty have a better track record or reputation and, most important, better contacts which can enhance fame and fortune. Professors earn about $200 to $400 per month which is not enough to live on; thus, they openly teach at several institutes or seek other work, with a preference for business/government consulting, tutoring or translating. Instructors at private schools earn up to $900 per month, but in exchange must promise not to moonlight at other posts. Reputation of other professors rests little on teaching, more on publishing, and most of all on connections with business and government leaders. In Eastern Europe ministers often come from the ranks of senior faculty at the old-line universities.

We have already commented on programs and courses offered; but the real meaning of the new curriculum unfolds on a day-to-day basis in each and every class. What is happening here? Instructor-student relations are still stiff. Professors enjoy a high reputation and tend to lecture much of the time. Informal seminars with interaction are more likely for short courses and in executive development programs. Even in such cases participants are reluctant to speak out, to analyze, or to engage in a dialogue. Basic entrepreneurial instincts are present, but they need much cultivation. Students, especially at the graduate level, are starting to demand a good blend of conceptualization and smart business practice.

There are many signs of progress. Professors, pressed for time in preparing for a course, are beginning to draw their students into a dialogue. With co-op programs and internships encouraged, students bring their own examples from the business world. In turn, instructors are not reluctant to cite their consulting experiences. Where there is a mix of domestic and foreign students, classes are especially lively. Guest speakers, particularly those from foreign firms and from the areas of finance and marketing are welcomed. In our classes, we have seen a resurgence of enthusiasm and interest.

A wealth of information is becoming available from East and West, including new case studies from the home front and textbooks translated from English and German. Textbook prices are held down by publishing in paperback format; even so, many foreign authors must waive royalty rights in order to place their translated books in the hands of the students. Films and videotapes are now more abundant; overhead projectors have been available. Libraries are starting to feature Western business journals, streamlined catalogs and electronic access to online databases. However, the copying of articles by/for students or handouts in class by professors is still cumbersome to achieve.

Possibly, the greatest progress has been achieved in regard to tests and examinations. In the past, it was usual at most East European universities to conduct final exams based on oral interrogation of each student. These "make or break" examinations would last from 5 to 15 minutes. This was time-consuming for both instructors and students; most of all, the process was highly subjective. Written essay and multiple choice exams are now coming in vogue, though some instructors still favor the old ways. We think oral presentations, but not exams, make sense as do oral defenses of papers, theses, and dissertations.

PERFORMANCE

How can we evaluate the performance of business schools in East Central Europe, their programs and their achievements? To do such an evaluation is complex under the best of circumstances, because there is no strong agreement as to what constitutes success and failure. Here the task is made doubly difficult by the relatively short track record since 1989. Some contend that it is too early to come to judgment, that it will take until 2000 when we can sort out the achievements of institutes, faculties, student bodies, programs, and so forth.

Scattered evidence available to us gives reason to be optimistic about what business schools are accomplishing now and what they seek to achieve in the future. First, student evaluations are now conducted at both old-line universities and the new management schools. With all their shortcomings, such ratings give some insights. Base on the results so far, instructors, specific courses, and teaching material receive favorable comments and relatively high rankings. For example, both short and long programs at the privately-sponsored international management centers of Budapest and Prague were rated at about 4. plus on a 1 to 5 scale. Second, both invited and drop-in visitors from academic institutes, ministries, and corporations give favorable comments about what they observed in and out of classrooms. Finally, the popular media, East and West, report in generally positive terms about the major transformations which resulted in the move away from Communist ideology and Marxist economics toward modern management training.

Recently, in the USA, some popular magazines (news weeklies such as *U.S. News & World Report* and business journals such as *Business Week*) began a ranking of colleges and universities, including business schools.

At first there was much hue and cry from academia; but then, as the magazines refined their rating methods, reluctance gave way to acceptance to such an extent that schools are now quoting their rankings. (The *USN&WR* rating scheme now includes: student test scores; reputation of schools judged by alumni, deans, directors, practitioners; and faculty resources, activities and achievements.) Such rankings are still difficult to ascertain in the East, but *Table 4* gives us a first glimpse at ten business schools in Poland. A wide variety of indicators were used by the author, with detailed results discussed in a book in press now (TESAR 1994).

Table 4. Ranking of new business schools, Poland, 1993

School	Location	Type	Year	Score*
Managers Training Foundation Regional Management Center	Gdańsk	Foundation	1990	85.4
Polish International Management School	Warsaw	Foundation	1989	67.7
International Management Center @ U. of Warsaw	Warsaw	Joint Stock company	1989	62.7
International Management School	Warsaw	Joint Stock company	1989	60.1
Poznań School of Management	Poznań	Foundation	1988	57.1
International School of Commerce	Rynia	Company Limited	1990	56.8
Lublin Business School at Catholic Univ. of Lublin	Lublin	Foundation	1990	53.8
International Management School-Marco Ltd.	Kludzlenko	Company Limited	1990	51.2
Rzeszow Management School @ Rzeszow Polytechnic	Rzeszow	Foundation	1990	50.9
Katowice Management School	Katowice	N.A.	1990	50.5

Note:

* Maximum Score = 100. Factors included in evaluation are: course quality; selection of topics; availability and quality of teaching materials; cooperation with foreign institutions; available staff and instructor competence; school location; teaching/training facilities and technical equipment (computers, copiers, telecomm); accommodation facilities; forms of recruitment; and scope of faculty activities (research, consulting, publishing, etc.).

Source:

T. GOLEBIOWSKI, "Transformation of the Management Education and Training System in Poland: Needs and Reality." (GEORGE TESAR, ed.)

Reprinted with permission: TESAR, *Management Education and Training: Understanding Eastern European Perspectives,* 1994, Krieger Publishing Company, Malabar, Florida.

Just as important as the scattered evidence and the rankings are the signs from the "placement front". The majority of recent graduates from both the old-line universities and the new management schools are able to find attractive positions, although not as easily as they hoped for. (Many students hold part-time or full-time positions even before graduation.) Numerous conversations with graduates, professors, and employers indicate to us that there is "meat on the bone" and that value has been obtained from their course of studies. Actual utilization of every facet is not easily achieved, but the overall training appears to have been worthwhile from both employees' and employers' view. Applications for admission are still running strong.

How to make the courses and programs even more attractive? Our recommendations are shown in *Table 5*. We see need for increased emphasis or new offerings in these areas:

(1) entrepreneurship, because this fits closely with the need for economic rejuvenation;
(2) marketing, because consumers' needs must be taken into account and because distribution and promotion schemes need to be more sophisticated; and
(3) ethics and social responsibility, because there is increased concern with business practices and with the environment.

As for internationalizing the curriculum, this will be an on-going issue, but with a change in focus. The classical economics courses, offered during 1945–1989, put the stress on theory, on terminology, on regulations, and on arcane dealings in the Eastern Bloc. Now, as the firms in the East look to the West (which must be receptive and not hostile to the region), new conceptual and practical steps must be acquired. We think that as graduates leave the universities and management schools they will be better equipped to deal with their Western counterparts.

What we advocate is an education initiative within an international setting. This implies a range of small, but important steps, such as: gathering a good mix of domestic and foreign case studies; translating both textbooks and popular business volumes; student and faculty exchanges. All of these events are happening, but an added thrust seems highly useful. Possibly the most significant and least costly step is making international business information available at the university and college libraries. This is starting to happen; for example, the leading university (BUES) and private management school (IMC) in Budapest both subscribe to dozens of

Table 5. Prescriptions for eastern business schools:
what to retain, what to change

	Instill New	More Emphasis	Retain As Is	Less Emphasis
General:				
Quantitative skills			X	
Language skills			X	
Curriculum:				
Econ. theory				X
Applied economics for business		X		
Entrepreneurship	X			
Computers: hardware, software, telecommunications			X	
Marketing: consumer orientation, promotion	X			
Ethics and social responsibility	X			
Environmental concerns	X			
Teaching:				
Skills and preparation		X		
Classroom participation	X			
Informality with students; office hours		X		
Written exams, especially essay		X		
Foreign exchanges			X	
Consulting				X
Faculty evaluations	X			
Administration:				
Streamline bureaucracy	X			
Link functional areas better	X			
Link w/Academy of Science				X
Freedom to departmental units		X		
Exchange with other institutes		X		
Rigor in discipline and grading			X	
Selected admission			X	
Internationalizing curriculum		X		
Alumni donations	X			
Student social life		X		
Policymakers (Ministries):				
Surveys of comparable schools		X		
Budget setting		X		
Self-government for universities		X		

Source:

Primary research by the authors.

foreign journals, receive many annual reports, feature films or videos, and offer access to online and e-mail.

In regard to teaching techniques, we recommend that professors encourage and even demand class participation. We also advocate greater reliance on written exams; the oral interrogations are too subjective, too traumatic, and too time-consuming. Faculty members will also have to accept evaluation of their teaching performance and may have to decrease their consulting activities (if the school pays them well). A greater student orientation is needed, with more informality and less bureaucracy as a rule (and with more office hours). Finally, if placement and alumni offices are established, these will bring payoffs in the form of donations.

CONCLUSION

In this paper we have taken a look at business education in the new East Central Europe. Our analysis rested on three legs: a literature review; informal interviews in different nations and of different audiences; and our own observations in and out of the classroom, also in different countries. We conclude that business education in the region rests on decades of tradition which are not only unique to the region, but to each country. Thus, the cultural and social milieu must be taken into account and programs, policies and facilities must be tailored accordingly. In addition, the economic and business environment – for example, the unique strengths and weaknesses of different sectors in each nation – do affect and in turn are impinged upon by the management training which is undertaken.

We then looked at the business education "industry" in the region in terms of structure, conduct and performance. We found that old-line universities of economics transformed themselves, while new management schools or centers – aided by private sector funds at home and abroad – were being established. Competition between existing institutes is rather keen as they seek the right mix of student bodies and faculties. The expansion phase is ending and entry barriers are increasing. There is some evidence that the new curricula and related policies are appropriate to the local circumstances and responsive to the desires of the various constituencies. But it will take at least the rest of this decade, before management education in the region can be called mature or streamlined.

REFERENCES

AACSB: *The Internationalization of Business Education in the 1990s.* St. Louis: American Association of Collegiate Schools of Business (1993).

AACSB and AAC: *Beyond Borders: Profiles in Internationalization.* St. Louis: American Assembly of Collegiate Schools of Business (1993).

BALTKI, M.: East bloc meets mysterious west; Hungary's International Management Center, a new business school. *U.S. News and World Report,* 107 (5), p. 42 (1989, July 31).

BEAMISH, P. W., CALOF, J. L.: International business education: A corporate view. *Journal of International Business Studies,* 20, pp. 553–564 (1989).

BENTLEY, J. C.: Turning a world upside down: Reflections on change in graduate management education. *Selections,* Autumn, pp. 32–39 (1992).

BOLLAG, B.: An ambitious program aims to revive higher education in Eastern Europe. *Chronicle of Higher Education,* pp. A46–A48 (1992, October 21).

BOYATZIS, R. E. et al.: Implementing curricular innovation in higher education. *Selections,* Autumn, pp. 1–9 (1992).

BYRT, W. J.: *Management Education: An International Survey.* London: Routledge Kegan (1989).

CELLICH, C.: Designing effective international programmes for senior export executives. *Journal of Teaching in International Business,* 1 (3–4), pp. 7–27 (1990).

CHAN, T. S.: Teaching marketing in China: Implications for effective marketing education. *Journal of Teaching in International Business,* 1 (1), pp. 33–46 (1989).

CZAKÓ, E.: Lessons of the U.S. business schools for Hungary: A comparison. *Journal of Management Development,* 11 (3), pp. 48–55 (1992).

Economic Staff.: Educating Milos: Business Education in Eastern Europe. *The Economist,* 323 (7759), p. 86 (1992, May 16).

EFMD: *Guide to Eastern European Business Education.* Brussels: European Foundation for Management Development (1992).

FOGEL, D. S. (ed.): *Management Education and Training in Central and Eastern Europe and the Soviet Union.* Deans and Directors Conference, Budapest, Hungary (1991).

Fortune Staff.: MBA program to be offered at Karl Marx University in Budapest. *Fortune,* 118 (2), p. 16 (1988, July 16).

GRIEVES, R. T.: Teaching socialists to merge: GEORGE SOROS and IMC. *Forbes,* 142 (10), p. 161 (1988, October 3).

HASKINS, G. (ed.): Special issue: Management education in Eastern and Central Europe. *EFMD Forum,* pp. 1–66 (1993).

KASPERSON, C. J., OBLOJ, K.: Training Polish managers in a new economic era. *FRE-RL Research Report,* 11, pp. 64–67 (1992, March 13).

KOZMINSKI, A. K.: Management Studies in Poland: Past history, present state, requirements, and future prospects (in French). *Revue d'Etudes Comparatives Est-Ouest,* 22 (4), pp. 121–130 (1991).

KRUGLOV, V. V.: Recent developments in management education in the USSR: Business and Education. *Soviet Education,* 33 (11), pp. 37–44 (1991).

KUBR, M.: *Managing a Management Development Institution.* Geneva: International Labour Office (1987).

KWIATKOWSKI, S., KOZMINSKI, A. K.: Paradoxical country-management education in Poland. *Journal of Management Development*, 11 (5), pp. 28–33 (1992).

LARSON, L. S., SCHMERHORN, J. S. JR.: Alternative instructor roles in cross-cultural business and management training. *Journal of Teaching in International Business*, 1 (1), pp. 7–21 (1989).

MADHAVAN, R., FOGEL, D. S.: In support of reform: Western business education in Central and Eastern Europe. *Review of Business*, 13 (4), pp. 4–9 (1992).

MANOUKOVSKY, A.: The outlook for Soviet business schools. *European Management Journal*, 9, pp. 182–186 (1991, June).

MASSEY, S.: Soviet plans for a market economy already in focus at some of Moscow's higher education institutes. *Chronicle of Higher Education*, 37 (4), pp. A49–A50 (1990, September 26).

MCNULTY, L.: Management education in Eastern Europe. *Academy of Management Executive*, 6 (4), pp. 78–87 (1992).

Ministry of Education (Hungary), Coordination Office for Higher Education: *Concept for Higher Education Development in Hungary.* Budapest: Ministry of Education (1991).

NEHRT, L.: The internationalization of the curriculum. *Journal of International Business Studies*, 18 (1), pp. 83–90 (1987).

NICOLESCU, O.: Management education in Romania. *Journal of Management Development*, 11 (5), pp. 34–40 (1992).

O'CONNOR, R.: Retraining Eastern Europe. *Training*, 29 (11), pp. 41–45 (1992).

PORTER, L. W., MCKIBBIN, L. E.: *Management Education and Development: Drift or Thrust into the 21st Century.* New York: McGraw-Hill (1988).

PRESTEL, D. K.: The integration of business-related materials into the undergraduate Russian program. Paper presented at the 11th Annual Eastern Michigan University Conference on Languages and Communication for World Business and the Professions (available as EDRS Reprint) (1992).

PURG, D.: Past, present and future management development in the former republics of Yugoslavia. *Journal of Management Development*, 11 (3), pp. 56–64 (1992).

SARATHY, R.: Internationalizing MBA education: The role of overseas programs. *Journal of Teaching in International Business*, 1 (3–4), pp. 101–118 (1990).

SZCZEPANSKI, J.: Higher education in Eastern Europe. *Occasional paper, No. 12.* New York: Interlock for ICED (1974).

TESAR, G. (ed.): *Management Education and Training: An Eastern European Perspective.* Melbourne, FL: Krieger Publishing (1994).

THANOPOULOS, J., VERNON, I.: International business education in the AACSB schools. *Journal of International Business Studies*, 18 (1), pp. 91–98 (1987).

TIMÁR, J.: The development of Hungarian higher education (in Hungarian). *Közgazdasági Szemle*, XXXIX (9), pp. 824–836 (1992).

VECSENYI, J.: Management for Hungarian Transition. *Journal of Management Development*, 11 (3), pp. 39–47 (1992).

VIKHANSKI, O. S.: Let's train managers for the market economy. *Soviet Education*, 33 (11), pp. 31–36 (1991).

WALTERS, P. G. P.: The significance of foreign language skills for initial entry positions in international firms. *Journal of Teaching in International Business,* 1 (3–4), pp. 71–83 (1990).

WANKEL, C., ADVOCATE, M.: Management education in Poland. *Review of Business,* 13 (4), pp. 13–15 (1992).

WOLFE, J.: On the transfer of market-oriented business games to eastern bloc cultures. *Social Science Computer Review,* 9 (2), pp. 202–214 (1991).

WOODARD, C.: Hungary moves to streamline its universities and eliminate vestiges of its Soviet-style system. *Chronicle of Higher Education,* pp. A35–A36 (1992, September 23).

WYND, W. R., REITSCH, A. G.: Soviet and American business students: Similarities and differences. *Journal of Education for Business,* 66 (6), pp. 338–341 (1991).

IV

ECOLOGICAL AND SOCIAL RESPONSIBILITY: ENVIRONMENT AND ETHICS

INTRODUCTION TO PART FOUR

Public opinion in the former socialist countries – because of the one-sidedness of the mass media – cherished such illusions as the belief that as a result of the institutionalization of social responsibility they possessed a relatively advanced system of environment protection. After the change in the régime, when objective data became available about the real environment-polluting activities of companies and various institutions, it became apparent that these countries were significantly backward in many fields compared with the developed countries.

We find this problem explored and systematized in the KEREKES–WELFORD article in Chapter 22. They show that in Hungary a relatively small proportion of GDP is spent on environment protection compared with the developed countries. Its foreign trade product structure is such that it specifically increases environmental pollution, therefore encouraging export has negative external effects. But the changes in the structure of industry resulting from competition, the withering of certain branches (e.g. heavy industry) have beneficial effects. The authors make recommendations as to what sort of role the state should fulfil in a developing country.

With the growing role of the market economy, there is increasing pressure on company management with regard to environment protection expenditure. On the basis of an empirical survey carried out among company executives, VASTAG–KEREKES–RONDINELLI tested four possible management approaches: reactive, proactive, strategic and crisis preventive. Their results showed that the approaches mentioned are closely related to companies' environment protection risks. In companies requiring the strategic approaches (e.g. big chemical firms in the vicinity of towns), where both the endogenous and the exogenous environmental hazards are great, senior management deals with the issue. Protection permeates the everyday work; there is an advanced monitoring system, and the company's publications also reveal awareness of the environment.

Hungarian company executives' environmental awareness is evaluated by means of international comparisons by VASTAG–RONDINELLI–KEREKES in Chapter 24. Their international and Hungarian surveys produced fairly similar results. With regard to direction, despite the fact that the answers pointed in the same direction, there were differences. For instance, 54% of Hungarian managers agreed with the international survey were of this opinion. In the field of environment protection campaigns, however, Hungarian executives have more modest programs than their foreign counter-parts.

A higher degree of environmental awareness is represented by environmental ethics in business. In Chapter 25, starting out from ecological considerations ZSOLNAI applies the stakeholder concept in formulating environmental ethics. The ethical approach is reinforced by the fact that even in the most advanced countries the law on environment protection is fragmented and frequently favours narrow interest groups. The forces seeking to implement green ideas do what they can within a company to turn ethics into business practice.

In the last article, Chapter 26, ZSOLNAI raises to the theoretical level the concept of moral responsibility and economic choice. Bringing in psychology as well, he attempts to work out a normative model capable of counterbalancing traditional rational decision-making behaviour, and accords a central role to the responsible decision-maker.

22

ECONOMIC DEVELOPMENT AND ENVIRONMENTAL PERFORMANCE IN HUNGARY*

By

SÁNDOR KEREKES, RICHARD WELFORD

The transformation of the economies of Central and Eastern Europe could represent a watershed in European environmental policy. By learning from the experiences of the West, they could set new standards in sustainable development. This is especially evident in Hungary, although as SÁNDOR KEREKES and RICHARD WELFORD discuss, social and economic priorities are likely to prevent this opportunity from being realised.

INTODUCTION

The Central and Eastern European region is living through a period with no parallel in history. Many specialists from around the world are offering advice and guidance to assist the region in a rapid transition to a market economy. While this may have a number of advantages, careful consideration of the political, social and environmental ramifications would suggest that a slower and more gradual approach would be more appropriate (KINDLER 1992 and VAN ZON 1992). This article will attempt to prove the necessity of a gradual transition, taking into account achievable economic development and the interests of environmental protection.

Rapid economic development is only possible if the conditions for fast technological transfer are created. But because of low income levels and a very low modern capital base, rapid forms of technological transfer can operate only through foreign investments which also bring with them social tensions. Moreover, with the world recession, it is increasingly

* In *European Environment*, 1993, Vol. 3, Part 2, pp. 14–17.

apparent that the initial euphoria directed towards the East has been short lived.

Central and Eastern Europe has reached the third year of its transitional period. Many of the changes are radical, at least in the eyes of external observers and the limited statistics available. The real picture undoubtedly varies between countries and is as yet superficial. Therefore it is our intention to try to avoid the generalisations so often found in papers of this sort and to concentrate our analysis on the environmental consequences of the changing structure of the Hungarian economy. In so doing we will argue that there is a need for a much more consistent and longer term plan for the sustainable development of the Hungarian economy.

PRECONDITIONS AND POSSIBILITIES

According to many commentators (e.g. WELFORD and PRESCOTT 1992), in comparison with the other Central and Eastern European countries, Hungary is in a relatively advantageous position. It is much further down the line towards the market economy with foreign confidence relatively high and there are favourable conditions for privatisation and foreign market entry. Hungarian managers are familiar enough with Western management methods to be able to adopt them right away, and this is helped by a culture which is much more liberal, tolerant and adaptable than in the neighbouring countries of the region. Moreover, Hungarian society appears to have been more able to live with social uncertainty associated with transition than expected. Thus neither the rise in prices, nor unemployment, has thrown the Hungarian economy totally out of control.

Another advantage which Hungary has over its neighbours is that the establishment of the institutional system necessary for the operation of the market economy (the banking system, stock exchange, etc.) began some time ago and is now relatively well developed. Budapest is fast becoming the financial centre of the region with significant inward investment from the EC, America and Japan. However, considerable uncertainty still exists and, in general, international conditions for transition are much less favourable than expected.

Presently, the impact for Hungary of the world recession is compounded by the instability of the neighbouring countries and the virtual economic collapse of the former Soviet Union. But in spite of unfavourable conditions and the initial failures, there are increased expectations that the current development path will work. These expectations themselves encourage the acceptance of the market economy amongst the population and an increased willingness for foreign companies to invest in the region.

THE ENVIRONMENTAL RISKS OF ECONOMIC DEVELOPMENT

In 1989, Hungarian GDP per capita was US$2,730. The comparable figure in the developed countries was between US$14,000 and US$20,000. Hungarian GDP has decreased steadily since this time, although, as stated, of the countries in Central and Eastern Europe, Hungary is perhaps in the best position to expand its economy. However, expectations of economic development have a range of associated environmental risks and achieving environmentally sustainable economic growth will not be easy for a number of reasons.

Firstly, there may be a temptation to follow the model of western consumerism which we know to be unsustainable and environmentally damaging. While to some Hungarians Western levels of income and wealth may seem unachievable, in general the population does aspire towards Western consumption patterns. We need therefore to avoid a development path which would put huge pressure on already inefficient energy production and raw materials consumption.

Secondly, expectations are naively short term. The Government's response is increasingly short-termist, trying understandably to rectify problems such as growing unemployment. Longer term thinking and strategic planning consistent with sustainable development have perceptibly fallen in priority and there is a need to rectify that situation.

The economic situation therefore encourages many of Hungary's policy makers to take the view that it is not possible or necessary to do anything other than manage current problems such as the debt crisis, unemployment and inflation, and if these variables can be controlled then the market will solve structural problems itself. However, experience from market-driven economies in the 1980's indicates that such expectations overestimate the power and flexibility of the market and continue to treat the environment as a free good unless the "polluter pays" principle can be forcefully applied.

We would argue therefore that not enough emphasis is being given to longer term problems such as improving the overall efficiency and therefore the environmental performance of industry. The question of natural resource use and the problems of environmental protection and nature conservation must also be addressed.

INDUSTRY AND THE ENVIRONMENT

Undoubtedly urgent action is required to address the environmental impact of industry for two reasons. Firstly, economic transformation offers an excellent opportunity to achieve environmental aims at the lowest cost with many of the most polluting industries closing in the competitive marketplace. Secondly, a growing number of new firms are appearing. It would seem timely to introduce environmental measures which these firms can adapt to at the outset. Without this sort of initiative, it will be very difficult to estimate and control the environmental effects of these small and medium size enterprises.

Unfortunately, many of the fundamental environmental and structural problems of Hungarian industry have not been solved by the drastic fall in production. Although industrial production has fallen to 51% of its value in 1985 [and this is even more striking in metallurgy, considered to be the most polluting branch (44%), the building material industry (50%), and in the chemical industry (68%)], there is still a lack of infrastructure and there continues to be an acute pollution problem which is a disincentive to inward investment.

THE ENVIRONMENTAL CONSEQUENCES
OF UNDERDEVELOPMENT

Most developed economies of the world have seen consistent structural shift from high volume to high value production. This has had associated benefits in terms of environmental efficiency. These trends have not been reflected in the economies of Central and Eastern Europe which saw the rise of raw material and energy prices to be only temporary and thus, in the absence of free market competition, failed to encourage structural change and hence fell behind the trends of development of the world economy (JANICKE et al. 1991).

As well as leading to unsuccessful modernisation, this mistaken development policy of the 1970s was based on the expansion of outdated and uncompetitive heavy industry. While market economies entered a period of development based on the information revolution, Hungary attempted to borrow in order to transform its obsolete economic structure. These investments merely increased the gap in technical development between it and the developed countries. Consequently, it is no accident that while the structural changes in the developed countries resulted in significant improvements in environmental efficiency, aptly called the "environmental gratis effects" (JANICKE et al. 1991), in the countries of Central Europe structural environmental pollution had to be endured. Thus, the Hungarian economy was structurally distorted and showed a predominance of heavy industry and an underdevelopment of the service sector.

While significant proportions of the heavy industry sector have closed since 1989, the remainder is out of date, using obsolete and inefficient technology and continually causing environmental damage. The problems stemming from outdated technology are intensified by the fact that 33% of employees, the majority of whom are skilled, are working in manufacturing industry. Therefore, the best trained workforce is employed in a field which uses out of date technology. However, those economic sectors that are commonly considered as environmentally harmful have been in decline since 1985. In part this was caused by significant energy price increases between 1980 and 1990 which caused crisis in some sectors of heavy industry with some environmental improvements. Since 1985, carbon dioxide and sulphur dioxide emissions from Hungarian industry have fallen, although clearly not as a result of direct environmental protection measures. This fall reflects decreases in GDP, again underlining the central relationship between economic structure and environmental damage. On the many occasions where the government has tried to support industry, environmental considerations have been a low priority. Also, the "environmental gratis effect" brings with it severe social and economic problems with increased closures and unemployment. As a result, these environmental benefits have not been entirely welcome and are increasingly leading to deep social tensions.

ENVIRONMENTAL PROTECTION IN HUNGARY

A common way of assessing the degree of environmental protection in an economy is to measure environmental protection investment as a share of GDP. Given the structural bias of the Hungarian economy toward heavy industry, this figure should be relatively high if protection were at western European levels. We know that in heavily polluting branches, environmental protection investments in Hungary have been significant, although at lower levels than in the West. However, there is a now real danger that the heavily polluting branches of industry will simply not be able to maintain levels of environmental investment. It is also increasingly likely that a blind eye will be turned to the environmental impacts of heavy industry to improve its chances of survival. In high earning branches of the economy such as tourism and the retail sector, environmental investments are virtually non-existent.

Further, applying the important "polluter pays principle" runs into difficulties not only from the bankrupt industries but also from those to be privatised. Pollution taxes and controls are too often seen as an impediment to the sales of assets to the private sector. In addition, the question of whether new private owners or the state should accept liability for past pollution is still unresolved and continues to add uncertainty to the move towards the market economy. The dominant ideology at the moment is one of do nothing, pushing environmental considerations further down the country's agenda.

THE ENVIRONMENTAL IMPACT OF FOREIGN TRADE

The success of transition depends to a large part on the Hungarian economy's productive capacity. Hungary's relative political stability is largely based on the relatively positive achievements of the economy. We have already noted that foreign investment and technology transfer are vital to the continued transformation of the economy. However, such foreign investment has been significantly lower than that hoped for throughout all eastern European economies. There is still a fear of economic colonialisation that does not bring the best technology to eastern Europe but industry which relocates as environmental protection tightens in the West (KADERJAK and LEHOCZKI 1991).

As yet, however, such fears appear to be unfounded. New investment has not been dominated by investment in the most polluting branches.

Indeed the bulk of new investment has been in retail and other service sectors which are generally accepted as less environmentally damaging. However, the majority of foreign capital investments do not enter the country as working capital but rather as a result of high domestic interest rates. Thus, in truth, we cannot fully evaluate the impact of foreign capital investment on economic structure and on environmental quality. In the limited number of cases where investment has been in the heavily polluting sector (e.g. General Motors, General Electric and Suzuki), the experience nevertheless tends to be favourable.

One has also to be wary about assuming that much of the foreign investment in sectors which are not regarded as heavily polluting are in fact environmentally friendly. In the tourism sector for example we are increasingly aware of the environmental damage done through increased energy and water consumption and the generally harmful effects of the vast number of tourists now entering the country and particularly Budapest.

Examining foreign trade rather than inward investment paints a rather different picture, however. Hungarian trade is typically dominated by the quantity and not the quality of goods. In the first half of 1992, 38% of a growing export volume was composed of materials and semi-manufactured goods where environmental damage was significant in their extraction and processing (Hungarian Central Statistics Office 1993). Thus in terms of foreign trade, the environmental impacts associated with exports have grown.

THE ROLE OF THE STATE

We would argue that the paternalistic attitude of the state still exists in Hungary. In the past, society justifiably expected the state, as the owner of industry, to solve the environmental problems created by companies. Paradoxically, environmental regulation in Hungary has always been very strict, perhaps stricter than some EC measures and certainly more strict than that which might be expected given the stage of development of the economy. However, for standards to be effective, they have to be reasonable and they have to be enforced. Neither criteria was ever achieved in Hungary.

Plans for the future are shrouded in uncertainty with the dominant aim being to move towards the market economy. Economic transformation is affecting ownership, the size of companies and the types of activities being undertaken. It is difficult to map out the future direction of the Hungarian economy and therefore equally difficult to design appropriate environmental protection measures. In addition environmental protection is too often seen as an impediment to economic improvement. Although the new Environmental Protection Act begins to move Hungary in the direction of equalising environmental standards with the West, the overriding consideration is still whether Hungary will be able to achieve compliance with its conditions.

The privatisation process and the transformation of the economy has to date led to an even more hands-off approach by the government towards environmental protection. Government is increasingly of the view that it no longer has to take responsibility for the environmental damage caused by the (private) business sector. Instead, it is more intent on trying to solve the environmental damage inflicted in the past, particularly by the Soviets. But this is a very expensive strategy and meanwhile environmental damage continues to build up. There is a need for a more strategic approach to the environmental situation.

The government's approach to dealing with the past's environmental damage is important but to neglect the present simply means that damage will reproduce itself and investment will be worthless. In addition, because industry finds itself able, at present, to export goods which have been environmentally damaging in their extraction and production, there is a view that this is a viable long term economic strategy. Certainly, it is a strategy of sorts, but it is not consistent with the aims of sustainable development, rather it illustrates the contradictions which run through the whole of Hungarian environmental policy.

THE FUTURE OF ENVIRONMENTAL POLICY

What the government can achieve is clearly limited by the Hungarian economy's indebtedness, increasing unemployment and loss of markets. The prospects for any real environmental improvement in the short run even with the so-called "gratis" effects are low. With falls in GDP, the government is further hampered by a decreasing budget with which to invest in environmental improvements and in any case these are of a lower priority than issues such as privatisation. For environmental protection to be a success it also requires the support of enterprises and society as a whole and again, other issues appear to take priority.

Such phenomena are typical of any underdeveloped region. Too often the quality of the environment only becomes important when a threshold material quality of life is attained. In Hungary, due to deteriorating living conditions, the significance of the environment and even of people's own health is driven into the background compared with consumption. To challenge the implicit societal resistance which this implies, it is important to challenge the view that environmental protection is first and foremost a financial question. A pre-condition of successful environmental policy is the creation of strong societal support.

In addition, because of the transformation of the Hungarian economy, future environmental policy will have to be based largely on local instruments. This will be aided if people actually adopt a "not in my backyard" approach which is so commonly derided elsewhere. A municipal approach will be more successful than directives from central government. Indeed this approach is occurring in Hungary with local government taking over more responsibility for planning. Hopefully this will lead to a more rational use of resources and the achievement of a greater consensus between the public and producers. There is still a role for central government, however, in putting in place an institutional system to protect the public interest.

Finally, we must recognise that the sort of environmental policies adopted in the West may not be applicable in Hungary in the short run. Poor living conditions and not environmental damage constitute the most serious risk to human health in Hungary at present. Whilst western economies have had the luxury of embarking on environmental policies within a framework of democracy, a functioning market economy and an up-to-date technological infrastructure, this is not the case in eastern Europe. Nevertheless, the environment does matter in countries such as Hungary and whilst the ideas and principles of sustainable development remain the same, their implementation will have to be different. However, it is our assertion that effective environmental protection measures are simply not consistent with the quick fix approach. Such an approach will continue to sideline environmental issues. A gradualist strategic approach needs to be developed with the cooperation of the population if we are to begin to deal with the environmental problems of the region.

REFERENCES

[1] Hungarian Central Statistical Office: *Yearbook of Economic Statistics,* Budapest (1992).

[2] JANICKE, M., MONCH, H., RANNEBERG, T., SIMMONIS, U.: *Economic Structure and Environmental Impact,* WZB, Berlin (1990).

[3] KADERJAK, P., LEHOCZKI, Z. S.: "Economic Transition and Environmental Protection: Foreign Investment and the Environment in Hungary", Budapest University of Economics, Department of Business Economics Working Paper, 1991/5 (1991).

[4] KINDLER, J. et al.: *A Study of the Environmental Protection Bill from an Economic Viewpoint,* Regional Environmental Centre for Central and Eastern Europe, Budapest (1992).

[5] VAN ZON, H.: *Alternative Scenarios for Eastern Europe,* Commission for the European Communities, Science Research and Development, FAST, FOP 226 (1992).

[6] WELFORD, R. J., PRESCOTT, C. E.: *European Business: An Issue Based Approach,* Pitman Publishing, London (see Chapter 10) (1992).

23

EVALUATION OF CORPORATE ENVIRONMENTAL MANAGEMENT APPROACHES: A FRAMEWORK AND APPLICATION*

By

GYULA VASTAG, SÁNDOR KEREKES, DENNIS A. RONDINELLI

This article proposes a framework to evaluate corporate environmental strategies. In the proposed framework, a company's environmental risks are analyzed on two dimensions. One dimension, the endogenous environmental risks, arises from the internal operations of the company. The other dimension, the exogenous environmental risks, are determined by the company's external world: its location, its ecological setting, and the demographic characteristics of the physical environment in which it operates. Four environmental management approaches are defined as a function of endogenous and exogenous environmental risks: reactive, proactive, strategic, and crisis preventive. The framework was applied in a survey of 141 company representatives in Hungary. A relationship was sought between the a priori defined environmental management approaches based on technology and location and the companies environmental management characteristics defined by senior managers. Variables that differentiated among the four environmental management approaches were identified and ranked. The study concludes that there is a relatively well-defined relationship between the environmental risks of companies and the nature of their environmental management approaches. Implementing a strategic environmental management approach may not be the best option for all companies – although there is a growing pressure to do so.

1. INTRODUCTION

A general consensus is emerging among business managers and environmental protection advocates that the economic impacts of the worldwide movement toward environmental management are becoming increasingly important for international corporations [1]. Often, however, observers see the results differently. Environmentalists increasingly emphasize the

* In *International Journal of Production Economics*, 1996, Vol. 43, pp. 193–211.

strong business opportunities inherent in the growing concern with environmental protection and management while business executives often see the threats to their companies of diminishing market opportunities, rising costs, decreasing competitiveness, and increasing uncertainties and legal challenges [2].

The most direct impacts may arise from the fact that with greater frequency individual executives are being held responsible under criminal laws for their companies environmental damage, especially in the United States and Canada. And as the concern with environmental issues spreads, governments in other countries are also beginning to impose legal liabilities on managers for the environmental degradation caused by their companies [3]. This generally results in defensive reactions from managers, who either demand changes in legal requirements or seek stronger personal protection against the potentially illegal consequences of their companies' activities [4].

The threat of criminal prosecution, however, is not the only force driving companies to create environmental management strategies. Increasingly, customers are reacting negatively to corporate environmental mismanagement, shareholders are abandoning companies caught in environmental crises, and financial institutions are including environmental risks in their assessments of loan requests [5]. The ISO 14000 standards now being drafted by the International Organization for Standardization (ISO) will set criteria for multinational companies to develop environmental management systems that are similar to the ISO 9000 standards for total quality management. But the compulsion to avoid legal liabilities that exists among executives and corporations is in itself a strong motivation to adopt environmental management strategies [6].

Developing a sophisticated, comprehensive, and well-documented environmental management strategy, usually with the help of outside experts seems, in most cases, to be the best (although not necessarily the safest) way for most managers to avoid legal liabilities [7]. A proper reaction to the environmental challenge is also crucial to ensure the survival of companies in an era of heightened environmental sensitivities. Bad environmental management, resulting in serious environmental damages or health hazards, can destroy a company as quickly as bad financial management. Moreover, the social risks of environmental mismanagement is a globalizing and increasingly competitive economy may be even greater. But there are also serious financial risks in developing an overly sophisticated and constraining environmental management strategy – even if it does protect the managers who demand it – when it is not really needed or justified.

This paper describes a framework to evaluate corporate environmental management approaches. We first discuss the issues that a company must address in developing an appropriate environmental management strategy and then provide a framework for choosing the best alternative. We test the framework in an international business setting by drawing on a survey of Hungarian companies to see how well the characteristics of companies and the perceptions of their executives about the importance of environmental challenges can predict the approaches that companies have adopted. We use two methodologies to test the validity of framework: one analyzes the management attitudes and characteristics of companies assigned to each group in the framework based on their technology and location; the other classifies companies into four groups using all variables and a new, powerful methodology of classificiation and regression trees (CART).

2. WHAT IS AN APPROPRIATE ENVIRONMENTAL MANAGEMENT APPROACH?

Any corporation facing environmental management challenges must deal with two questions. First, what is the appropriate level of environmental standards to which a company should comply or the most prudent environmental managements approach that a company should adopt? Second, at what level of the organization should environmental issues be addressed?

Companies can commit two types of errors in adpoting an environmental management approach:

(1) they can underestimate or overestimate the *business opportunities* offered by the growing worldwide concern for environmental protection; or

(2) they can underestimate or overestimate the *costs and constraints* created by legal and market dermands for environmental management.

Both mistakes can have serious impacts on a company's competitiveness and profitability. If management does not recognize the business opportunities created by increasing public demand for environmental protection, it may overlook a growing market segment and eventually lose market share to more sensitive and agile competitors. One report from the Organization for Economic Cooperation and Development (OECD) put the value of environmental-technology markets at $200 billion in 1990. The OECD projects that this market will grow to $300 billion by the end of the decade, and some experts are even more optimistic in predicting an enormous demand for clean-up services from fast-growing countries such as China, Taiwan and South Korea, and from the former Soviet Union as they clean up more than 40 years of industrial pollution [8]. On the other hand, overestimating environmental threats may result in unnecessarily costly expenditures or constrain the company from undertaking otherwise profitable activities. If the business opportunities offered by increasing demands for environmental protection are overestimated, a company may initiate projects that do not produce revenues. But if the company does not spend enough to comply with regulations, it may be unable to meet new or stricter requirements in the future, which could result in catastrophic costs, fines, penalties, or other legal liabilities that may threaten its competitiveness, profitability or survival [9].

Unfortunately, companies are often led to make such errors by regulatory experts or consulting firms that try to impose common guidelines on companies that do not all have the same characteristics and needs or that do not operate in the same economic and social environments. The growing movement toward adopting international environmental charters or standards that seek to impose universal principles of sustainable development and environmental management – which is a very positive development in itself – often push corporations to adopt environmental management approaches that may be either inappropriate or imprudent for their circumstances [10]. As Barthman points out, "no bright line standard exists for an environmental-compliance management framework" [11]. Legal requirements often impose on companies what regulators consider to be ideal universal standards. Although a sound environmental management approach should be based on widely accepted general principles, it must also be specifically designed to reflect the characteristics of the company and the external conditions that affect its operations.

2.1 ENDOGENOUS AND EXOGENOUS ELEMENTS OF ENVIRONMENTAL RISK

The primary criterion for designing an appropriate environmental management approach is the company's ability to manage its environmental risks. A company's environmental risks can be defined as the probability of causing environmental damage and the seriousness of that damage. A company's environmental risk depends not only on its own activities but also on the environmental consequences of its activities that are determined by external factors. The broad environmental consequences include not only those influenced by the physical environment but also those resulting from the social environment in which the company operates. Public reaction to environmental damages is often shaped not so much by the facts as by the public's perceptions of the facts [12]. This difference explains much of the debate that takes place between managers and engineers and the rest of the population after environmentally damaging incidents. The "experts" and the public often perceive and evaluate the same facts differently because their knowledge of the facts, perceptions of damage, and "social environments" are different.

In reality, the environmental risk of an activity is always somewhat uncertain. As WYNNE concluded from his studies of hazardous wastes:

"The scientific uncertainties about what happens chemically, physically, and biologically in a landfill site are huge, and the opportunities for examining and reducing them extremely limited. Thus, the effects of putting a given waste into a site can only be approximately known; these effects are not in any case determinate, but depend *(inter alia)* upon how the site is operated and managed. At which site a waste ends up, and in what condition, also depends upon many social unknowns and contingencies" [13].

A similar level of uncertainty attends the environmental consequences of other company activities, and attempting to predict either the real impacts or the public reactions to them is often impossible for managers. However, in practice, due diligence and responsible care may be sufficient strategies for most companies; scientific exactness may not be required.

Based on these assumptions we propose that a company's environmental risks be analyzed on two dimensions, although we are fully aware of the multidimensional nature of the problem. One dimension – the *endogenous environmental* risks – includes the internal operations of the company, including the materials, technologies, and human resources used in the manufacturing process. The other dimension – the *exogenous environmental* risks – is determined by the company's external world: its location, the ecological characteristics (biodiversity, winds, topography) of the physical environment in which it operates, the demographics (population density, age, income distribution), infrastructure (roads, telecommunication networks), education levels of the population, and their attitudes toward environmental hazards. Political institutions play an especially important role in exogenous environmental risks. As Wynne points out, in analyzing hazardous waste practices of the United States and the United Kingdom, the impact of regulatory agencies in environmental risk is a function of political culture [14].

It is not always easy to decide if a company's suppliers and customers are part of the internal risks or the external risks. We can argue that suppliers are selected by a company and therefore it should be responsible for the potential damages caused by its transactions with them. The situation is different for customers because a company has far less influence on them. But if customers use a company's products (e.g. fertilizers) improperly it may cause significant pollution and destroy its environmental image.

Both endogenous and exogenous dimensions of environmental risk are complex, but they differ in their implications. Endogenous risks are more clearly under the control of management and regulatory authorities. Risks created by externalities usually are beyond the influence or control of either the company or regulators. As a result, environmentalists and managers debate whether multinational companies should comply with the requirements of the host country in which they operate or the home country of their headquarters [15].

The proposed framework does not evaluate the fine individual differences between companies, such as results of previous environmental projects. Its focus is rather general: it considers the technology used in the industry and the location and surrounding of the plant.

The importance of considering both endogenous and exogenous factors in determining a company's potential environmental risks can be illustrated by an example from Hungary. In Hungary, many chemical companies that had originally been located well outside of cities were later surrounded by the spread of urban centers into suburbs and rural hinterlands. At the beginning, even the heavily polluting companies did not cause a problem because they were relatively far from the city. Today even those companies that meet all environmental regulations but are now surrounded by a city may have environmentally related conflicts and problems. The 1987 explosion in a Budapest chemical plant – although the damage from the explosion did not go beyond the fence – produced serious conflicts with city officials. Many people in Budapest demanded that the plant be closed, whereas 40 years earlier people living in Budapest would not even have noticed that something had happened on the plant's grounds.

2.2 ENVIRONMENTAL MANAGEMENT AS FUNCTION
OF ENVIRONMENTAL RISK

We propose four environmental management approaches – shown in *Fig. 1* – as explanations of how companies respond to their endogenous and exogenous risks.

Endogenous environmental risks along the vertical axis and exogenous environmental risks along the horizontal axis are, for purposes of illustration, divided into small and large. The cells describe four environmental management approaches with combinations of large and small exogenous and endogenous risks.

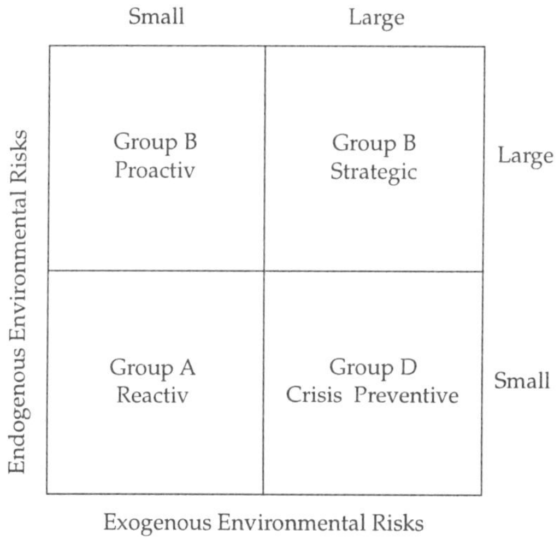

Figure 1. Classification of environmental management approaches

2.2.1 Reactive environmental management approach (Group A)

Group A would consist of those companies, for example, that are in an industry that has low levels of pollution emission in which the pollutants are not environmentally dangerous and the number of people affected is small. These companies may use nonexhaustible resources as raw materials, production is not energy-intensive, and their activities do not involve transportation of massive volumes of hazardous materials. Mass production industries that use well-developed technologies such as textiles, precision instruments, or some food producers (bakeries, for example) could appropriately adopt a reactive environmental management strategy. In these companies, environmental management calls merely for complying with local environmental regulations whithout taking extraordinary precautions to prevent highly unlikely environmental damages. This approach does not have a significant influence on the company's operations and responsibility for monitoring compliance can be carried out at middle management levels by an environmental and safety officer.

2.2.2 Proactive environmental management approach (Group B)

Group B consists of companies in industries whose technologies involve high levels of pollution or emit pollutants that are environmentally dangerous. However, because of location, climate conditions, or good environmental infrastructure, the adverse ecological and health consequences of these pollutants are small. Distilleries or sugar factories from the food processing industry, for example, might be assigned to this proup. At these companies, the environmental function is more significant than in Group A; managers have to anticipate future changes in environmental regulations, technology, and public opinion. The environmental management of these companies is often highly decentralized to the plants where the critical technologies are concentrated. These plants, however, may be located in or around smaller towns where the inhabitants are less sensitive to environmental issues (in most cases the plant may be the only major employer in the town) and the population density is much smaller than in or around major cities.

2.2.3 Strategic environmental management approach (Group C)

This group consists of companies in industries that are highly polluting and that operate in a social or physical context in which risks are further increased by external conditions or public attitudes toward environmental hazards. Large chemical companies in cities are good examples. In these companies, environmental management must be an important part of the company's overall business strategy and should be dealt with at the senior management level. These companies must often go beyond compliance with environmental regulations and take more aggressive safeguards to prevent or reduce environmental damage. Their environmental management strategy should be well defined, highly visible in company publications, and monitored carefully to protect managers against legal actions.

2.2.4 Crisis preventive environmental management approach (Group D)

In this group, the companies are not high-level polluters either because they do not use large volumes of inputs or because the pollution happens indirectly (e.g. tourism, fast food chains) and the direct effect is not significant. Whatever pollution does occur, however, may be highly visible and affect large numbers of people or a wide territory. Other examples include electric energy plants, and hydroelectric stations (except flatland-based ones) or poultry processing plants located in big cities. The environmental management approach can be best characterized as crisis preventive where public education campaigns are combined with elaborate technical procedures to assure that neither the pollution worsens nor the public misperceives the dangers of the low-level pollution that is taking place.

2.3 COMPARING ENVIRONMENTAL MANAGEMENT APPROACHES

The reactive and strategic environmental management approaches represent two extremes where the external and internal environmental risks are balanced, both of them are at the same qualitatively defined level (either low or high). In the former, there is no pressure to do anything beyond complying with regulations – there are no urgent environmental issues, and the companies can wait to adopt new management guidelines. In the latter, a company is under enormous pressure to go beyond compliance – environmental issues are extremely important; they cannot wait any longer to develop a strategy; and they cannot afford to make mistakes. In the other two approaches (proactive and crisis preventive), the environmental risks are unbalanced. In both cases, companies can wait; they are not pressed to do anything immediately. But this situation may change, and they may have to plan their moves very carefully.

This classification of environmental management approaches gives a static description of companies at a specific point in time. Obviously, their situations may change quickly.

Although there is a growing international pressure for companies to develop and use strategic environmental management approaches in all cases, it may not be necessary or profitable to move from *proactive* or *crisis preventive* approaches to the *strategic* management approach. Through technology modifications and better emission control (for companies in Group B) and through public opinion monitoring (for companies in Group D), moving toward a *reactive* environmental management ap-

Table 1. Comparison of reactive and strategic
environmental management

Reactive	Activity	Strategic
Middle level management involvement; environmental committee less critical	*Management seniority level*	Senior management leadership, environmental committee in key position
Low	*Environmental management reporting level*	Very high (Chairman or CEO level)
There is time to fix it	*Uneven performance of environmental management*	Serious and immediate intervention is required
Cost optimization is important	*Cost control*	Risk reduction is the critical issue; cost does not matter
Special training for experts and for middle management	*Training and education*	Corporation-wide, specific training for senior and middle management
Pollution reduction	*Management focus*	Outstanding environmental performance
Monitoring and control	*Main activity of environmental management*	Innovation and communication
Complying with regulations	*Regulatory focus*	To be the standard for the industry
A few years behind state-of-the-art technologies is acceptable	*Innovation in pollution prevention*	Innovation to state-of-the-art technologies is crtical to stay in business; it is part of competitiveness

proach may be another option. The difference in costs and requirements between the reactive and strategic environmental management approaches are enormous, as illustrated in *Table 1.*

Adopting a reactive environmental management approach does not mean that companies pay no attention to opportunities for emission reduction, waste management, or more stringent sanitary practices. But because they are not central to the operations of the company, they can be dealt with by middle managers or outside experts rather than by senior management. Problems normally do not require immediate intervention because their noncrisis nature leaves time to fix them. Not all employees would necessarily be given environmental education and training; it may be enough to have activies monitored by experts in the company. Pollution emission reduction using monitoring equipment or "end-of-pipe" filters is the primary goal of these companies. Demand for environmental investments comes from stricter regulations and norms. These regulations and norms are the main forces driving these companies to make environmental improvements.

At those companies where environmental performance is a crucial element of business activities, environmental management has to be part of the company's overall business strategy, formulated and implemented by top management. For this reason, companies like 3M, McDonalds, Volvo, Kodak, Allied Signal, and many of the world's leading chemical companies have adopted principles of industrial ecology and pervasive environmental management strategies [16]. A high-level environmental committee including outside experts should play an important role in environment-related decisions. The objectives of environmental management are derived from the company's long-term strategy and not from current environmental regulations. All employees should be educated about environmental hazards, and environmental investments should include state-of-the-art technology and intensive attempts to reduce waste and pollution in the manufacturing process rather than relying on end-of-pipe controls.

3. TESTING THE FRAMEWORK: ENVIRONMENTAL MANAGEMENT IN HUNGARIAN COMPANIES

The purpose of this section is to test empirically the validity of the proposed framework for assessing environmental management approaches. We have argued that the most appropriate environmental management approach chosen by a company should be a function of the company's environmental risks. Therefore, companies from different industries and in different locations may be better off following different paths. To measure the endogenous and exogenous environmental risks of a company – the basis of this framework – we use the industry (technology) and the location of its plants. A priori classificiation of a plant's processing technology will divide them into "large" and "small" endogenous risk categories, while population density, closeness to cities, dominant winds, environmental sensitivity and attitude of neighboring communities will determine whether a plant faces large or small exogenous risk. Thus, plants from the same industry could be in different cells.

Central Europe and, specifically, Hungary, were chosen as test sites because executives there must operate in complex and uncertain economic conditions as their countries undergo a transition from socialist to market systems. The transition affects every segment of the society. One of the most critical challenges facing Hungarian managers, for example, is how to resolve the conflicting pressures of attaining financial stability for their companies while at the same time coping with potentially serious environmental risks [17].

A survey of corporate executives' perceptions of environmental challenges was carried out in Hungary in late 1992 and early 1993 and was based on a similar worldwide survey undertaken by McKinsey a year earlier [18]. The questions were translated from English to Hungarian, and some new questions about company ownership were added to those used in the McKinsey survey. The translation was made by a doctoral candidate at the Budapest University of Economic Sciences and was verified by one of the authors. Questionnaires were sent to 400 medium- or large-sized companies that were on the membership list of the Hungarian Chamber of Commerce. The 42% response rate – 169 company executives, mostly senior managers – was itself an indicator of the strong interest in this topic among Hungarian companies. However, as is common in surveys, not all of the respondents answered all of the questions; and, thus, the actual number of respondents varies from question to question [19].

To test the validity of the approaches described in *Fig. 1*, 141 companies were selected from the 169 responses. The selection was based on readily available information about the location and technology of the company. Most of the companies had only one plant, but if the company had multiple plants then the most significant plant was selected to represent the company. Therefore, "company" and "plant" are used interchangeably in the paper. The authors then determined the exogenous risks based on the location of the plant and the endogenous risks based on prevalent technology in the industry. The exogenous risks were considered small if the company was located in or around smaller cities where the population density was low and the company was a major employer in the region. Similarly, if the company was in major cities with high population denstiy and generally with higher levels of environmental awareness, the exogenous risks were considered large. The endogenous risks of mass production industries that use well-developed technologies with low emissions such as textiles, precision instruments, or bakeries, for example, were considered low. Chemical companies, distilleries, or sugar factories with high emissions of pollutants were considered to have large endogenous risks. The characteristics of the selected companies by group are shown in *Table 2*.

Based on their technology and location as surrogates for endogenous and exogenous risks, Group A included textile and some machine tool companies that manufacture precision instruments. Group B included com-

Table 2. Sample characteristics

Endogenous/exogenous risks	Small/small	Large/small	Large/large	Small/large
Characteristics	Group A reactive	Group B proactive	Group C strategic	Group D crisis preventive
Number of companies	38	12	50	41
Industrial sector				
Light industries (manufacturers of textiles, leathers, furs, shoes)	15	2	–	3
Machine factory	15	–	1	1
Food processing	5	7	3	13
Chemicals (oil refineries and manufacturers of rubber, cosmetics, and pharmaceuticals)	–	2	23	1
Construction materials	–	–	6	–
Mining	–	–	1	–
Metallurgy	–	–	7	–
Wood processing	–	–	–	4
Paper production	–	–	2	–
Printing	1	–	–	8
Other	2	1	7	11
Number of employees				
Did not answer	1	0	3	1
Fewer than 50	1	0	2	3
Between 50 and 250	14	0	5	2
Between 251 and 500	4	1	6	6
Greater than 500	18	11	34	29
Company sales (million HUF)				
Did not answer	1	0	2	0
Less than 50	1	0	6	5
Between 50 and 250	14	1	9	9
Between 251 and 500	10	3	6	7
Greater than 500	12	8	27	20
Average foreign ownership (%)	12.1	23.0	11.6	12.4

panies that were heavy polluters, such as leather processing plants that emit high levels of chrome in their waste, and food, sugar, and distillating plants located outside of major urban centers. These companies are polluting but they are not perceived to be dangerous. Group C included pharmaceutical and heavy chemical companies, and waste incinerators with technologies that emit high levels of pollutants and located in or near cities. Food processing, wood processing and printing companies that do not have serious environmental problems now but could have in the future if public opinion about the environmental impacts of their operations changes or if regulations further constrain their significant emissions of wastewater fell into Group D. Generally, companies in groups C and D were larger than in the other two groups. The low foreign investment in Group C, where companies needed it the most, can be explained by the fact that foreign investors in Hungary may at some time be required to assume liability for past environmental pollution – a risk that is very high for almost all investors.

Some industries include companies that fall into more than one category. In *Table 2* there are companies from the food processing industry for example in all four groups. Food processing is a very broad category and it includes a variety of activities, nonetheless this scattered distribution of companies in all categories requires some explanation. The five companies in Group A are bakeries with no environmental problems. They did not pay any pollution charges in the past and their location is not really an issue. The seven companies in Group B are distilleries (3), sugar plants (3) and a canning plant – all located around small towns. All of them paid water pollution charges – there is high water consumption and potential or actual water pollution in these plants that is reduced by their remote location and the fact that they are major employers in the region. Three large dairy companies located in major cities were assigned to Group C. They require large amounts of water and if they have the infrastructural support (cleaning facilities for the waste water) they are environmentally safe. These plants did not have such facilities and paid high water pollution charges. Poultry and meat processing companies with slaughter houses located in major cities are assigned to Group D. Their situation may change at any time. Animal protection leagues may sue them for keeping the animals in unacceptable conditions, customers may boycott their products (smoked ham, for example), and water pollution is a threatening issue for them.

There are significant differences in environmental investments and pollution charges paid by the different groups. *Table 3* shows the actual and anticipated percentages of environmental investments from total company investments in 1992 and in 2000 and the average air and water pollution charges in 1992. In 1992, the percentage of environmental investments from total company investments (which, in general, were much lower than in previous years due to the recession in the Hungarian economy) was significantly higher in Group C than in the other groups. These numbers show two clear trends: first, generally, with the notable exception of Group C, companies plan to spend more on environmental investments in

Table 3. Environmental investments and pollution charges

Characteristics	Group A reactive	Group B proactive	Group C strategic	Group D crisis preventive
Environmental investments (% of total investments)				
in 1992	3.7	4.6	19.0	5.1
in 2000	12.2	12.0	19.9	15.7
Pollution charges paid in 1992 (in Hungarian Forints)				
Average air pollution charge	135,250	905,000	3,679,867	293,833
(number of companies fined)	(4)	(2)	(15)	(6)
Average water pollution charge	23,126	1,060,000	118,883,000	3,763,931
(number of companies fined)	(3)	(3)	(17)	(6)

Table 4. Hierarchical level of environmental manager

Hierarchical level	Group A	Group B	Group C	Group D
CEO or President	12	3	14	10
COO or Chief Engineer	13	6	21	20
Middle manager	8	8	8	5
Did not answer	5	2	7	6
Number of responses	38	12	50	41

the future; and, second, the differences between the groups are decreasing. As expected, a higher, portion of companies in Group C paid fines than the others.

Table 4 shows that a senior manager (the respondent to this questionnaire) was responsible for environmental management in all groups.

The high level of direct participation of senior managers in Hungarian companies can be explained by past experience as well. Before 1989, the political forces in opposition to the government used environmental issues to legitimize their criticisms. As a result, company managers representing the economic power of the state learned early on that they had to prove that they used due diligence and reasonable care in their operations to offset criticism from a relatively well-organized social environmental movement favored by the media.

If the initial theoretical classification described in *Fig. 1* is a valid one, then the groups should show different environmental management atti-

tudes and they should have different environmental management profiles. Considering the immediate and enormous pressure that managers in
Group C face, it is reasonable to assume that this group should show a
significantly different environmental profile from the others.

3.1 ENVIRONMENTAL MANAGEMENT PROFILES
OF THE GROUPS

To measure the managerial characteristics of the companies, respondents
were asked about the following topics: general environmental attitude;
key environmental concerns within the industry; seriousness of environmental issues at different phases of product creation; the most effective
ways to protect the environment; the environmental policy component
that is currently installed at their companies; and the familiarity of employees with company objectives in environmental protection. Most of the
questions were worded as statements, and respondents were asked the
extent of their agreement or disagreement with the statement on a five-
point scale. Based on the proposed theoretical framework, several hypotheses about the environmental management profiles of the groups were
tested. We hypothesized that Group C is more advanced in managerial
characteristics related to the environment than other groups and that companies in Group C would be fundamentally different from the others.
Table 5 gives more details about these questions and shows the hypotheses
for each section.

Managers were asked about seven statements related to different aspects of environmental management. The *strongly agree* answers on a five-
point Likert-scale showed a positive environmental attitude, while the
strongly disagree answers reflected a negative attitude. First, using Cronbach's alpha coefficient, the reliability of the scale was analyzed. Cronbach's alpha for the seven statements was 0.64, which is slightly lower
than the average of this indicator in psychology and marketing research
but it is acceptable in preliminary research situations like ours [20]. Moreover, considering that we relied on an international survey instrument,
this level of internal consistency is quite acceptable.

Table 5. Variables and hypotheses related to managerial
characteristics of companies

Variable description	Hypothesis
General environmental attitude: Managers were asked about seven statements related to different aspects of environmental management. The scale ranged from 1 (strongly disagree) to 5 (strongly agree), where 5 showed a positive environmental attitude. The managers general attitude was measured as the average of the seven answers.	The environmental attitudes of Groups B and C (where the endogenous environmental risks are large) are more positive than those of Groups A and D.
Key environmental concerns within the industry: (1) Complying with regulations; (2) Preventing incidents; (3) Realizing new market opportunities; (4) Enhancing positive image; (5) Integrating environment into corporate strategy. The scale ranged from 1 (not important) to 5 (very important). The level of environmental concern was defined as the average of the five answers.	Overall, Group C has a higher level of concern about the environment than the other groups, which are about at the same level.
Seriousness of environmental issues at the following phases of product creation: (1) Sourcing of (raw) materials; (2) Production (including transportation, storage); (3) Product use; (4) Disposal/Recycling. The scale ranged from 1 (not serious) to 5 (very serious). The level of seriousness of environmental issues in product creation is the average of the four answers.	Group C faces more serious environmental problems in the broadly defined production process than the others. In the other groups, the seriousness of environmental issues are approximately equal.
Most effective options to protect the environment: (1) Improve manufacturing technology; (2) Improve end product; (3) Improve waste management. The scale ranged from 1 (not effective) to 5 (very effective).	Improving manufacturing technology and the end product are considered the most effective in Group C and are about equal in the other groups. Improvement in waste management is the most (and about equally) important in Groups A, B, and D and less important in Group C.
Environmental policy component that is currently installed at the company: (1) Written company policy statement; (2) Board member with specific responsibility; (3) Environmental performance evaluation of suppliers; (4) Hiring external experts in environmental affairs; (5) Public communication programs; (6) Environmental marketing program (e.g. green products, green labeling, special promotions, advertising). The options to answer this question were yes or no. The overall portion of yes answers shows the strategic content of the company's environmental policy.	Group C has the most strategic environmental policy content: the other groups are about equal.
Familiarity with company objectives in environmental protection: Managers were asked to indicate on a five-point scale the extent (1 = not at all, 5 = to a great extent) to which the employees are familiar with company objectives in environmental protection.	In Group C, employees are more familiar with the company objectives in environmental protection than in other groups, which are approximately at the same level.

Second, the general environmental attitude of the groups (as the average of the answers to the seven statements) was tested. The hypothesis tested was that the environmental attitudes of respondents in Groups B and C (groups with large endogenous environmental risks) would be more positive than those in Groups A and D. Managers who know the environmental dangers of their technologies should be more sensitive to environmental issues than those working with environmentally safe technologies. *Table 6* shows the average level of agreement with the statements in each group and the tests of our hypothesis.

Table 6. General environmental attitude
(1 = strongly disagree, 5 = strongly agree)

Statement	Group A	Group B	Group C	Group D
The environmental challenge is one of the central issues of the 21st century	4.5	4.9	4.7	4.6
The industry will have to re-think its entire conception of the industrial process if it is to adapt profitably to an increasingly environment oriented world	3.8	3.8	3.9	3.8
Where environmental or health considerations demand it, the sale of our products will be curtailed or their production halted, regardless of our economic interests	2.3	2.3	2.9	2.5
Pollution prevention pays	3.3	3.4	4.0	3.4
There is a need to assume responsibility for one's products even after they left the plant	4.7	4.8	4.7	4.7
In the long-term, our spending on environmental R&D will give us a competitive advantage	3.2	3.8	4.1	3.6
To minimize the chance of future (environmental) tragedies, we should pursue a partnership of government, industry and academia	4.3	4.5	4.3	4.2
General environmental attitude (average of the seven answers)	3.71	3.94	4.07	3.80
Does the hypothesis hold? (ANOVA results)		Yes[a] ($F_{128:1} = 3.726$; $p = 0.056$)		

[a] The significance level is slightly higher than the customary 5%, however, the difference is so small that we accepted the hypothesis that environmental attitudes in Groups B and C are more positive than in Groups A and D.

Overall, as shown by the average of seven statements, managers in Groups B and C had a much more positive environmental attitude than the others – our hypothesis holds at 5.6% significance level that is slightly higher than the customary 5%. The two areas where managers in Group C showed a far more positive attitude than the other groups were the willingness to stop production if environmental or health considerations demand it and their belief that "pollution prevention pays". All groups agreed at a very high level (minimum 4.5 on a scale of 1 to 5) that the environmental challenge is one of the central issues of the 21st century and companies should assume responsibility for their products even after they have left the plant.

Key environmental concerns included four areas (complying with regulations, preventing incidents, enhancing positive image, and integrating environment into corporate strategy) – all of them are very important for an environmentally conscious company. For these four statements the Cronbach's alpha was 0.72 – a generally accepted level of consistency. We hypothesized that, overall, group C would have a higher level of concern about the environment than the other groups. The overall level of environmental concerns was measured as the average of the four answers. *Table 7* shows that there was a significant difference between Group C and the others.

Because of the external and internal factors described earlier, companies in Group C face more serious environmental problems in the production process than those in the other groups. The seriousness of environmental issues in the broadly defined production process was measured as

Table 7. Key environmental concerns
(1 = not important, 5 = very important)

Statement	Group A	Group B	Group C	Group D
Complying with regulations	4.3	4.0	4.2	4.3
Preventing incidents	4.4	4.3	4.8	4.6
Enhancing positive image	4.4	4.6	4.6	4.5
Integrating environment into corporate strategy	4.0	4.1	4.6	4.1
Level of environmental concerns (average of the four answers)	4.31	4.25	4.55	4.36
Does the hypothesis hold? (ANOVA results)	Yes $(F_{132:1} = 4.661; p = 0.033)$			

Table 8. Seriousness of environmental issues
(1 = not serious, 5 = very serious)

Phases of product creation	Group A	Group B	Group C	Group D
Sourcing of (raw) materials	3.2	2.3	3.2	2.7
Production (including transportation, storage)	2.9	3.0	3.6	3.0
Product use	2.0	1.7	2.4	2.4
Disposal and recycling	3.5	3.3	4.0	3.9
Seriousness of environmental issues (average of the four answers)	2.91	2.57	3.27	2.99
Does the hypothesis hold? (ANOVA results)		Yes $(F_{128:1} = 6.442; p = 0.006)$		

Table 9. Most effective options to protect the environment
(1 = not effective, 5 = very effective)

Options to protect the environment	Group A	Group B	Group C	Group D	Does the hypothesis hold? (ANOVA results)
Improve manufacturing technology	3.9	4.0	4.4	3.9	Yes $(F_{132:1}=4.412; p=0.019)$
Improve end product	3.0	2.9	3.2	2.7	No $(F_{126:1}=1.901; p=0.085)$
Improve waste management	4.4	4.3	4.0	4.5	Yes $(F_{133:1}=4.080; p=0.023)$

the average of four answers, each related to one phase of production. The reliability of this scale was 0.73 – an acceptable level. *Table 8* shows that this hypothesis holds.

We also discerned differences in the attitudes of respondents about the most effective ways to protect the environment. We hypothesized that improving manufacturing technology and end products – the most strategic options – would be considered the most effective in Group C and about equal in the other groups. Moreover, improving waste management – the most conservative approach – would be considered the most effective in all groups but C. *Table 9* shows that at 5% significance level our hypothesis about the end product (the only exception) did not hold – it holds at an 8.5% significance level showing the same tendency.

Table 10. Scope of environmental programs

Environmental policy component installed at the company	Percentage of *yes* answers			
	Group A	Group B	Group C	Group D
Environmental protection is part of the company (written) philosophy	52.6	66.7	76.0	46.3
Board member with specific responsibility	34.2	16.7	38.0	41.5
Environmental performance evaluation of suppliers	5.3	16.7	6.0	2.4
Hiring external experts in environmental affairs	10.5	8.3	32.0	9.8
Public communication program	5.3	0.0	10.0	2.4
Environmental marketing program	26.3	41.7	28.0	19.5
Scope of environmental programs (average of the six indicators above)	22.4	25.0	31.7	20.3
Does the hypothesis hold? (ANOVA results)	Yes			
	$(F_{137:1} = 13.448; p = 0.000)$			

Table 10 shows the scope of environmental programs currently adopted by companies in the four groups. The yes answers indicate a more strategic orientation in the company's environmental policy. In Hungary, as shown by the low percentage of yes answers in our sample, many of these strategic management approaches are not yet generally used. The overall proportion of yes answers to the six questions in the Hungarian sample is 25.7% with Group C having a significantly higher portion of them. Our hypothesis about Group C as having the most strategic environmental management approach holds.

Managers were also asked to indicate on a five-point scale the extent (1 = not at all, 5 = to a great extent) to which their employees are familiar with company objectives in environmental protection. In Group C, employees are significantly more informed ($F_{129:1} = 18.873; p = 0.000$) than in the other groups (the mean in Group A was 2.91; 2.90 in Group B; compared to 3.80 in Group C, and 3.00 in Group D).

These analyses showed the validity of the proposed framework, namely that companies with different exogenous and endogenous risks – proxied as industry technology and location – follow different environmental management approaches. In all sections described in *Table 5*, companies in Group C have differentiated themselves from the others and expresed attitudes congruent with a strategic environmental management approach.

3.2 CLASSIFICATION OF ENVIRONMENTAL MANAGEMENT
APPROACHES USING ALL VARIABLES

The objective of this section is to validate the proposed framework in a different way. In the previous section, we compared the environmental management characteristics of the groups and tested several hypotheses about the differences – variable by variable. In this section, we classify the companies based on their environmental management characteristics into the four groups predetermined by the company's environmental risks – using all variables at the same time. We are looking for a relationship between the physical characteristics of the company (exogenous and endogenous environmental risks) and environmental management characteristics, which – if the framework is valid – should match. However, there are serious limitations that damped our expectations about this classification:

(1) the original assignment was based on proxy variables, and there may have been some errors in assigning companies to different groups;
(2) the variable set we used had only environmental management characteristics; and, moreover, it reflected the opinion of one senior manager from each company; and
(3) the variable set contained only eight variables. A random classification would yield about a 25% success rate. This analysis could only be considered successful if it resulted in a significantly higher success rate.

The data base used in the analysis was relatively small (141 observations and 8 variables), but it hald missing data points and a presumably nonhomogeneous data structure. A nonhomogeneous data structure means that relationships among variables in different parts of the measurement space (for example, in different industries) are, or can be, different. Thus, we sought an approach that would help us to sort out these complexities and that would assist us in understanding the true nature of differences across environmental management approaches. We sought to answer three questions:

- How can companies be classified into the four environmental management groups (in other words, what is the recipe for classification)?
- What is the relative importance of variables making the classification?
- How accurate is this classification?

We used a binary recursive partitioning method, the CART procedure, to classify the data set of 141 observations into four groups and used all variables about environmental management characteristics as predictors. CART (Classification *and* Regression *Trees*) is an andvanced statistical procedure for tree-structured nonparametric data analysis that performs about 10–15% better than stepwise logistic regressions or discriminant analyses [21]. The process is binary because parent nodes are always split into exactly two child nodes and is recursive because the process can be repeated by treating each child node as a parent.

The CART method looks at all possible splits for all variables included in the analysis. Since there are, at most, 141 different values for each variable in this data set (one for each case) and eight variables, CART has to consider up to 141×8 splits; and it conducts searches through them all. The process is considerably simplified because CART always asks questions that have a yes or no answer. The next step is to rank each splitting rule on the basis of a goodness-of-split criterion. One criterion commonly used is a measure of how well the splitting rule separates the classes contained in the parent node. Once a best split is found, CART repeats the search process for each child node and continues recursively until further splitting is impossible or stopped for some other reason (e.g. the node has too few cases). Because each node has the potential for being a terminal node, a class assignment is made for every node whether it is terminal or not. Considering that we did not have any a priori information about distribution of group memberships in the population, the classes were treated as they were uniformly distributed in the population regardless of the observed sample proportions.

We chose CART because it offers many advantages over traditional discriminant analysis:

(1) it is a nonparametric procedure;
(2) it can handle data sets with complex, nonhomogeneous structure;
(3) it is extremely robust in identifying the effects of outliers;
(4) it can use any combination of categorical and continuous variables;
(5) it can adjust for samples stratified on a categorical dependent variable;
(6) it can reveal context dependence and interactions by using the same variable in different parts of the tree; and
(7) it can process cases with missing values for predictors because it develops alternative splits (surrogates), which can be used to classify an object when the primary splitting variable is missing.

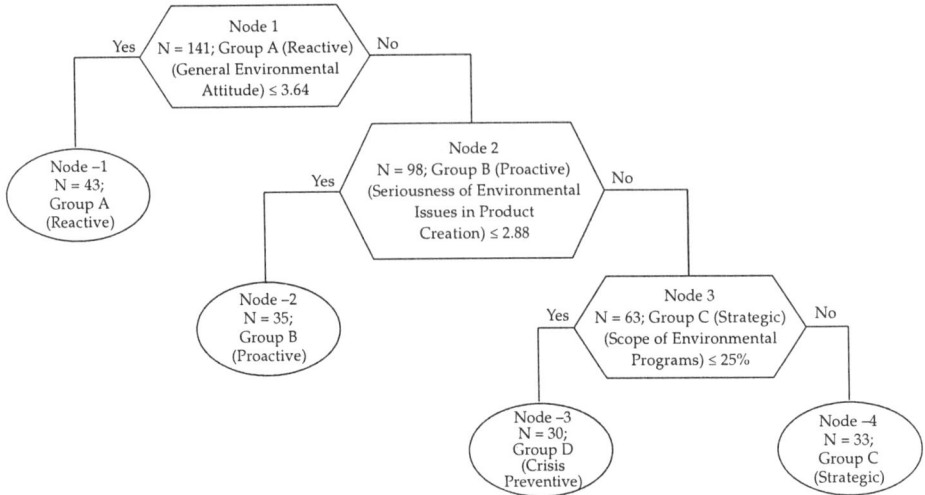

Figure 2. Classification of environmental management approaches

We used the CART procedure to classify the data set of 141 observations into four groups described earlier using all eight variables related to environmental management as predictors. *Fig.* 2 shows the resulting classification scheme.

Figure 2 is drawn in the form of an inverted tree and is read like a flow chart. The trapezoids are nonterminal nodes denoted by a positive number. The ellipsoids show the terminal nodes and are denoted by negative numbers. The number of terminal nodes depends on the selected tree, and it is not related directly to the number of groups to be classified. At the beginning, all companies, in this case 141, are in node 1. This node is classified as Group A because this is the first group and we assumed that the groups are uniformly distributed in the population so the misclassification rate would be the same independently of the group chosen. The first variable selected to make the first split was the general environmental attitude of the company measured by the average of seven variables. For each company, the question asked at node 1 is the following: Is this variable, the general environmental attitude of the company, less than or equal to 3.64 measured on a five-point scale where 5 represented the positive extreme? If the answer to this question is *yes*, then the company is assigned to the first terminal node (node −1). If the answer is *no*, then node 2 follows where the seriousness of environmental issues in product creation is questioned. Companies are assigned to node −4 – classified as Group C or Strategic – if the general environmental attitude is greater

Table 11. Relative importance of variables

Variable name and description	Relative importance
Familiarity of employees with company objectives in environmental protection	100.0
General environmental attitude	94.2
Seriousness of environmental issues in the broadly defined production process	82.9
Strategic content of the company's environmental policy	79.3
Improving the end product is the most effective way to protect the environment	70.9
Improving manufacturing technology is the most effective way to protect the environment	59.3
Level of environmental concerns	24.3
Improving waste management is the most effective way to protect the environment	7.6

Table 12. Classification table of companies

Actual Group Membership	Predicted group membership				Actual total
	Group A: reactive	Group B: proactive	Group C: strategic	Group D: crisis preventive	
Group A: reactive	19	10	11	5	38
Group B: proactive	1	7	3	1	12
Group C: strategic	9	8	25	8	50
Group D: crisis preventive	14	10	1	16	41
Predicted total	43	35	33	30	141
Correct (%)	50.0	58.3	50.0	39.0	47.5

than 3.64, the seriousness of environmental issues in production is greater than 2.88 and the scope of environmental programs is greater than 25%. *Table 11* shows the relative importance of variables. This list should be read as a checklist for diagnosis: *these variables differentiate between the four environmental management approaches.*

In this table, we can find variables that did not show up in *Fig. 2* as primary splitting variables (familiarity of employees with company objectives in environmental protection, for example). The reason for this is that CART tracks surrogate splits in the tree-growing process and the contribution a variable can make in prediction is not determined only by primary splits. The phenomenon of one variable hiding the significance of another is known as masking and is addressed in CART's variable importance measure. *Table 11* shows, for example, that the employees familiarity with environmental objectives of the company is the most important variable and it is about four times as important as the level of environmental concerns.

The most important issue of any classification is the accuracy of the prediction. In this case, the question is whether there is a fit between a classification based on exogenous and endogenous environmental risks and the company's environmental management characteristics. *Table 12* shows the results of the CART classification.

The overall correct classification rate of 47.5% is good considering the difficulties of this task and the fact it was a four-group classification problem. The most problematic group was the crisis preventive Group D where only 39.0% of the cases were classified correctly. Classification rates for the other groups were 50% or higher.

4. CONCLUSIONS

Based on survey results, we can conclude that there is a relatively well-defined relationship between companies environmental risks and the nature of their environmental management approaches. The external and internal physical characteristics of companies determine their exogenous and endogenous environmental risks, wich in return have an impact on a company's environmental management characteristics. This impact is the most significant on companies with strong and immediate environmental pressures, companies that have to have a strategic environmental management approach to avert risks. Although there is pressure to develop and use strategic environmental management approaches in all companies, it may not be cenessary or profitable to move from proactive or crisis-preventive management approaches to the strategic management approach. Through technology modifications and better emission controls (for companies using a proactive approach) and through public opinion monitoring (for companies using crisis preventive approach), moving toward a reactive environmental management approach may be another option. There is little debate over the fact that for a hazardous waste incinerator, environmental management is of strategic importance. On one hand, stricter environmental regulations may mean new business opportunities for the company because demand for the incinerator grows. On the other hand, because of the stricter regulations, requirements for technologies used in the incinerator change and the emission limits are set at lower levels. In order to remain a competitive player, the company has to meet these requirements, have a good environmental performance record, and maintain good communications with people living in the surrounding areas.

A logical extension of this research would be to test the framework using an international data set, including companies from developed market economies as well. This can be done most effectively by focusing on fewer industries and extending the number of environmental management characteristics.

ACKNOWLEDGEMENTS

The authors would like to thank three anonymous referees, and North American editor D. CLAY WHYBARK for their valuable comments and suggestions that led to the improvement of this paper.

REFERENCES

[1] FISCHER, K., SCHOT, J. (eds): Environmental Strategies for Industry: International Perspectives on Reserach Needs and Policy Implications. Island Press, Washington, DC (1993).

[2] PORTER, M. K.: America's Green Strategy. Scientific American. Vol. 264, No. 4 and WELFORD, R. and GOULDSON, A., 1993. Environmental Management and Business Strategy. Pittman, London (1991).

[3] SIMMONS, P., COWELL, J.: Liability for the environment – lessons from the development of civil liability in Europe. In: T. JACKSON (ed.): Clean Production Strategies. Lewis Publishers, Boca Raton, FL, pp. 345–364; VÁRI, A., TAMÁS, P. (eds), 1993. Environment and Democratic Transition: Policy and Politics in Central and Eastern Europe. Kluwer, Boston, pp. 120–145 (1993).

[4] PRICE, K. S.: What gets measured gets done – the criminalization of technical decision-making. Proc. 47th Ind. Waste Conf. Lewis Publishers, Boca Raton, FL. The penalties resulting from criminal law procedures in the United States against managers of companies with violations of environmental regulations have reached tens of millions of dollars a year. In 1992 for example, penalties of more than $38 million were imposed, not counting the $125 million in fines and more than 37 years in prison sentences levied against those found responsible for the Exxon Valdez incident. As these penalties have grown, however, so too have the debates over their legitimacy. BARTHMAN reflects a widely shared opinion in pointing out that "...the standard for imposing criminal liability on an individual employee or officer and on a corporation for environmental offenses is low, requiring proof only that the employee intended to place a drum of waste where he placed it, not that

the employee knew the law was being violated, nor that the waste was regulated". Even an employee's negligent discharge of a nonhazardous pollutant into a water-way can be criminally prosecuted and officers of the corporation can be held liable for employee error. Richard Harris, President of KPMG Environmental Services, concluded after the Bata Industries case was decided in Canada that "the public has become less tolerant of environmental misdeeds, and regulators... are increasingly looking for ways to make examples of corporate polluters". Considering these circumstances, Harris concluded that managers had only one option and that was to protect themselves against environmental risks. "Company owners, directors and managers need to show that they have exercised all reasonable care to prevent any environmental problem form occurring." He argued that every company will have to establish a system of environmental management that provides the documentation needed to defend the company's executives against government prosecution.

See T. R. BARTHMAN, Dodging Bullets. Fortnightly, Vol. 131, Issue 18 (October 1993); 21–25, quote at p. 21, and RICHARD HARRIS, ignoring the Environment is Bad for Business. Canadian Manager, Fall 1993, quote at p. 21 (1992).

[5] Business International and ARTHUR D. LITTLE Inc. Managing the Global Environmental Challenge. Business International, New York (1992).

[6] The case of Bata Industries in Canada generated a strong public debate in 1993 over the environmental responsibilities of senior management. At one extreme, some lawyers argued that company directors should become totally proficient in all matters relating to Ontario regulations on air and water standards. Others countered that in order to comply with Canadian law every director would have to have a strong science background to understand the environmental implications of the company's operations. Still others asserted that directors should personally review for accuracy and completeness the environmental audits routinely conducted for Canadian corporations. Although these obligations have never been formally imposed on directors, either before or after the Bata case, the courts demanded that directors "understand what due diligence means and establish policies and systems to ensure the corporation remains in compliance with environmental laws". (See E. ROVET, Making Sense of Due Diligence. CA Magazine. Vol. 126. Issue 9 (October 1993): 55–57. quote at p. 55.

[7] In the United States, "to attain a high level of environmental compliance (recognizing that the breadth and complexity of environmental compliance requirements make 100% compliance unattainable for most utility and industrial companies), their [companies'] efforts must proceed beyond what is specifically required." One legal expert argues. See BARTHMAN, "Dodging Bullets", quote at p. 22.

[8] Unsigned article, How to make lots of money, and save the planet too. The Economist. June 3rd 1995, pp. 57–58.

[9] NORTH, K.: Environmental Business Management: An Introduction. International Labor Organization. Geneva, Switzerland (1992).

[10] See, for example, British Standard (BS 7750) for Environmental Management Systems. described in SMITH, J. and WATTS, G. A framework for Environmental Management. Focus on Physical distributions and Logistics Management, 12: 2–5 (1993).

[11] BARTHMAN, Dodging Bullets, p. 22 (1993).

[12] JUHÁSZ, J., VÁRI, A., TÖLGYESI, J.: Environmental conflict and political change: Public perception on low level radioactive waste management in Hungary. In: A. VÁRI, P. TAMÁS (eds). Environment and Democratic Transition, Kluwer, Boston, pp. 227–248 (1993).

[13] WYNNE, B.: Uncertainty and environmental learning – reconceiving science and policy in the preventive paradigm. In: JACKSON, T. (ed.): Clean Production Strategies. Lewis Publishers, Boca Raton, FL, pp. 63–84, quote at p. 73–74 (1993).

[14] WYNNE, Uncertainty and Environmental Learning, p. 72.

[15] An issue that became critical after the Bhopal accident, for example, was "whether the Union Carbide affiliate was operating with equivalent procedures, safeguards, and equipment to those at comparable facility in the United States". But even if Union Carbide had implemented the American standards in India it would have been inadequate because of the lower levels of education of the workers, less developed infrastructure, and other factors creating higher exogenous environmental risks for a chemical company operating in this region of India. To lower the environmental risks of the Bhopal plant, Union Carbide would have had to adopt a more stringent and constraining environmental management strategy than in its American plants in order to compensate for the differences in infrastructure and education levels in India. The education level and training of people living around a plant are at least as important as the internal operations of the company in determining environmental risks. The Bhopal accident or the Chernobil incident in the former Soviet Union would have caused much less damage if the neighboring population had been more concerned about environmental hazards and better trained in emergency procedures.

   For the quotation see Union Carbide Fights for its life. Business Week, December 24, 1984.

[16] NEWMAN, J. C., BREEDEN, K. M.: Managing in the environmental era:L essons from environmental leaders. The Columbia J. of World Bus., 210–221: SCHMIDHEINY, S. and the Business Council on Sustainable Development. 1992. Changing Course: A Global Business Perspective on Development and the Environment. MIT Press, Cambridge, MA (1992).

[17] The stereotype of managers from third world or formerly communist countries as being oblivious to or unconcerned about the dangers of environmental degradation arises from the belief that the government and the private sector continue to avoid the costs of environmental protection and cleanup. Although Hungary's economy is just emerging from a long period of stagnation and its GNP per capita ranks only 52 among the 173 countries for which the United Nations Development Program provides comparative economic statistics, its human development index (the combination of GNP per capita, adult literacy rate, average number of years spent in school and life expectancy at birth) ranks 28, higher than some Western European countries. Because education levels and environmental awareness are correlated, the concern for a clean environment should be relatively high in a country like Hungary. Given Hungary's human development index and its desire to become a member of the European Economic Community, its corporate executives should be willing to adopt higher environmental standards as quickly as possible.

[18] McKINSEY and Company: The Corporate Response to the Environmental Challenge: Summary Report. McKinsey and Company. Amsterdam the Netherlands (1991).
[19] VASTAG, G., RONDINELLI, D. A., KEREKES, S.: How corporate executives perceive environmental issues: Hungarian and global companies. J. Euromarketing, 5 (3) (1995).
[20] PETERSON, R. A.: A Meta-analysis of Cronbach's coefficient alpha. J. Consumer Res., 21: 381–391 (1994).
[21] BRIEMAN, L., FRIEDMAN, J., OLSHEN, R., STONE, C.: Classification and Regression Trees. Wadsworth, Pacific Grove, CA (1984).

24

HOW CORPORATE EXECUTIVES PERCEIVE ENVIRONMENTAL ISSUES: COMPARING HUNGARIAN AND GLOBAL COMPANIES*

By

GYULA VASTAG, DENNIS A. RONDINELLI, SÁNDOR KEREKES

This article reports the results of a survey conducted in Hungary to compare the environmental perceptions of Hungarian corporate managers with those of other executives form around the world who had earlier responded to a similar survey conducted by McKinsey and Company. The results showed virtually no differences in how Hungarian managers perceived the importance of environmental challenges, but they did reveal stronger differences in perceptions between Hungarian and international respondents and among Hungarian respondents from companies in different ownership groups on how companies were putting their environmental concerns into practice. Although there seems to be a wider gap between executives of Hungarian companies and those from Western Europe and North America in adopting environmental practices, the survey revealed that Hungarian manageres are acutely aware that their companies will have to invest more heavily to achieve higher levels of environmental protection in the future. *[Article copies available from The Haworth Document Delivery Service: 1-800-342-9678. E-mail address: getinfo@haworth.com.]*

INTRODUCTION

Executives in Central Europe most operate in complex and uncertain economic conditions as their countries undergo a transition from socialist to market systems. The transition affects every segment of society (JACKSON et al. 1993). One of the most critical challenges facing Hungarian managers is how to resolve the conflicting pressures of attaining financial stability for their companies while at the same time coping with potentially serious problems such as environmental pollution. The stereotype of managers from third world or formerly communist countries as being oblivious to or unconcerned about the dangers of environmental degradation

* In *Green Marketing in a Unified Europe.* The Haworth Press, 1996, pp. 5–27.

arises from the belief that the government and the private sector continue to avoid the costs of environmental protection and cleanup (PEARSON 1987). Although Hungary's economy is just emerging from a long period of stagnation and its GDP per capita ranks only 56 among the 160 countries for which the World Bank and the United Nations Development Program provide comparative economic statistics, its human development index (the combination of GDP per capita, illiteracy rate, average number of years spent in school and life expectancy) ranks higher than some Western European countries (World Bank 1994). Because education levels and environmental awareness are correlated, the concern for a clean environment should be relatively high in a country like Hungary. Given Hungary's human development index and its desire to become a member of the European Economic Community, its corporate executives should be willing to adopt higher environmental standards as quickly as possible.

Although many Hungarian managers may still consider the costs of meeting environmental challenges a threat to their companies' competitiveness, the growing pressures from nongovernment organizations and consumers for environmentally sound production processes and environmentally-friendly products are likely to push them more quickly toward meeting global market requirements (CAIRNCROSS 1992; SCHMIDHEINY 1992). Moreover, government officials and business leaders in Central Europe are coming to realize that stricter environmental regulations and stronger enforcement can protect the region from the transfer of obsolete and highly polluting production technologies (FROSCH & GALLOPULAS 1989; KEMP 1993).

Pressures on Hungarian companies interested in attracting foreign investment also arise from the fact that over the past few years multinational corporations have become increasingly sensitive to the environmental impacts of their business practices and operations (SCHOT & FISCHER 1993). An increasing number of companies recognize that in the global marketplace, their environmental image affects the demand for their products, their ability to obtain loans from international financial institutions, and the sale of their shares on international stock exchanges (UNCTC 1990). Even in formerly socialist countries and in developing economies where governments and the private sector paid little attention to the environmental consequences of industrial activity during the past half century, governments are increasingly being pressured by international organizations and local interest groups to adopt stronger environmental regulations and to encourage companies to use "green" business practices (PANAYOTOU 1993).

Although there seems to be a growing consensus among corporate executives in multinational companies that they must take environmental impact into account, little is known about how extensively such perceptions are shared by companies that are not owned by or that do not generally trade with multinational firms, or about how the perceptions of environmental issues are translated into business policy and operations within manufacturing firms in emerging market countries. Many questions remain about the significance of environmental issues in business practice. Do multinational companies operate differently in countries such as Hungary that less stringently enforce environmental regulations than they do in countries with stronger environmental laws and enforcement? Do widespread perceptions of the need for companies to be sensitive to the environmental impacts of their operations extend deeply into firms in formerly communist countries in Central and Eastern Europe, where environmental problems are severe and the environmental impacts of their operations were largely ignored for more than 40 years? Do managers of multinational companies in Central and Eastern European countries such as Hungary perceive any differently the need to improve environmental conditions than managers of their parent companies in Western Europe or North America?

This article explores answers to some of these questions by examining the perceptions of corporate executives throughout the world of the importance of environmental protection to their business strategies and operations; by comparing international perceptions with those of executives in one country, Hungary, that is in transition from a socialist to a market-oriented economy and that suffers from serious environmental problems; and by comparing the environmental perceptions of executives of companies within Hungary under different forms of ownership. The impact of ownership on the way in which executives and managers perceive environmental issues has received little attention in the literature.

ENVIRONMENTAL PROBLEMS AND ECONOMIC CONDITIONS IN HUNGARY

The challenges facing multinational and local companies around the world in dealing with environmental issues are no more critical than in the former socialist countries of Central and Eastern Europe (VÁRI & TA-MÁS 1993). Since 1989 the economic situation and the political map of Central Europe have changed dramatically, and the implications of these changes will be critical for multinational companies seeking to invest in or export to the region. Among the new democracies of this region, Hungary, Poland, and the Czech Republic have the best chance to become an integral part of the European Community, but do so they must address their environmental problems and pursue higher environmental standards.

Although Central European countries have made relatively good progress toward economic reform and the restructuring of the ownership of their industries since 1990, they face two critical challenges in the decade ahead. First, they must restructure their domestic industries and attract investment by multinational companies (MNCs) in order to become competitive in world markets (RONDINELLI 1993). The ongoing privatization and the growing number of joint ventures in Hungary, for example, are already changing the way many companies are managing their internal functions, including manufacturing (RONDINELLI & FELLENZ 1993). But more profound and widespread changes will have to occur in the future in order for Central European countries such as Hungary to meet the stricter standards of quality, flexibility, delivery time, and service required by global markets. Second, both domestic and multinational manufacturing companies in Hungary and in other Central European countries will have to adjust to growing demands by both local residents and international organizations for environmental protection and clean-up (HANSEN 1989). Traditionally, environmental issues played a minor role in decisions of companies in centrally planned economies. Because they were state-owned enterprises against which environmental regulations were not stringently enforced by the government, manufacturing and mining industries in Hungary, for example, could largely ignore the environmental impacts of their operations under the socialist regime. Now, with the adoption of stricter environmental regulations and the growing demand for environmental cleanup there is a chance that this situation will change, and industrial enterprises will have to modify their manufacturing processes accordingly. Although Hungary has environmental protection laws and regulations, they have only been casually enforced since the demise of the communist regime. The desire of Hungary to join the European Economic Community and the pressures of international financing organizations such as the World Bank and the European Bank for Reconstruction and Development on the Hungarian government to clean up environmental pollution and enact and enforce more stringent regulations will increase the pressures on businesses to address environmental management issues.

New legislation on environmental protection is being considered by the Hungarian Parliament along with new regulations that require environmental impact assessments for a wide range of industries, new land use and construction regulations, and new legislation on handling, storage, and disposal of chemical hazardous materials. In the early 1990s Hungary upgraded regulatory standards for air quality and defined more clearly monitoring and control requirements, placed limits on vehicular air emissions, and increased fines for polluting rivers, lakes and groundwater. Since the late 1980s, the Hungarian government has also signed international conventions on environmental impact assessment, control of transboundary movements of hazardous wastes and their disposal, and long-range transboundary air pollution, and signed the Montreal Protocol on Substances that Deplete the Ozone Layer (WHITE & CASE, Inc., 1994). If the new legislation and agreements are enforced, those industries that have the highest potential for polluting air and water resources will have to find ways of building environmental restrictions and targets into their manufacturing processes.

COMPARING ENVIRONMENTAL PERCEPTIONS INTERNATIONALLY AND IN HUNGARY

The purpose of this article is to assess the perceptions of environmental challenges and practices among executives of manufacturing firms in three ownership groups in Hungary and to compare them with perceptions of corporate executives in other parts of the world. A questionnaire for Hungarian corporate executives was developed to compare their responses with those of executives who participated in a worldwide survey conducted by MCKINSEY and Company in 1991 (MCKINSEY & Company 1991).

The MCKINSEY study elicited responses from corporate executives who attended three international conferences and from targeted groups to ensure sufficient responses from developing countries in Latin America, Southeast Asia, and other regions (26% of respondents) and from Central and Eastern Europe (12%) in addition to those received from executives from Western Europe (34%), North America (17%) and Japan (11%). The five regions were based on the geographic location and the GNP per capita of the country where the company's headquarters were located. MCKINSEY sent out about 1,400 questionnaires, and received a total of 447 completed forms, a 30% response.[1]

The Hungarian survey was carried out about a year after the McKINSEY international survey. Many of the same questions were translated from English to Hungarian and some new questions about company owner-ship were added. The translation was made by a Hungarian doctoral can-didate at the Budapest Unviersity of Economic Sciences and verified by one of the authors. Questionnaires were sent to 400 medium- or large-sized companies that were on the membership list of the Hungarian Chamber of Commerce. The 42% response rate in Hungary–169 company executives-was itself an indicator of the strong interest in this topic. How-ever, as is quite common in surveys, not all of the respondents answered all of the questions and, thus, the actual number of respondents varies from question to question.

CHARACTERISTICS OF THE HUNGARIAN SAMPLE

As in the McKINSEY survey, the respondents to the Hungarian question-naires were mostly senior manageres, including managing directors, CEOs, and corporate department heads. The McKINSEY international responses were largely from executives in companies in the chemicals, energy, metals, processing, consumer goods and durables industries.[2] The international survey did not identify respondents by their companies' ownership characteristics. In the Hungarian sample, shown in *Table 1*, companies were divided into three ownership groups based on the as-sumption that foreign ownership probably has some influence on the management style of the company. This differentiation makes it possible to verify whether or not foreign investment is dominant in highly pol-luting industries.

The majority of the companies – 125 establishments – were domestic Hungarian companies and were fully owned by Hungarian institutions. The second group, 30 companies, represented mixed ownership. In this group the average foreign ownership was 52%. The third group consisted of six companies fully owned by foreign investors. Those companies that did not give information about their ownership were not included in this analysis.

Table 2 lists the industries included in the survey. *Table 3* shows that most of the companies in all ownership groups were involved in manu-facturing, although a few were engaged in assembling, trading, forward-ing or warehousing. *Table 4* indicates the size categories of companies by number of employees.

Table 1. Legal structures by ownership types

Legal type	Ownership					
	domestic		mixed		foreign	
Limited liability company	29	(23.2%)	11	(36.7%)	5	(83.3%)
Joint stock company	52	(41.6%)	19	(63.3%)	1	(16.7%)
Cooperative	5	(4.0%)	0	(0%)	0	(0%)
State-owned company	34	(27.2%)	0	(0%)	0	(0%)
No answer	5	(4.0%)	0	(0%)	0	(0%)
Total	125	(100.0%)	30	(100.0%)	6	(100.0%)

Table 2. Industries of companies surveyed

Industry	Domestic	Mixed	Foreign
Mining	1	1	0
Electric energy production	2	0	0
Metallurgy	7	0	0
Machine factory	15	3	0
Construction materials	1	3	2
Chemicals	20	2	0
Light industries	30	3	0
Food industry	20	9	2
Transportation	4	1	0
Trade	7	3	1
Other	11	3	1

Table 3. Activities of companies

Type of activity	Domestic	Mixed	Foreign
Mining	1	0	0
Manufacturing	84	22	5
Assembling	8	2	0
Trade	8	3	1
Forwarding, warehousing	1	2	0
Construction	1	0	0
Other	20	1	0

Table 4. Number of employees by ownership
(percentage distribution)

Number of employees		Domestic	Mixed	Foreign
Fewer than 50		9.8	16.7	16.7
Between 50 and 250		26.0	20.0	50.0
Between 250 and 500		17.9	10.0	0.0
More than 500		46.3	53.3	33.3
	Total	100.0	100.0	100.0

Domestic Companies. The largest subsample of executives was from domestically-owned companies (78.7% of all companies in the sample), including light industries such as wood processing, paper, and textiles. Executives from companies in the chemical industry (e.g., pharmaceutical, rubber, and cosmetics) and the food industry made up 17.2 and 16.4% respectively of the sample. Respondents from machine factories represented 12.9% in this ownership category. Hardly any foreign investment was found in the chemical industry because Hungary's environmental liability regulations make new owners of privatized companies fully liable for clean-up of the site. Many of the domestic companies were still either state-owned enterprises (27%) or joint stock companies in which the government may still own a portion of the shares (41.6%). About 46% of these enterprises were large, with more than 500 employees, and about 64% had more than 250 employees.

Mixed-Ownership Companies. Respondents from most companies with mixed ownership were in the food industry. The other sectors-machine factories, construction materials, light industries, and trade-were about equally represented by about 10.7% of the respondents. A majority of these enterprises were joint stock companies. More than 53% of these mixed-ownership companies had more than 500 employees. Only about 17% were small companies with less than 50 workers.

Foreign-Owned Companies. Two of the six foreign-owned companies produced construction materials, two others were in the food industry, and the remaining two were engaged in trade. As might be expected, five of the six wholly foreign-owned companies were limited liability corporations and one was a joint stock company. Two of the companies had more than 500 employees; the other four had fewer than 250 workers.

PERCEPTIONS OF ENVIRONMENTAL ISSUES

Both the McKinsey international survey and the Hungarian corporate survey sought to understand how strongly corporate executives recognized environmental issues and their perceptions of how government and the business community can begin to deal with them. In both questionnaires, executives were asked about their reactions to seven statements and to indicate on a five-point scale (1 = fully disagree, 5 = fully agree) the extent to which they agreed with these statements. The results show a high level of recognition of how serious environmental problems are in countries around the world. The Hungarian responses also allowed differences between perceptions of executives in companies in different ownership groups to be tested. The Kruskal–Wallis non-parametric test was used to indicate differences among the ownership groups in Hungary. This powerful test is the nonparametric equivalent of the analysis of variance and it is more appropriate for the analysis of data with potential outliers (Daniel 1990). *Table 5* shows the statements posed to corporate executives in both surveys and the significance level of the test for the Hungarian group where significant differences appeared. In order to make the Hungarian study comparable with the McKinsey survey, the data were rescaled and the ratings were converted into percentages.

Importance of Environmental Challenges. The results of both surveys show strong recognition of the importance of environmental challenges (statement 5-1). In the McKinsey international survey, 92% of the respondents agreed that "the environmental challenge is one of the central issues of the 21st century". Overall, 94% of the Hungarian respondents also agreed that environmental issues will be crucial in the coming century and there was relatively little difference among the responses of executives of companies in different ownership groups, with all of the executivs of foreign-owned companies strongly agreeing. Perceptions were similar about responsibility for the environmental impacts of products (statement 5-5 in *Table 5*).

Need for New Partnerships to Solve Environmental Problems. A strong consensus also existed in both surveys on the need for new partnerships to solve environmental problems and prevent new ones in the future (statement 5-7). About 80% in the international survey and 79% in the Hungarian survey, agreed on the need to pursue partnerships among government, industry, and academia in order to minimize the chance of future tragedies. However, in Hungary this statement was viewed differently – at 11.0% significance level using the Kruskal–Wallis test – among res-

Table 5. Differences in perceptions of environment
(percentage of respondents who agreed with the statement)

Statement (Significance level)	Domestic	Mixed	Foreign	Hungary Total	McKinsey Survey
5-1. The environmental challenge is one of the central issues of the twenty-first century	94	93	100	94	92
5-2. The industry will have to rethink its entire conception of the industrial process if it is to adapt profitably to an increasingly environment-oriented world	67	72	50	67	63
5-3. Where environmental or health considerations demand it, the sale of our products will be curtailed or their production halted, regardless of our economic interests ($p=0.044$)	23	24	67	25	NA
5-4. Pollution prevention pays	56	33	50	54	76
5-5. There is a need to assume responsibility for one's products even after they left the plant	95	97	100	96	83
5-6. In the long-term our spending on environmental R&D will give us a competitive advantage	65	63	50	64	76
5-7. To minimize the chance of future tragedies, we should pursue a partnership of government, industry and academia ($p=0.110$)	83	62	67	79	80

pondents from companies in different ownership groups. Executives from the domestic companies, having had long experience with government involvement, agreed the most (83%) about the need for new types of partnerships that include academia and the private sector. The other two groups – 62% of those from mixed-ownership companies and 67% from foreignowned companies – agreed, but somewhat less strongly.

Benefits of Environmental Management. A majority of corporate respondents agreed in both the international and Hungarian samples – although at a somewhat lower level of consensus than existed on broader issues – that actions to manage environmental problems would benefit their companies. However, differences appeared in both the strength of agreement between international and Hungarian executives, and about ways in which environmental actions would benefit companies among managers of different types of companies in Hungary. About 76% of the executives responding to the McKinsey survey agreed that long-term spending on environmental R&D (statement 5-6) would give their companies a compative advantage. In Hungary only about 64% of all executives and only about half of those from foreign-owned companies agreed with the statement.

About 76% of international respondents also agreed that pollution prevention pays for companies (statement 5-4). But in Hungary only 54% of the executives thought that pollution prevention would result in benefits for the company, and among those from mixed-ownership companies only one-third agreed. Small differences also appeared when respondents were asked how extensively their companies would have to reorient their practices and procedures. About 63% of the international respondents and 67% of the Hungarian respondents agreed to the statement (5-2) that "industry will have to re-think its entire conception of the industrial process if it is to adapt profitably to an increasingly environment-oriented world". Perhaps because to some degree foreign-owned companies had already adopted more environmentally-friendly manufacturing processes and because they are operating mostly in the less environmentally sensitive industries, only half of the executives in this ownership group agreed.

PERCEPTIONS OF APPROPRIATE COMPAY
POLICIES AND PRACTICES

Given the relatively strong consensus among corporate executives internationally and in Hungary on the critical environmental challenges facing companies in the future, both the McKinsey and the Hungarian surveys sought to clarify how executives perceived these challenges in their own companies and what types of changes they were prepared to support.

Key Environmental Concerns. Some differences appeared in the responses of executives throughout the world who were survewed by McKinsey, and in those of Hungarian executives from companies in different ownership groups, on the operational implications of their concenrns. In the McKinsey survey, "complying with regulations" was the main environmental concern followed by "preventing incidents". Both are typical of traditional "defensive" environmental management approaches. About half as much importance was assigned to the next two (more proactive) concerns, "enhancing positive image" and "integrating environment into corporate strategy". The least important consideration for the international companies was "realizing new market opportunities", while for the companies operating in Hungary it was the key concern. Interestingly, the participants in the Hungarian study and the international survey agreed on the importance of the next two items: "preventing incidents" and "enhancing positive image". "Complying with regulations" and "integrating environment into corporate strategy" were the least important issues for the respondents from Hungary, perhaps because of the uncertain circumstances they had to deal with during the economic transition. Complying with regulations may have seemed less important because Hungary's regulations are strict but not effectively enforced. The economic crisis largely focused Hungarian managers' attention on issues of survival and they may have therefore underestimated the importance of corporate strategy.

Curtailing Environmentally Harmful Products. Although a majority of respondents to both surveys agreed with general staterments about the seriousness of environmental challenges and the benefits to companies of taking positive actions to improve environmental management, only 25% of Hungarian respondents agreed that companies should curtail production of or remove products for helalth or environmental reasons. The results show that statement 5-3 was viewed significantly differently (at 4.4% significance level) by respondents in the three ownership groups. Managers from foreign-owned companies tended to agree more strongly (67%) that if environmental considerations demand it, the sale or manufacture of a product should be halted regardless of the economic interests of the company. Only about 23% and 24%, respectively, of the executives from domestic and mixed-ownership companies agreed with that statement.

Seriousness of Environmental Issues in Value-added Chain. Respondents were asked in the MCKINSEY study to identify the phase of a product's life cycle where environmental issues were most serious. The international respondents reported production as being the most critical phase; followed by disposal and recycling. Product use and sourcing were at the end of the list. Hungarian executives had somewhat different perceptions. They felt that environmental issues were most serious in disposal and recycling and showed less concern about production, sourcing of raw materials, and product use. This difference can be explained by the fact that Hungary's 1986 hazardous waste law created a large gap between the volume of waste production and the level of waste disposal capacity. There was strong agreement in all ownership categories in Hungary on the need for improving waste management and manufacturing technology and far less agreement on improving end products. A much higher percentage of executives from foreign-owed companies thought that improvements in end products would improve environmental protection than did their counterparts in domestic or mixed-ownership companies.

Most Effective Government Policy Instruments. A question about the most effective government policy instruments for addressing major environmental issues was unique because differences in political culture should influence the attitudes of managers. The MCKINSEY survey showed that 63% of the Japanese respondents (double the average response) preferred direct regulation, while self-regulation and market mechanisms were strongly favored by North American managers. Direct regulation may be more strongly preferred by managers of companies in countries with stable political situations or with governments having more transparent economic policies. Indirect regulation and self-regulation were mainly favored in stable market economies like the United States. The international and Hungarian surveys also sought to elicit executives' preceptions about the most effective means of achieving environmental protection. The major differences between international and Hungarian respondents appeared to be on the efficacy of direct regulation (e.g. command and control) and positive indirect regulation (e.g. subsidies, tax breaks). Hungarian managers were less disposed toward direct regulation – not because they preferred indirect regulation, which was even more problematic for them – but because Hungarian environmental protection legislation started with the command and control instruments and Hungarian managers may have better understood how unrealistic that approach really was. After 1989 the new government introduced some economic instruments such as fuel taxes, deposits for tires, and ecotaxes on packaging, and it reduced subsidies for public transport and elminated tax breaks for environmental protection investments. Perhaps this experience led Hungarian managers to prefer positive incentives over indirect regulation through negative incentives (e.g. taxes, pollution charges) and "self-regulation" (e.g. voluntary restraint of production).

About 59% of the respondents in Hungary thought that the current legal regulations greatly contributed to environmental protection. However, this overall response masked large differences among the three ownership groups. The level of agreement ranged from 33% for foreign-owned companies and 58% for Hungarian owned estamblishments to 69% for companies with mixed ownership. These differences were significant at the 14.3% level on the KRUSKAL–WALLIS test for the original five-point scale responses. One possible explanation for the joint ventures' high level of satisfaction with current regulations is the number of concessions made by the government in order to attract foreign investment. The desire on the part of the Hungarian government to increase foreign investment in order to improve economic conditions may have temporarily superseded its concern about environmental conditions. Joint venture managers would be reluctant to change the regulations under which they negotiated their arrangements and to curtail production of environmentally damaging products.

Environmental Practices Currently Used. Finally, the greatest differences between international and Hungarian respondents were seen in the types of environmental practices already adopted. Hungarian companies lagged behind in all categories. Significant differences were also seen among Hungarian companies in different ownership groups. For example, while 79% of international companies have written environmental policy statements, only about 57% of domestic Hungarian companies and 67% of foreign-owned Hungarian companies have adopted such policies. About half of the international respondents reported that their companies have a board member with specific responsibility for environmental issues; but in Hungary only one-third of the foreign-owned firms, 8% of the domestic firms, and 13% of the mixed-ownership companies have such programs *(Table 6)*. Only a very small percentage of domestic (6.4) and mixed companies (3.3) and none of the foreign companies in Hungary used environmental performance evaluations for their suppliers, while 22% of the executives in the international survey reported that their company followed this practice.

Although about one third of the companies had some kind of an environmental program in place, the use of these programs differed from market to market among the companies operating in Hungary. In the Hungarian questionnaire several additional questions addressed the issue of environmental marketing. Generally, these questions asked managers what they thought about their customers and the potential for marketing green products. There was no statistically significant difference in any of these questions among the different ownership groups, showing that although the managers disagreed on several environmental issues, they saw their operating environment, the Hungarian market and their Hun-

Table 6. Environmental policy component that is currently installed
at the company

Policy component	Percentage of companies with the component			
	Domestic (Hungary)	Mixed (Hungary)	Foreign (Hungary)	McKinsey Survey
1. Written company policy statement	57	77	67	79
2. Board member with specific responsibility	39	23	33	52
3. Environmental performance evaluation of suppliers	6	3	0	22
4. Hiring external experts in environmental affairs	19	13	17	27
5. Public communication program	8	13	33	43
6. Environmental marketing program	26	27	33	32

garian customers quite similarly. The first question was about the importance of the green nature of a product for customers. Only about 7% of the domestic companies and joint ventures, and about 17% of the foreign companies thought that the green nature of the product is important or very important for their customers. Similarly, only a minority of the respondents thought that their customers would pay 5% more for a "green" product. This agreement was further supported when the managers were asked about the importance of emphasizing the green nature of the products in developed market economies, in other foreign markets, and in the domestic market. The answers showed a clear trend: an overwhelming majority of the respondents thought that it is very important to emphasize the green nature of a product in the developed market economies, somewhat less important in other foreign markets, and not very important in the Hungarian market.

FINDINGS AND CONCLUSIONS

The Hungarian survey showed that there is virtually no difference between the environmental perceptions of Hungarian and international managers of the importance of environmental challenges. If anything,

Hungarian executives are slightly more sensitive to the importance of environmental issues and more strongly agree that companies are responsible for the environmental impacts of their products even after they leave the factory. Hungarian executives also strongly agree with their international counterparts on the need for new partnerships of government, business, and academia to address environmental issues, and seem to be less trusting that government or businesses alone can solve environmental problems. Although Hungarian managers agree with their international counterparts that environmental actions will benefit companies, the level of that agreement was much weaker than that of international executives on the statements that their industries would have to entirely rethink their industrial processes and that pollution prevention would result in benefits for their companies.

It was surprising, however, that respondents to the MCKINSEY survey saw very little distinction between Central and Eastern European and third world countries in terms of the most appropriate approaches to developing clean technologies or the environmental barriers to foreign acquisition of companies. Despite some large economic, political and social differences in the two regions, executives from around the world had virtually the same attitudes toward the appropriate approaches to developing clean technologies in Central and Eastern Europe and third world countries. A little over 40% believed that training local management and staff in clean technologies was the best approach for both regions; about 20% thought that subsidies, soft loans, and tax provisions would promote the adoption of clean technologies; and smaller percentages favored transfer of expatriate experts to operate facilities, development of special "fool-proof" technologies, and access to patents at minimal or no charge. Their perceptions of the barriers to higher foreign investment in Central and Eastern Europe and third world countries were also similar, except on two dimensions: more than twice as many international respondents thought that potential environmental liabilities would be barriers to foreign acquisition of companies, and a far larger percentage thought that the cost of upgrading facilities would be a stronger barrier to foreign investment in Central and Eastern Europe than in third world countries.

When attention was focused on the specifics of how companies should deal with environmental issues, there were some strong differences in perceptions between Hungarian and international respondents and among Hungarian respondents from companies in different ownership groups.

Only a minority of Hungarian executives from domestic and mixed-ownership companies, for example, agreed that the production or sale of a product should be halted because of environmental considerations.

Most Hungarian managers saw the most serious environmental implications in disposal and recycling and in production processes, whereas for international respondents disposal and recycling were perceived to be less urgent problems, perhaps because in Western European, Japanese, and American companies these problems were no longer as compelling. More than their international counterparts, Hungarian managers favored indirect regulation and use of incentives as the most effective means of protecting the environment. Generally the managers of joint ventures and domestic companies in Hungary thought that current legal regulations were contributing to environmental protection, while executives of foreign companies did not strongly agree. This disagreement might be attributed in part to the small number of foreign-owned companies in the sample, but it is more likely due to the current economic conditions in Hungary where managers focus more on "marketization" and attracting foreign investment than on strengthening environmental controls.

When asked about environmental actions currently used by their companies, the responses of Hungarian executives showed that their companies lagged behind their international counterparts in all categories of actions. Beyond having adopted environmental policy statements or designated a board member to be concerned with environmental issues, a relatively small percentage of Hungarian companies have adopted other means of meeting environmental challenges. A realtively high percentage of companies reported the existence of environmental marketing programs. However, marketing "green" products or the "green" nature of the products was thought to be much more important in developed market economies than in the Hungarian market.

Although there seems to be a wider gap between Hungarian and Western European and North American companies in adopting more effective environmental practices, the survey revealed that Hungarian managers are acutely aware that their companies will have to invest more heavily to achieve higher levels of environmental protection in the future. As *Table 7* indicates, more than 77% of the respondenst from domestic companies predicted an increase or a significant increase in environmental protection-related company investments in the future, as did 80% of those from mixed-ownership companies, and 88% from foreign-owned companies. If these predictions are accurate reflections of the plans these

Table 7. Change of environmental protection
related company investments in the immediate future
(percentage distribution)

Investment trend forecast	Domestic	Mixed	Foreign
Decrease	4.9	6.7	0.0
Constant	17.1	13.3	16.7
Increase	68.3	70.0	50.0
Significant increase	9.7	10.0	33.3

executives are making for future investment, it seems to indicate that neither domestic companies nor multinationals anticipate operating in Hungary in a way that can evade or ignore the increasing pressures to address environmental challenges in the future.

Finally, the evidence from these surveys indicates that executives from around the world are highly sensitive to the importance of environmental issues, and that foreign-owned companies in Hungary are not seeking a "pollution haven" in which to manufacture at a lesser standard environmentally than they do in Europe or North America. A recent survey of foreign investors in joint ventures undertaken by the Hungarian Academy of Science's Institute for World Economics for a Japanese aid organization confirms this impression (CSÁKI 1993). It concludes that "most companies think about environmental protection as a normal feature [of doing business], a necessary condition of production, and are ready to equip their facilities with up-to-date equipment". Indeed, the study found that the lack of clear and enforceable environmental regulations leaves most multinational companies uncertain about how to make those investments and about their future liability for environmental degradation. American companies were particularly concerned about the impact of weak environmental regulations on their decisions and on their ability to sell products made in Hungary in Western European markets. They generally saw the move toward more transparent environmental regulations and more effective enforcement in Hungary as a way of improving the business climate.

END NOTES

[1] The MCKINSEY "Corporate Response" questionnaire was distributed to participants of the Annual Meeting of the World Economic Forum (held in Davos in February 1991), the Second World Industry Conference on Environmental Management (WICEM II, organized by the International Chamber of Commerce in Rotterdam, April 1991), and the 19th Annual General Meeting of the International Primary Aluminum Institute (held in Amsterdam in May 1991). Efforts were made to generate responses from specific geographic regions in order to ensure a sufficient response from these areas. The five regions were based on the geographic location and the GNP per capita of the country where the company headquarters were located:

- North America (consisting of Bermuda, Canada, and the United States), Japan, Western Europe (consisting of the European Community and the EFTA countries);
- Central and Eastern Europe (consisting of former centrally planned economies of Bulgaria, Czechoslovakia, Hungary, Poland, Soviet Union and Yugoslavia); and
- Third World (consisting of the developing countries in South America, Africa, and Asia).

Responses from Australia, Hong Kong, New Zealand, Singapore, Taiwan and the United Arab Emirates were included in the overall analysis but they were excluded from any regional segmentation because of lack of sufficient numbers relative to the variety of countries.

The industrial classification of the sample included six groups:

(1) chemicals (covering chemicals, rubber, and plastic);
(2) energy (including utilities, energy distributors and oil, coal, and gas companies);
(3) metals (including primary metals, metal products and machinery);
(4) process industries (including paper and paper products, glass, construction and building materials);
(5) consumer goods (including food, beverage and tobacco, tectiles and apparel, and pharmaceuticals/diagnostics);
(6) durables (including transport equipment, electrical machinery/appliances, electronics/telecommunications, aviation, and environmental technology).

In many parts of the questionnaire the respondents were asked how strongly they agreed or disagreed with certain statements or whether an issue was critical or unimportant. The scale used ranged from 1 (disagree or unimportant) to 5 (agree or critical). The ratings were converted into percentages (1 and 2 as disagree, 3 as neutral, 4 and 5 as agree).

[2] The overall results of the McKINSEY survey may be somewhat optimistic on corporate executives' perceptions of the environmental challenge because:

(1) most of the responses were from senior executive who are, generally, more strategically oriented and more optimistic about environmental matters than their lower level, more operational counterparts;

(2) about 59% of the respondents were from large, international companies that may have had greater exposure to environmental issues, and therefore were more environmentally sensitive; and

(3) respondents who attended the World Industry Conference on Environmental Management, WICEM II, can be expected to be more positive about environmental issues than those who did not attend.

REFERENCES

CAIRNCROSS, F.: *Costing the Earth: The Challenges for Governments, the Opportunities for Business*, Cambridge, Mass.: MIT Press (1992).

CSÁKI, G.: *Foreign Direct Investments and Joint Ventures in Hungary: A Basic Issue of Transformation Towards a Market Economy.* Budapest, Hungary: Hungarian Academy of Sciences, Institute for World Economics (1993).

DANIEL, W. W.: *Applied Nonparametric Statistics* (2nd ed.). Boston, Mass.: PWS-Kent (1990).

FROSCH, R., N. GALLOPULAS: Strategies for Manufacturing. *Scientific American* (September), pp. 144–153 (1987).

HANSEN, P.: Criteria for Sustainable Development Management of Transnational Corporations. *Industry and Environment*, Vol. 12, Nos 3–4, pp. 32–42 (1989).

JACKSON, T., COSTANZA, R., OVERCASH, M., REES, W.: The Biophysical Economy – Aspects of the Interaction Between Economy and Environment. In: T. JACKSON (ed.): *Clean Production Strategies*. Boca Raton, Fla.: Lewis Publishers, pp. 3–28 (1993).

KEMP, R.: An Economic Analysis of Cleaner Technology: Theory and Evidence. In: K. FISHER, J. SCHOT (eds): *Environmental Strategies for Industry*. Washington, D.C.: Island Press, pp. 79–113 (1993).

McKINSEY & Company: *The Corporate Response to the Environmental Challenge, Summary Report*. Amsterdam, The Netherlands: McKINSEY & Company (1991).

PANAYOTOU, T.: *Green Markets: The Economics of Sustainable Development*. San Francisco, Calif.: ICS Press (1993).

PEARSON, C. S.: *Multinational Corporations, Environment and the Third World: Business Matters.* Durham, N.C.: Duke University Press (1987).

RONDINELLI, D. A.: *Privatization and Economic Reform in Central Europe: The Changing Business Climate.* Westport, Conn.: Quorum Books (1993).

RONDINELLI, D. A., FELLENZ, M. R.: Privatization and Private Enterprise Development in Hungary: An Assessment of Market Reform Policies. *Business & The Contemporary World, 5* (4), pp. 75–88 (1993).

SCHMIDHEINY, S. and the Business Council on Sustainable Development: *Changing Course: A Global Business Perspective on Development and the Environment.* Cambridge, Mass.: MIT Press (1992).

SCHOT, J., FISCHER, K.: The Greening of the Industrial Firm. In: K. FISCHER, J. SCHOT (eds): *Environmental Strategies for Industry.* Washington, D.C.: Island Press, pp. 3–33 (1993).

United Nations Commission on Transnational Corporations (UNCTC): *Transnational Corporations and Issues Relating to the Environment.* New York: United Nations (1990).

VÁRI, A., TAMÁS, P. (eds): *Environment and Democratic Transition: Policy and Politics in Central and Eastern Europe.* Boston, Mass.: Kleuwer Academic Publishers (1993).

WHITE & CASE Inc.: Hungary in European Bank for Reconstruction and Development, *Investors' Environmental Guidelines.* London: Graham & Trotman Publisheers, pp. 223–288 (1994).

World Bank: *Social Indicators of Development.* Washington, D.C.: World Bank (1994).

25

ENVIRONMENTAL ETHICS FOR BUSINESS*

By

LÁSZLÓ ZSOLNAI

In our technological age business is one of the greatest destroyers of the natural environment. At present, we do not have any appropriate theory of business that would be consistent with ecology, that is, contains a well-articulated *ecological point of view*. This article is an attempt to meet this need.

Conventional theories of business hold that business is to serve the interests of the owners. As MILTON FRIEDMAN has so suggestively stated: the only social responsibility of business is to increase its profit within the actually existing framework of law [1]. This view can hardly be reconciled with the demands of ecology. The emerging *stakeholder theory of business* seems to offer a much more adequate approach in an age of rapidly deteriorating natural environment. The stakeholder theory states that business is to serve the interests of all the parties that are affected by its functioning [2].

1. THE NATURAL ENVIRONMENT AS A STAKEHOLDER OF BUSINESS

The standard definition of the "stakeholder" concept excludes the natural environment among the stakeholders of business. According to EDWARD R. FREEMAN "a stakeholder in an organisation is (by definition) any group or individual who can affect or is affected by the achievement of the organisation's objectives" [3].

* In *Management Research News*, 1996, Vol. 19, No. 10, pp. 9–15.

FREEMAN lists *environmentalist groups*, but not the natural environment itself, among the stakeholders of a business firm. This is a rather paradoxical position, since it implies that managers should consider the environmental impacts of their decisions, if and only if they violate the actual standards of law or there are environmentalist groups to advocate for and voice the "interest" of the natural environment.

In modern societies neither legal regulation nor environmentalist groups can provide satisfactory defence for nature from business activities.

Environmental law, even in the most advanced countries, is fragmented, issue-centred and mostly expresses solely the interests of people living in a particular environment. Until now environmental legislation has proved to be rather ineffective from the point of view of nature because it does not follow the logic and organisation of nature. In most cases actual standards of law cannot avoid the free riding practice of business concerning the natural environment [4].

It is known from the sociological literature that the environmental awareness of people is highly correlated with the level of social welfare. The higher the welfare of people, the higher the environmental awareness that can be expected from people. In modern societies strong environmental preferences only appear once a certain level of material welfare has been reached [5]. The present state of the green movement in Eastern Europe provides a clear illustration of this point. East European environmentalist groups received much stronger social support during the former Communist regimes than they can get now. With the considerable decrease in their standard of living Eastern European people are displaying a more limited interest in environmental problems.

The logic of collective action analysed by MARCUR OLSON and others presents another obstacle for environmental activism. People, even with high level environmental awareness, tend to not participate in joint environmental actions when the cost of their participation is high and the effect of their participation is marginal.

One may argue that other stakeholders of business, namely the *customers* and especially the *government,* might be able to force business towards environmentally sound practices. But, unfortunately, this is often not the case. *Green consumerism* has an important but somewhat limited role in orienting business decisions and policies. *Government politicians* always and necessarily function within the framework of their short term election period. Political decisions are, not surprisingly, more or less myopic, that is, environmental problems which endure beyond the election period are usually overdiscounted. There is an additional and extremely important fact whereby neither environmentalist law and environmentalist groups nor the customers and the government can be guarantor of the ecological integrity of the natural environment. This fact is the *irreversibility* of much of the environmental damage done. Loss of biodiversity, degradation of the structure and form of ecosystems and other drastic environmental effects are more or less irreversible. I think irreversibility is the ultimate reason why business should voluntarily adopt an ecological point of view.

The "interest" of the natural environment is under-represented, or even not represented at all, by the usual stakeholders of business. However, the natural environment has a very *existential stake* in the functioning of business. The survival and health of many parts and segments of nature depends on:

(i)   what business extracts from the natural environment as inputs;
(ii) what business emits as outcome into the natural environment;
(iii) how business changes the function and structure of the natural environment *(Fig. 1)*.

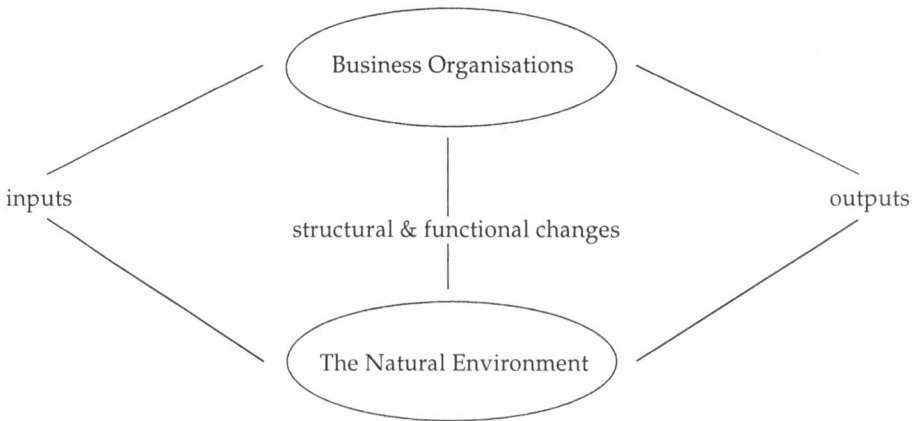

Figure 1. The Interaction of Business and the Natural Environment

The stakeholder concept can be redefined in a way that is appropriate to include the natural environment among the stakeholders of business. I propose an *ecological generalisation* and, at the same time, an *ethical restriction* of the notion. According to the new definition: *stakeholders are those living systems that are affected by and can affect the functioning of business.*

In this definition the term "living system" refers to self-creating (auto-poietic) entities. The natural environment, human individuals and their groups and organisations are all living systems [6].

The proposed definition excludes those parties among the stakeholders that are not affected by the functioning of business, but just affect it. Those parties are kibitzers, not stakeholders. This conceptualisation meets the theoretical demand of KENNETH E. GOODPASTER: all the stakeholders are *morally considerable,* and *only those entities* are stakeholders that are morally considerable [7].

Hence, the most important stakeholders of an average business firm can be listed as follows:

(i)   owners;
(ii)   employees;
(iii)   customers;
(iv)   suppliers;
(v)   competitors;
(vi)   the government;
(vii) the local community;
(viii) the natural environment *(Fig. 2).*

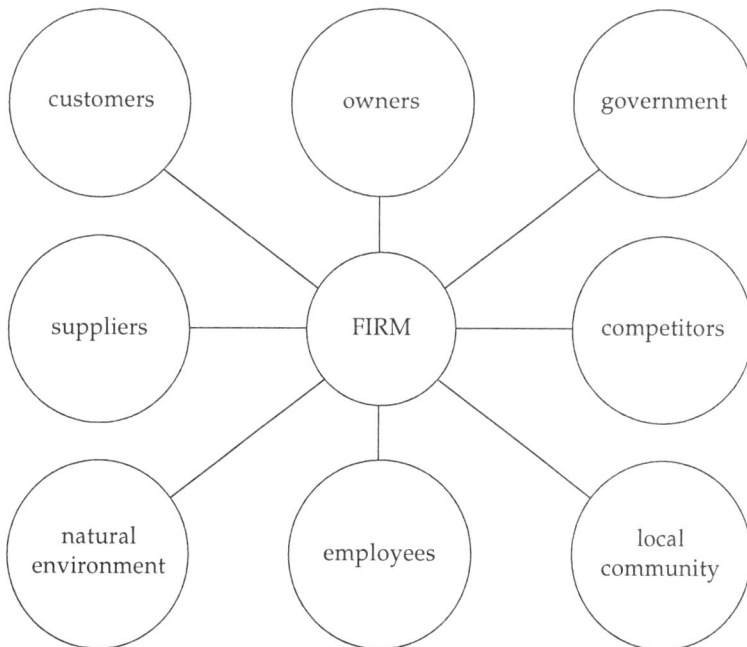

Figure 2. Stakeholders of an average firm

2. ENVIRONMENTAL ETHICS APPLIED TO BUSINESS

The underlying principle of environmental ethics is that *all living things have intrinsic value.* That is, living things are not merely means for accomplishing one's purposes but are ends in and of themselves [8]. This statement can be called "the categorical imperative of ecology".

Business affects the natural environment at three levels of the organisation of nature.

- *Individual biological creatures* are affected by business (hunting, fishing, husbandry, animal testing, etc.).
- *Natural ecosystems* are affected by business (mining, regulating rivers, agriculture, polluting the air, water and land, etc.).
- *The Earth as a whole* is affected by business (exterminating species, contributing to global warming and acid rain, etc.).

The categorical imperative of ecology applies to business at all the above mentioned levels, since individual biological creatures, natural ecosystems, and the Earth as a whole, are all alive. While this is evident as regards the individual biological creatures, it requires some explanation at the level of natural ecosystems and the Earth.

Natural ecosystems are co-existing populations of plants, animals, and micro-organisms in close interaction with sunlight, air, water, and soil. Such natural regions like, for example, the Rocky Mountains or the San Francisco Bay are large-scale ecosystems.

Natural ecosystems are supra-individual entities which means that their key players are not individual biological creatures but *population.* The co-existence of populations are regulated in natural ecosystems: some populations multiply and flourish while other populations migrate or become extinct.

The long-term dynamics of natural ecosystems is called *succession,* that is a directional change in the structure, form and function of co-existing populations over time. They develop new emphases, as well as different bases and forms. During the succession process we find that the total biomass production progressively increases; the decomposer elements - become large and more important, and the diversity of species and complexity of their balance grow. In early developmental stages the biomass production exceeds the biomass consumption; there are some niches for new populations. When biomass production and biomass consumption become equal then natural ecosystems reach their mature, climax state [9].

Now let us turn to the Earth as a whole. In his Gaia theory, JAMES LOVE-LOCK demonstrated that the Earth is not a passive substratum of life but plays a very active role in conditioning and sustaining life itself [10]. A simple thought-experimented proposed by LOVELOCK can illustrate this point.

Let Daisyworld be a planet like the Earth. Over billions of years its Sun gets warmer. Daisyworld has nothing but soil and two species or daisy, black and white, competing with each other. Early on, when the Sun is young and cool, only the black daisies flourish because they absorb more of the sun's warmth than white daisies do. Their competitive advantage ensures that they spread over the planet. That makes the planet dark, more absorbent of sunlight, and thus warmer. As time goes on, the white daisies, capable of reflecting away more sunlight and thus keeping cool, gain the upper hand. The warming effect, of black daisies and the cooling effect of white daisies complement each other and the daisies keep the planet at the temperature most suited to them.

The Earth should be viewed as a giant network of all the terrestrial and aquatic ecosystems. It does have *systemic patterns* and *global mechanisms* above and beyond any particular ecosystem.

At the level of individual biological creatures the *awareness-based ethics* seems to be adequate for business. The most eloquent protagonist of this branch of environmental ethics is PETER SINGER. He writes: "If a being suffers there can be no moral justification for refusing to take this suffering into consideration. (...) If a being is not capable of suffering, or of experiencing enjoyment or happines, there is nothing to be taken into account" [11].

Awareness-based ethics implies that *business should assure natural life conditions and relatively painless existence for animals and other sentient beings* that are affected by its activities.

At the level of natural ecosystems the so-called *ecosystem ethics* is relevant for business. The maxim of ecosystem ethics was first stated by ALDO LEOPOLD in his classic "Sand County Almanach". He writes: "A thing is right when it tends to preserve the integrity, stability, and beauty of the biotic community. It is wrong when it tends otherwise" [12].

Ecosystem ethics implies that *business must use natural ecosystems in a sustainably way*, that is, keeping statistically invariant the most important structural and functional properties of the ecosystems during use.

At the level of the Earth, *Gaian ethics* is demanded for business. The essence of Gain ethics is reverence for the self-regulating character and evolutionary (or even cosmic) uniqueness of the biosphere [13].

Gaian ethics implies that *business should not violate the systemic patterns and global mechanisms of the Earth.* This means stopping the production of greenhouse gases, and the balancing the CO_2/O_2 account, among other things.

3. CORPORATE ENVIRONMENTALISM

Corporate environmentalism shows some promising signs to turn environmental ethics into business practice. Companies like *3M,* the *Body Shop, Rhone-Poulenc, Dow, AT&T,* the *Ferruzzi Group* are recognised as being in the frontline of the greening of business.

Corporate environmentalism is based on *green corporate vision.* A green scenario on the future development of the company can encourage managers to search for *cost-effective methods in environmental preservation,* to adapt some version of *environmental impact analyses* in plant planning, to introduce *clean production technologies,* and to take the *product stewardship approach* [14].

It would be wrong to state that corporate environmentalism, and more deeply, environmental ethics are fully consistent with the pursuit of self-interest of business. But it is the same with other value-commitments of business as well. For example, protecting human rights within and outside the company.

From DAVID HUME we know that moral behaviour is based on sentiments, rather than on reason. Finally, I would like to list some *moral sentiments* that can motivate business managers to consider the natural environment as a stakeholder in their practice.

First, the natural environment contributes to the profit of business. It is a matter of *fairness* to return this contribution in the form of moral considerations. Second, nature is more or less defenceless against injuries and violations caused by business. Here the matter of *compassion* emerges. Third, the natural environment is the home of the employees, customers, and local neighbours of business. This is the matter of *love.*

Business organisations which destroy nature at various levels *cannot be authentic* and *integral* in any sense.

REFERENCE

[1] FRIEDMAN, M.: "The Social Responsibility of Business Is to Increase Its Profit." *The New York Times Magazine.* September 13 (1970).

[2] DONALDSON, TH., PRESTON, L. E.: *The Stakeholder Theory of the Corporation: Concepts, Evidence, Implications.* CIBER University of Maryland at College Park (1994).

[3] FREEMAN, E. R.: *Strategic Management: A Stakeholder Approach.* PITMAN (1984).

[4] HOFFMAN, M. W.: "Business and Environmental Ethics." *Business Ethics Quarterly,* No. 2 (1991).

[5] COTGROVE, S.: *Catastrophe or Cornucopia?* JOHN WILEY (1982).

[6] PRUZAN, P., THYSSEN, O.: "Conflict and Consensus: Ethics as Shared Value Horizon for Strategic Planning." *Human Systems Management,* No. 1 (1991).

[7] GOODPASTER, K. E.: "Business Ethics and Stakeholder Analyses." *Business Ethics Quarterly,* No. 1 (1991).

[8] FOX, W.: *Towards a Transpersonal Ecology.* Shambhala (1990).

[9] PUTMAN, R. J., WRATEN, S. D.: *Principles of Ecology.* University of California Press (1984).

[10] LOVELOCK, J.: *Gaia. A New Look at Life on Earch.* Oxford University Press (1979).

[11] SINGER, P.: *Animal Liberation: A New Ethics for our Treatment of Animals.*

[12] LEOPOLD, A.: *A Sand County Almanac.* University of Chicago Press (1947).

[13] FOX, W.: *Op. cit.*

[14] ELKINGTON, J., KNIGHT, P.: *The Green Business Guide.* VICTOR GOLLANZ Ltd. (1992).

26

MORAL RESPONSIBILITY
AND ECONOMIC CHOICE*

By

LÁSZLÓ ZSOLNAI

Moral responsibility emerges in choice situations where the choice has wide-ranging consequences and not only the decision maker but also other parties are affected by the outcome of the choice. In this paper I will refer to such situations as complex choice situations.

The purpose of this paper is to present a normative but realistic model of responsible choice. The model is normative in the sense that it prescribes the way a morally responsible decision maker should behave in complex choice situations. However, the model is intended to be realistic in the sense that it does not require anything from the decision maker that would be contrary to the psychology of human choice behaviour.

The basic fault of the national choice model is its lack of psychological realism. Rational decision makers should maximize their utility functions under perfect information. This is a highly unrealistic requirement for human beings.

By more than 50 years of research HERBERT A. SIMON has demonstrated that real-word decision makers are not capable of maximizing their utility functions, partly because of their strongly bounded computing capacities, partly because of the strictly limited information they usually have. Real-word decision makers are only capable of making satisficing choices (SIMON 1979).

DANIEL KAHNEMAN'S recent research shows that decision makers are unable to foresee the real experienced utility of their chosen decision alternatives. For this reason their choices are not rational for most cases (KAHNEMAN 1994).

* In *International Journal of Social Economics*, 1997, Vol. 24, No. 4, pp. 355–363.

THE IDEA OF MORAL RESPONSIBILITY

HANS JONAS, the outstanding German–American philosopher, has injected the problem of moral responsibility into the modern moral discourse.

For JONAS moral responsibility is essentially substantive in nature. The actor displays moral responsibility if he/she cares about the subject of his/her action. Power is inherent in responsibility relationship; there is an asymmetrical relation between the actor and the subject of his/her action.

The actor can enter into a responsibility relationship either in a natural way or by contract. In the first case the subject becomes a subject of the actor's action independently from his/her will. In the second case the subject becomes a subject of the actor's action because he/she has established a contract with the actor.

JONAS cites the parent and the statesman as ideal types of natural responsibility and contractual responsibility, respectively. The parent is responsible for his/her child not because of the child's own will or even contrary to it. But the responsibility of the statesman comes from the political contract that he/she has established with his/her constituencies.

The economic decision maker is somewhere in between the role of the parent and the role of the statesman. For example, while a corporate manager has a number of stakeholders (customers, employees, suppliers, creditors) with whom his/her company has contractual relationship, there are usually other stakeholders (the local community, the natural environment) who are affected by the company's operations but towards whom the company has no contractual, only a natural responsibility.

Consider the following famous case from business ethics. In 1978 three girls died in Winamac, Indiana because of the explosion of their Ford Pinto car. This was not the first case when this Ford model caused a serious accident by explosion. There were several law suits filed against Ford since it was proven that the top managers had been informed about the design problem of the model. Despite the warnings of their engineers, Ford managers decided to manufacture and sell the car (HOFFMAN 1985).

Our ethical intuition suggests that the Ford managers behaved in a non-responsible way since they decided to put an unsafe model on the market. But how can this ethical intuition be defended on a more systematic ground?

In the Ford Pinto case all the important components of complex choice situation can be identified. First, the decision maker has more than one decision alternative, that is, he/she can choose among different courses of action. Second, the decision maker or his/her organization has some goals that he/she wants to achieve. Third, in the choice situation there are ethical norms that represent the duties of the decision maker. Finally, other parties (stakeholders) are present who can be greatly affected by the outcome of the choice.

In a complex choice situation the following components are the most important.

$$A_1, ..., A_i, ..., A_m \quad (m \geq 2) \tag{1}$$

There are at least two decision alternatives for the decision maker.

$$G_1, ..., G_j, ..., G_n \quad (n \geq 1) \tag{2}$$

The decision maker or his/her organization has at least one goal to achieve.

$$D_1, ..., D_k, ..., D_p \quad (p \geq 1) \tag{3}$$

There exists at least one ethical norm that represents the duty of the decision maker.

$$S_1, ..., S_q, ..., S_r \quad (r \geq 1) \tag{4}$$

At least one stakeholder is present in the situation.

Responsible choice involves finding and implementing the decision alternative which corresponds to the idea of moral responsibility in the given context.

$$A_i^* = \Omega[A_1, ..., A_i, ..., A_m] \tag{5}$$

We need to define the decision rule Ω that selects the responsible course of action among the feasible ones.

DEONTOLOGY, RATIONALITY
AND RESPECT

In the context of economics KENNET E. GOODPASTER has presented the most developed model of responsible choice (GOODPASTER 1983, 1990; GOODPASTER and MATTHEWS 1982).

Using the conception of WILLIAM K. FRANKENA (1980) GOODPASTER distinguished two basic components of moral responsibility, namely rationality and respect.

Rationality involves the following attributes:

(1) lack of impulsiveness;
(2) care in mapping out alternatives and consequences;
(3) clarity about goals and purposes; and
(4) attention to details of implementation.

Rationality described by the attributes (1)–(4) differs strikingly from the rationality postulate of standard economics. The rationality concept used here is procedural in nature and does not require to maximize anything.

Respect means a special awareness of and concern for the effects of one's decisions and policies on others, special in the sense that it goes beyond the kind of awareness and concern that would ordinarily be part of rationality, that is, beyond seeing others merely as instrumental to accomplishing one's own purposes. Respect for others involves taking their needs and interests seriously. It is what KANT meant by the "categorical imperative" to treat others as valuable in and for themselves.

In GOODPASTER'S model responsible choice is to combine rationality and respect for others in decision making. In this model respect is basically, if not exclusively, a consequentialist account. This means that the decision maker considers the effects of his/her choice on the stakeholders. However, there are complex choice situations where a pure consequentialist account is not enough.

In complex choice situations there might be marginal contributions, unforeseeable consequences, and distant effects. These phenomena create decision traps if the choice is based solely on consequentialist considerations.

It is possible that the choice of the decision maker produces marginal contributions to the wellbeing of stakeholders but cumulative or aggregate effects of these marginal contributions might be detrimental for the stakeholders. GARRET HARDIN'S famous "tragedy of the commons" model describes such situations (HARDIN 1968). If the consequences of a certain course of action are partly or completely unforeseeable then the decision maker necessarily neglects them. Here lies another decision trap. If the consequences are foreseeable but distant in space and/or time then the decision maker discounts them. Effects beyond the normal (usually very narrow) space and time reference-frame of the decision maker are highly overdiscounted.

Phenomena of marginal contributions, unforeseeable consequences, and distant effects show that non-consequentialist considerations are also required in complex choice situations.

Deontological, that is non-consequentialist, considerations are based on ethical norms. Ethical norms can be understood as heuristic devices which help to avoid decision traps in complex choice situations. These devices capture the essence of evolutionary stable strategies of human communities.

In a deontological account the value of decision alternatives does not depend on the real-world outcomes. It depends only on the correspondence of decision alternatives to the applying ethical norms.

A number of well-known philosophers, sociologists and economists have emphasized the importance of deontological considerations in economic and political decision making (ELSTER 1989; EPSTEIN 1987; ETZIONI 1988; FRANK 1988; MANSBRIDGE 1990; NOZICK 1974; RAWLS 1971; SEN 1982).

GOODPASTER'S responsibility model can be enlarged to include the deontological aspect of choice. Hence responsible choice can be defined as a synthesis of deontology, rationality as goal achievement, and respect for stakeholders. Responsible decision makers try to make choices that involve applying ethical norms, promoting the achievement of their goals, and showing respect for affected parties.

In complex choice situations three kinds of decision variables play a role. Decision alternatives have deontological value ($D(A_i)$), Instrumental (goal achievement) value ($G(A_i)$), and external value, that is value for the stakeholders ($S(A_i)$).

The question is how can the value functions $D(.), G(.)$, and $S(.)$ be defined?

THE PSYCHOLOGY OF CHOICE

In the last few decades psychologists have discovered some basic regularities of human choice behaviour that should be taken seriously in developing a normative but realistic model of responsible choice.

Based on a series of well-designed experimental studies AMOS TVERSKY and DANIEL KAHNEMAN have stated the general features of the value functions of decision makers (KAHNEMAN and TVERSKY 1979). Decision makers display important differences in valuing positive and negative decision prospects. The value function is much steeper for negative outcomes than it is for positive outcomes.

TVERSKY and KAHNEMAN found that people are more sensitive to losses than to gains.

$$|V(x)| < |V(-x)| \qquad (6)$$

The magnitude of the value of a positive outcome x is smaller than the magnitude of the value of the corresponding negative outcome $-x$.

Other experimental studies show that the loss aversion coefficient of decision makers is about 2, that is, a negative outcome can be compensated for them by a twice greater positive outcome (KAHNEMAN 1994).

$$|V(2x)| \approx |V(-x)| \tag{7}$$

Harvard psychologist RICHARD J. HERRNSTEIN has discovered the so-called "Matching law" after decades-long experimental research. The main finding is that it is the average reinforcement value of the decision alternatives that really counts for decision makers (HERRNSTEIN and PRELEC 1991).

Finally, the same experimental results of REINHARD SELTEN should be mentioned. He found that decision makers try to avoid trade-offs among different value dimensions (SELTEN 1994).

To be realistic, the normative model of responsible choice should be consistent with the above listed regularities of human choice behaviour.

MODELLING RESPONSIBLE CHOICE

Let $D_k(.)$ be deontological value function as follows:

$$D_k(A_i) = \begin{cases} 1 & \text{if decision alternative } A_i \text{ correspond to ethical norm } D_k; \\ 0 & \text{if decision alternative } A_i \text{ is neutral regarding ethical} \\ & \text{norm } D_k; \\ -2 & \text{if decision alternative } A_i \text{ violates ethical norm } D_k; \end{cases} \tag{8}$$

$D_k A_i$ characteristically shows the deontological value of decision alternative A_i regarding ethical norm D_k.

Let $G_j(.)$ be instrumental value function as follows:

$$G_j(A_i) = \begin{cases} 1 & \text{if decision alternative } A_i \text{ is positive for the achievement} \\ & \text{of goal } G_j; \\ 0 & \text{if decision alternative } A_i \text{ is neutral for the achievement} \\ & \text{of goal } G_j; \\ -2 & \text{if decision alternative } A_i \text{ is negative for the achievement} \\ & \text{of goal } G_j; \end{cases} \tag{9}$$

$G_j(A_i)$ characteristically shows the deontological value of decision alternative A_i regarding the achievement of goal G_j.

Finally, let $S_q(A_i)$ be external value function as follows:

$$S_q(A_i) = \begin{cases} 1 & \text{if decision alternative } A_i \text{ good for stakeholder } S_q; \\ 0 & \text{if decision alternative } A_i \text{ is neutral for stakeholder } S_q; \\ -2 & \text{if decision alternative } A_i \text{ is bad for stakeholder } S_q; \end{cases} \quad (10)$$

$S_q(A_i)$ characteristically shows the external value of decision alternative A_i regarding stakeholder S_q.

The above-defined value functions are TVERSKY and KAHNEMAN-type value functions since (8), (9), and (10) satisfy both (6) and (7).

How can the aggregate value functions $D(.)$, $G(.)$ and $S(.)$ be construed?

Let $w_1, ..., w_k, ..., w_p$ be weights that represent the relative importance of ethical norms $D_1, ..., D_k, ..., D_p$ for the given society. It is required that

$$\sum_k w_k = 1 \quad (11)$$

Then

$$D(A_i) = \sum_k \left[w_k D_k(A_i) \right] \quad (12)$$

$D(A_i)$ shows the average deontological value of decision alternative A_i.

Let $u_1, ..., u_j, ..., u_n$ be weights that represent the relative importance of goals $G_1, ..., G_j, ..., G_n$ for the decision maker. It is required that

$$\sum_j u_j = 1 \quad (13)$$

Then

$$G(A_i) = \sum_j \left[u_j G_j(A_i) \right] \quad (14)$$

$G(A_i)$ shows the average instrumental value of decision alternative A_i.

Finally, let $v_1, ..., v_q, ..., v_r$ be weights that represent the relative stakes of stakeholders $S_1, ..., S_q, ..., S_r$ in the choice situation. It is required that

$$\sum_q v_q = 1 \quad (15)$$

Then

$$S(A_i) = \sum_q \left[v_q S_q(A_i) \right] \quad (16)$$

$S(A_i)$ shows the average external value of decision alternative A_i.

The following vector gives a multiple evaluation of decision alternative A_i.

$$\underline{V}(A_i) = [D(A_i), G(A_i), S(A_i)] \tag{17}$$

In contemporary moral philosophy three distinct viewpoints are identified from which an act can be evaluated, namely the viewpoint of the actor (doer relativity), the viewpoint of society (observer relativity), and the viewpoint of the stakeholders (receiver relativity) (SEN 1982).

In (17) the first component of the vector represents the evaluation of the decision alternative from the viewpoint of society. The second component of the vector represents the decision maker's evaluation while the third component represents the evaluation of the stakeholders.

The rule of responsible choice is stated as follows:

$$A_i = \text{maximin } [D(A_i), G(A_i), S(A_i)] \tag{18}$$

Responsible choice demands the choice of the least worst alternative in the multidimensional space of deontological, instrumental, and external values.

If here are two decision alternatives, A and B, then the responsible choice is A if and only if

$$\text{min } [D(A), G(A), S(A) > \text{min } [D(B), G(B), S(B)].$$

The underlying principle of responsible choice is that decision makers should make optimal compromises among the applying ethical norms, their own goals, and the interests of the stakeholders.

Let us consider again the Ford Pinto case. The following simplified analysis serves as illustration only.

The Ford managers' main goal was to introduce the model without time delay and at no extra cost (G_1). The applying ethical norm is to supply a safe product for the customers, to avoid jeopardizing their lives (D_1). Stakeholders were the actual and potential buyers and users of the car (S_1).

Essentially two alternatives were available for the managers. A_1 = manufacturing and selling the car without re-engineering; A_2 = re-design the model and manufacturing and selling the safer version.

Table 1 shows the multiple evaluation of the decision alternatives. It is easy to discover that A_2 is the responsible course of action as it is suggested by our ethical intuition. Namely $\underline{V}(A_1) = [-2, 1, -2]$ while $\underline{V}(A_2) = [1, -2, 0]$. A_1 and A_2 are equal in their worst components (-2) but the second worst component of A_2 is better than that of A_1 (0 versus -2). Using the maximum rule A_2 is preferable to A_1.

Table 1. Multiple evaluation of the decision alternatives
in the Ford Pinto case

	Deontological value (D)	Instrumental value (G)	External value (S)
A_1 alternative	-2	1	-2
A_2 alternative	1	-2	0

It is important to demonstrate that the rational choice model is a degenerate form of the responsible choice model. The rule of rational choice is as follows:

$$\max G(A_i) \tag{19}$$

(19) is equivalent to (18) if there are no applying ethical norms as well as no stakeholders in the choice situation, that is, $D_1, ..., D_k, ..., D_p$ and $S_1, ..., S_q, ..., S_r$ simply do not exist in the given context. From this it follows that responsible choice is the general case while rational choice is a special case only.

THE RESPONSIBLE DECISION MAKER

The procedural model of responsible choice can be summarized as follows:

(1) identifying the ethical norms which apply in the given choice situation;
(2) mapping out the stakeholders;
(3) defining the goals to be achieved;
(4) generation of decision alternatives;
(5) multiple evaluation of each alternative regarding the ethical norms, the decision maker's goals and the stakeholders;
(6) finding the least worst alternative in the multidimensional space of deontological, instrumental, and external values.

There is always conflict or at least some tension among the ethical norms of society, the decision maker's own goals, and the interests of the stakeholders. Making responsible choice is not an easy business at all.

Responsible decision makers have some common character traits. On the one hand, they are rightly socialized persons, that is, they have interiorized the ethical norms of society (ETZIONI 1988). On the other hand, they have developed responsiveness towards their stakeholders (FREEMAN 1984). In short, responsible decision makers display social commitment and empathy. These character traits us of the moral make up that ADAM SMITH presupposed about his fellow-businessmen (SEN 1987). However, social commitment and empathy are such scarce resources in our economies that ethical awards and other prizes have been established for decision makers who have them.

Rational choice does not produce satisficing outcomes in complex choice situations. Such situations require multiple considerations and optimal compromises across diverse value dimensions.

REFERENCES

ELSTER, J.: *The Cement of Society*, Cambridge University Press, Cambridge (1989).

EPSTEIN, E. M.: "The corporate social policy process: beyond business ethics, corporate social responsibility, and corporate social responsiveness", *California Management Review*, No. 3 (1987).

ETZIONI, A.: *The Moral Dimension*, The Free Press, New York, NY (1988).

FRANK, R.: *Passions within Reason*, W. W. NORTON, New York, NY (1988).

FRANKENA, W. K.: *Thinking about Morality*, University of Michigan Press, Ann Arbor, MI (1980).

FREEMAN, E. R.: *Strategic Management: A Stakeholder Approach*, Pitman, Boston, MA; London (1984).

GOODPASTER, K. E.: "The concept to corporate conscience", *Journal of Business Ethics*, No. 1 (1983).

GOODPASTER, K. E.: "PASCAL and corporate conscience", *Strategic Direction*, November (1990).

GOODPASTER, K. E., MATTHEWS, J. B.: "Can a corporation have a conscience?", *Harvard Business Review*, January–February (1982).

HARDIN, G.: "The tragedy of the commons", *Science*, Vol. 162, pp. 1243–1248 (1968).

HERRNSTEIN, R. J., PRELEC, D.: "Melioration: a theory of distributed choice", *Journal of Economic Perspectives*, No. 3 (1991).

HOFFMAN, M. W.: "The Ford Pinto." In: M. W. HOFFMAN, R. E. FREDERICK: *Business Ethics*, McGraw-Hill, Inc., New York, NY, pp. 552–558 (1995).

JONAS, H.: *The Imperative of Responsibility*, University of Chicago Press, Chicago, IL (1984).

KAHNEMAN, D.: "New challenges to the rationality assumption", *Journal of Institutional and Theoretical Economics*, No. 1 (1994).

KAHNEMAN, D., TVERSKY, A.: "Prospect theory: an analyses of decision under risk", *Econometrica*, No. 2 (1979).

MANSBRIDGE, J. (ed.): *Beyond Self-Interest*, University of Chicago Press, Chicago, IL (1990).

NOZICK, R.: *Anarchy, State, and Utopia*, Basic Books, New York, NY (1974).

RAWLS, J.: *A Theory of Justice,* Harvard University Press, Cambridge and Boston, MA (1971).

SELTEN, R.: "New challenges to the rationality assumption", *Journal of Institutional and Theoretical Economics,* No. 1 (1994).

SEN, A.: "Rights and agency", *Philosophy and Public Affairs,* No. 1 (1982).

SEN, A.: *On Ethics and Economics,* Blackwell, Oxford (1987).

SIMON, H. A.: "Rational decision making in business organizations", *American Economic Review,* September (1979).

BUDAPEST UNIVERSITY OF
ECONOMIC SCIENCES
1948-1998

University-level instruction in Hungarian economics and business education started in 1920. 1998 was a jubilee year in Hungarian economics education, as the independent Hungarian University of Economic Sciences was established in 1948. The history of the university is closely linked to the political and economic events of the period. The university was named after Karl Marx in 1952 and in 1990 it was re-named the Budapest University of Economic Sciences (BUES).

In the past ten years the BUES has started to apply a curriculum which is in harmony with international standards. We are members of organisations which incorporate the best European management schools and we work together on joint research projects with famous European business schools.

The jubilee year gives us an excellent chance to inform people about the past and present of the BUES. We are focusing on the future, though. With this publication we would like to introduce a university which is advancing towards the millennium with a mentality (represented by its instructors) which is a guarantee that the most harmonious area of accession to the European Union will be that of research and education.

The aim of the University is to be the leading institution in economic and business sciences in the region. In 1990 the management of the university decided to advertise its degree program in English, which is the international language of economics, making it more accessible. The International Studies Center is the trustee of this mission.

The ISC is the only institution in East Central Europe which offers instruction in economics, business and social sciences in English at undergraduate, graduate and Ph.D. levels. Students graduating from any ISC degree program are highly valued in today's extremely competitive job market, equipped as they are not only with high-quality, internationally accepted academic knowledge, but also with a special advantage, a deep understanding of Hungary and the region.

Acta Oeconomica

Periodical of the Hungarian Academy of Sciences

Editor: Tamás Földi

Aims and scope

Acta Oeconomica publishes articles mainly on Hungary's economic development, economic policy and on certain issues of the transition period, and on mathematics applied in economics. Extra space is devoted to issues dealing with recent phenomena of world economy, East-West trade and integration (place of Hungary and East and East-Central Europe in the international division of labour).

Founded in 1966

Papers in English
Publishes book reviews and advertisements

Size: 17 × 25 cm
HU ISSN 0001-6373

Publication:
one volume of four issues annually

1999: Vol. 50

Subscription price per volume:
USD 164.00

Manuscripts and editorial correspondence should be addressed to
Acta Oeconomica
P.O.Box 262
H-1502 Budapest
Hungary
Phone: (36 1) 319 3126
Fax: (36 1) 319 2617